MystikU

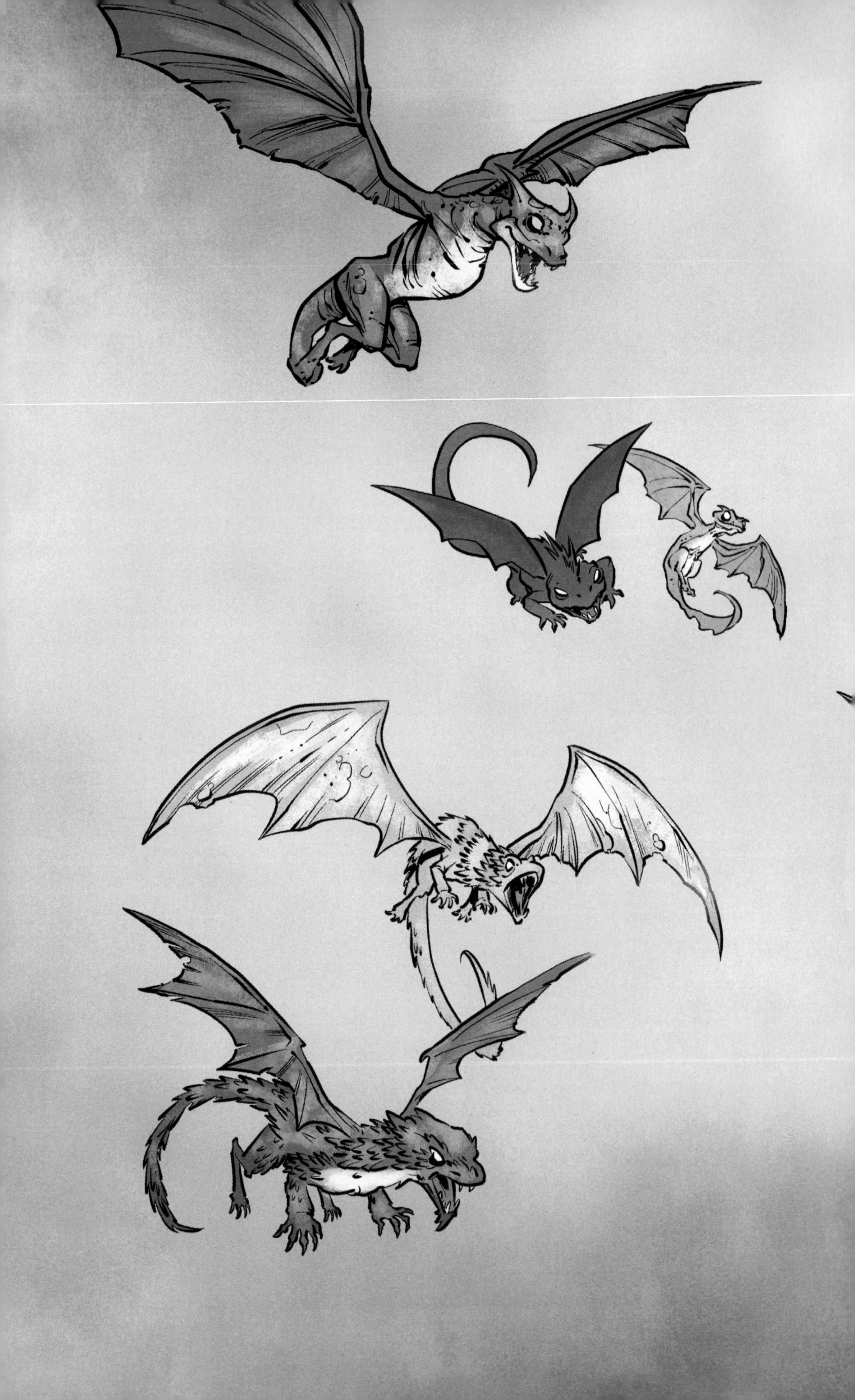

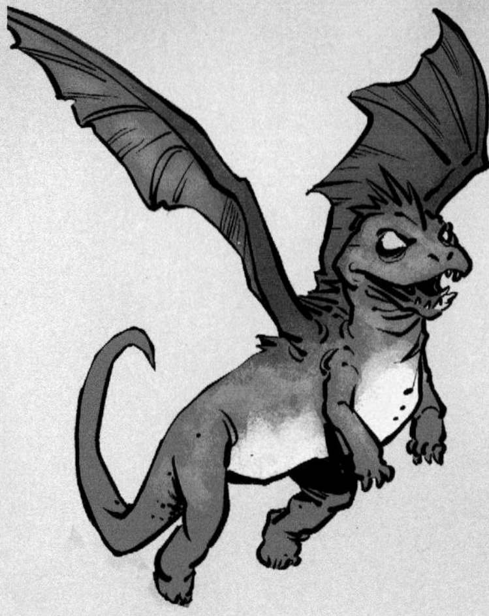

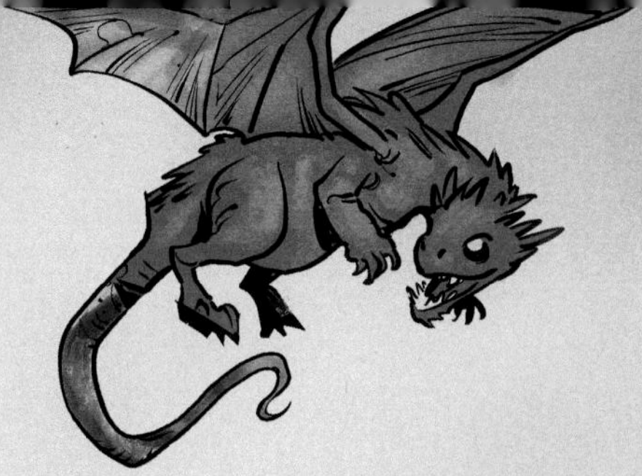

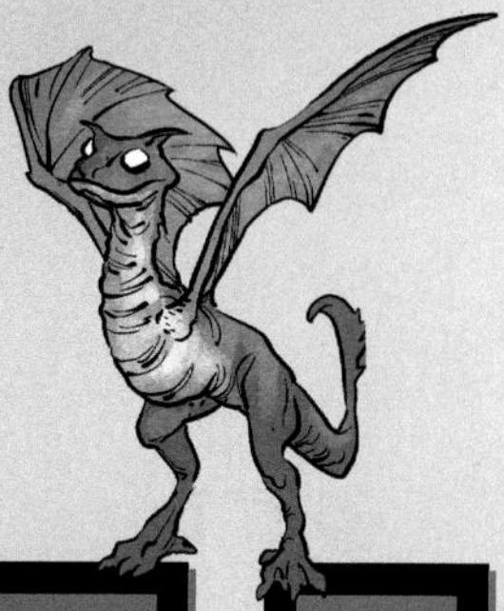

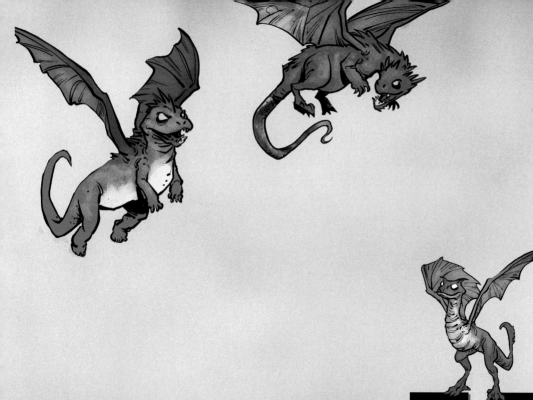

Mystik U

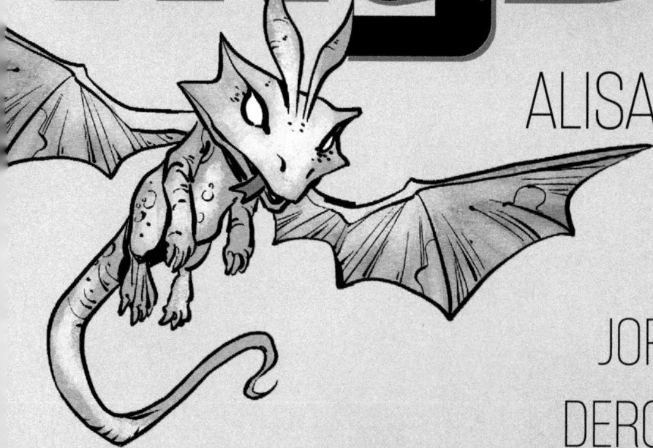

ALISA KWITNEY *writer*
MIKE NORTON *artist*

JORDIE BELLAIRE *colorist*
DERON BENNETT *letterer*
JULIAN TOTINO TEDESCO
cover art and original series covers

ZATANNA *created by* GARDNER FOX
and MURPHY ANDERSON

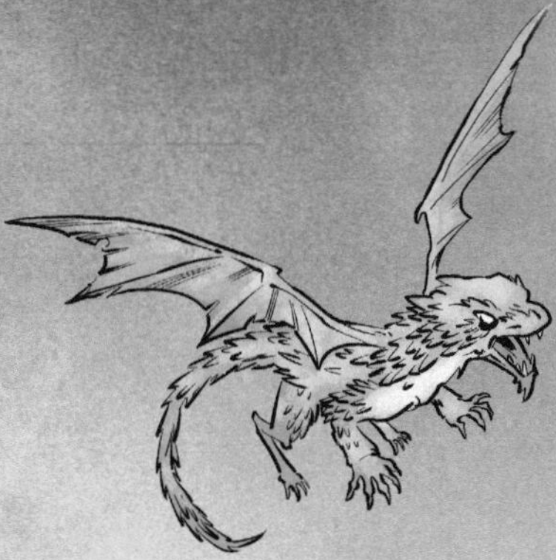

ALEX ANTONE	Editor – Original Series
BRITTANY HOLZHERR	Associate Editor – Original Series
JEB WOODARD	Group Editor – Collected Editions
SCOTT NYBAKKEN	Editor – Collected Edition
STEVE COOK	Design Director – Books
AMIE BROCKWAY-METCALF	Publication Design

BOB HARRAS	Senior VP – Editor-in-Chief, DC Comics
PAT McCALLUM	Executive Editor, DC Comics

DIANE NELSON	President
DAN DiDIO	Publisher
JIM LEE	Publisher
GEOFF JOHNS	President & Chief Creative Officer
AMIT DESAI	Executive VP – Business & Marketing Strategy, Direct to Consumer & Global Franchise Management
SAM ADES	Senior VP & General Manager, Digital Services
BOBBIE CHASE	VP & Executive Editor, Young Reader & Talent Development
MARK CHIARELLO	Senior VP – Art, Design & Collected Editions
JOHN CUNNINGHAM	Senior VP – Sales & Trade Marketing
ANNE DePIES	Senior VP – Business Strategy, Finance & Administration
DON FALLETTI	VP – Manufacturing Operations
LAWRENCE GANEM	VP – Editorial Administration & Talent Relations
ALISON GILL	Senior VP – Manufacturing & Operations
HANK KANALZ	Senior VP – Editorial Strategy & Administration
JAY KOGAN	VP – Legal Affairs
JACK MAHAN	VP – Business Affairs
NICK J. NAPOLITANO	VP – Manufacturing Administration
EDDIE SCANNELL	VP – Consumer Marketing
COURTNEY SIMMONS	Senior VP – Publicity & Communications
JIM (SKI) SOKOLOWSKI	VP – Comic Book Specialty Sales & Trade Marketing
NANCY SPEARS	VP – Mass, Book, Digital Sales & Trade Marketing
MICHELE R. WELLS	VP – Content Strategy

MYSTIK U

DC Comics, 2900 West Alameda Ave., Burbank, CA 91505
Printed by LSC Communications, Kendallville, IN, USA. 5/18/18. First Printing.
ISBN: 978-1-4012-8056-7

Library of Congress Cataloging-in-Publication Data is available.

PEFC Certified
Printed on paper from sustainably managed forests, controlled sources
PEFC
PEFC/29-31-337
www.pefc.org

introduction

Writing is a form of witchcraft.

At least, that's what it feels like to me. I have my rituals—first draft with a fountain pen, project writing on the right side of the page, notes for revision on the left, getting up and working before all the dream stuff is gone from my head—but these are all subject to change. I invent different rituals for different projects, borrowing freely from what other writers say works for them. After consulting various writing shamans and grimoires, there is always the critical moment when I have to go sit on my own and attempt to conjure alternate realities.

Occasionally, it works the way I hope it will.

When it works, I feel like I'm tapping into something outside of myself, or channeling other voices. Sometimes I feel like I've slipped out of the regular time stream and I'm just chronicling the story I see in my head. Hours feel like minutes.

Mostly, though, it doesn't work like that. Instead, I find myself staring at the empty screen or the empty page and minutes feel like hours. I get distracted by a ladybug landing on my coffee cup. After relocating the insect, I force myself back to the work, doggedly trying to assemble a bunch of mundane elements in the blind hope that somehow, they will come together in a way that feels a little surprising, and yet so right and fitting that it doesn't seem as though the story could have happened any other way.

MYSTIK U was a particularly magical project for me, but it spent a lot of time baking in mundane ways.

It began more than three years ago, when I was teaching high school English at a school for students with dyslexia. That summer, Marie Javins had hired me to write a Stephanie Brown Batgirl story for DC's big "Convergence" crossover event, which led to Bobbie Chase asking me if I wanted to pitch some ideas.

Of course I did—I was very excited that Bobbie and Marie liked my take on Batgirl—but I was also teaching high school students at a rural boarding school, which took up an enormous amount of my brain. (I had taught a semester of graphic novel writing at Fordham University, but nothing prepared me for teaching high school. I was also expected to come up with my own curriculum—but that's a whole other story.)

That first MYSTIK U was a very different creature. The mandate I was given was to come up with mostly original characters, and that version skewed a bit darker—possibly because I was swimming in a sea of angsty teenage drama at the time. That older version still involved a university and magic, and one of the characters has emerged more or less intact, but other than that, almost everything changed as the idea developed and evolved.

I think part of the magic of MYSTIK U was that it had time to marinate, and a lot of the earlier ingredients enriched the final brew. Amedeo Turturro, then an assistant editor with Brian Cunningham's group, worked with me on the original version, and it seems fitting that he went on to become part of Vertigo. (Funny story: when I asked Amedeo how he knew so much about old HOUSE OF MYSTERY comics from the seventies, he said that DC had put out a collection, WELCOME BACK TO THE HOUSE OF MYSTERY, in the nineties. To which I replied, "That wasn't DC. That was me!" Back when I was a staff editor with Vertigo in the nineties, that is.)

I also wound up talking constantly with Alain Mauricet, the Belgian artist who was originally tapped to draw MYSTIK U. Alain and I became so addicted to these calls—and our mutual love of obscure old comics characters—that we continue to talk and discuss plots and characters and potential projects on a near-weekly basis. I'm also in touch with the lovely and talented Yishan Li, who was also involved in the earlier incarnation.

MYSTIK U really began to come together, however, when Dan DiDio decided that DC needed a bit of gothic romance, and editor Alex Antone declared that gothic romance was his catnip, and Marie Javins reminded everyone that MYSTIK U had elements of both the gothic (horror, classic faux-medieval architecture, young innocents subject to arcane evil influence) and romance.

Both Alex and Brittany Holzherr, who worked with him editing the book, seemed as enthusiastic as I was about the project. When we talked through the edits of a script over the phone, I felt a heady sense of being in really good hands—so it was probably for the best that neither Alex nor Brittany told me they had been transferred to different editorial groups halfway through the book's journey to publication. Insulated from the news that neither of my editors was actually supposed to be working on the book, I only found out later that they had fought to keep our team intact.

(Funny story #2: Alex said, "Legal wants to know why it's MYSTIK U, not MYSTIC U." And I said, "Is this the same legal that asked us to change the name from MYSTIC U because of copyright issues, which made us spend weeks trying to come up with another name, until I realized we could just change the C to a K and all would be well?")

Two of the biggest differences between the final MYSTIK U and the original version were that a) I was told that I should

MYSTIK U
URTA VI TAMITU

use established DC magical characters and b) I was told specifically that I could use Zatanna. When I first heard this, I was afraid to get too excited. "Zatanna as a student? Are you sure about this?" For weeks, I kept waiting for a follow-up call telling me that someone had made a mistake.

Sometimes I still have to pinch myself to believe it.

I knew that what I wanted to do with Zatanna and the others was create a storyline that incorporated elements of what made these characters cool to someone who was familiar with them, but that also felt accessible to a reader who didn't know Zatanna's backstory or hadn't read about Rose Psychic in THE BOOKS OF MAGIC.

I also wanted to convey something of the sense of going to college with the sense of being good at something—and then having to reassess your identity as you discover that you are not as proficient as you thought you were, while others are far more adept and seem to be learning without even trying.

One idea that I keep coming back to in my writing is college as a kind of theater where people go to improvise themselves. Of course, some arrive with their props and personas already firmly in place, like Sebastian Faust, while others, like June Moone, are deliberately trying on new ways of performing themselves in the world. There will always be students, like Davit Sargon and Pia Morales, who arrive on campus with a firm sense of who they are and what they want to do after graduation. At some point, they will have to question some of their assumptions—whether they stay with their original plan or not.

(The character of Davit Sargon, who is essentially an original character, was also informed by a student from my year of teaching high school. K, as he was called by many of his friends, came from Saudi Arabia and was a huge comic book fan. Davit's family is not from Saudi Arabia—I wanted to keep him in the area where the original, historical Sargons lived and ruled—but there's definitely a bit of K in there.)

In the end, MYSTIK U wound up being a strange concoction that combined elements of old horror comics, gothic romance and the weirdness and drama of freshman year. (One member of the cast was influenced by some of my favorite old horror comics—spoiler alert!—including DC's own weird humor/horror hybrid, PLOP! But it was also inspired by my daughter's description of the effluvia she encountered in her coed dorm shower. I later discovered that I was prescient when the *New York Times* ran an article on a giant fat-berg menacing the sewers of London's east end.)

Yet it was still just words on a page. It was only when Mike Norton started drawing the artwork that the real magic happened. I was able to write the scripts for issues two and three knowing that Mike would be drawing them, which filled me with something I rarely feel as a writer—confidence. Mike seemed to know more about the world of MYSTIK U than I knew myself, and his incredible location shots—filled with glorious and quirky details (the pipe-smoking frog is his brainchild)—forced me to go back over my final lettering proofs to delete every unnecessary word so that more of his art would show.

Mike also enthusiastically embraced my unspoken motto by keeping Faust as undressed as possible, while making sure Zatanna was always stylish, but not sirenish. (My motto was, "No cheesecake. Beefcake.") He is also a master at conveying the subtle play of emotions in a scene—what comics editors call acting.

And then there is Jordie Bellaire, our colorist. Who is also an incredible writer. And brilliant, and funny, and so much fun to work with that I have to end with the e-mail conversation we had on the day she joined the team:

Mike: WHOA! Jordie! I was almost positive you'd already be booked! SO STOKED! MAKE ME BEAUTIFUL!!!!!!

Jordie: I'm gonna paint you like one of my French girls!

Alisa: Wait, wait, if Mike is Kate and Jordie is Jack, then I...I...wanna be the door! Which is to say... welcome on board, Jordie...

Alex: I would like to be Billy Zane. Not the character he plays in *Titanic*, though. Just Billy Zane.

Brittany: Can I be Molly Brown a.k.a. Kathy Bates? Welcome aboard, Jordie!

Alex: You're unsinkable, Brittany! And an American treasure!

So there you have it—the genesis of the book you hold in your hands. It was conceived with hope and angst and a little bit of craziness, but it came together as a labor of love. My gratitude to all the witches and warlocks who helped me bring this weirdness to life.

—Alisa Kwitney
March 2018

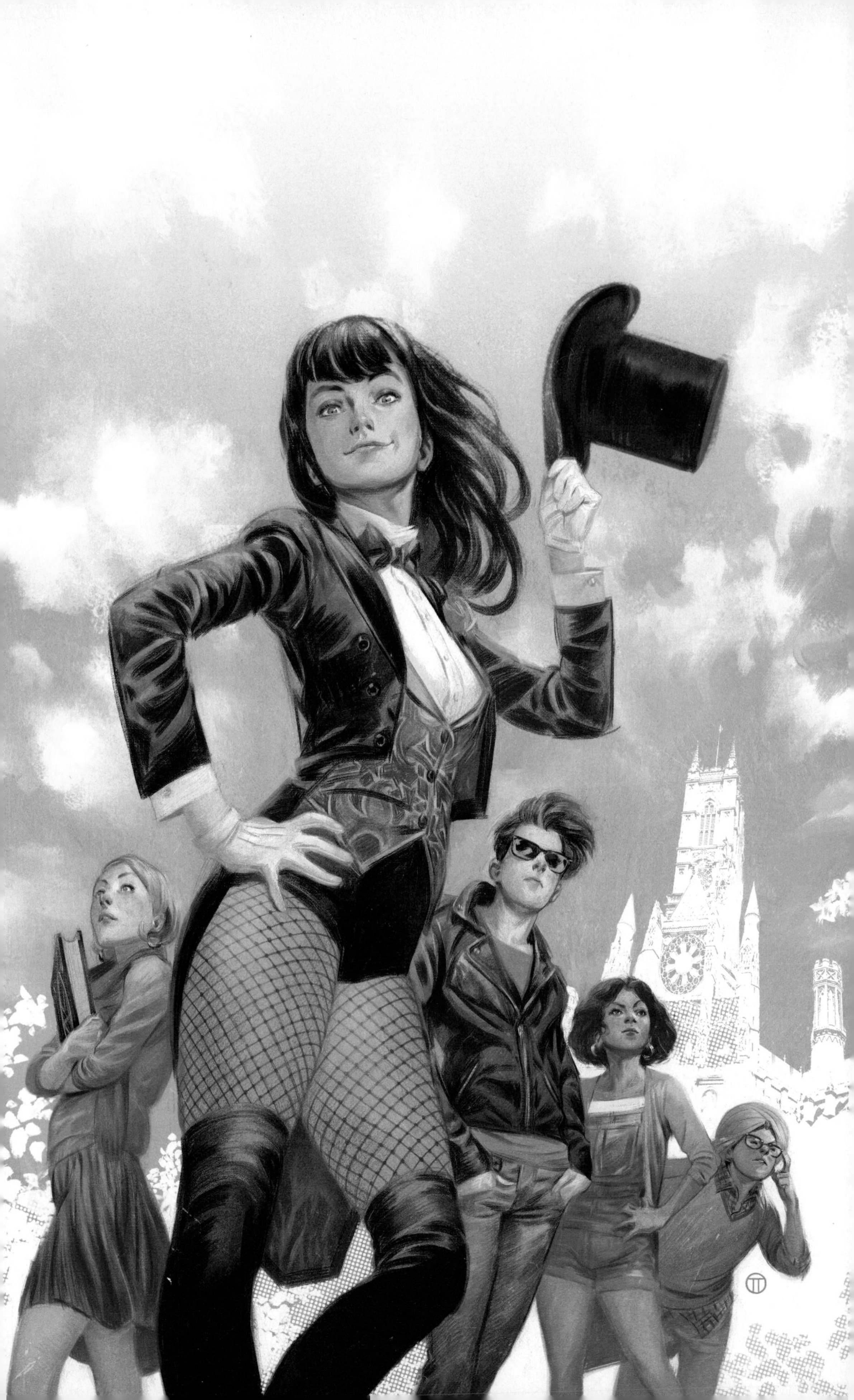

"Sometimes, the thoughts
I have...they frighten me."

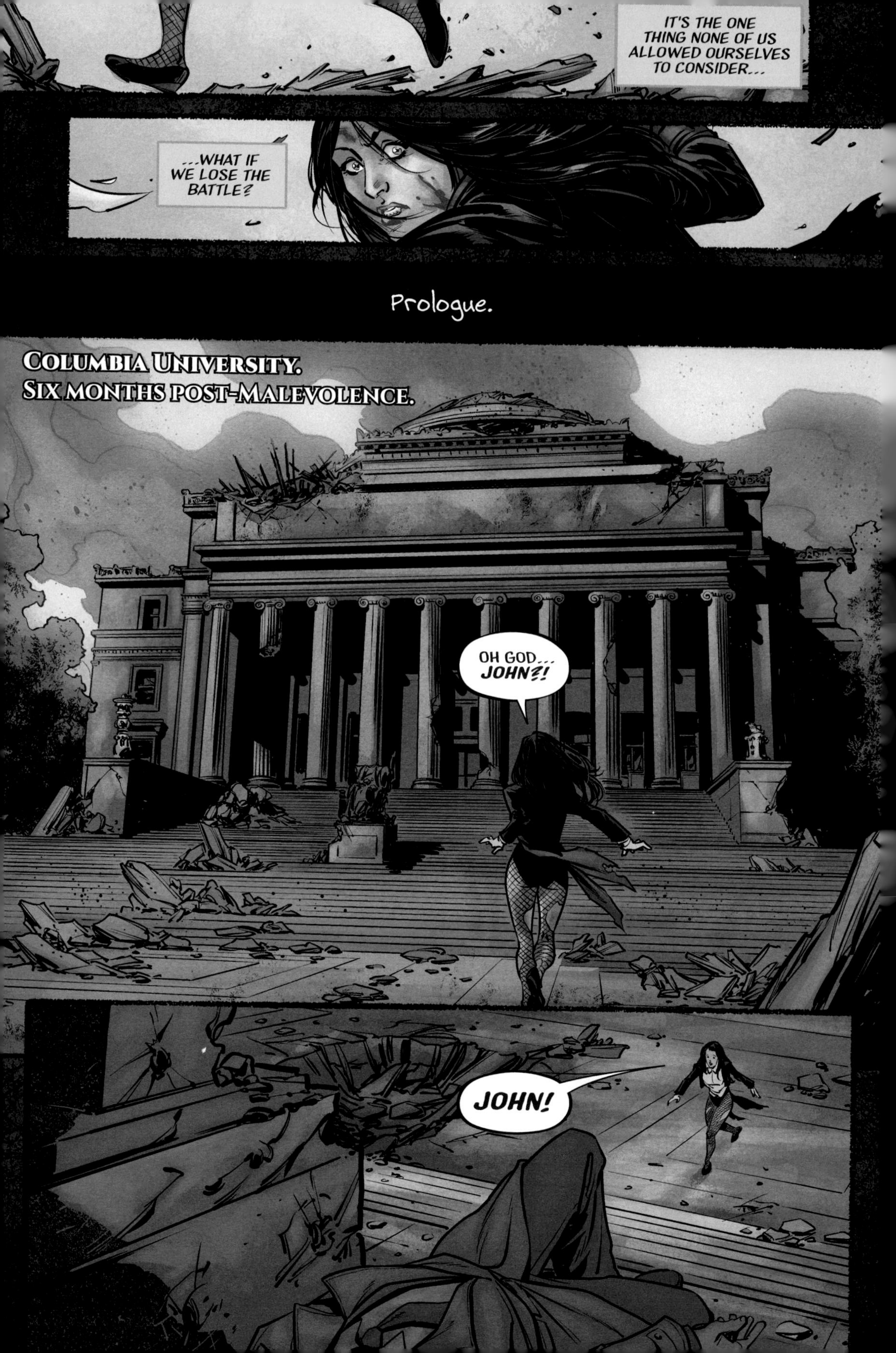
IT'S THE ONE THING NONE OF US ALLOWED OURSELVES TO CONSIDER...
...WHAT IF WE LOSE THE BATTLE?
Prologue.
COLUMBIA UNIVERSITY.
SIX MONTHS POST-MALEVOLENCE.
OH GOD... JOHN?!
JOHN!

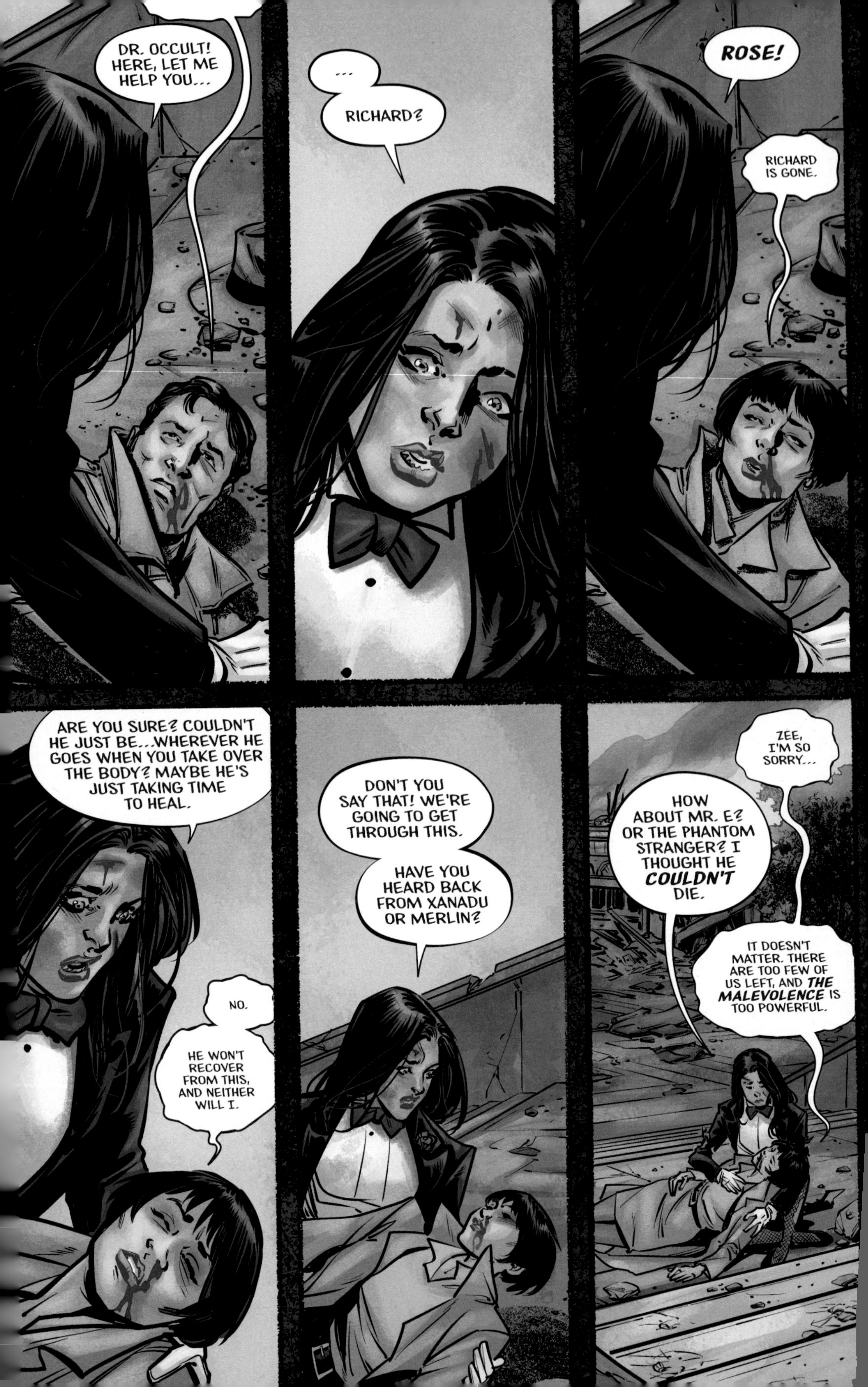
DR. OCCULT! HERE, LET ME HELP YOU...
...
RICHARD?
ROSE!
RICHARD IS GONE.
ARE YOU SURE? COULDN'T HE JUST BE...WHEREVER HE GOES WHEN YOU TAKE OVER THE BODY? MAYBE HE'S JUST TAKING TIME TO HEAL.
NO.
HE WON'T RECOVER FROM THIS, AND NEITHER WILL I.
DON'T YOU SAY THAT! WE'RE GOING TO GET THROUGH THIS.
HAVE YOU HEARD BACK FROM XANADU OR MERLIN?
ZEE, I'M SO SORRY...
HOW ABOUT MR. E? OR THE PHANTOM STRANGER? I THOUGHT HE COULDN'T DIE.
IT DOESN'T MATTER. THERE ARE TOO FEW OF US LEFT, AND THE MALEVOLENCE IS TOO POWERFUL.

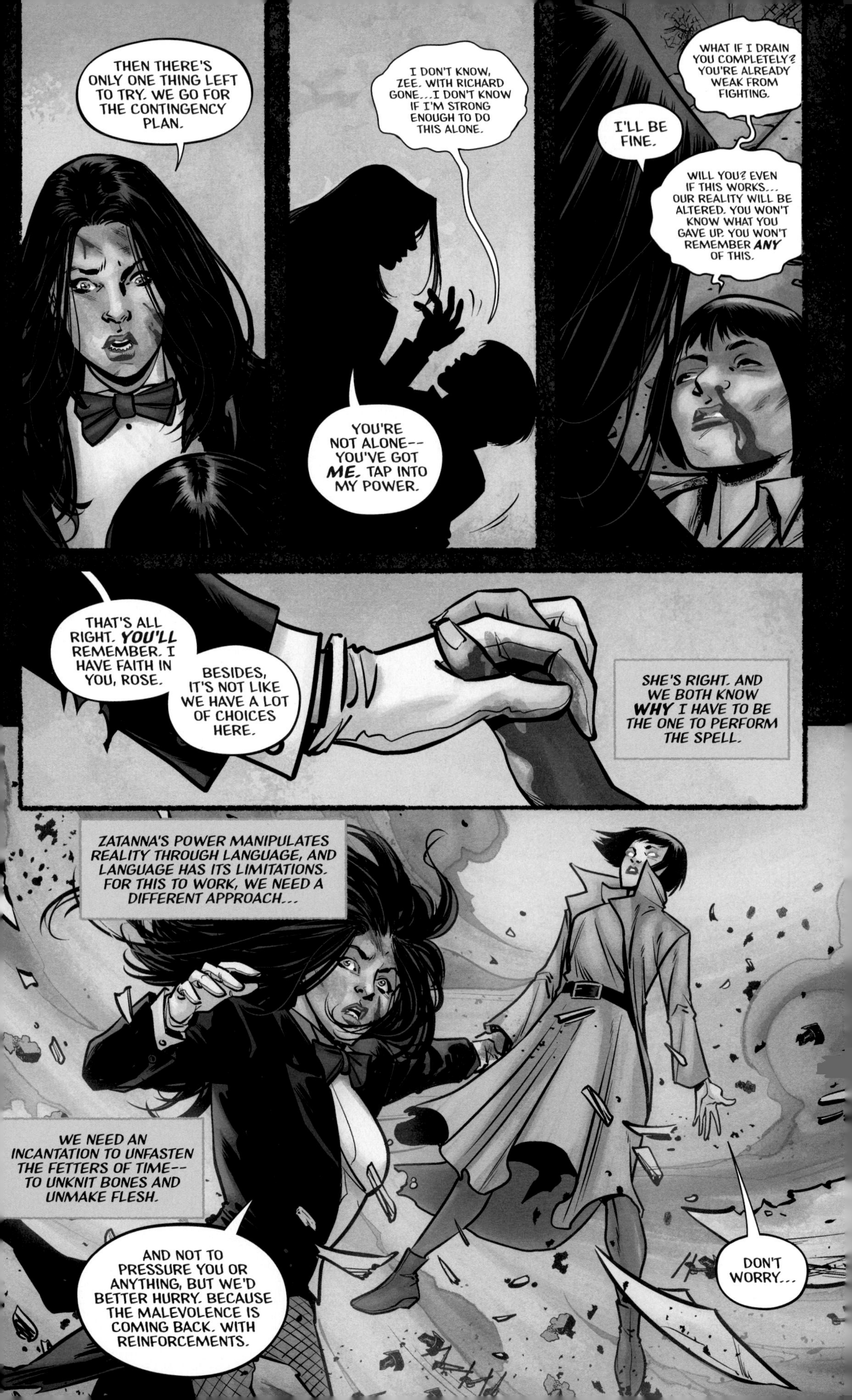
THEN THERE'S ONLY ONE THING LEFT TO TRY. WE GO FOR THE CONTINGENCY PLAN.
I DON'T KNOW, ZEE. WITH RICHARD GONE... I DON'T KNOW IF I'M STRONG ENOUGH TO DO THIS ALONE.
YOU'RE NOT ALONE-- YOU'VE GOT ME. TAP INTO MY POWER.
WHAT IF I DRAIN YOU COMPLETELY? YOU'RE ALREADY WEAK FROM FIGHTING.
I'LL BE FINE.
WILL YOU? EVEN IF THIS WORKS... OUR REALITY WILL BE ALTERED. YOU WON'T KNOW WHAT YOU GAVE UP. YOU WON'T REMEMBER ANY OF THIS.
THAT'S ALL RIGHT. YOU'LL REMEMBER. I HAVE FAITH IN YOU, ROSE.
BESIDES, IT'S NOT LIKE WE HAVE A LOT OF CHOICES HERE.
SHE'S RIGHT. AND WE BOTH KNOW WHY I HAVE TO BE THE ONE TO PERFORM THE SPELL.
ZATANNA'S POWER MANIPULATES REALITY THROUGH LANGUAGE, AND LANGUAGE HAS ITS LIMITATIONS. FOR THIS TO WORK, WE NEED A DIFFERENT APPROACH...
WE NEED AN INCANTATION TO UNFASTEN THE FETTERS OF TIME-- TO UNKNIT BONES AND UNMAKE FLESH.
AND NOT TO PRESSURE YOU OR ANYTHING, BUT WE'D BETTER HURRY. BECAUSE THE MALEVOLENCE IS COMING BACK. WITH REINFORCEMENTS.
DON'T WORRY...

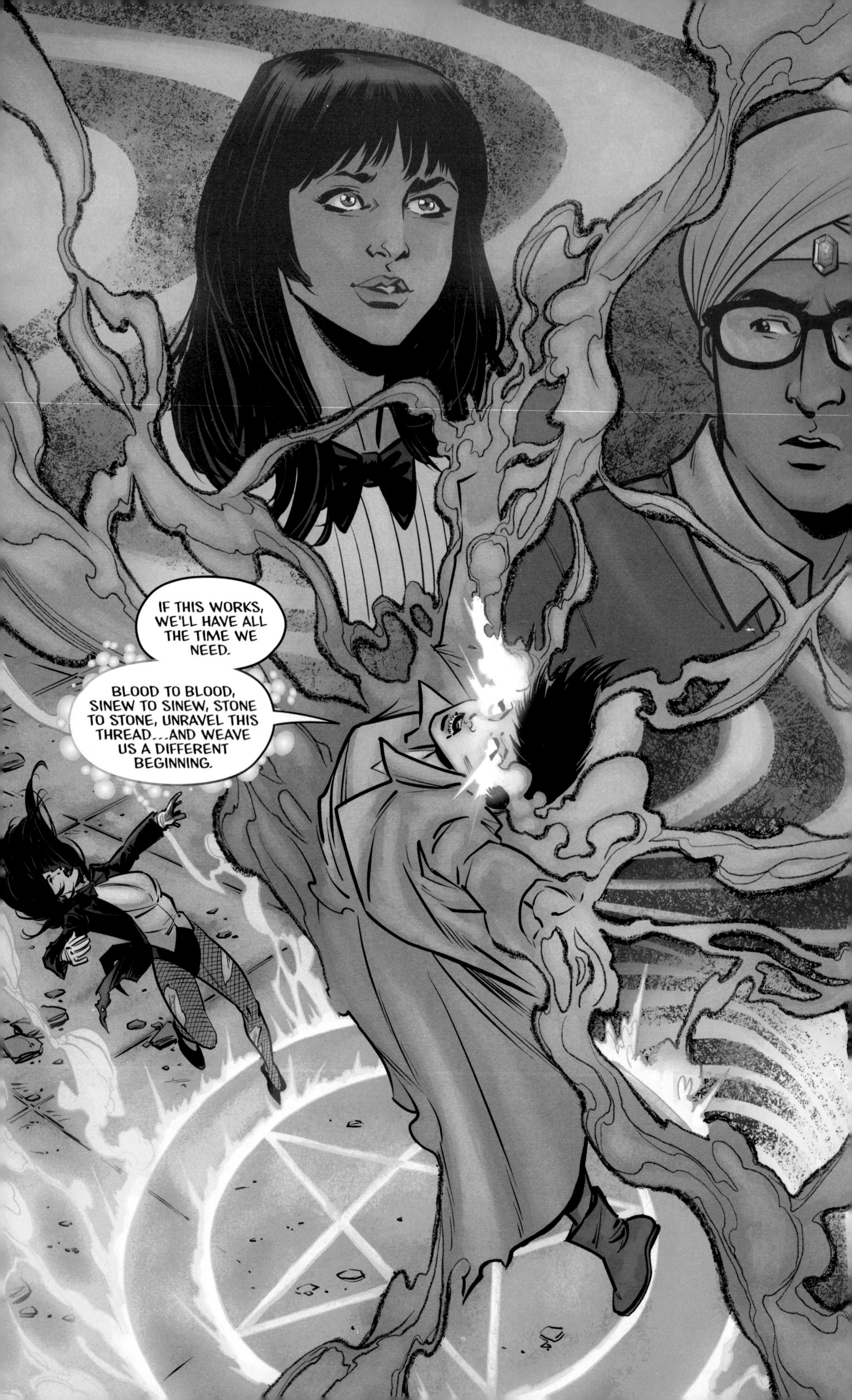
IF THIS WORKS, WE'LL HAVE ALL THE TIME WE NEED.
BLOOD TO BLOOD, SINEW TO SINEW, STONE TO STONE, UNRAVEL THIS THREAD...AND WEAVE US A DIFFERENT BEGINNING.

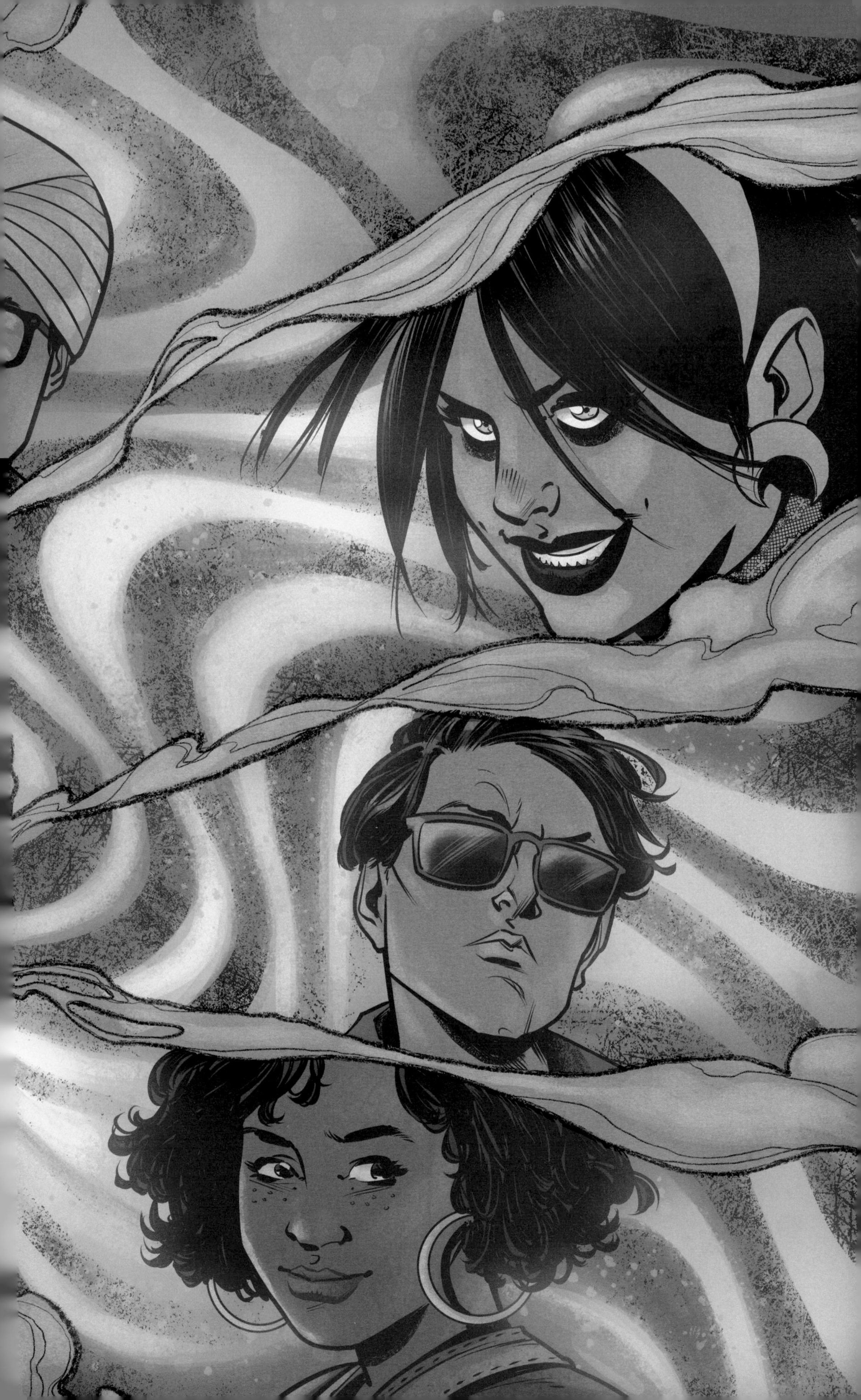

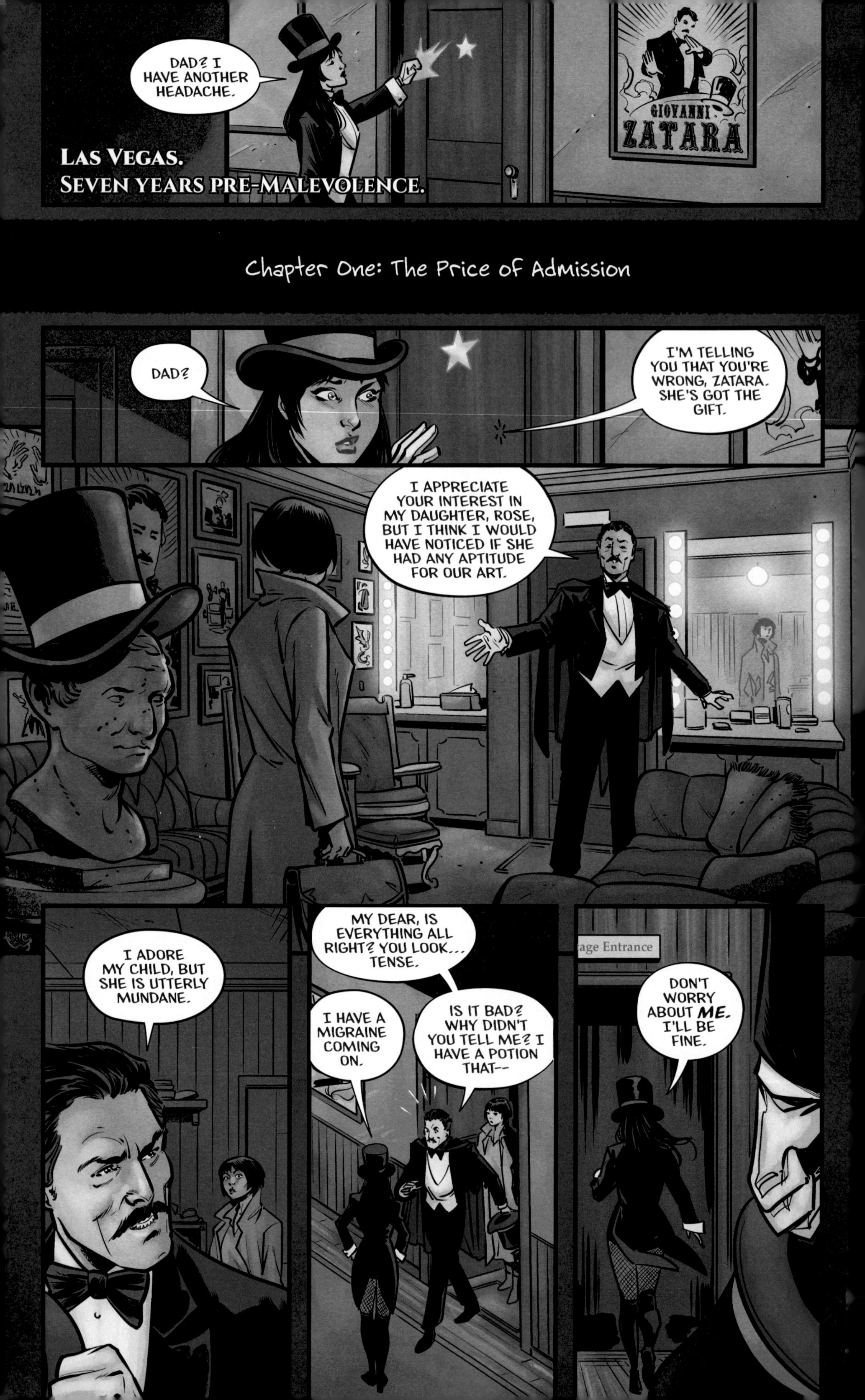
DAD? I HAVE ANOTHER HEADACHE.
LAS VEGAS.
SEVEN YEARS PRE-MALEVOLENCE.
GIOVANNI ZATARA
Chapter One: The Price of Admission
DAD?
I'M TELLING YOU THAT YOU'RE WRONG, ZATARA. SHE'S GOT THE GIFT.
I APPRECIATE YOUR INTEREST IN MY DAUGHTER, ROSE, BUT I THINK I WOULD HAVE NOTICED IF SHE HAD ANY APTITUDE FOR OUR ART.
I ADORE MY CHILD, BUT SHE IS UTTERLY MUNDANE.
MY DEAR, IS EVERYTHING ALL RIGHT? YOU LOOK... TENSE.
I HAVE A MIGRAINE COMING ON.
IS IT BAD? WHY DIDN'T YOU TELL ME? I HAVE A POTION THAT--
age Entrance
DON'T WORRY ABOUT *ME.* I'LL BE FINE.

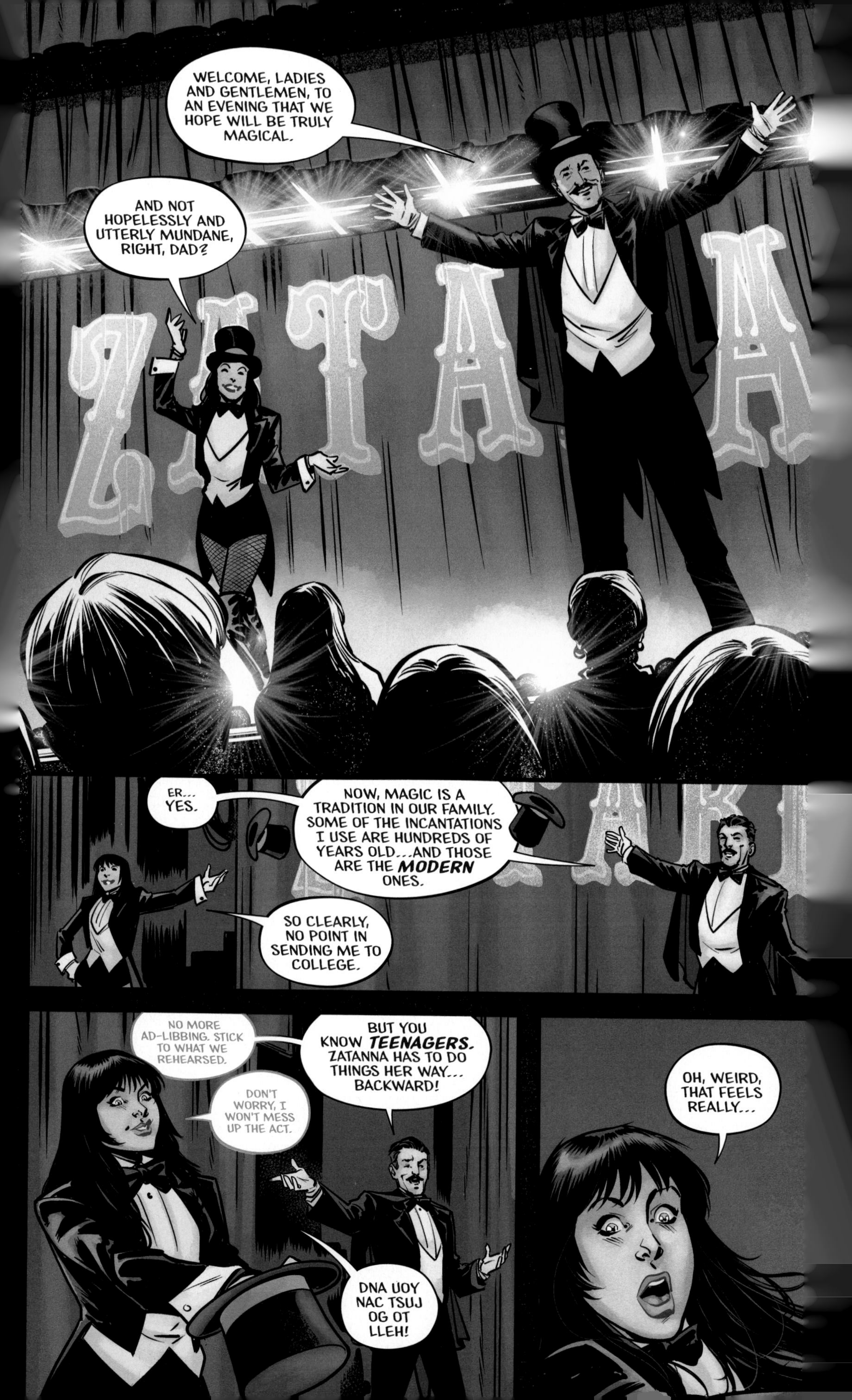
WELCOME, LADIES AND GENTLEMEN, TO AN EVENING THAT WE HOPE WILL BE TRULY MAGICAL.
AND NOT HOPELESSLY AND UTTERLY MUNDANE, RIGHT, DAD?
ER... YES.
NOW, MAGIC IS A TRADITION IN OUR FAMILY. SOME OF THE INCANTATIONS I USE ARE HUNDREDS OF YEARS OLD...AND THOSE ARE THE MODERN ONES.
SO CLEARLY, NO POINT IN SENDING ME TO COLLEGE.
NO MORE AD-LIBBING. STICK TO WHAT WE REHEARSED.
DON'T WORRY, I WON'T MESS UP THE ACT.
BUT YOU KNOW TEENAGERS. ZATANNA HAS TO DO THINGS HER WAY... BACKWARD!
DNA UOY NAC TSUJ OG OT LLEH!
OH, WEIRD, THAT FEELS REALLY...

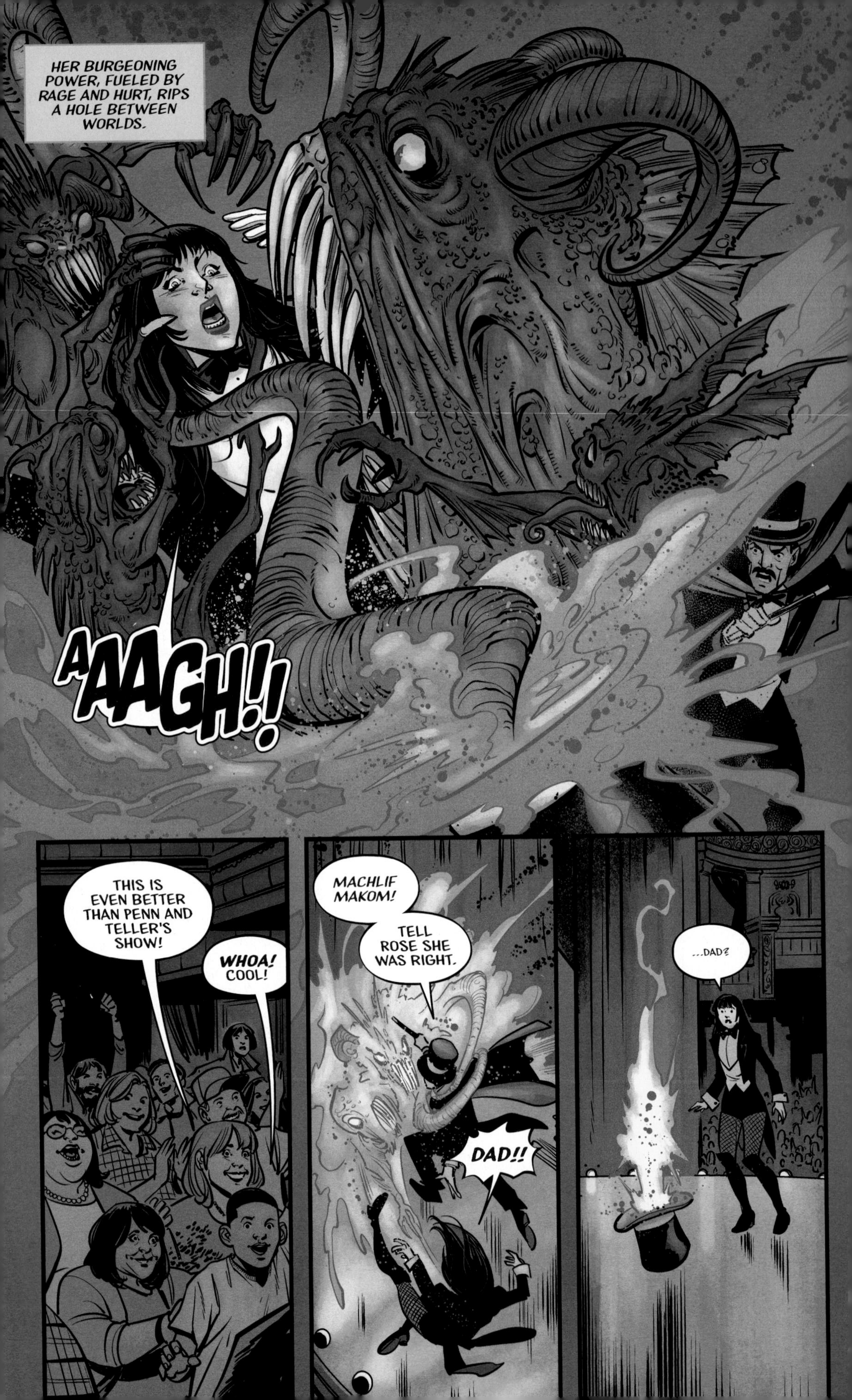
HER BURGEONING POWER, FUELED BY RAGE AND HURT, RIPS A HOLE BETWEEN WORLDS.
AAAGH!!
THIS IS EVEN BETTER THAN PENN AND TELLER'S SHOW!
WHOA! COOL!
MACHLIF MAKOM!
TELL ROSE SHE WAS RIGHT.
DAD!!
...DAD?

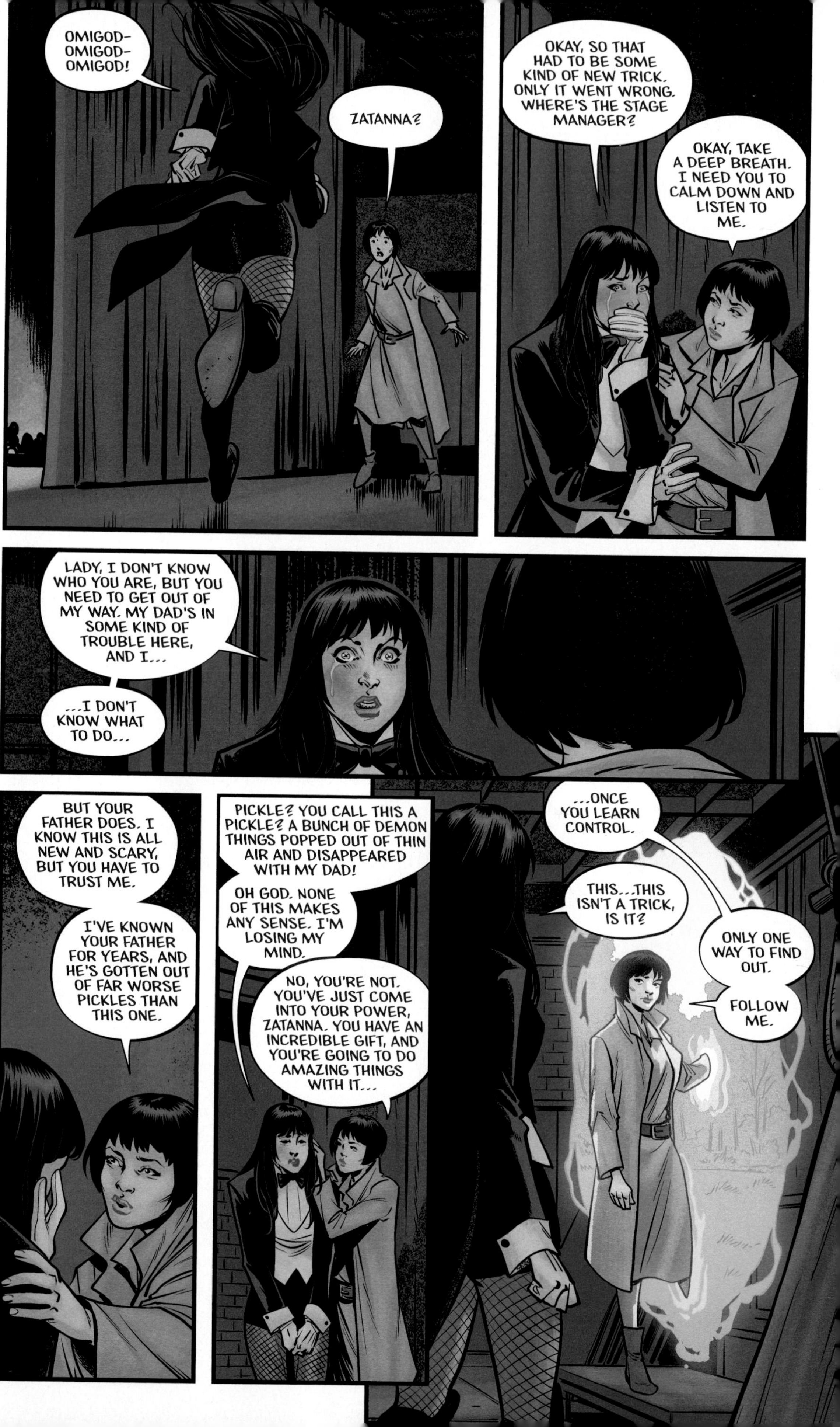
OMIGOD-OMIGOD-OMIGOD!
ZATANNA?
OKAY, SO THAT HAD TO BE SOME KIND OF NEW TRICK. ONLY IT WENT WRONG. WHERE'S THE STAGE MANAGER?
OKAY, TAKE A DEEP BREATH. I NEED YOU TO CALM DOWN AND LISTEN TO ME.
LADY, I DON'T KNOW WHO YOU ARE, BUT YOU NEED TO GET OUT OF MY WAY. MY DAD'S IN SOME KIND OF TROUBLE HERE, AND I...
...I DON'T KNOW WHAT TO DO...
BUT YOUR FATHER DOES. I KNOW THIS IS ALL NEW AND SCARY, BUT YOU HAVE TO TRUST ME.
I'VE KNOWN YOUR FATHER FOR YEARS, AND HE'S GOTTEN OUT OF FAR WORSE PICKLES THAN THIS ONE.
PICKLE? YOU CALL THIS A PICKLE? A BUNCH OF DEMON THINGS POPPED OUT OF THIN AIR AND DISAPPEARED WITH MY DAD!
OH GOD. NONE OF THIS MAKES ANY SENSE. I'M LOSING MY MIND.
NO, YOU'RE NOT. YOU'VE JUST COME INTO YOUR POWER, ZATANNA. YOU HAVE AN INCREDIBLE GIFT, AND YOU'RE GOING TO DO AMAZING THINGS WITH IT...
...ONCE YOU LEARN CONTROL.
THIS...THIS ISN'T A TRICK, IS IT?
ONLY ONE WAY TO FIND OUT.
FOLLOW ME.

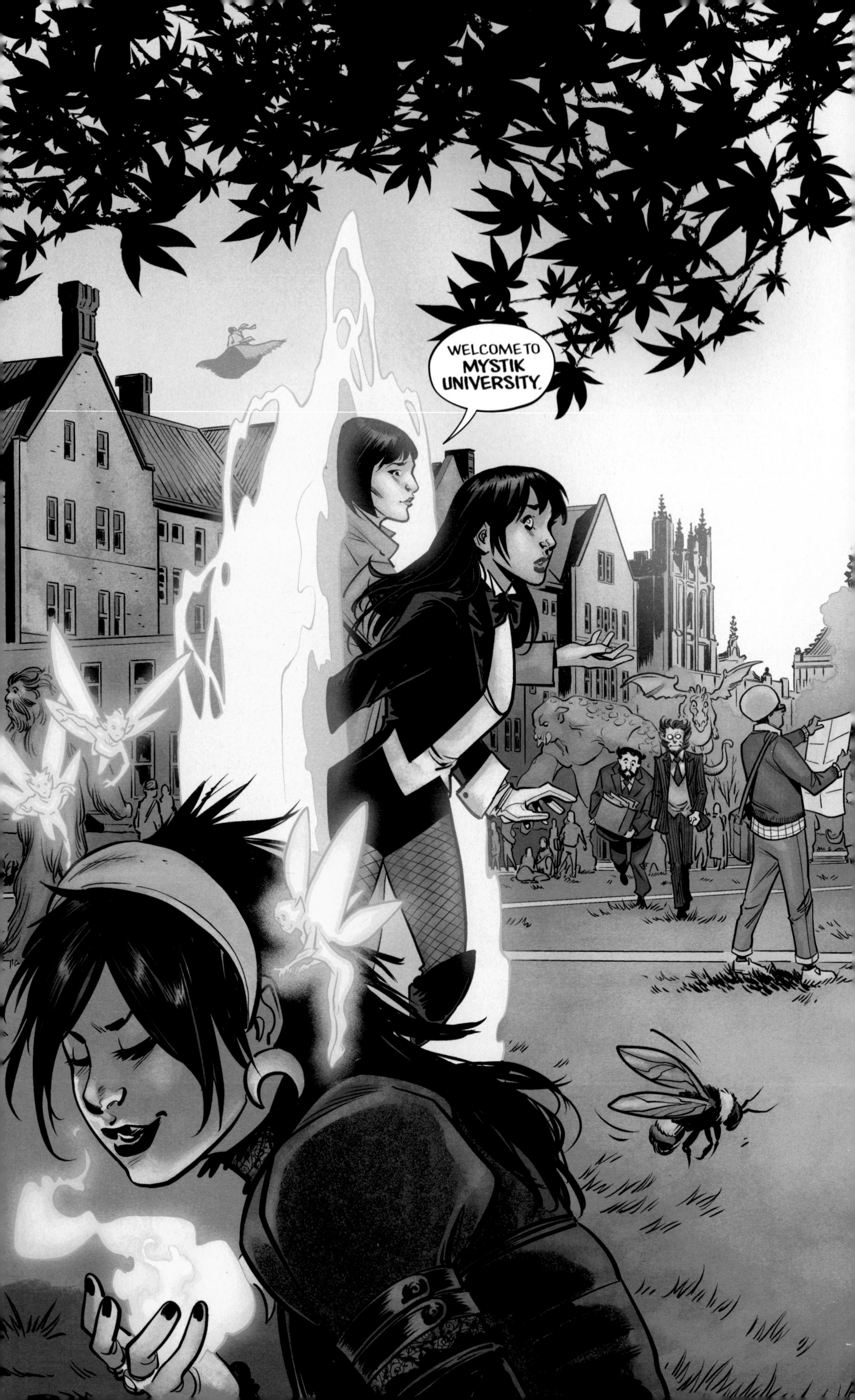
WELCOME TO MYSTIK UNIVERSITY.

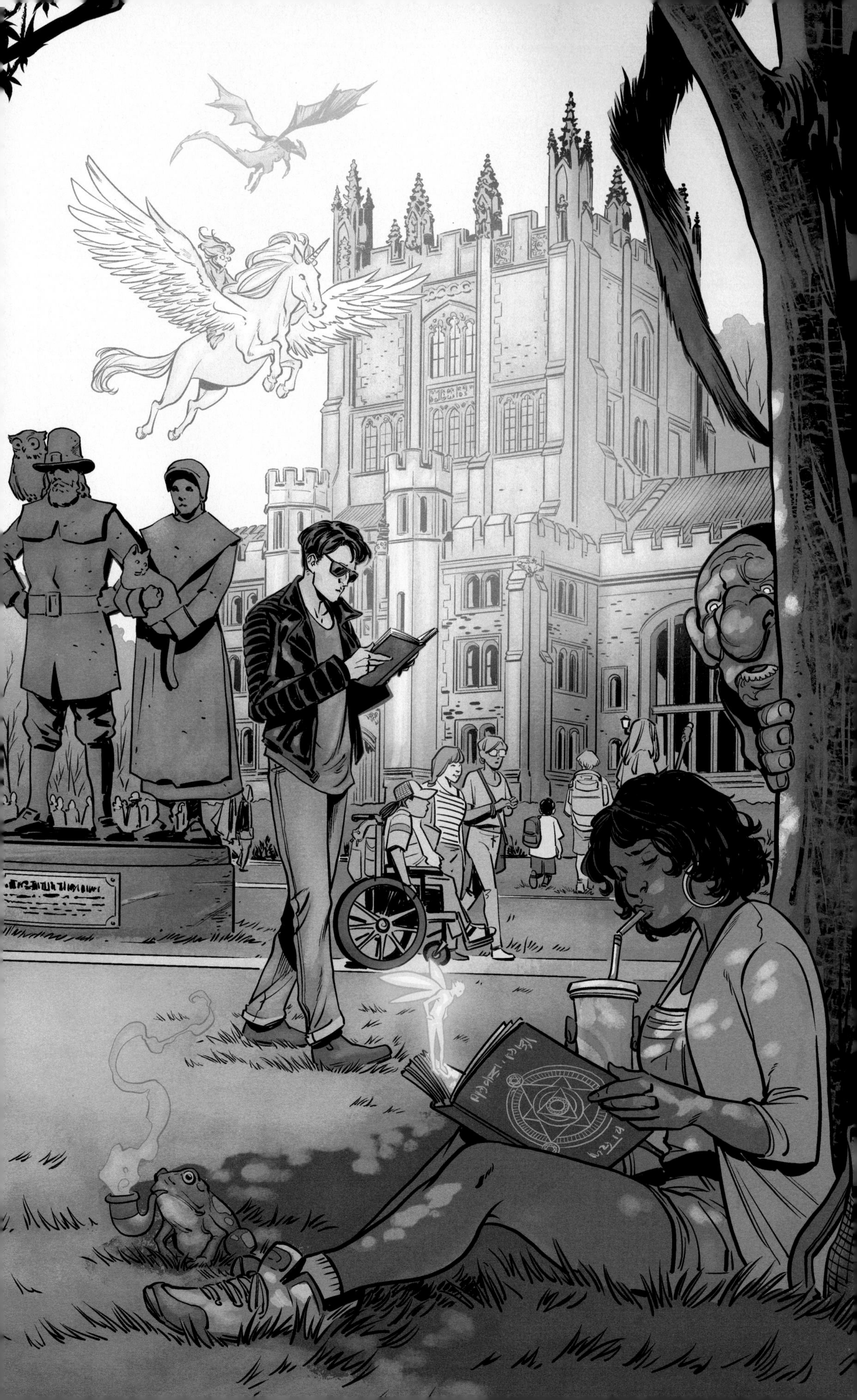

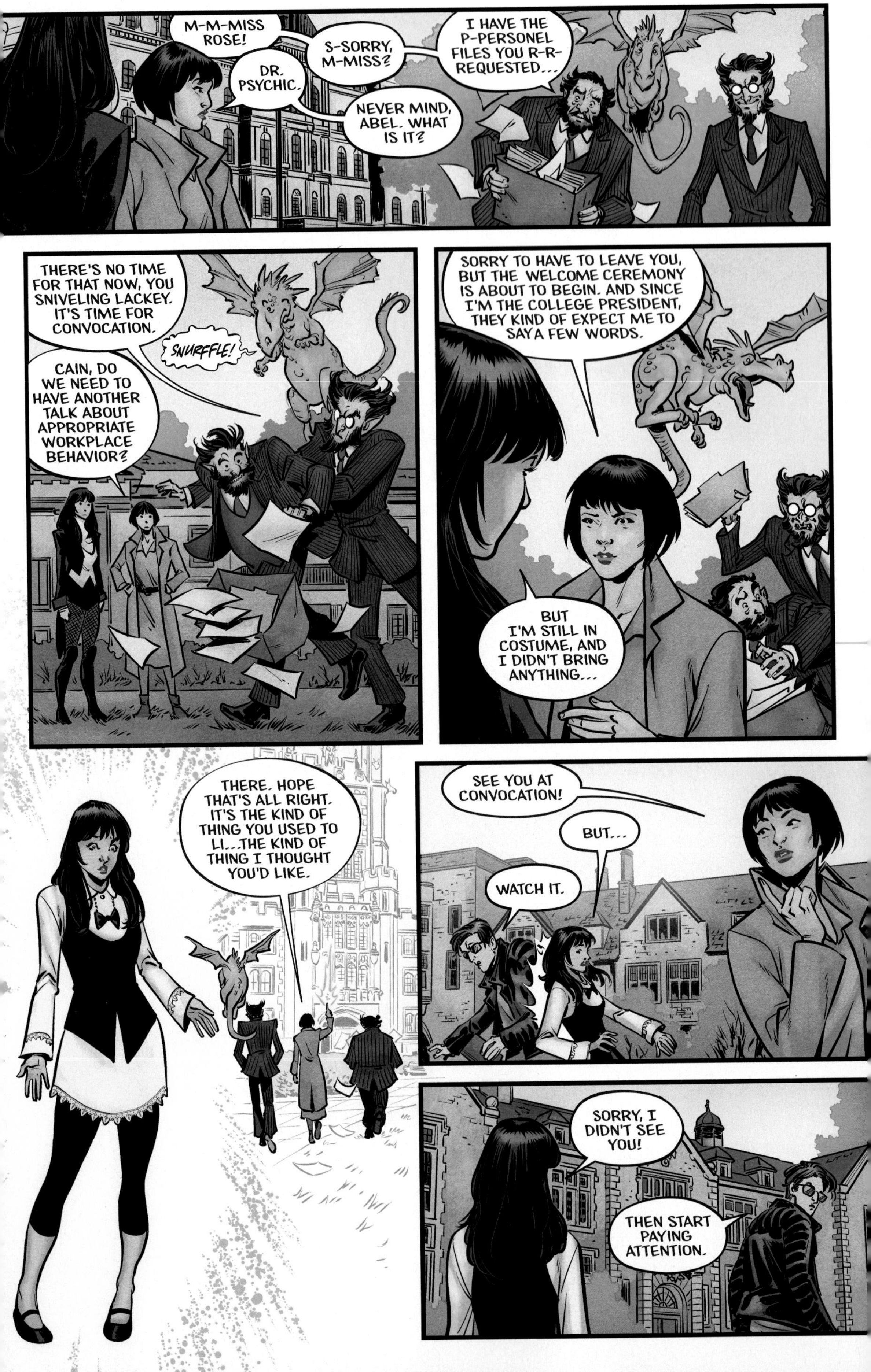
M-M-MISS ROSE!
DR. PSYCHIC.
S-SORRY, M-MISS?
NEVER MIND, ABEL. WHAT IS IT?
I HAVE THE P-PERSONEL FILES YOU R-R-REQUESTED...
THERE'S NO TIME FOR THAT NOW, YOU SNIVELING LACKEY. IT'S TIME FOR CONVOCATION.
SNURFFLE!
CAIN, DO WE NEED TO HAVE ANOTHER TALK ABOUT APPROPRIATE WORKPLACE BEHAVIOR?
SORRY TO HAVE TO LEAVE YOU, BUT THE WELCOME CEREMONY IS ABOUT TO BEGIN. AND SINCE I'M THE COLLEGE PRESIDENT, THEY KIND OF EXPECT ME TO SAY A FEW WORDS.
BUT I'M STILL IN COSTUME, AND I DIDN'T BRING ANYTHING...
THERE. HOPE THAT'S ALL RIGHT. IT'S THE KIND OF THING YOU USED TO LI...THE KIND OF THING I THOUGHT YOU'D LIKE.
SEE YOU AT CONVOCATION!
BUT...
WATCH IT.
SORRY, I DIDN'T SEE YOU!
THEN START PAYING ATTENTION.

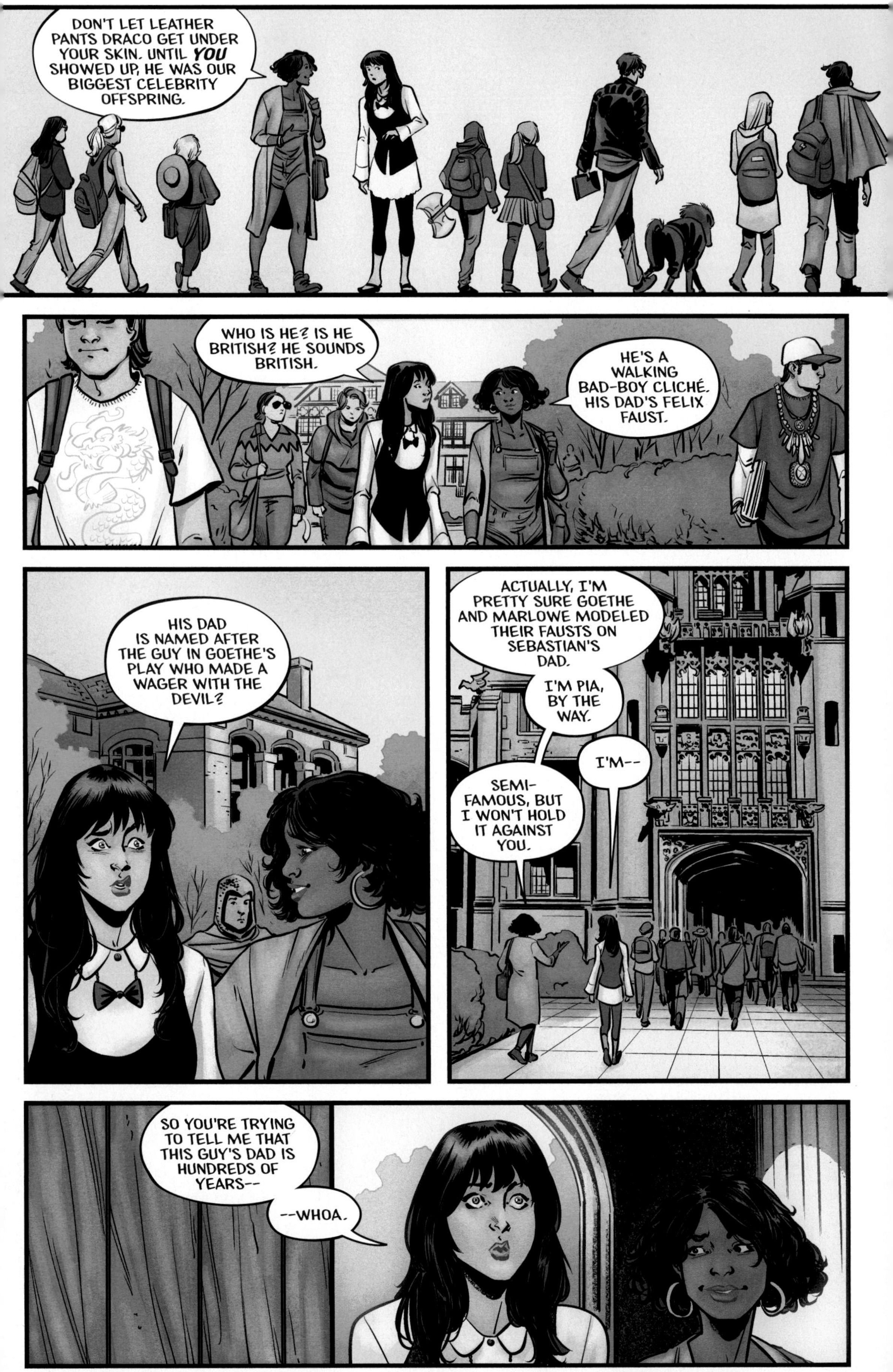
DON'T LET LEATHER PANTS DRACO GET UNDER YOUR SKIN. UNTIL YOU SHOWED UP, HE WAS OUR BIGGEST CELEBRITY OFFSPRING.
WHO IS HE? IS HE BRITISH? HE SOUNDS BRITISH.
HE'S A WALKING BAD-BOY CLICHÉ. HIS DAD'S FELIX FAUST.
HIS DAD IS NAMED AFTER THE GUY IN GOETHE'S PLAY WHO MADE A WAGER WITH THE DEVIL?
ACTUALLY, I'M PRETTY SURE GOETHE AND MARLOWE MODELED THEIR FAUSTS ON SEBASTIAN'S DAD.
I'M PIA, BY THE WAY.
I'M--
SEMI-FAMOUS, BUT I WON'T HOLD IT AGAINST YOU.
SO YOU'RE TRYING TO TELL ME THAT THIS GUY'S DAD IS HUNDREDS OF YEARS--
--WHOA.

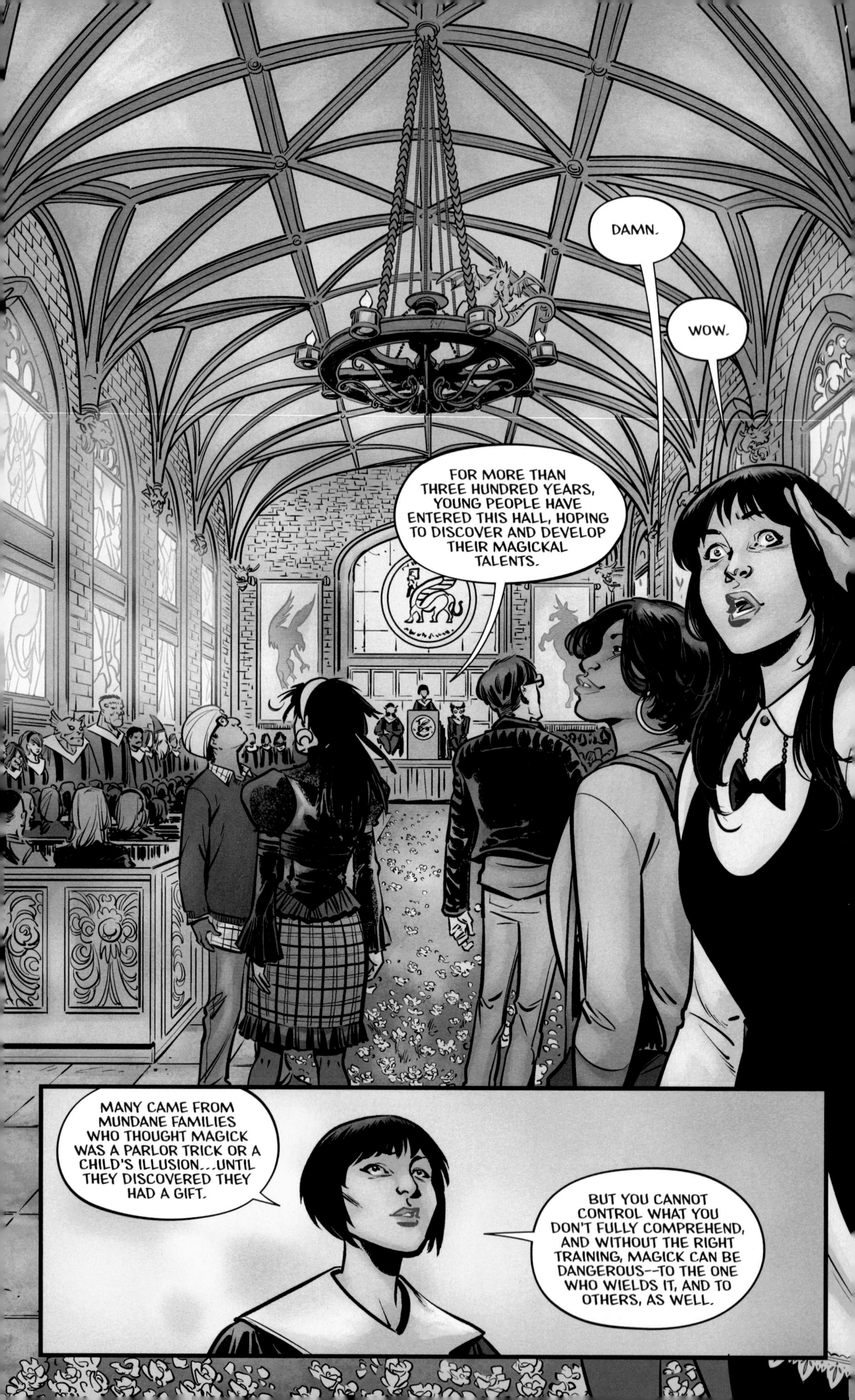
DAMN.
WOW.
FOR MORE THAN THREE HUNDRED YEARS, YOUNG PEOPLE HAVE ENTERED THIS HALL, HOPING TO DISCOVER AND DEVELOP THEIR MAGICKAL TALENTS.
MANY CAME FROM MUNDANE FAMILIES WHO THOUGHT MAGICK WAS A PARLOR TRICK OR A CHILD'S ILLUSION...UNTIL THEY DISCOVERED THEY HAD A GIFT.
BUT YOU CANNOT CONTROL WHAT YOU DON'T FULLY COMPREHEND, AND WITHOUT THE RIGHT TRAINING, MAGICK CAN BE DANGEROUS--TO THE ONE WHO WIELDS IT, AND TO OTHERS, AS WELL.

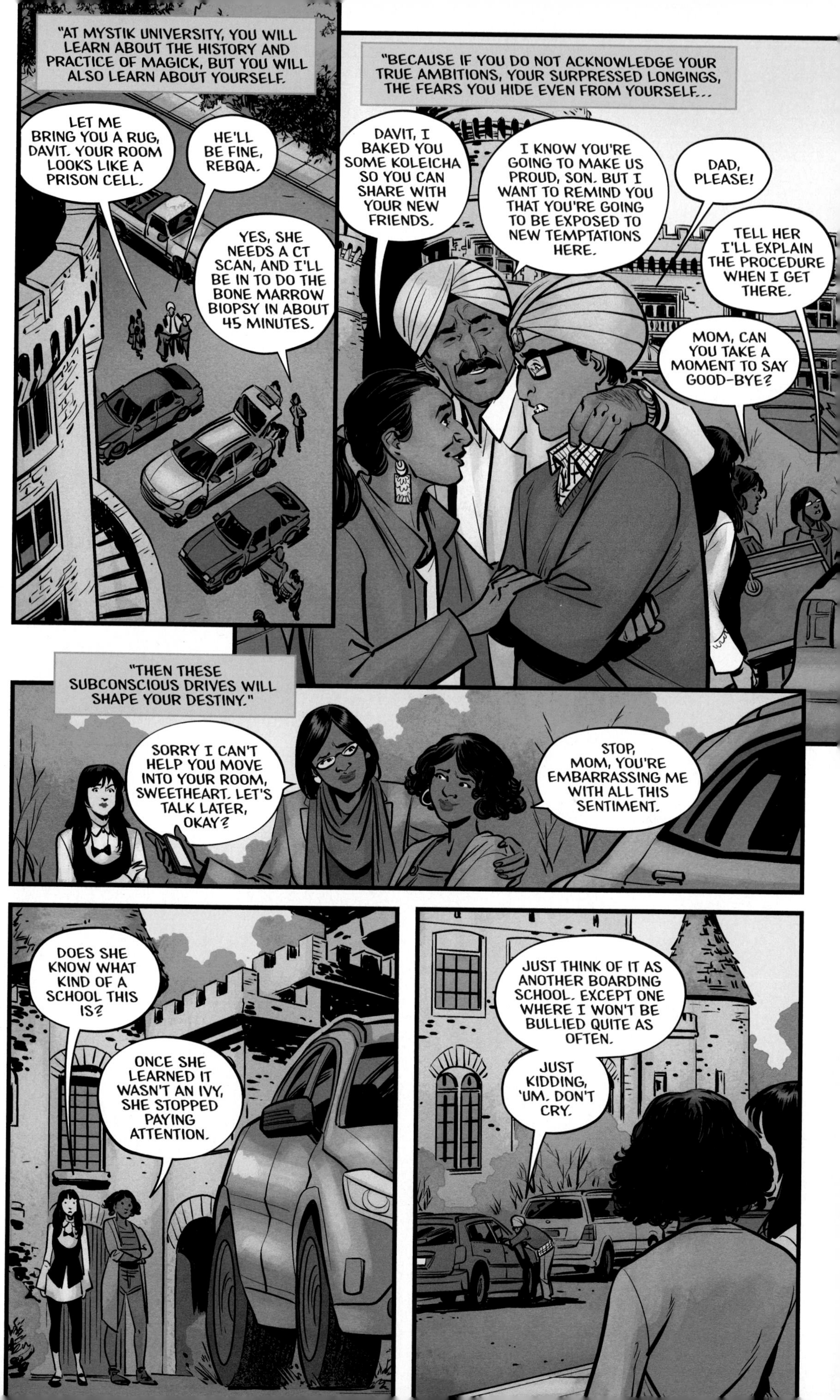
"AT MYSTIK UNIVERSITY, YOU WILL LEARN ABOUT THE HISTORY AND PRACTICE OF MAGICK, BUT YOU WILL ALSO LEARN ABOUT YOURSELF.
LET ME BRING YOU A RUG, DAVIT. YOUR ROOM LOOKS LIKE A PRISON CELL.
HE'LL BE FINE, REBQA.
YES, SHE NEEDS A CT SCAN, AND I'LL BE IN TO DO THE BONE MARROW BIOPSY IN ABOUT 45 MINUTES.
"BECAUSE IF YOU DO NOT ACKNOWLEDGE YOUR TRUE AMBITIONS, YOUR SURPRESSED LONGINGS, THE FEARS YOU HIDE EVEN FROM YOURSELF...
DAVIT, I BAKED YOU SOME KOLEICHA SO YOU CAN SHARE WITH YOUR NEW FRIENDS.
I KNOW YOU'RE GOING TO MAKE US PROUD, SON. BUT I WANT TO REMIND YOU THAT YOU'RE GOING TO BE EXPOSED TO NEW TEMPTATIONS HERE.
DAD, PLEASE!
TELL HER I'LL EXPLAIN THE PROCEDURE WHEN I GET THERE.
MOM, CAN YOU TAKE A MOMENT TO SAY GOOD-BYE?
"THEN THESE SUBCONSCIOUS DRIVES WILL SHAPE YOUR DESTINY."
SORRY I CAN'T HELP YOU MOVE INTO YOUR ROOM, SWEETHEART. LET'S TALK LATER, OKAY?
STOP, MOM, YOU'RE EMBARRASSING ME WITH ALL THIS SENTIMENT.
DOES SHE KNOW WHAT KIND OF A SCHOOL THIS IS?
ONCE SHE LEARNED IT WASN'T AN IVY, SHE STOPPED PAYING ATTENTION.
JUST THINK OF IT AS ANOTHER BOARDING SCHOOL. EXCEPT ONE WHERE I WON'T BE BULLIED QUITE AS OFTEN.
JUST KIDDING, 'UM. DON'T CRY.

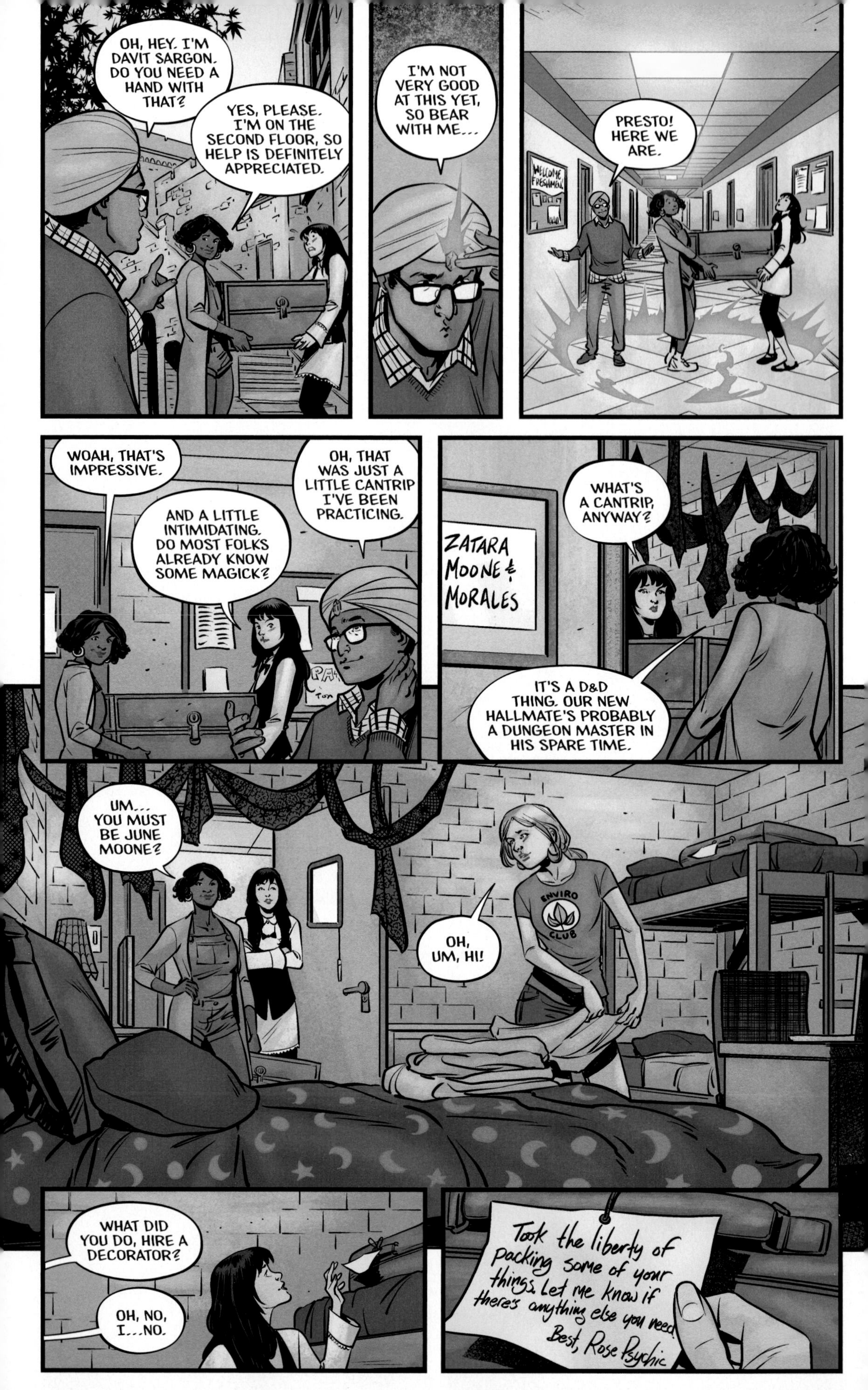
OH, HEY. I'M DAVIT SARGON. DO YOU NEED A HAND WITH THAT?
YES, PLEASE. I'M ON THE SECOND FLOOR, SO HELP IS DEFINITELY APPRECIATED.
I'M NOT VERY GOOD AT THIS YET, SO BEAR WITH ME...
PRESTO! HERE WE ARE.
WELCOME FRESHMEN
WOAH, THAT'S IMPRESSIVE.
AND A LITTLE INTIMIDATING. DO MOST FOLKS ALREADY KNOW SOME MAGICK?
OH, THAT WAS JUST A LITTLE CANTRIP I'VE BEEN PRACTICING.
ZATARA MOONE & MORALES
WHAT'S A CANTRIP, ANYWAY?
IT'S A D&D THING. OUR NEW HALLMATE'S PROBABLY A DUNGEON MASTER IN HIS SPARE TIME.
UM... YOU MUST BE JUNE MOONE?
OH, UM, HI!
ENVIRO CLUB
WHAT DID YOU DO, HIRE A DECORATOR?
OH, NO, I...NO.
Took the liberty of packing some of your things. Let me know if there's anything else you need. Best, Rose Psychic

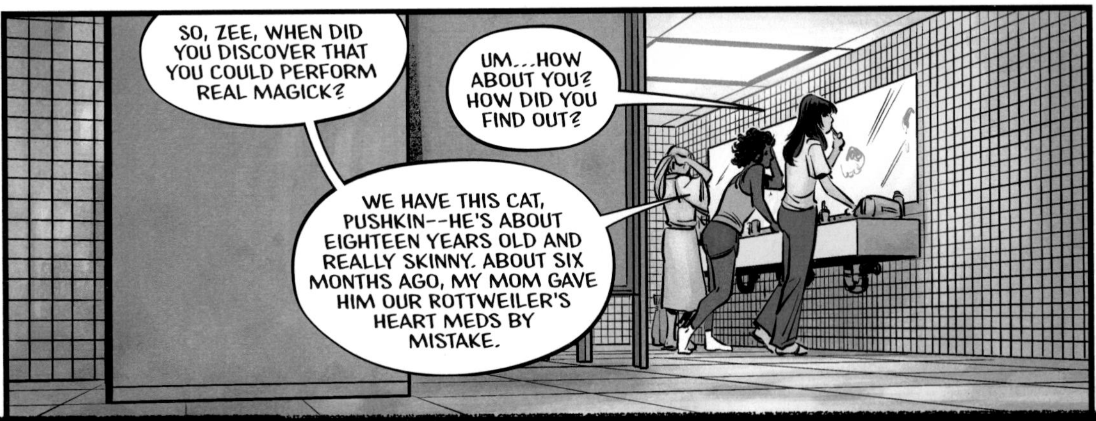
SO, ZEE, WHEN DID YOU DISCOVER THAT YOU COULD PERFORM REAL MAGICK?
UM...HOW ABOUT YOU? HOW DID YOU FIND OUT?
WE HAVE THIS CAT, PUSHKIN--HE'S ABOUT EIGHTEEN YEARS OLD AND REALLY SKINNY. ABOUT SIX MONTHS AGO, MY MOM GAVE HIM OUR ROTTWEILER'S HEART MEDS BY MISTAKE.

Chapter Two: Magickal Hygiene

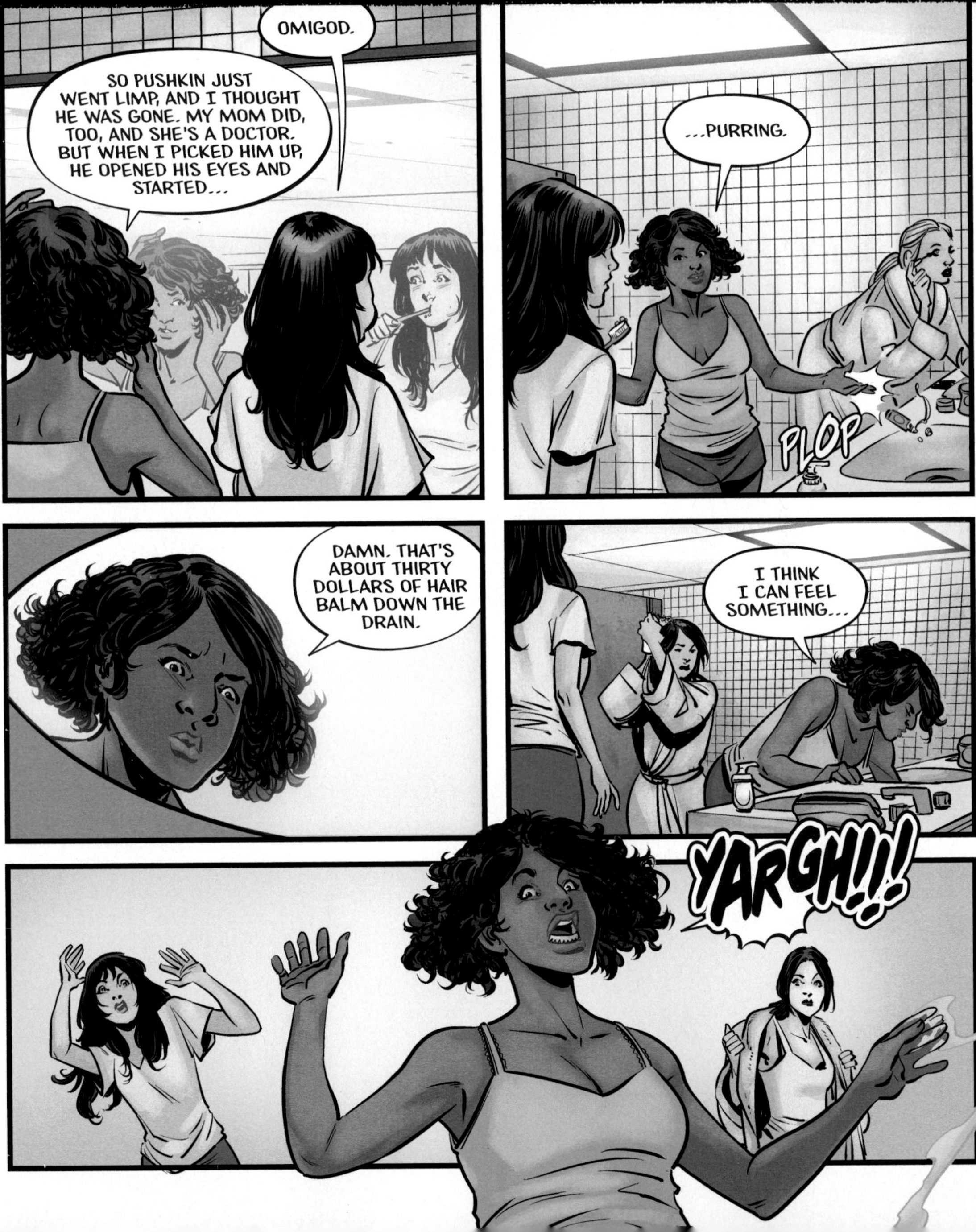
SO PUSHKIN JUST WENT LIMP, AND I THOUGHT HE WAS GONE. MY MOM DID, TOO, AND SHE'S A DOCTOR. BUT WHEN I PICKED HIM UP, HE OPENED HIS EYES AND STARTED...
OMIGOD.
...PURRING.
PLOP
DAMN. THAT'S ABOUT THIRTY DOLLARS OF HAIR BALM DOWN THE DRAIN.
I THINK I CAN FEEL SOMETHING...
YARGH!!!

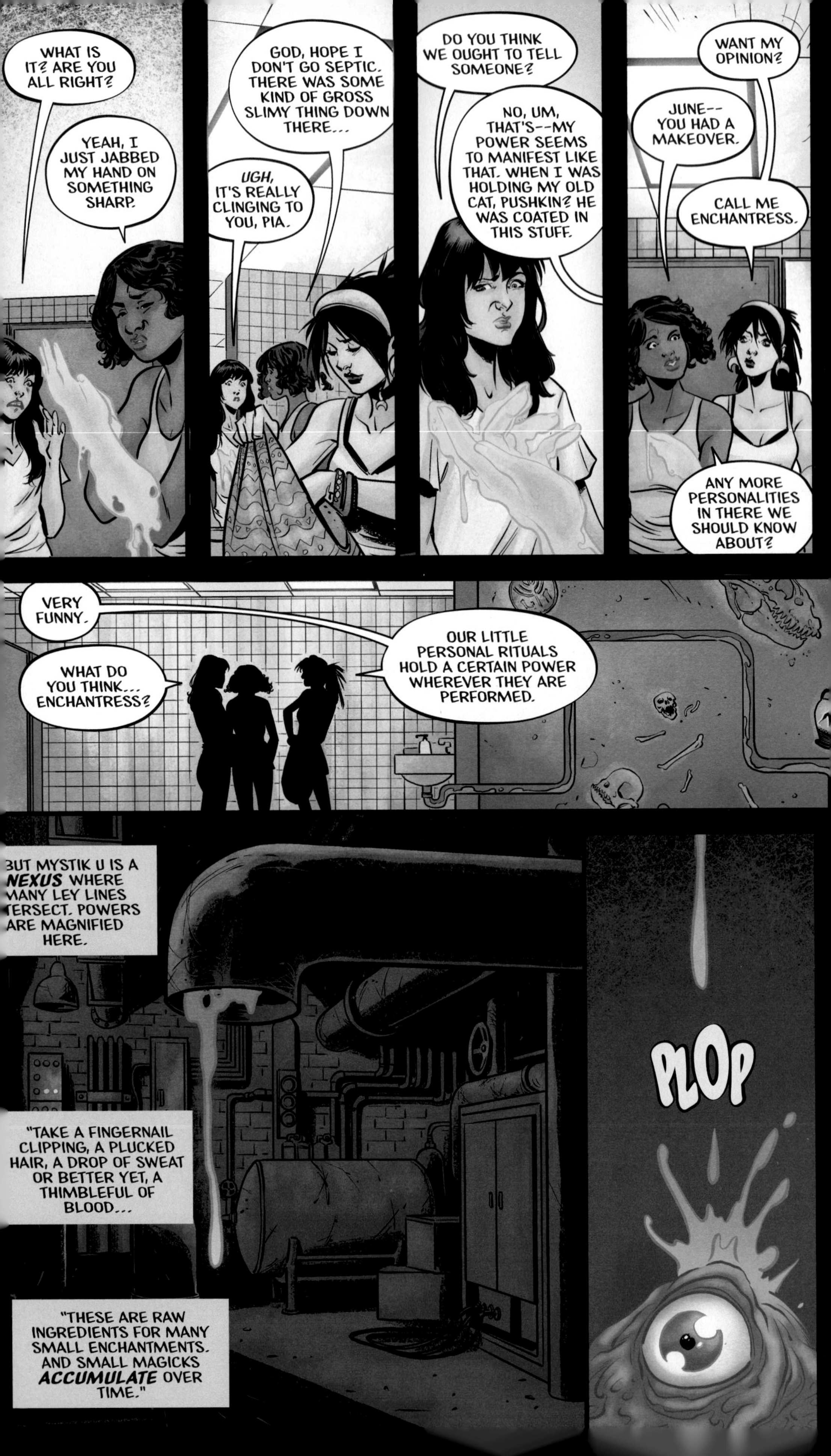

WHAT IS IT? ARE YOU ALL RIGHT?
YEAH, I JUST JABBED MY HAND ON SOMETHING SHARP.
GOD, HOPE I DON'T GO SEPTIC. THERE WAS SOME KIND OF GROSS SLIMY THING DOWN THERE...
UGH, IT'S REALLY CLINGING TO YOU, PIA.
DO YOU THINK WE OUGHT TO TELL SOMEONE?
NO, UM, THAT'S--MY POWER SEEMS TO MANIFEST LIKE THAT. WHEN I WAS HOLDING MY OLD CAT, PUSHKIN? HE WAS COATED IN THIS STUFF.
WANT MY OPINION?
JUNE--YOU HAD A MAKEOVER.
CALL ME ENCHANTRESS.
ANY MORE PERSONALITIES IN THERE WE SHOULD KNOW ABOUT?
VERY FUNNY.
WHAT DO YOU THINK... ENCHANTRESS?
OUR LITTLE PERSONAL RITUALS HOLD A CERTAIN POWER WHEREVER THEY ARE PERFORMED.
BUT MYSTIK U IS A NEXUS WHERE MANY LEY LINES TERSECT. POWERS ARE MAGNIFIED HERE.
"TAKE A FINGERNAIL CLIPPING, A PLUCKED HAIR, A DROP OF SWEAT OR BETTER YET, A THIMBLEFUL OF BLOOD...
"THESE ARE RAW INGREDIENTS FOR MANY SMALL ENCHANTMENTS. AND SMALL MAGICKS ACCUMULATE OVER TIME."
PLOP

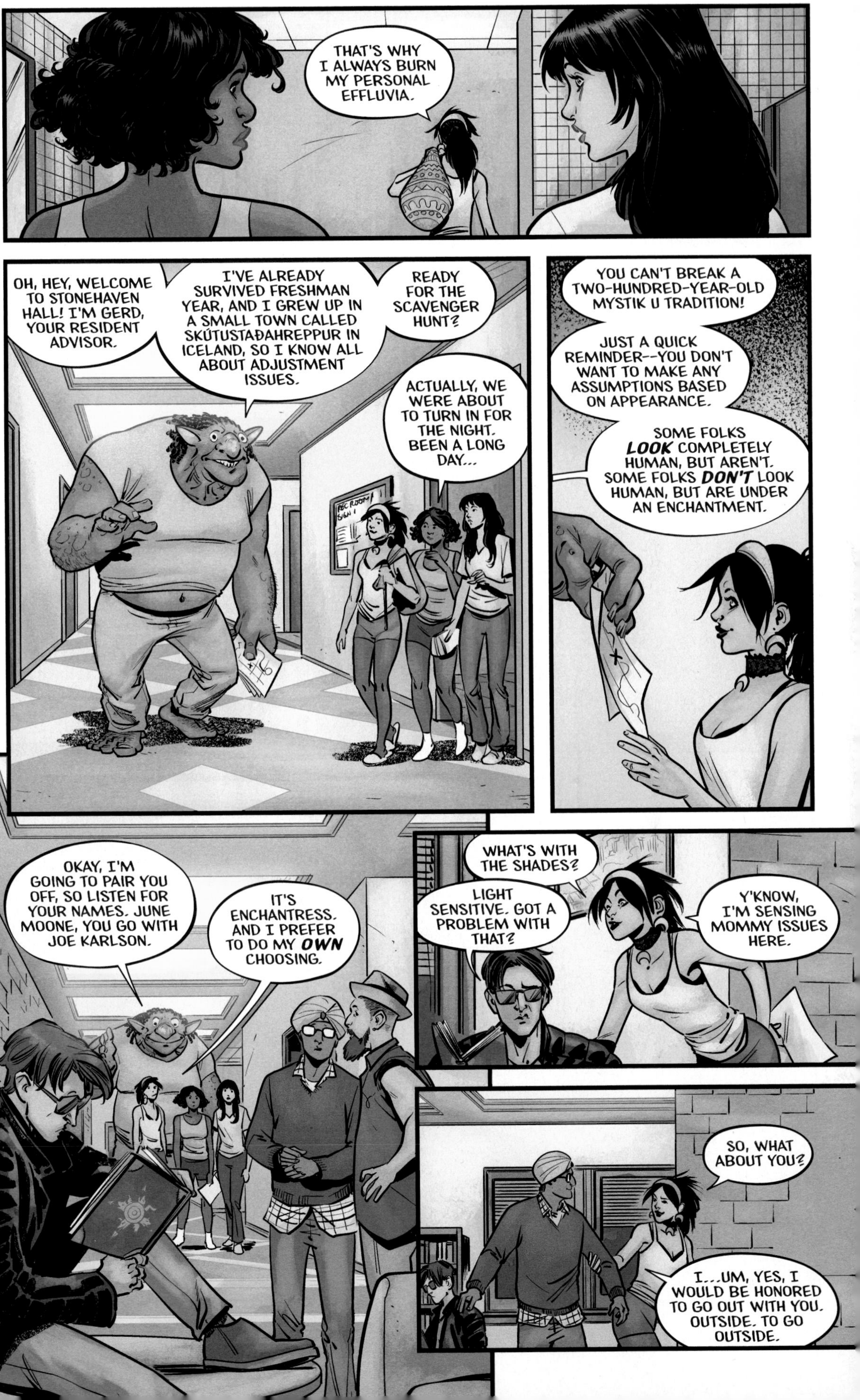
THAT'S WHY I ALWAYS BURN MY PERSONAL EFFLUVIA.
OH, HEY, WELCOME TO STONEHAVEN HALL! I'M GERD, YOUR RESIDENT ADVISOR.
I'VE ALREADY SURVIVED FRESHMAN YEAR, AND I GREW UP IN A SMALL TOWN CALLED SKÚTUSTAÐAHREPPUR IN ICELAND, SO I KNOW ALL ABOUT ADJUSTMENT ISSUES.
READY FOR THE SCAVENGER HUNT?
ACTUALLY, WE WERE ABOUT TO TURN IN FOR THE NIGHT. BEEN A LONG DAY...
REC ROOM SIGN I
YOU CAN'T BREAK A TWO-HUNDRED-YEAR-OLD MYSTIK U TRADITION!
JUST A QUICK REMINDER--YOU DON'T WANT TO MAKE ANY ASSUMPTIONS BASED ON APPEARANCE.
SOME FOLKS **LOOK** COMPLETELY HUMAN, BUT AREN'T. SOME FOLKS **DON'T** LOOK HUMAN, BUT ARE UNDER AN ENCHANTMENT.
OKAY, I'M GOING TO PAIR YOU OFF, SO LISTEN FOR YOUR NAMES. JUNE MOONE, YOU GO WITH JOE KARLSON.
IT'S ENCHANTRESS. AND I PREFER TO DO MY ***OWN*** CHOOSING.
WHAT'S WITH THE SHADES?
LIGHT SENSITIVE. GOT A PROBLEM WITH THAT?
Y'KNOW, I'M SENSING MOMMY ISSUES HERE.
SO, WHAT ABOUT YOU?
I...UM, YES, I WOULD BE HONORED TO GO OUT WITH YOU. OUTSIDE. TO GO OUTSIDE.

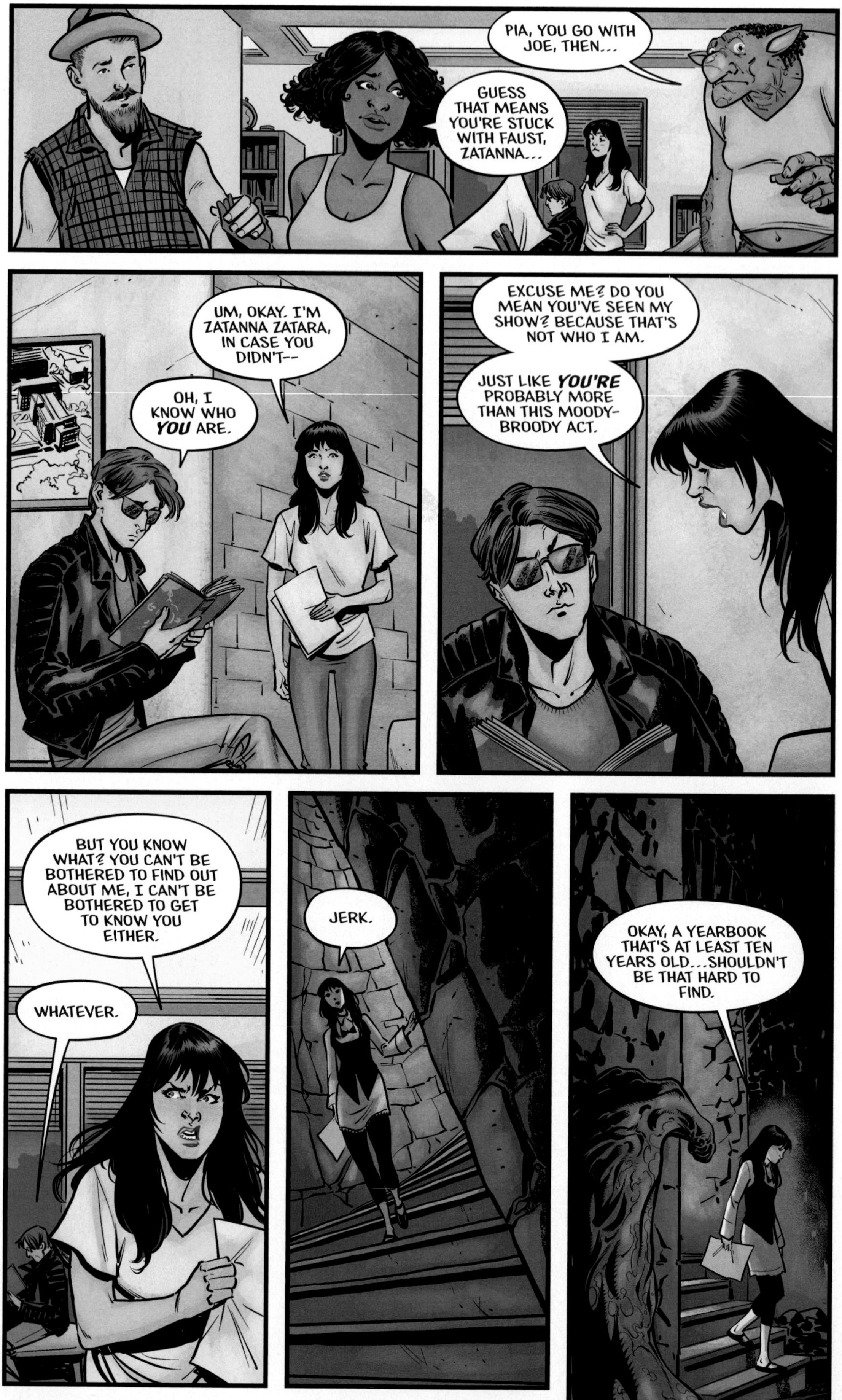
PIA, YOU GO WITH JOE, THEN...
GUESS THAT MEANS YOU'RE STUCK WITH FAUST, ZATANNA...
UM, OKAY. I'M ZATANNA ZATARA, IN CASE YOU DIDN'T--
OH, I KNOW WHO YOU ARE.
EXCUSE ME? DO YOU MEAN YOU'VE SEEN MY SHOW? BECAUSE THAT'S NOT WHO I AM.
JUST LIKE YOU'RE PROBABLY MORE THAN THIS MOODY-BROODY ACT.
BUT YOU KNOW WHAT? YOU CAN'T BE BOTHERED TO FIND OUT ABOUT ME, I CAN'T BE BOTHERED TO GET TO KNOW YOU EITHER.
WHATEVER.
JERK.
OKAY, A YEARBOOK THAT'S AT LEAST TEN YEARS OLD...SHOULDN'T BE THAT HARD TO FIND.

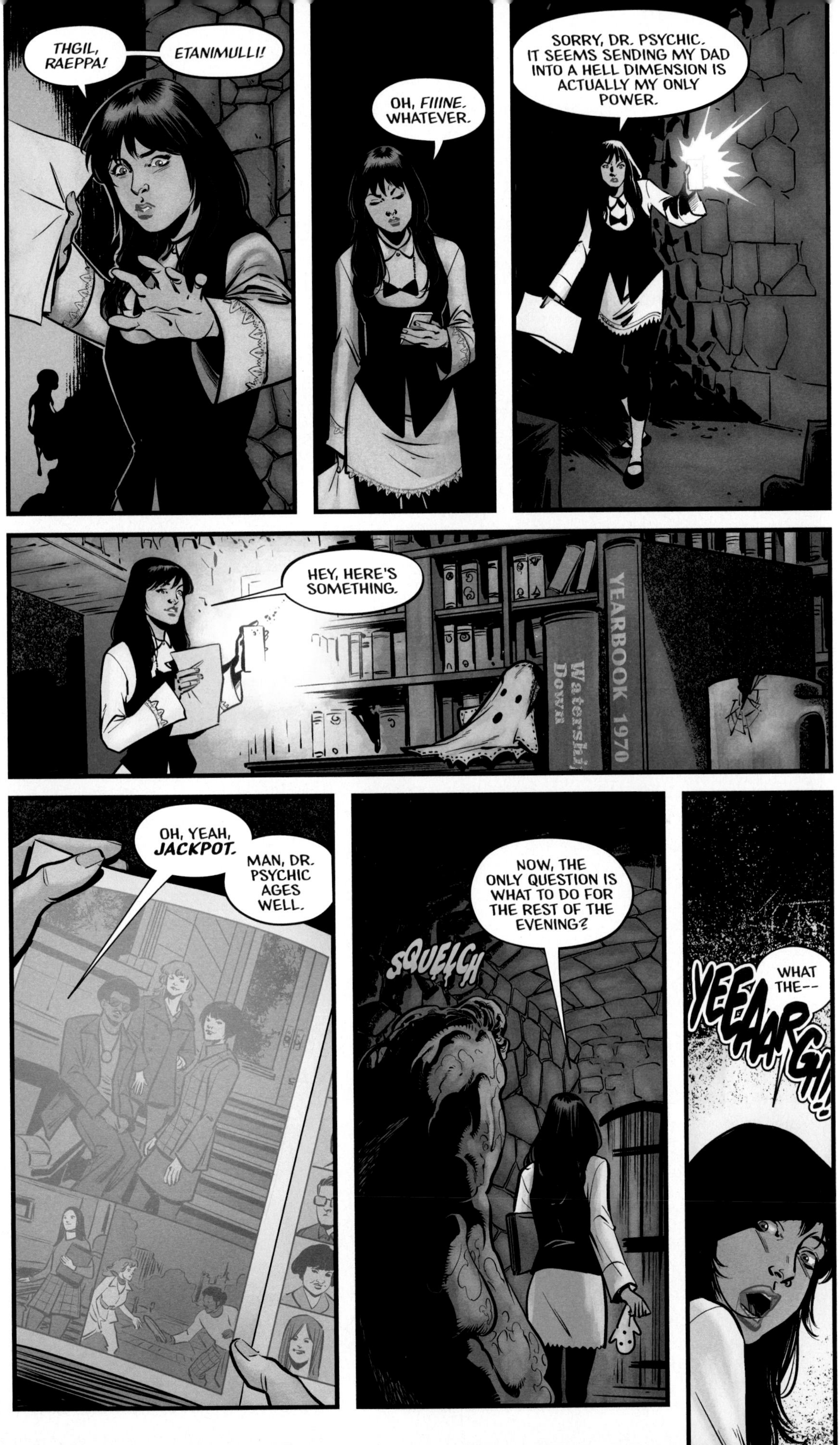
THGIL, RAEPPA!
ETANIMULLI!
OH, FIIINE. WHATEVER.
SORRY, DR. PSYCHIC. IT SEEMS SENDING MY DAD INTO A HELL DIMENSION IS ACTUALLY MY ONLY POWER.
HEY, HERE'S SOMETHING.
YEARBOOK 1970
Watership Down
OH, YEAH, JACKPOT.
MAN, DR. PSYCHIC AGES WELL.
NOW, THE ONLY QUESTION IS WHAT TO DO FOR THE REST OF THE EVENING?
SQUELCH
WHAT THE--
YEEAARGH!!

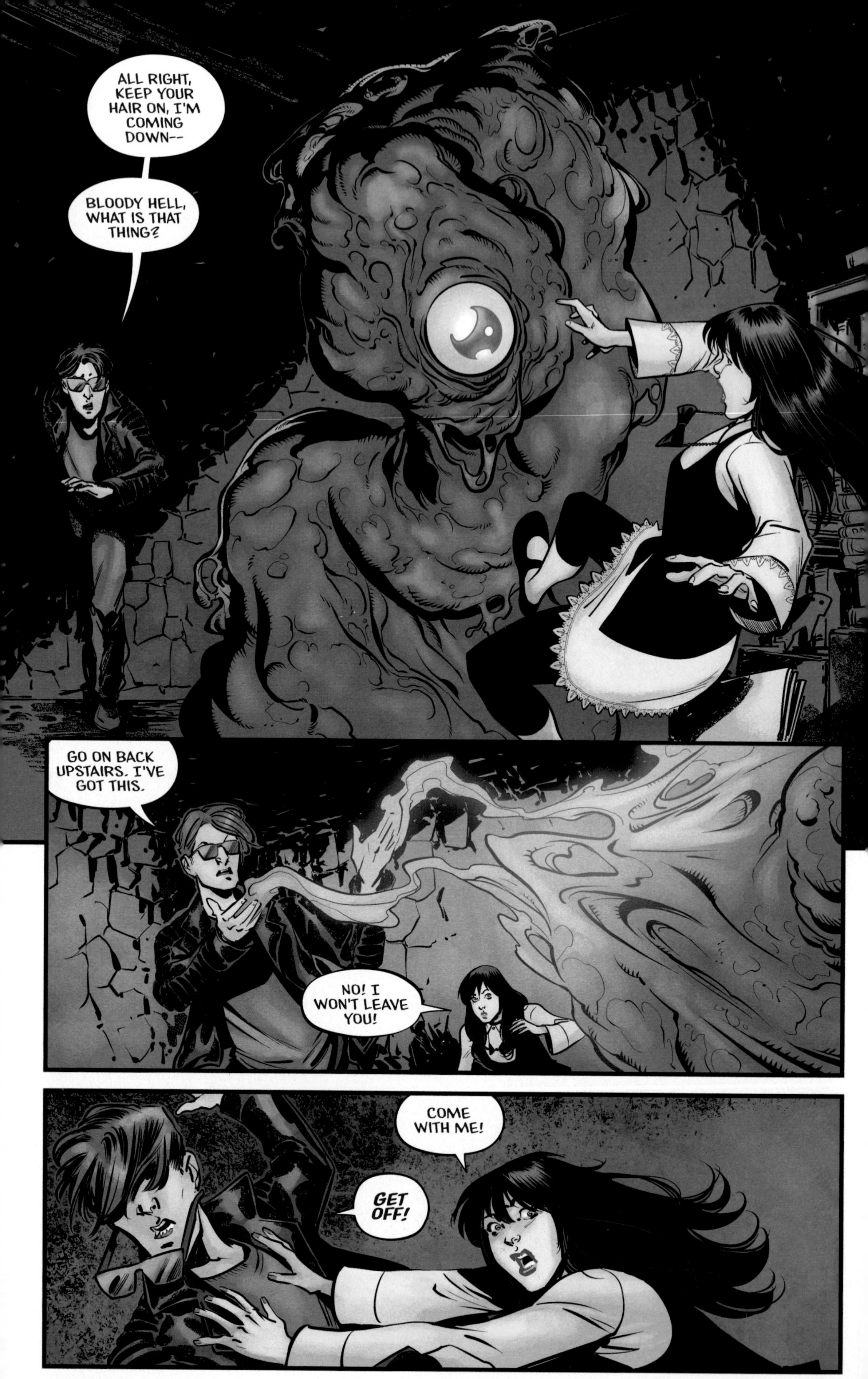
ALL RIGHT, KEEP YOUR HAIR ON, I'M COMING DOWN--
BLOODY HELL, WHAT IS THAT THING?
GO ON BACK UPSTAIRS. I'VE GOT THIS.
NO! I WON'T LEAVE YOU!
COME WITH ME!
GET OFF!

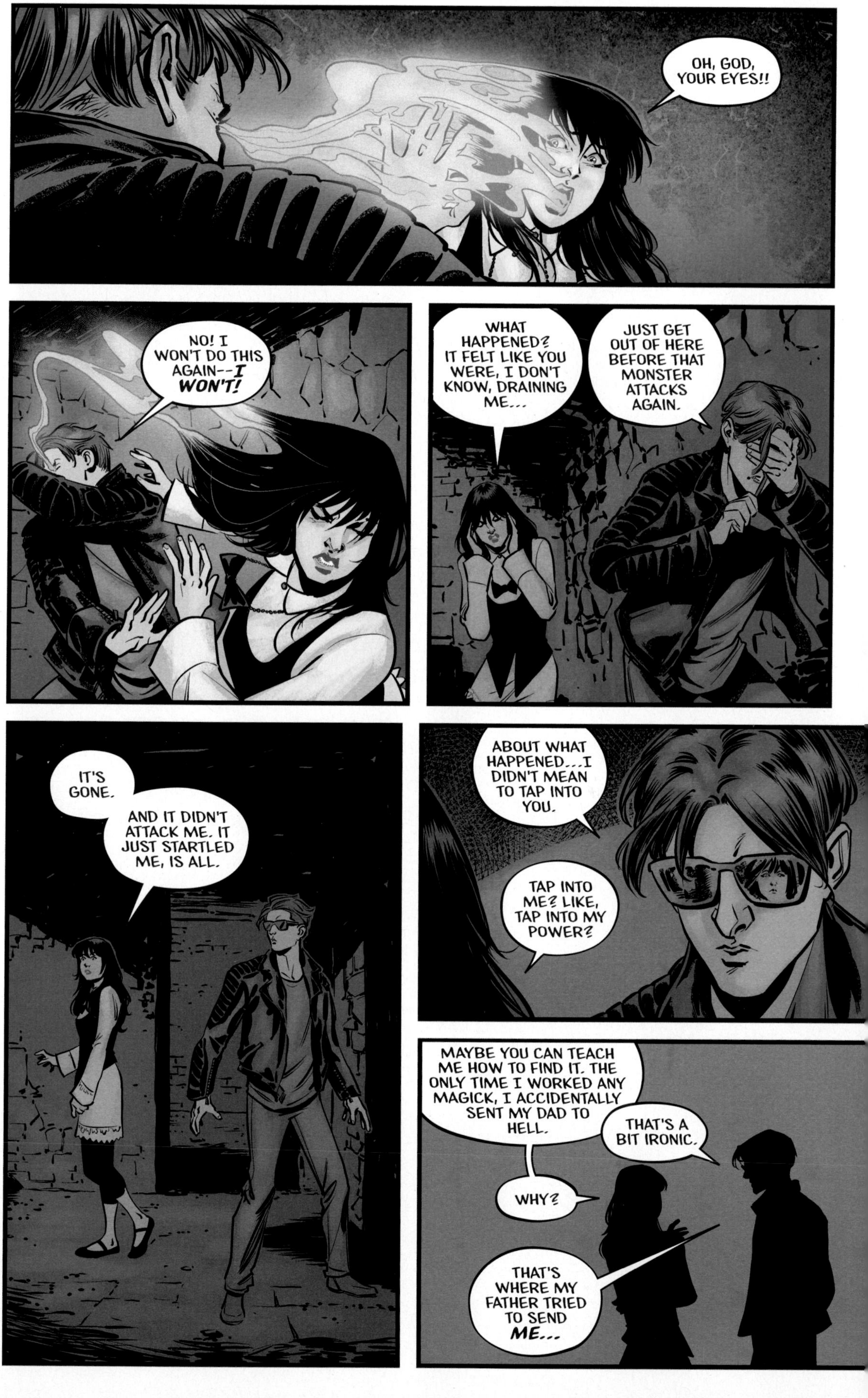
OH, GOD, YOUR EYES!!
NO! I WON'T DO THIS AGAIN--*I WON'T!*
WHAT HAPPENED? IT FELT LIKE YOU WERE, I DON'T KNOW, DRAINING ME...
JUST GET OUT OF HERE BEFORE THAT MONSTER ATTACKS AGAIN.
IT'S GONE.
AND IT DIDN'T ATTACK ME. IT JUST STARTLED ME, IS ALL.
ABOUT WHAT HAPPENED...I DIDN'T MEAN TO TAP INTO YOU.
TAP INTO ME? LIKE, TAP INTO MY POWER?
MAYBE YOU CAN TEACH ME HOW TO FIND IT. THE ONLY TIME I WORKED ANY MAGICK, I ACCIDENTALLY SENT MY DAD TO HELL.
THAT'S A BIT IRONIC.
WHY?
THAT'S WHERE MY FATHER TRIED TO SEND *ME...*

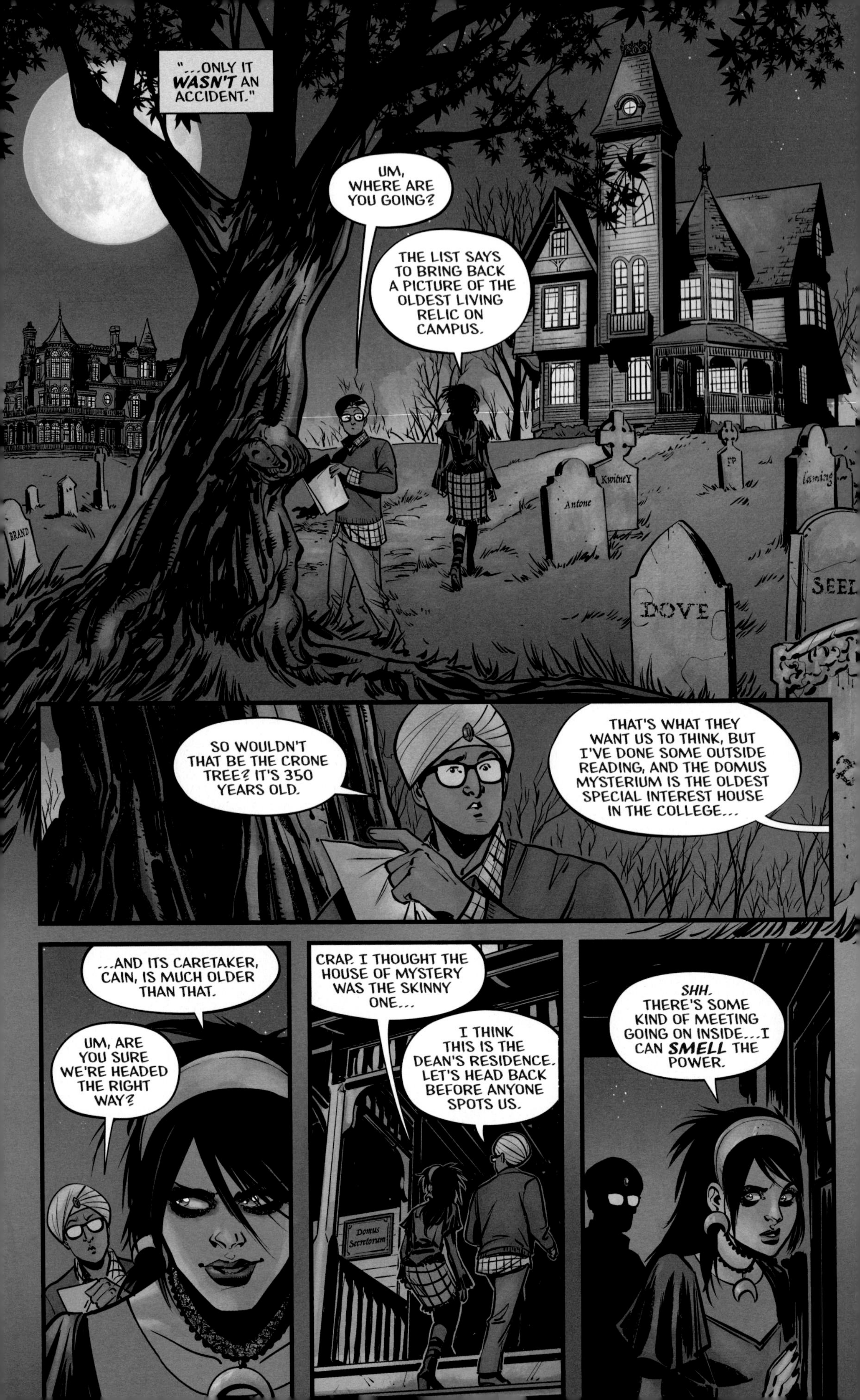
"...ONLY IT *WASN'T* AN ACCIDENT."
UM, WHERE ARE YOU GOING?
THE LIST SAYS TO BRING BACK A PICTURE OF THE OLDEST LIVING RELIC ON CAMPUS.
BRAND
Antone
KwitneY
DOVE
SEEL
SO WOULDN'T THAT BE THE CRONE TREE? IT'S 350 YEARS OLD.
THAT'S WHAT THEY WANT US TO THINK, BUT I'VE DONE SOME OUTSIDE READING, AND THE DOMUS MYSTERIUM IS THE OLDEST SPECIAL INTEREST HOUSE IN THE COLLEGE...
...AND ITS CARETAKER, CAIN, IS MUCH OLDER THAN THAT.
UM, ARE YOU SURE WE'RE HEADED THE RIGHT WAY?
CRAP. I THOUGHT THE HOUSE OF MYSTERY WAS THE SKINNY ONE...
I THINK THIS IS THE DEAN'S RESIDENCE. LET'S HEAD BACK BEFORE ANYONE SPOTS US.
Domus Secretorum
SHH. THERE'S SOME KIND OF MEETING GOING ON INSIDE...I CAN ***SMELL*** THE POWER.

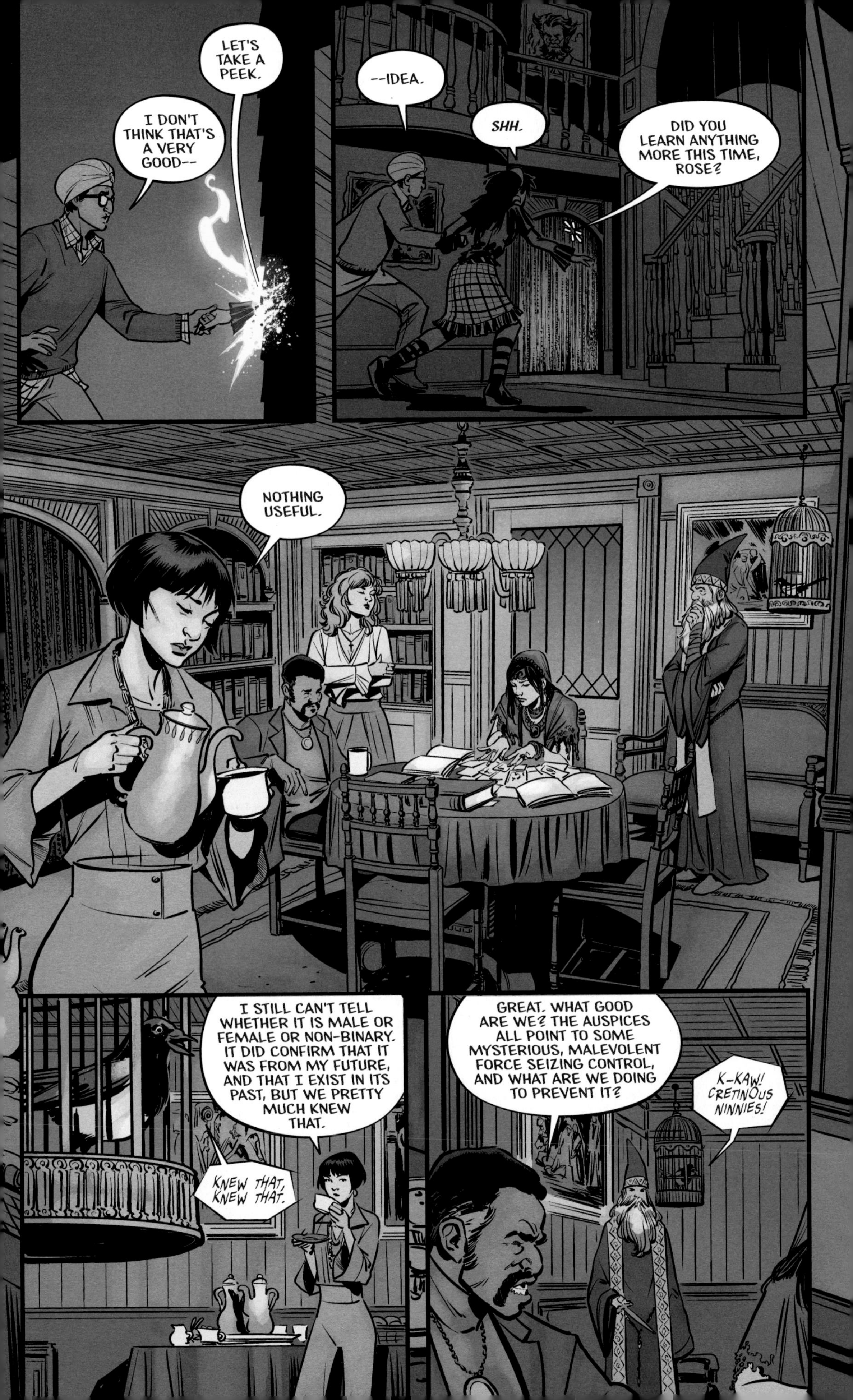
I DON'T THINK THAT'S A VERY GOOD--
LET'S TAKE A PEEK.
--IDEA.
SHH.
DID YOU LEARN ANYTHING MORE THIS TIME, ROSE?
NOTHING USEFUL.
I STILL CAN'T TELL WHETHER IT IS MALE OR FEMALE OR NON-BINARY. IT DID CONFIRM THAT IT WAS FROM MY FUTURE, AND THAT I EXIST IN ITS PAST, BUT WE PRETTY MUCH KNEW THAT.
KNEW THAT, KNEW THAT.
GREAT. WHAT GOOD ARE WE? THE AUSPICES ALL POINT TO SOME MYSTERIOUS, MALEVOLENT FORCE SEIZING CONTROL, AND WHAT ARE WE DOING TO PREVENT IT?
K-KAW! CRETINOUS NINNIES!

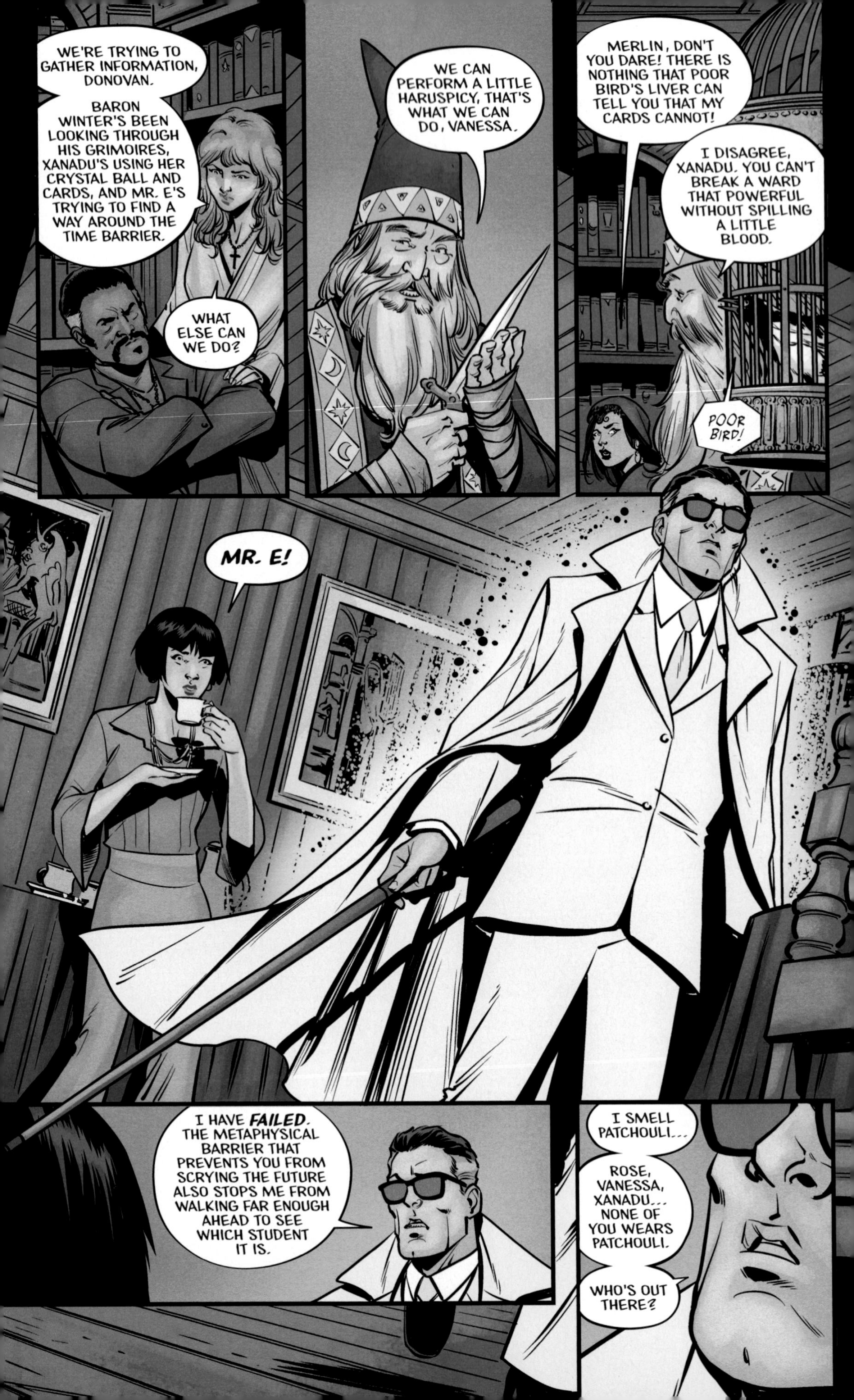
WE'RE TRYING TO GATHER INFORMATION, DONOVAN.
BARON WINTER'S BEEN LOOKING THROUGH HIS GRIMOIRES, XANADU'S USING HER CRYSTAL BALL AND CARDS, AND MR. E'S TRYING TO FIND A WAY AROUND THE TIME BARRIER.
WHAT ELSE CAN WE DO?
WE CAN PERFORM A LITTLE HARUSPICY, THAT'S WHAT WE CAN DO, VANESSA.
MERLIN, DON'T YOU DARE! THERE IS NOTHING THAT POOR BIRD'S LIVER CAN TELL YOU THAT MY CARDS CANNOT!
I DISAGREE, XANADU. YOU CAN'T BREAK A WARD THAT POWERFUL WITHOUT SPILLING A LITTLE BLOOD.
POOR BIRD!
MR. E!
I HAVE FAILED. THE METAPHYSICAL BARRIER THAT PREVENTS YOU FROM SCRYING THE FUTURE ALSO STOPS ME FROM WALKING FAR ENOUGH AHEAD TO SEE WHICH STUDENT IT IS.
I SMELL PATCHOULI...
ROSE, VANESSA, XANADU... NONE OF YOU WEARS PATCHOULI.
WHO'S OUT THERE?

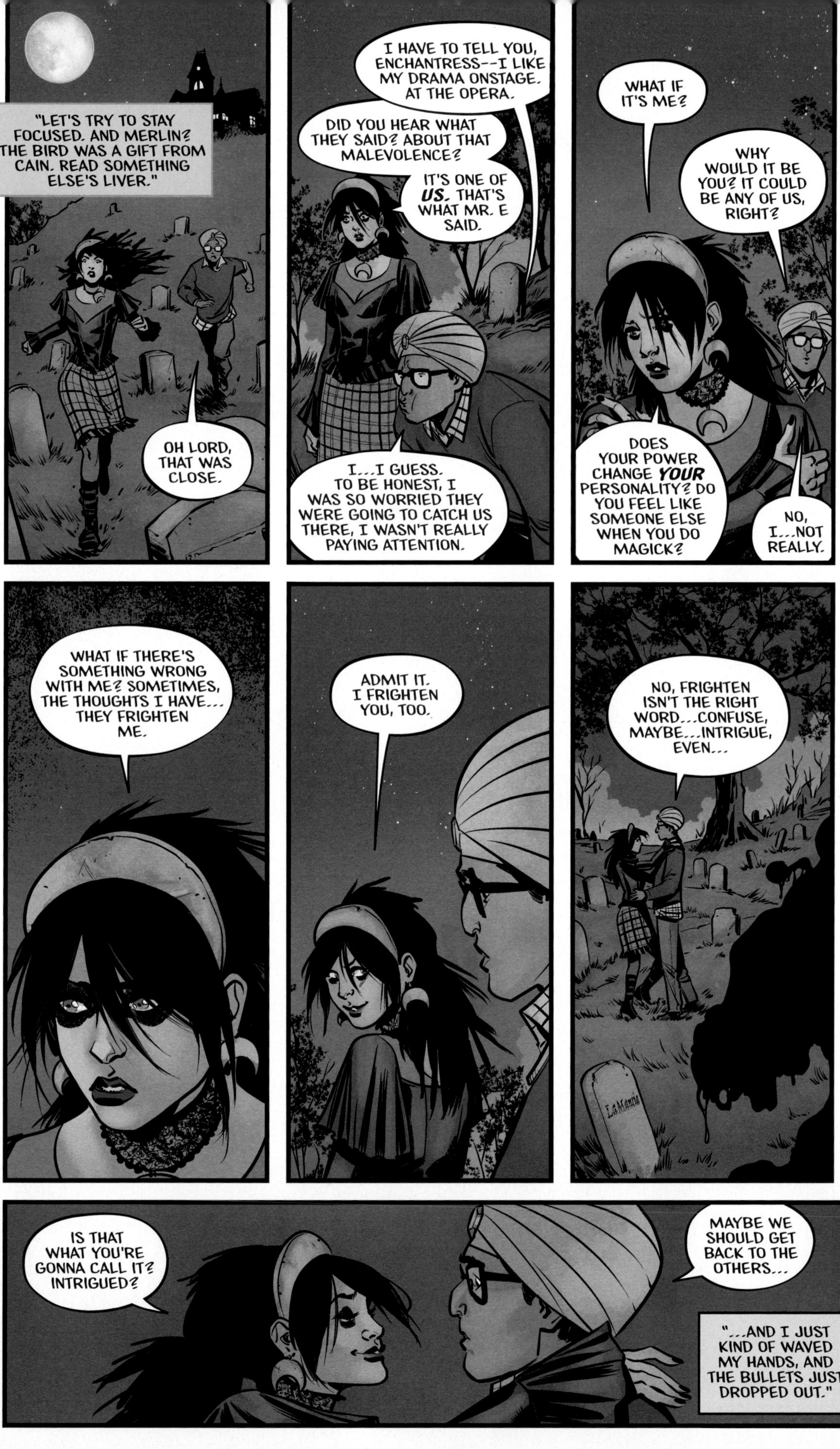
"LET'S TRY TO STAY FOCUSED. AND MERLIN? THE BIRD WAS A GIFT FROM CAIN. READ SOMETHING ELSE'S LIVER."
OH LORD, THAT WAS CLOSE.
I HAVE TO TELL YOU, ENCHANTRESS--I LIKE MY DRAMA ONSTAGE. AT THE OPERA.
DID YOU HEAR WHAT THEY SAID? ABOUT THAT MALEVOLENCE?
IT'S ONE OF US. THAT'S WHAT MR. E SAID.
I...I GUESS. TO BE HONEST, I WAS SO WORRIED THEY WERE GOING TO CATCH US THERE, I WASN'T REALLY PAYING ATTENTION.
WHAT IF IT'S ME?
WHY WOULD IT BE YOU? IT COULD BE ANY OF US, RIGHT?
DOES YOUR POWER CHANGE YOUR PERSONALITY? DO YOU FEEL LIKE SOMEONE ELSE WHEN YOU DO MAGICK?
NO, I...NOT REALLY.
WHAT IF THERE'S SOMETHING WRONG WITH ME? SOMETIMES, THE THOUGHTS I HAVE... THEY FRIGHTEN ME.
ADMIT IT. I FRIGHTEN YOU, TOO.
NO, FRIGHTEN ISN'T THE RIGHT WORD...CONFUSE, MAYBE...INTRIGUE, EVEN...
LaMonica
IS THAT WHAT YOU'RE GONNA CALL IT? INTRIGUED?
MAYBE WE SHOULD GET BACK TO THE OTHERS...
"...AND I JUST KIND OF WAVED MY HANDS, AND THE BULLETS JUST DROPPED OUT."

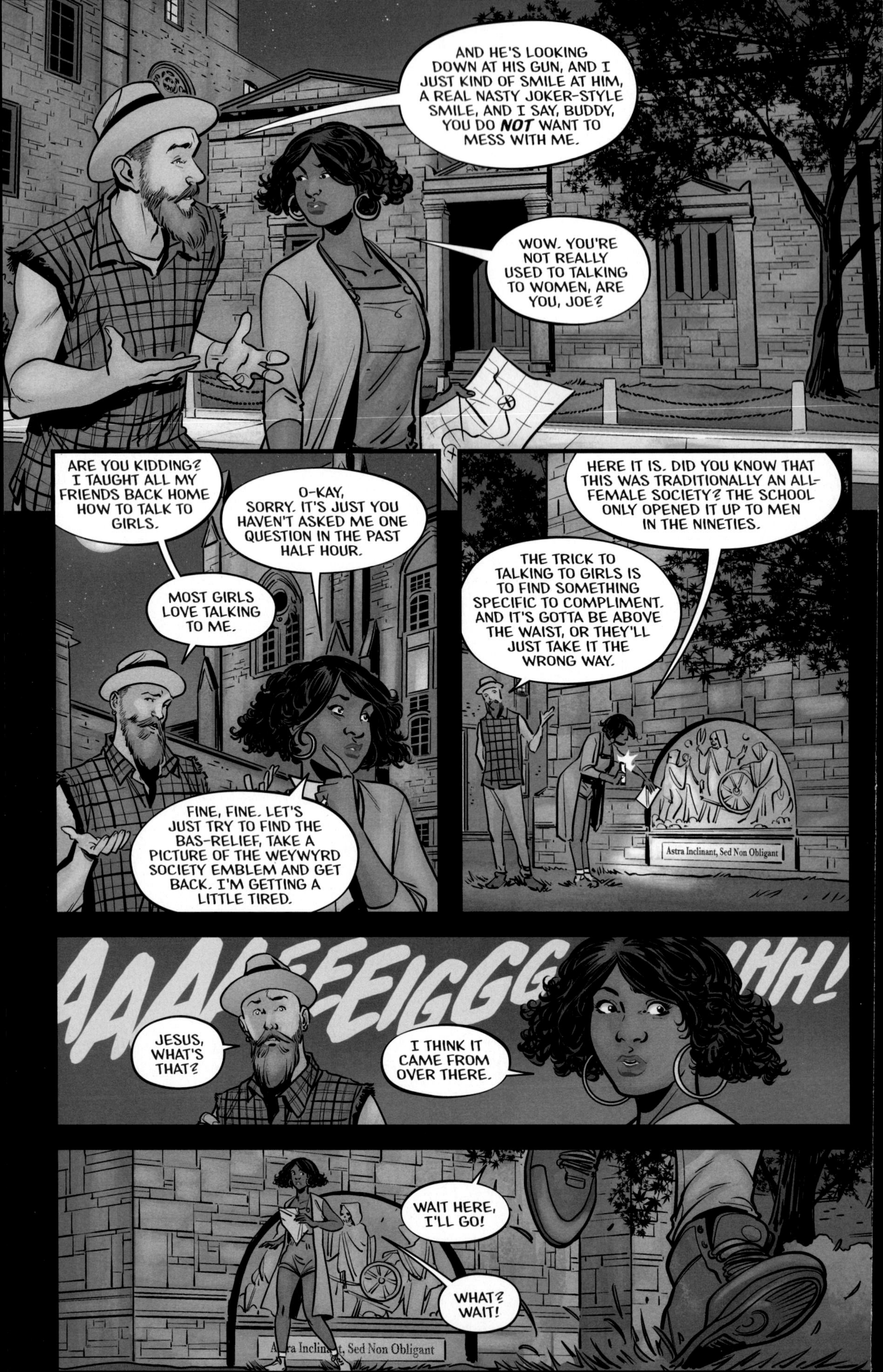
AND HE'S LOOKING DOWN AT HIS GUN, AND I JUST KIND OF SMILE AT HIM, A REAL NASTY JOKER-STYLE SMILE, AND I SAY, BUDDY, YOU DO NOT WANT TO MESS WITH ME.
WOW. YOU'RE NOT REALLY USED TO TALKING TO WOMEN, ARE YOU, JOE?
ARE YOU KIDDING? I TAUGHT ALL MY FRIENDS BACK HOME HOW TO TALK TO GIRLS.
O-KAY, SORRY. IT'S JUST YOU HAVEN'T ASKED ME ONE QUESTION IN THE PAST HALF HOUR.
MOST GIRLS LOVE TALKING TO ME.
FINE, FINE. LET'S JUST TRY TO FIND THE BAS-RELIEF, TAKE A PICTURE OF THE WEYWYRD SOCIETY EMBLEM AND GET BACK. I'M GETTING A LITTLE TIRED.
HERE IT IS. DID YOU KNOW THAT THIS WAS TRADITIONALLY AN ALL-FEMALE SOCIETY? THE SCHOOL ONLY OPENED IT UP TO MEN IN THE NINETIES.
THE TRICK TO TALKING TO GIRLS IS TO FIND SOMETHING SPECIFIC TO COMPLIMENT. AND IT'S GOTTA BE ABOVE THE WAIST, OR THEY'LL JUST TAKE IT THE WRONG WAY.
Astra Inclinant, Sed Non Obligant
JESUS, WHAT'S THAT?
I THINK IT CAME FROM OVER THERE.
WAIT HERE, I'LL GO!
WHAT? WAIT!

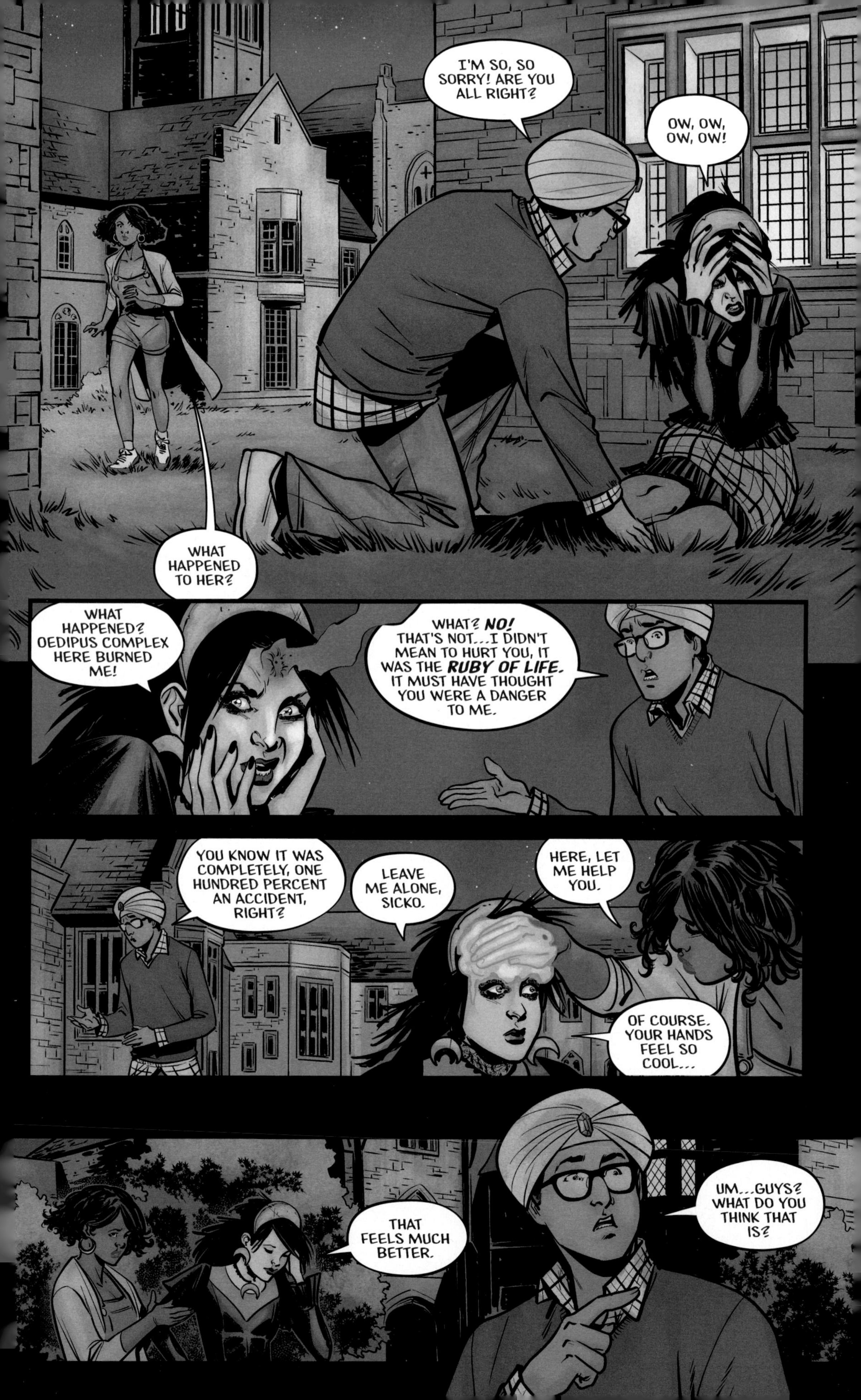
I'M SO, SO SORRY! ARE YOU ALL RIGHT?
OW, OW, OW, OW!
WHAT HAPPENED TO HER?
WHAT HAPPENED? OEDIPUS COMPLEX HERE BURNED ME!
WHAT? NO! THAT'S NOT... I DIDN'T MEAN TO HURT YOU, IT WAS THE RUBY OF LIFE. IT MUST HAVE THOUGHT YOU WERE A DANGER TO ME.
YOU KNOW IT WAS COMPLETELY, ONE HUNDRED PERCENT AN ACCIDENT, RIGHT?
LEAVE ME ALONE, SICKO.
HERE, LET ME HELP YOU.
OF COURSE. YOUR HANDS FEEL SO COOL...
THAT FEELS MUCH BETTER.
UM... GUYS? WHAT DO YOU THINK THAT IS?

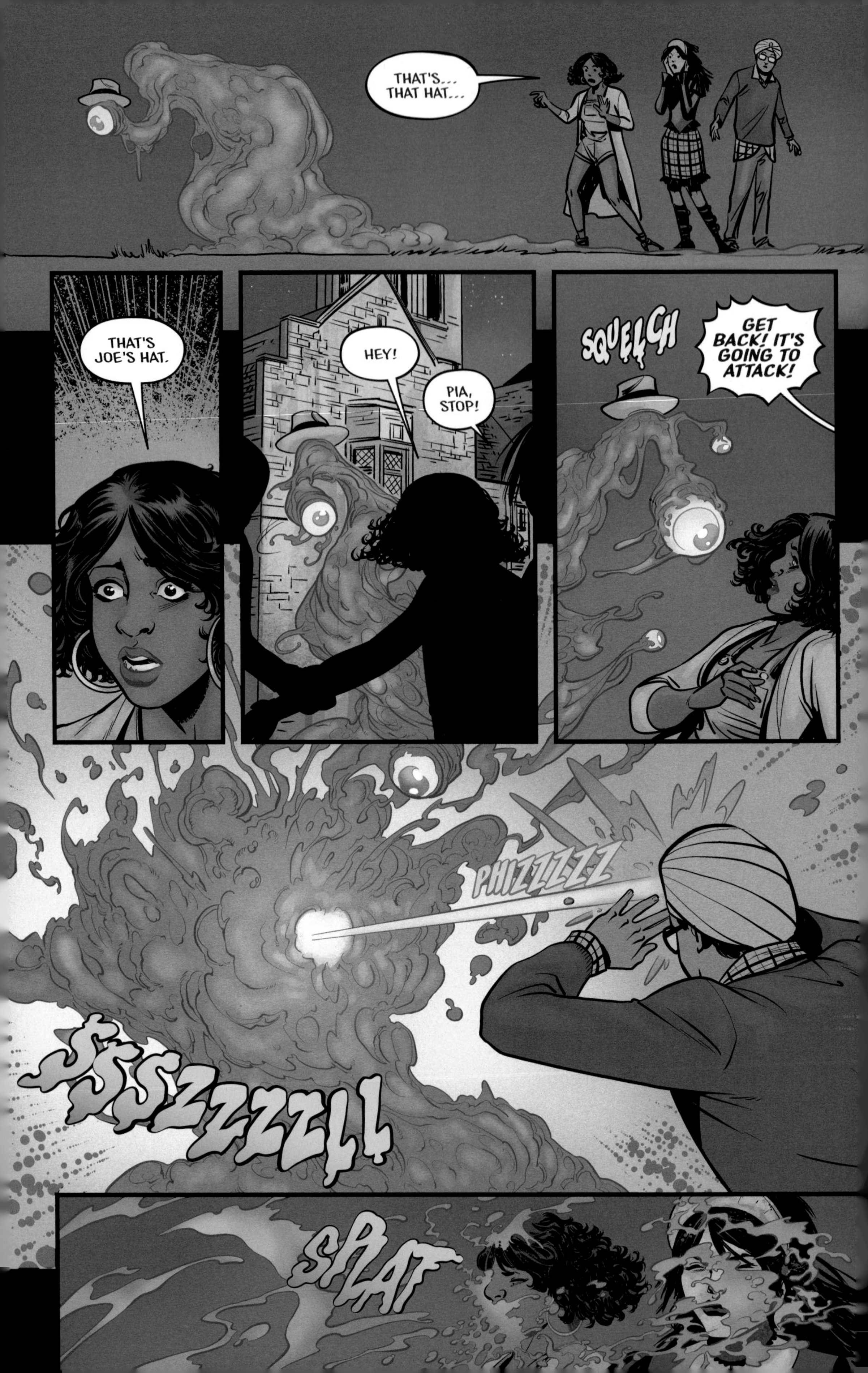
THAT'S... THAT HAT...
THAT'S JOE'S HAT.
HEY!
PIA, STOP!
SQUELCH
GET BACK! IT'S GOING TO ATTACK!
PHIZZZZZ
SSSZZZZLL
SPLAT

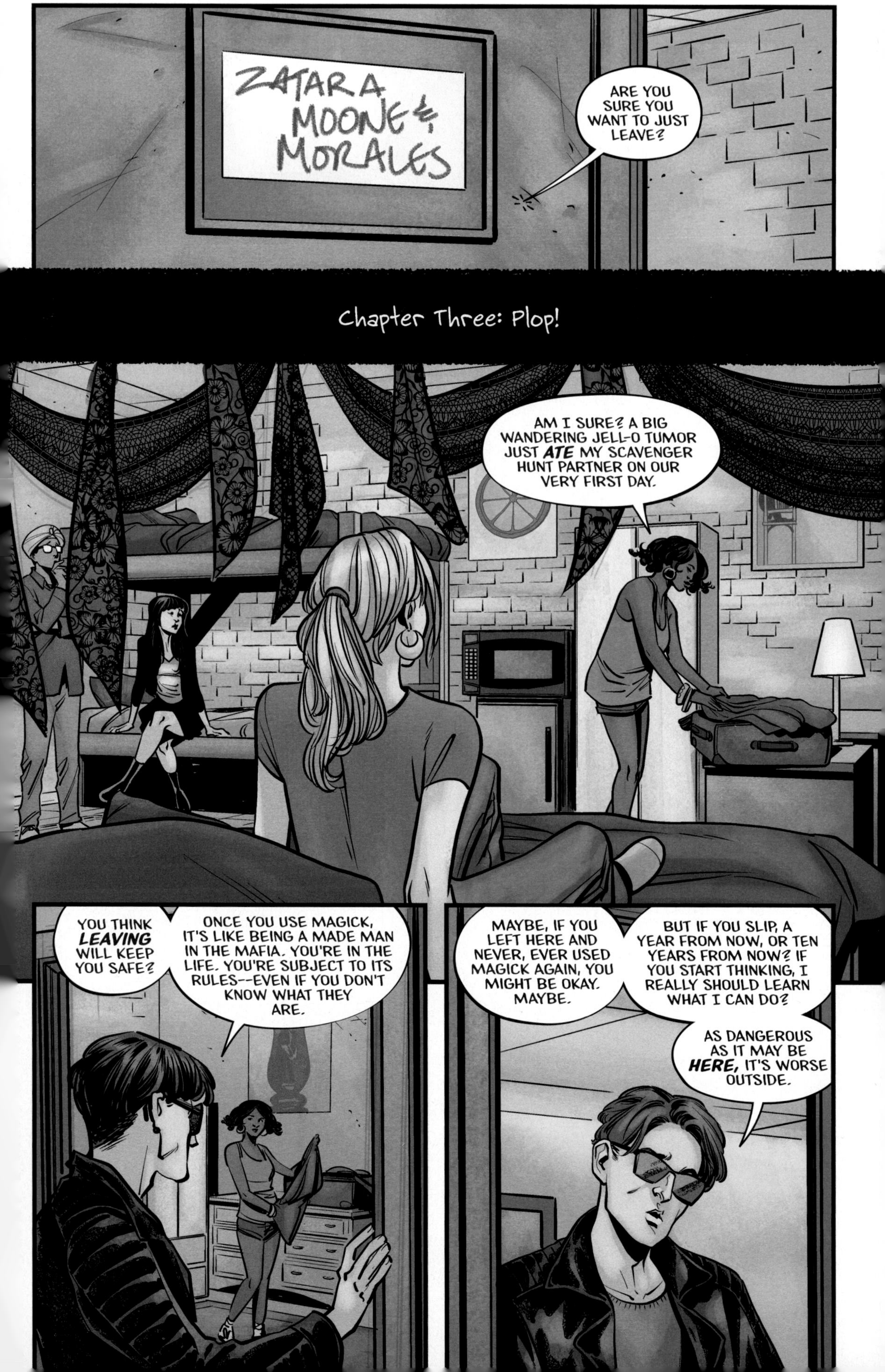
ZATARA MOONE & MORALES
ARE YOU SURE YOU WANT TO JUST LEAVE?
Chapter Three: Plop!
AM I SURE? A BIG WANDERING JELL-O TUMOR JUST ATE MY SCAVENGER HUNT PARTNER ON OUR VERY FIRST DAY.
YOU THINK LEAVING WILL KEEP YOU SAFE?
ONCE YOU USE MAGICK, IT'S LIKE BEING A MADE MAN IN THE MAFIA. YOU'RE IN THE LIFE. YOU'RE SUBJECT TO ITS RULES--EVEN IF YOU DON'T KNOW WHAT THEY ARE.
MAYBE, IF YOU LEFT HERE AND NEVER, EVER USED MAGICK AGAIN, YOU MIGHT BE OKAY. MAYBE.
BUT IF YOU SLIP, A YEAR FROM NOW, OR TEN YEARS FROM NOW? IF YOU START THINKING, I REALLY SHOULD LEARN WHAT I CAN DO?
AS DANGEROUS AS IT MAY BE HERE, IT'S WORSE OUTSIDE.

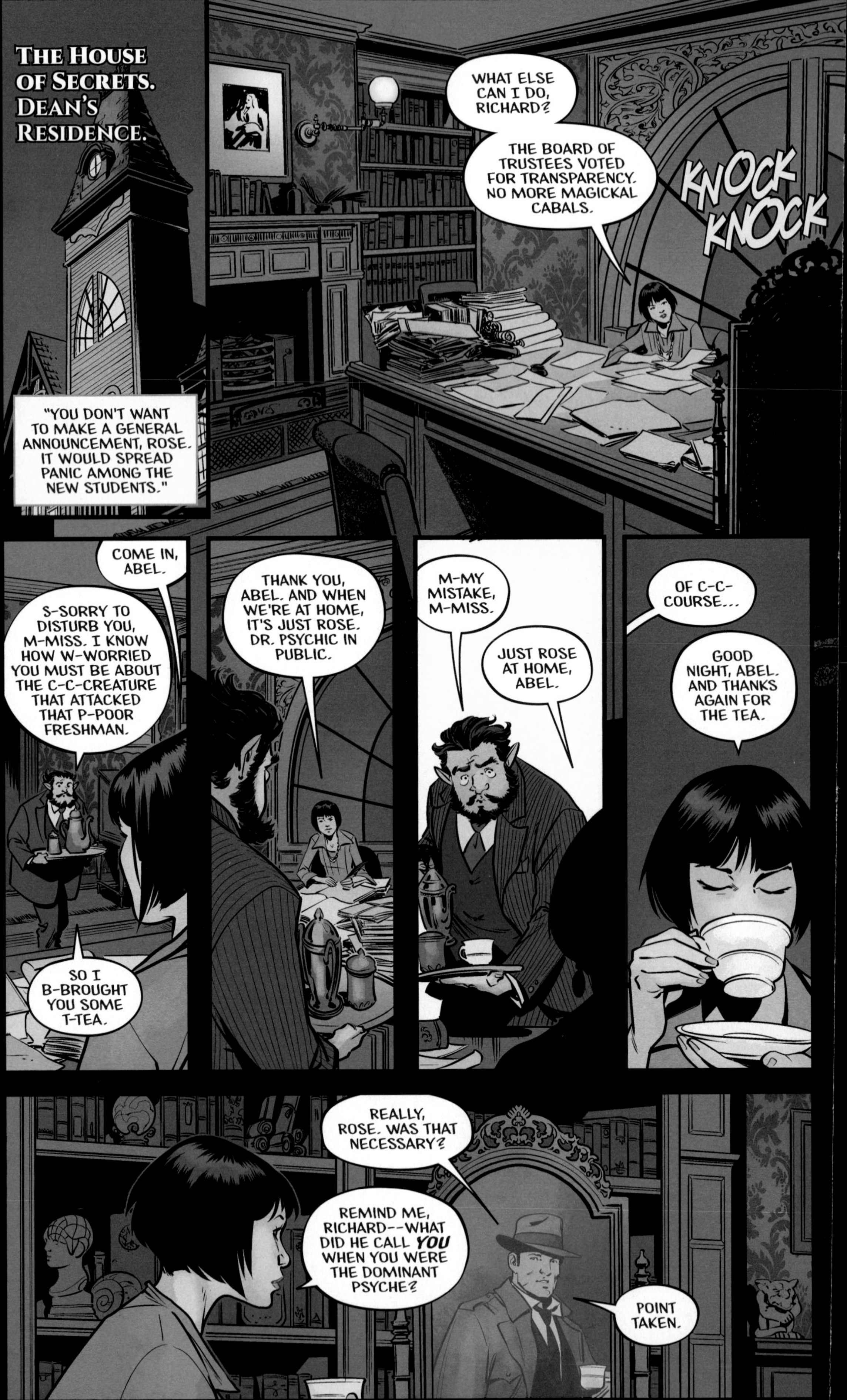
THE HOUSE OF SECRETS. DEAN'S RESIDENCE.
"YOU DON'T WANT TO MAKE A GENERAL ANNOUNCEMENT, ROSE. IT WOULD SPREAD PANIC AMONG THE NEW STUDENTS."
WHAT ELSE CAN I DO, RICHARD?
THE BOARD OF TRUSTEES VOTED FOR TRANSPARENCY. NO MORE MAGICKAL CABALS.
KNOCK KNOCK
COME IN, ABEL.
S-SORRY TO DISTURB YOU, M-MISS. I KNOW HOW W-WORRIED YOU MUST BE ABOUT THE C-C-CREATURE THAT ATTACKED THAT P-POOR FRESHMAN.
SO I B-BROUGHT YOU SOME T-TEA.
THANK YOU, ABEL. AND WHEN WE'RE AT HOME, IT'S JUST ROSE. DR. PSYCHIC IN PUBLIC.
M-MY MISTAKE, M-MISS.
JUST ROSE AT HOME, ABEL.
OF C-C-COURSE...
GOOD NIGHT, ABEL. AND THANKS AGAIN FOR THE TEA.
REALLY, ROSE. WAS THAT NECESSARY?
REMIND ME, RICHARD--WHAT DID HE CALL YOU WHEN YOU WERE THE DOMINANT PSYCHE?
POINT TAKEN.

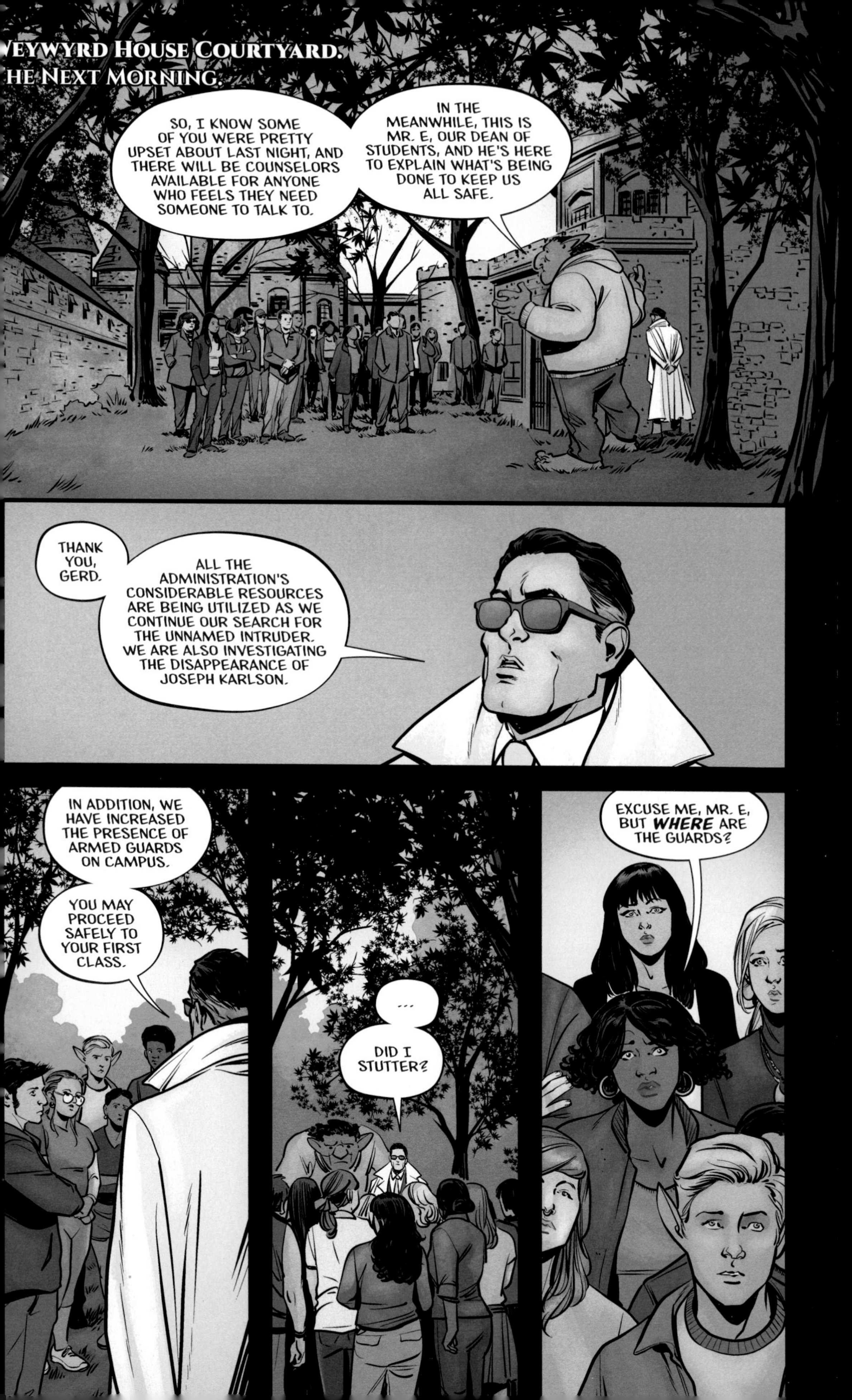
WEYWYRD HOUSE COURTYARD. THE NEXT MORNING.
SO, I KNOW SOME OF YOU WERE PRETTY UPSET ABOUT LAST NIGHT, AND THERE WILL BE COUNSELORS AVAILABLE FOR ANYONE WHO FEELS THEY NEED SOMEONE TO TALK TO.
IN THE MEANWHILE, THIS IS MR. E, OUR DEAN OF STUDENTS, AND HE'S HERE TO EXPLAIN WHAT'S BEING DONE TO KEEP US ALL SAFE.
THANK YOU, GERD.
ALL THE ADMINISTRATION'S CONSIDERABLE RESOURCES ARE BEING UTILIZED AS WE CONTINUE OUR SEARCH FOR THE UNNAMED INTRUDER. WE ARE ALSO INVESTIGATING THE DISAPPEARANCE OF JOSEPH KARLSON.
IN ADDITION, WE HAVE INCREASED THE PRESENCE OF ARMED GUARDS ON CAMPUS.
YOU MAY PROCEED SAFELY TO YOUR FIRST CLASS.
EXCUSE ME, MR. E, BUT *WHERE* ARE THE GUARDS?
...
DID I STUTTER?

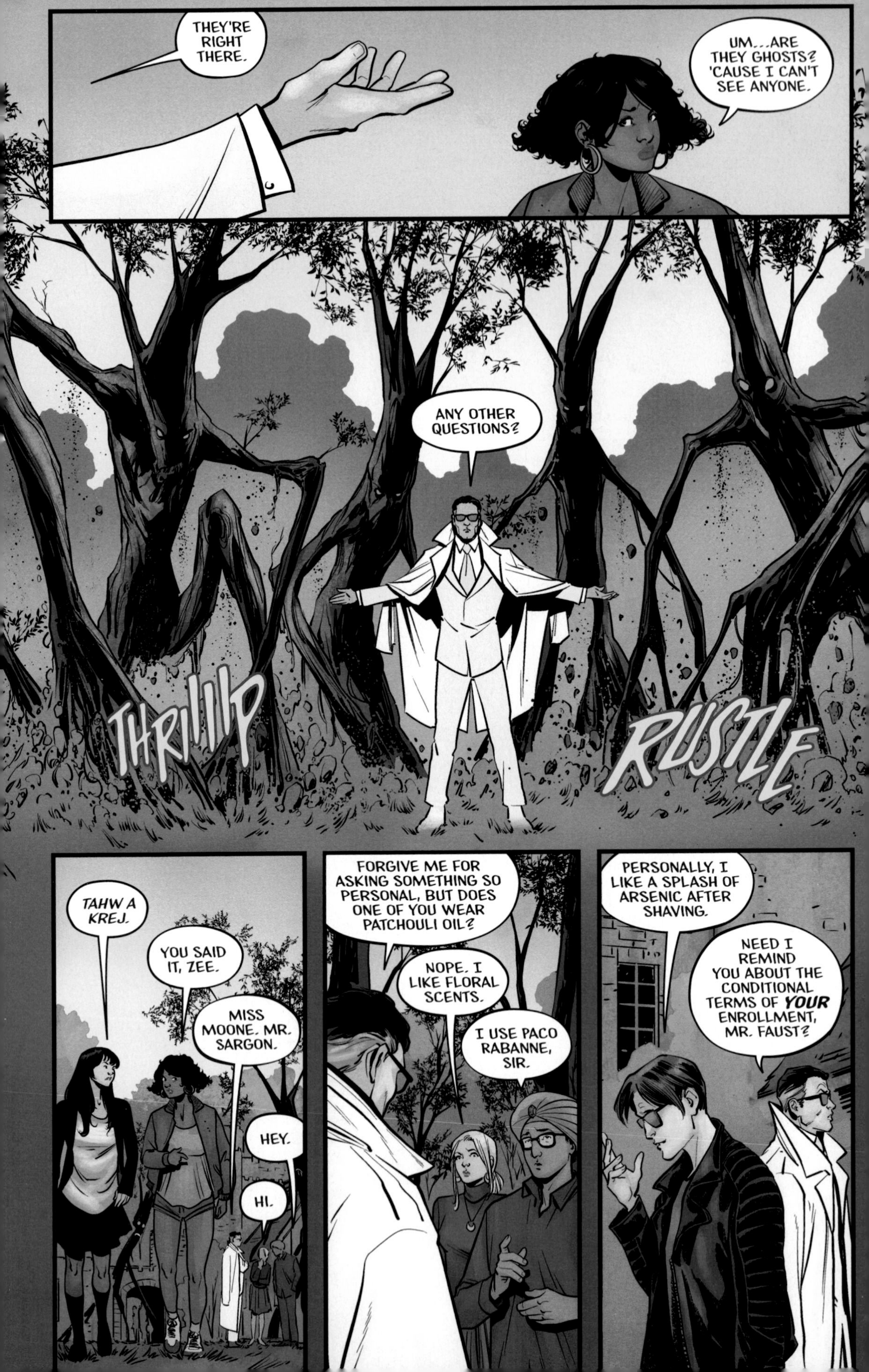
THEY'RE RIGHT THERE.
UM...ARE THEY GHOSTS? 'CAUSE I CAN'T SEE ANYONE.
ANY OTHER QUESTIONS?
THRIIIIP
RUSTLE
TAHW A KREJ.
YOU SAID IT, ZEE.
MISS MOONE. MR. SARGON.
HEY.
HI.
FORGIVE ME FOR ASKING SOMETHING SO PERSONAL, BUT DOES ONE OF YOU WEAR PATCHOULI OIL?
NOPE. I LIKE FLORAL SCENTS.
I USE PACO RABANNE, SIR.
PERSONALLY, I LIKE A SPLASH OF ARSENIC AFTER SHAVING.
NEED I REMIND YOU ABOUT THE CONDITIONAL TERMS OF *YOUR* ENROLLMENT, MR. FAUST?

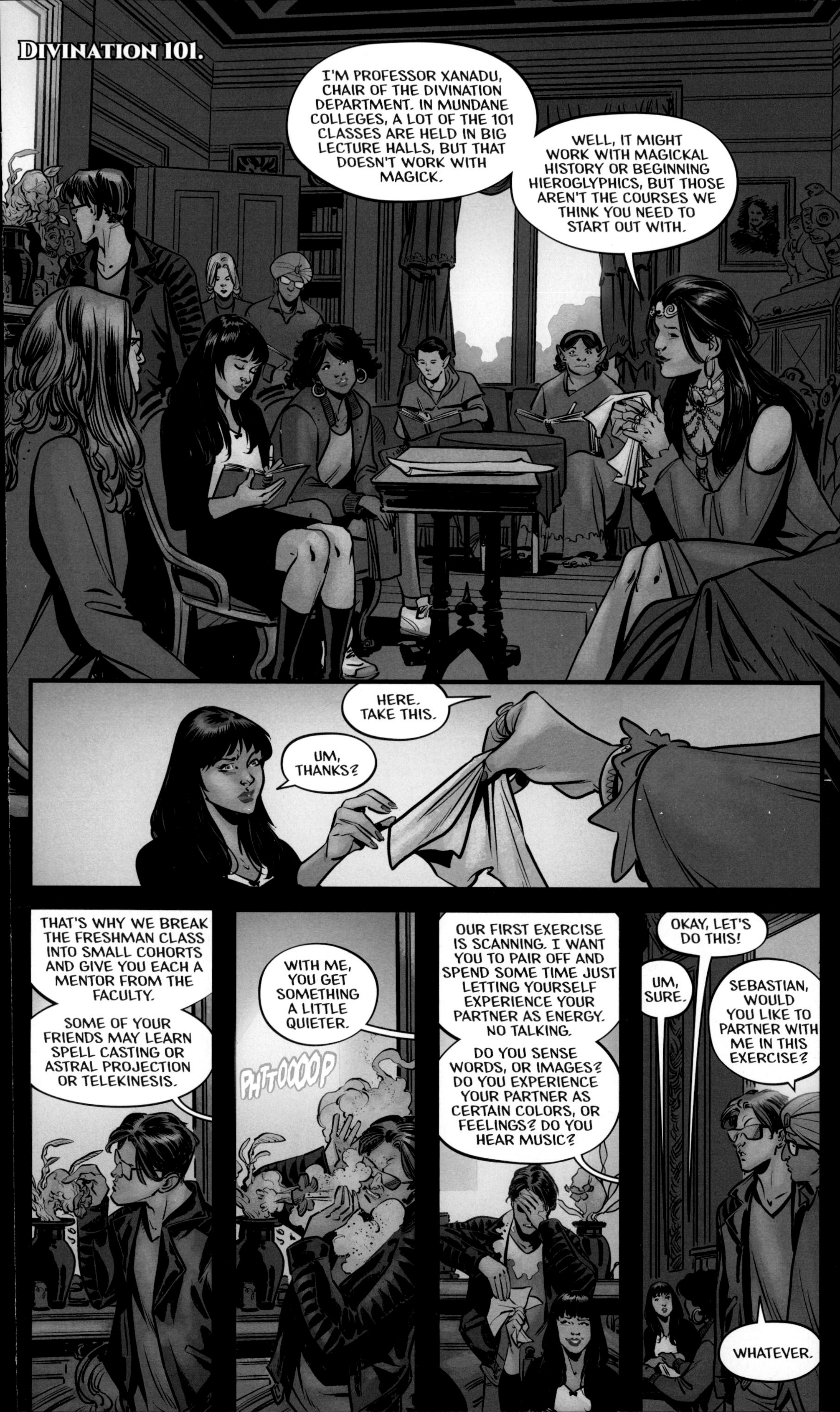
DIVINATION 101.
I'M PROFESSOR XANADU, CHAIR OF THE DIVINATION DEPARTMENT. IN MUNDANE COLLEGES, A LOT OF THE 101 CLASSES ARE HELD IN BIG LECTURE HALLS, BUT THAT DOESN'T WORK WITH MAGICK.
WELL, IT MIGHT WORK WITH MAGICKAL HISTORY OR BEGINNING HIEROGLYPHICS, BUT THOSE AREN'T THE COURSES WE THINK YOU NEED TO START OUT WITH.
HERE. TAKE THIS.
UM, THANKS?
THAT'S WHY WE BREAK THE FRESHMAN CLASS INTO SMALL COHORTS AND GIVE YOU EACH A MENTOR FROM THE FACULTY.
SOME OF YOUR FRIENDS MAY LEARN SPELL CASTING OR ASTRAL PROJECTION OR TELEKINESIS.
WITH ME, YOU GET SOMETHING A LITTLE QUIETER.
PHTOOOOP
OUR FIRST EXERCISE IS SCANNING. I WANT YOU TO PAIR OFF AND SPEND SOME TIME JUST LETTING YOURSELF EXPERIENCE YOUR PARTNER AS ENERGY. NO TALKING.
DO YOU SENSE WORDS, OR IMAGES? DO YOU EXPERIENCE YOUR PARTNER AS CERTAIN COLORS, OR FEELINGS? DO YOU HEAR MUSIC?
OKAY, LET'S DO THIS!
UM, SURE.
SEBASTIAN, WOULD YOU LIKE TO PARTNER WITH ME IN THIS EXERCISE?
WHATEVER.

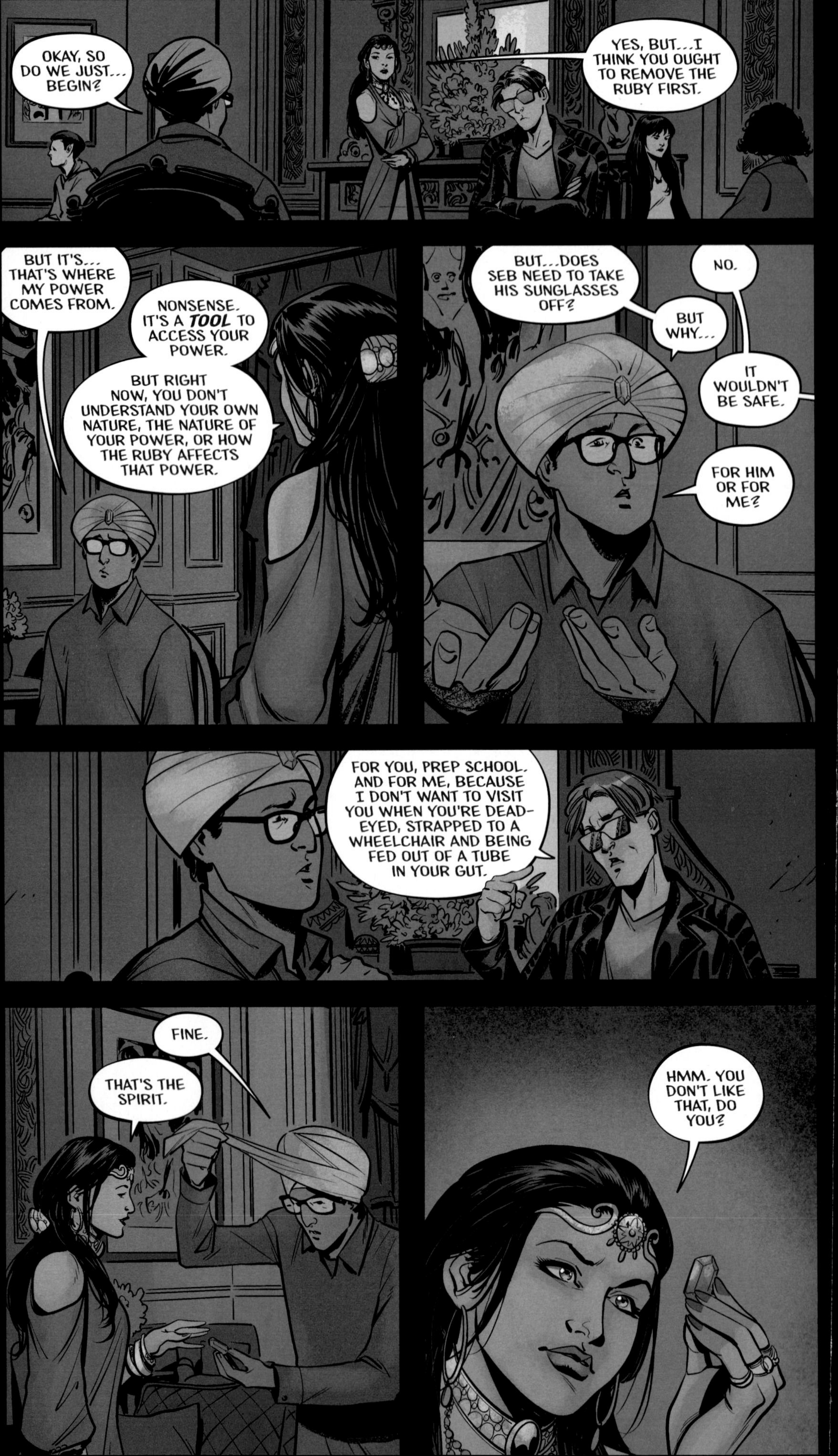
OKAY, SO DO WE JUST... BEGIN?
YES, BUT...I THINK YOU OUGHT TO REMOVE THE RUBY FIRST.
BUT IT'S... THAT'S WHERE MY POWER COMES FROM.
NONSENSE. IT'S A TOOL TO ACCESS YOUR POWER.
BUT RIGHT NOW, YOU DON'T UNDERSTAND YOUR OWN NATURE, THE NATURE OF YOUR POWER, OR HOW THE RUBY AFFECTS THAT POWER.
BUT...DOES SEB NEED TO TAKE HIS SUNGLASSES OFF?
NO.
BUT WHY...
IT WOULDN'T BE SAFE.
FOR HIM OR FOR ME?
FOR YOU, PREP SCHOOL. AND FOR ME, BECAUSE I DON'T WANT TO VISIT YOU WHEN YOU'RE DEAD-EYED, STRAPPED TO A WHEELCHAIR AND BEING FED OUT OF A TUBE IN YOUR GUT.
FINE.
THAT'S THE SPIRIT.
HMM. YOU DON'T LIKE THAT, DO YOU?

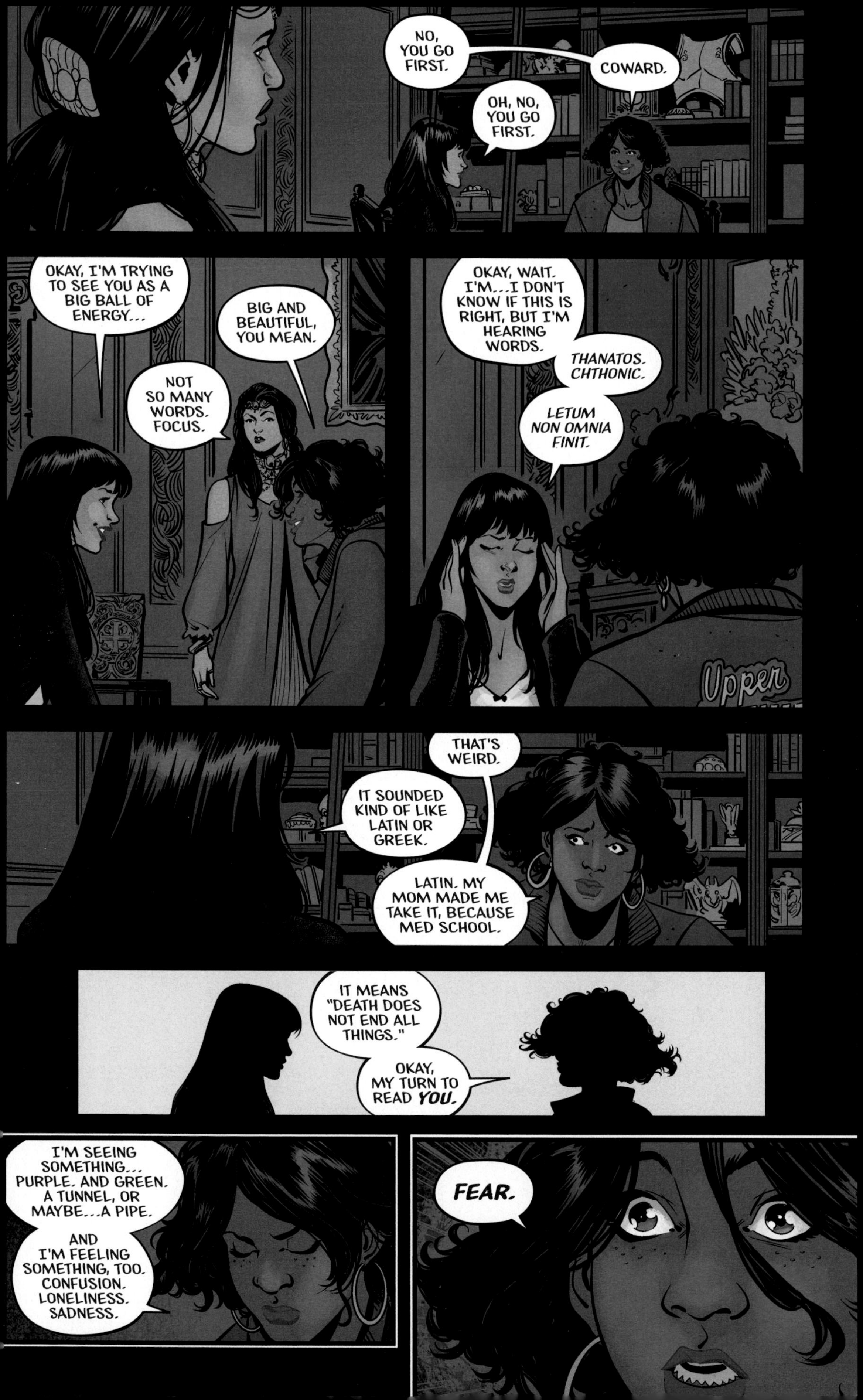
NO, YOU GO FIRST.
COWARD.
OH, NO, YOU GO FIRST.
OKAY, I'M TRYING TO SEE YOU AS A BIG BALL OF ENERGY...
BIG AND BEAUTIFUL, YOU MEAN.
NOT SO MANY WORDS. FOCUS.
OKAY, WAIT. I'M...I DON'T KNOW IF THIS IS RIGHT, BUT I'M HEARING WORDS.
THANATOS. CHTHONIC.
LETUM NON OMNIA FINIT.
Upper
THAT'S WEIRD.
IT SOUNDED KIND OF LIKE LATIN OR GREEK.
LATIN. MY MOM MADE ME TAKE IT, BECAUSE MED SCHOOL.
IT MEANS "DEATH DOES NOT END ALL THINGS."
OKAY, MY TURN TO READ *YOU.*
I'M SEEING SOMETHING... PURPLE. AND GREEN. A TUNNEL, OR MAYBE...A PIPE.
AND I'M FEELING SOMETHING, TOO. CONFUSION. LONELINESS. SADNESS.
FEAR.

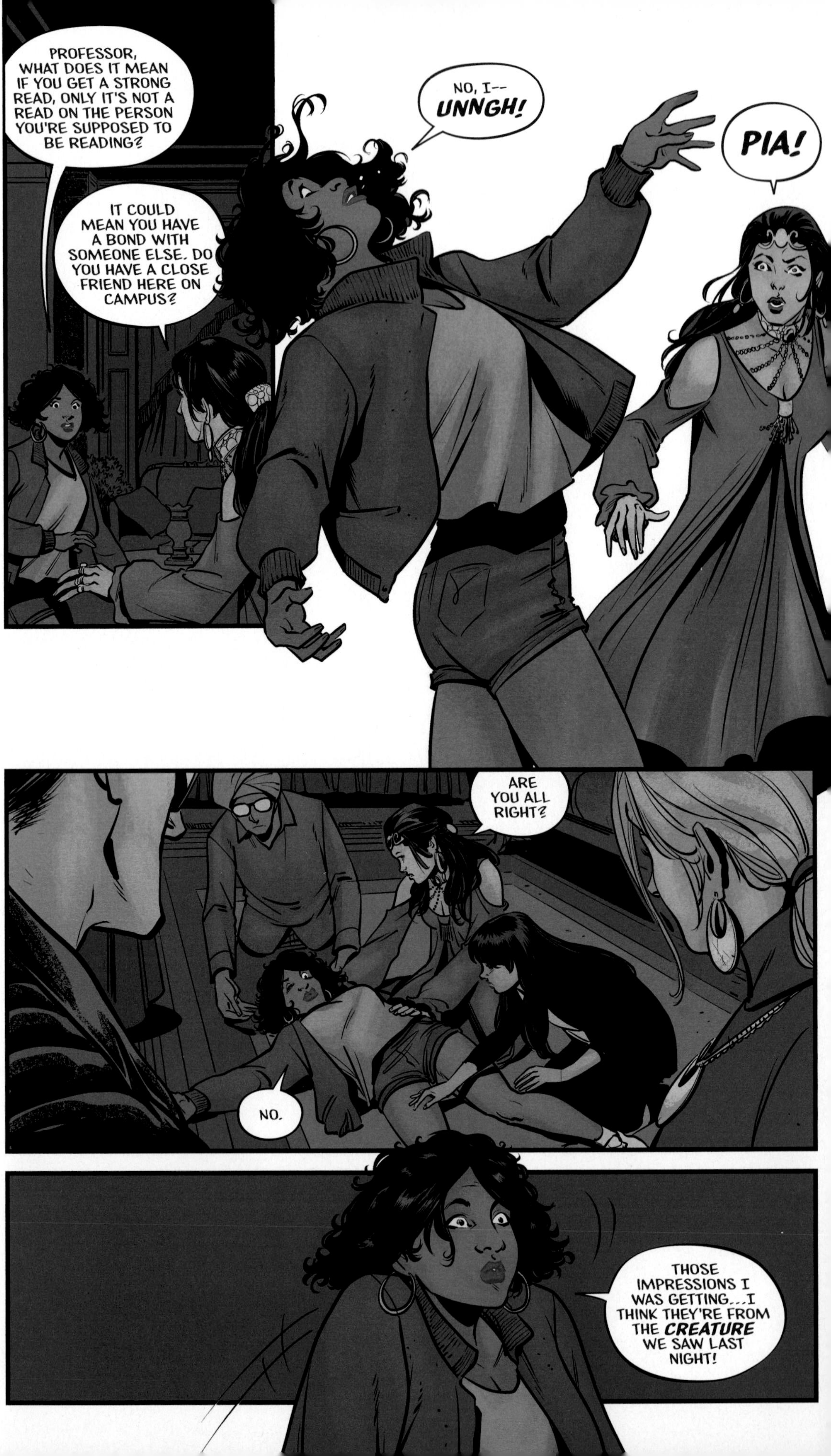

PROFESSOR, WHAT DOES IT MEAN IF YOU GET A STRONG READ, ONLY IT'S NOT A READ ON THE PERSON YOU'RE SUPPOSED TO BE READING?
IT COULD MEAN YOU HAVE A BOND WITH SOMEONE ELSE. DO YOU HAVE A CLOSE FRIEND HERE ON CAMPUS?
NO, I-- UNNGH!
PIA!
ARE YOU ALL RIGHT?
NO.
THOSE IMPRESSIONS I WAS GETTING...I THINK THEY'RE FROM THE CREATURE WE SAW LAST NIGHT!

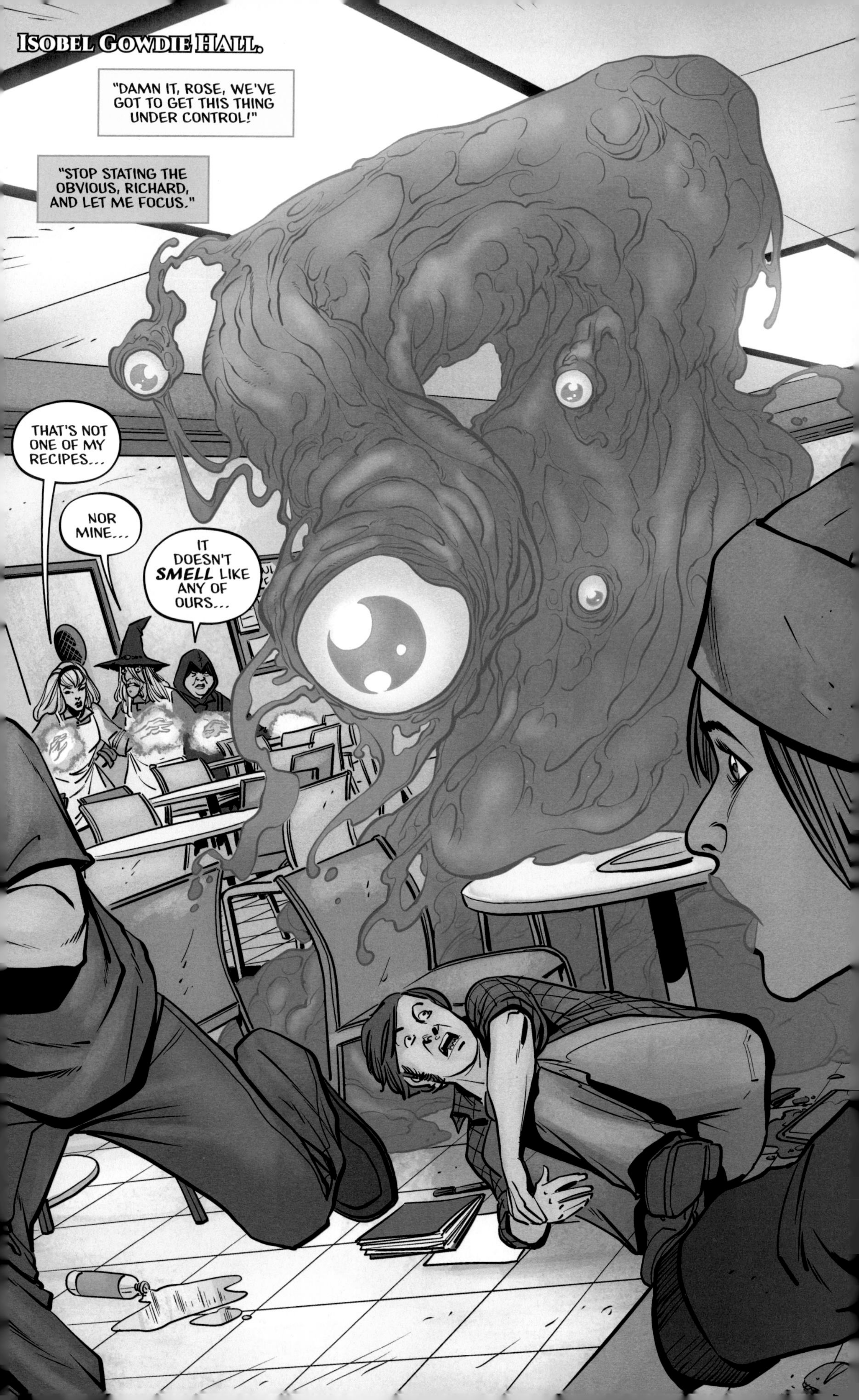
ISOBEL GOWDIE HALL.
"DAMN IT, ROSE, WE'VE GOT TO GET THIS THING UNDER CONTROL!"
"STOP STATING THE OBVIOUS, RICHARD, AND LET ME FOCUS."
THAT'S NOT ONE OF MY RECIPES...
NOR MINE...
IT DOESN'T SMELL LIKE ANY OF OURS...

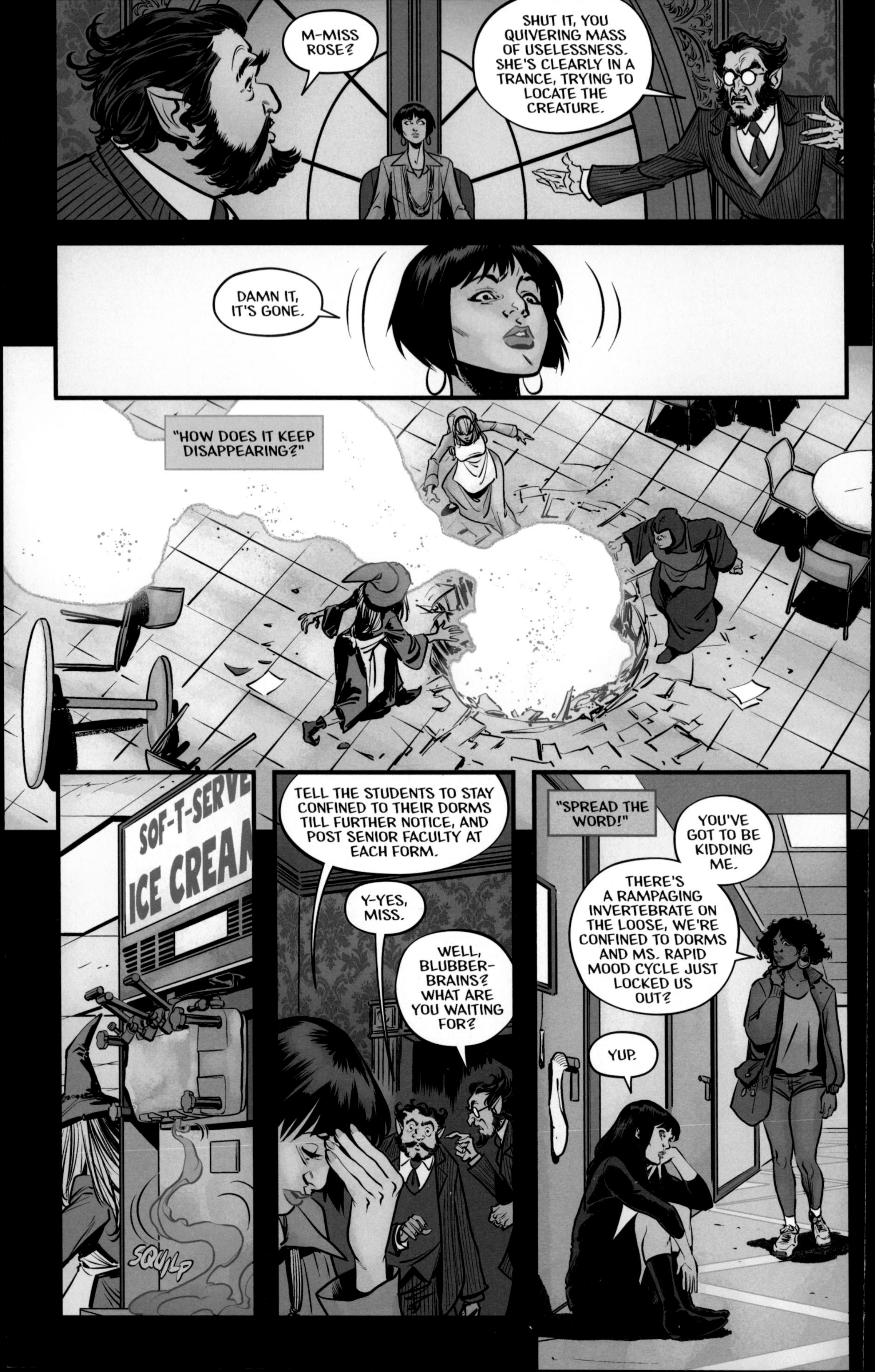
M-MISS ROSE?
SHUT IT, YOU QUIVERING MASS OF USELESSNESS. SHE'S CLEARLY IN A TRANCE, TRYING TO LOCATE THE CREATURE.
DAMN IT, IT'S GONE.
"HOW DOES IT KEEP DISAPPEARING?"
SOF-T-SERVE
ICE CREAM
SQUILP
TELL THE STUDENTS TO STAY CONFINED TO THEIR DORMS TILL FURTHER NOTICE, AND POST SENIOR FACULTY AT EACH FORM.
Y-YES, MISS.
WELL, BLUBBER-BRAINS? WHAT ARE YOU WAITING FOR?
"SPREAD THE WORD!"
YOU'VE GOT TO BE KIDDING ME.
THERE'S A RAMPAGING INVERTEBRATE ON THE LOOSE, WE'RE CONFINED TO DORMS AND MS. RAPID MOOD CYCLE JUST LOCKED US OUT?
YUP.

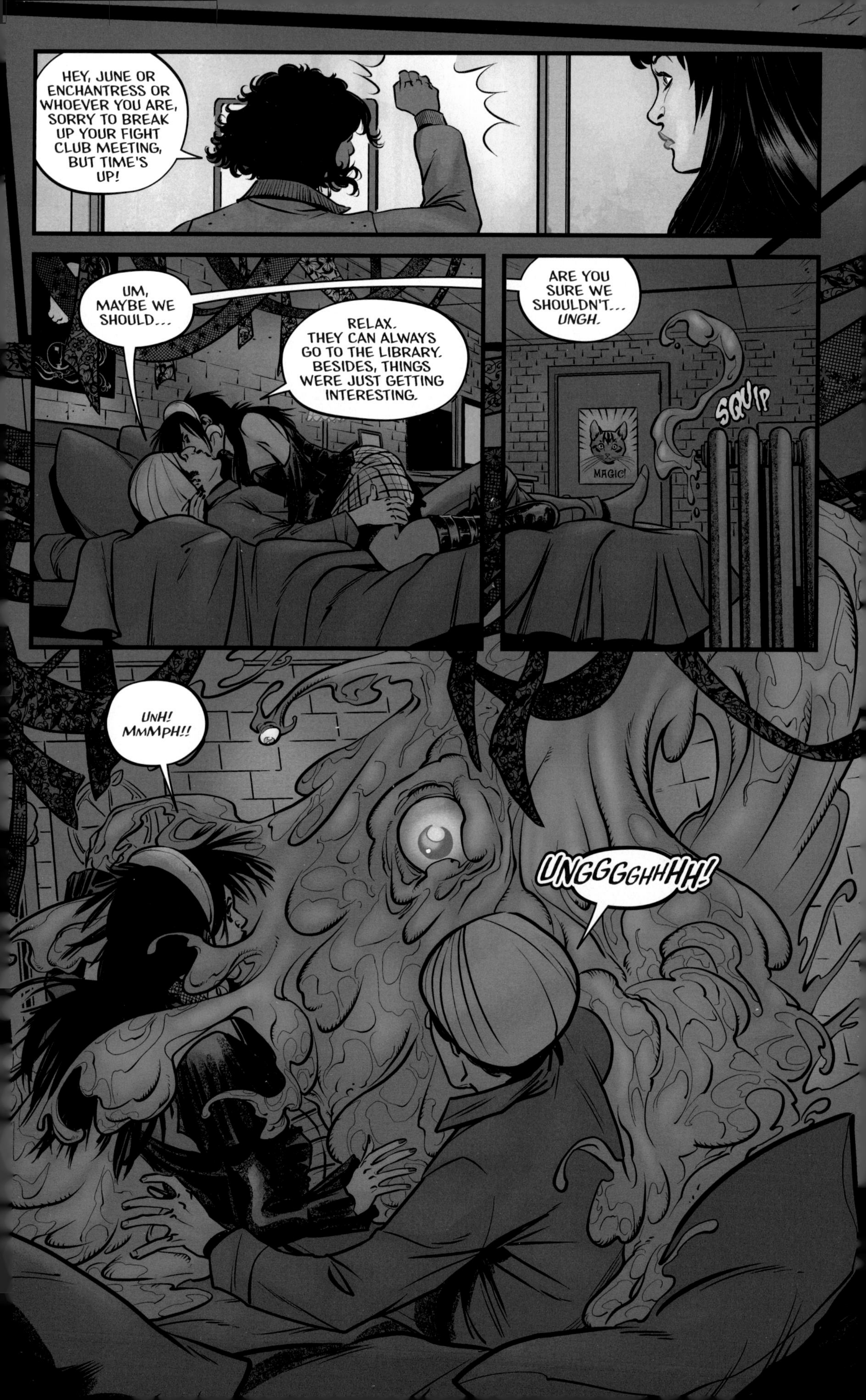
HEY, JUNE OR ENCHANTRESS OR WHOEVER YOU ARE, SORRY TO BREAK UP YOUR FIGHT CLUB MEETING, BUT TIME'S UP!
UM, MAYBE WE SHOULD...
RELAX. THEY CAN ALWAYS GO TO THE LIBRARY. BESIDES, THINGS WERE JUST GETTING INTERESTING.
ARE YOU SURE WE SHOULDN'T... UNGH.
MAGIC!
SQUIP
UNH! MMMPH!!
UNGGGGHHHH!

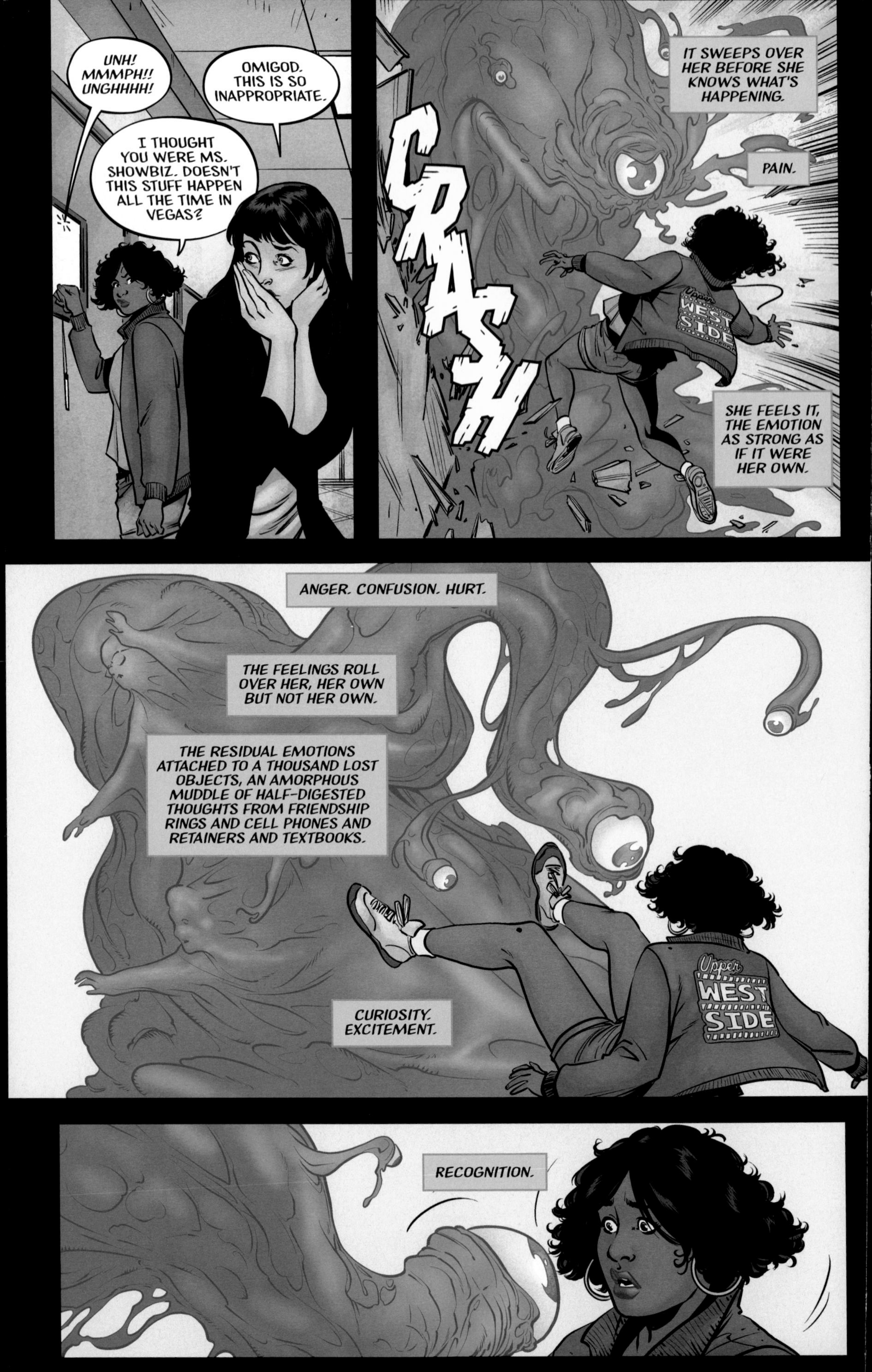
UNH! MMMPH!! UNGHHHH!
OMIGOD. THIS IS SO INAPPROPRIATE.
I THOUGHT YOU WERE MS. SHOWBIZ. DOESN'T THIS STUFF HAPPEN ALL THE TIME IN VEGAS?
CRASH
IT SWEEPS OVER HER BEFORE SHE KNOWS WHAT'S HAPPENING.
PAIN.
SHE FEELS IT, THE EMOTION AS STRONG AS IF IT WERE HER OWN.
Upper WEST SIDE
ANGER. CONFUSION. HURT.
THE FEELINGS ROLL OVER HER, HER OWN BUT NOT HER OWN.
THE RESIDUAL EMOTIONS ATTACHED TO A THOUSAND LOST OBJECTS, AN AMORPHOUS MUDDLE OF HALF-DIGESTED THOUGHTS FROM FRIENDSHIP RINGS AND CELL PHONES AND RETAINERS AND TEXTBOOKS.
CURIOSITY. EXCITEMENT.
Upper WEST SIDE
RECOGNITION.

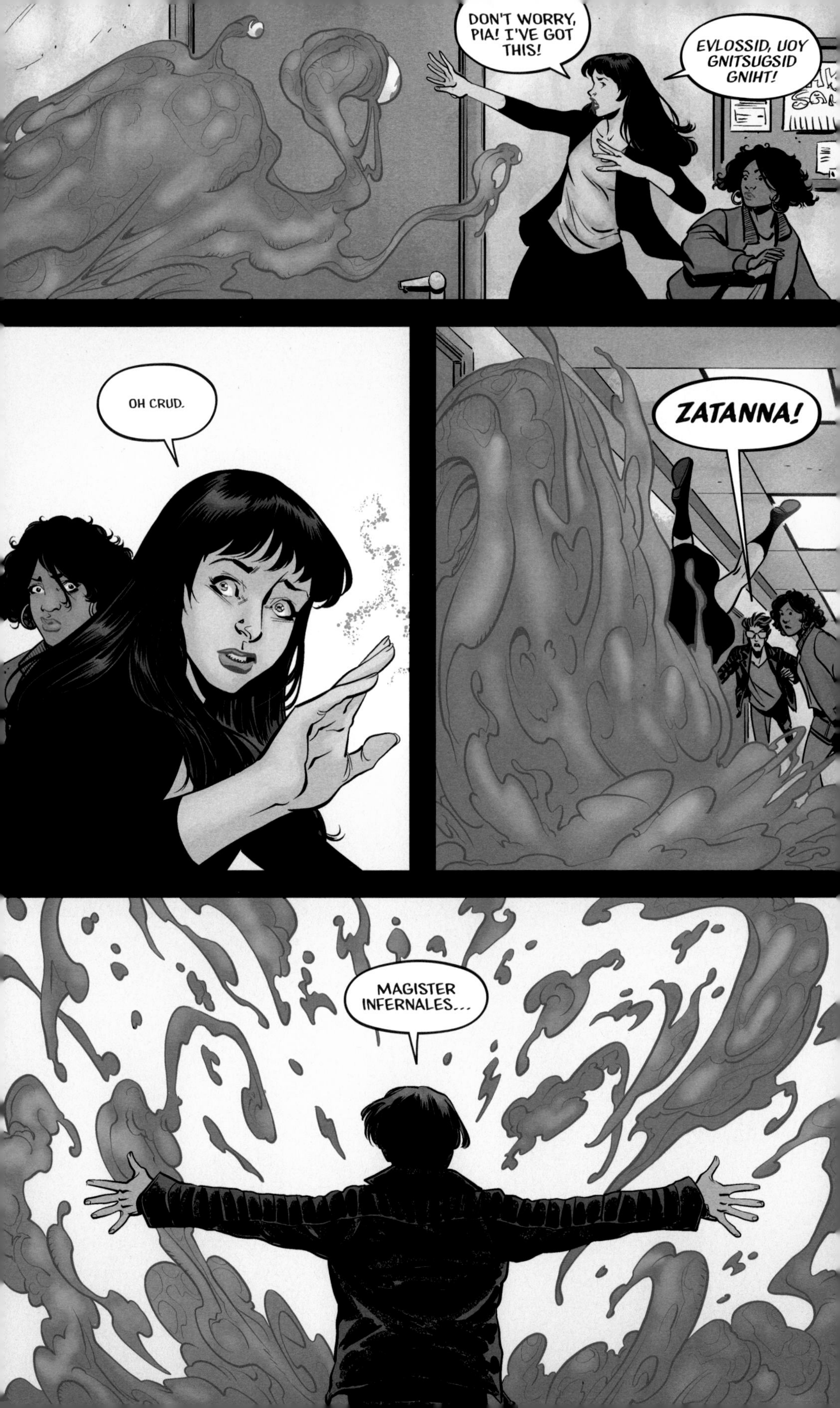
DON'T WORRY, PIA! I'VE GOT THIS!
EVLOSSID, UOY GNITSUGSID GNIHT!
OH CRUD.
ZATANNA!
MAGISTER INFERNALES...

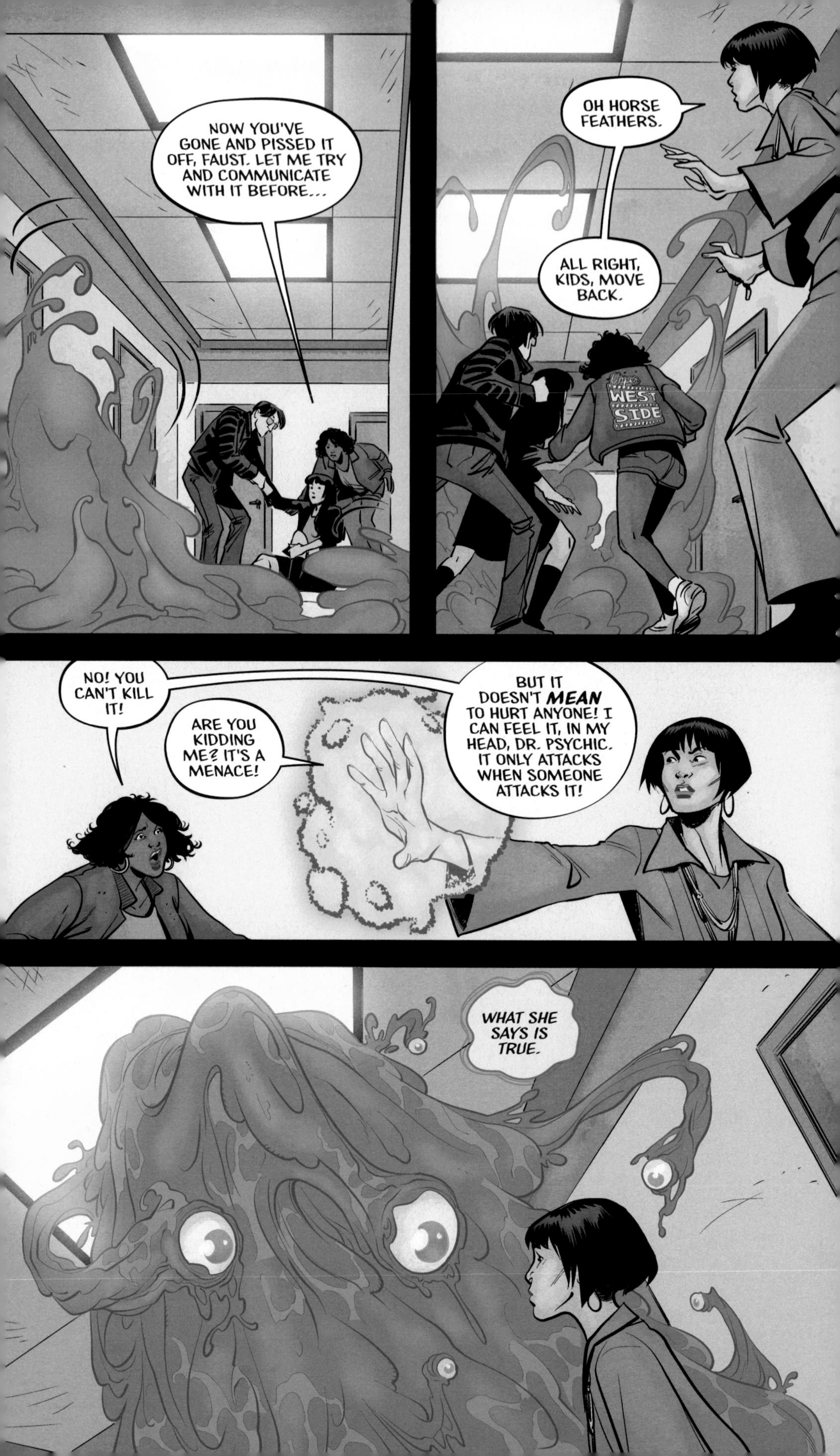
NOW YOU'VE GONE AND PISSED IT OFF, FAUST. LET ME TRY AND COMMUNICATE WITH IT BEFORE...
OH HORSE FEATHERS.
ALL RIGHT, KIDS, MOVE BACK.
WEST SIDE
NO! YOU CAN'T KILL IT!
ARE YOU KIDDING ME? IT'S A MENACE!
BUT IT DOESN'T MEAN TO HURT ANYONE! I CAN FEEL IT, IN MY HEAD, DR. PSYCHIC. IT ONLY ATTACKS WHEN SOMEONE ATTACKS IT!
WHAT SHE SAYS IS TRUE.

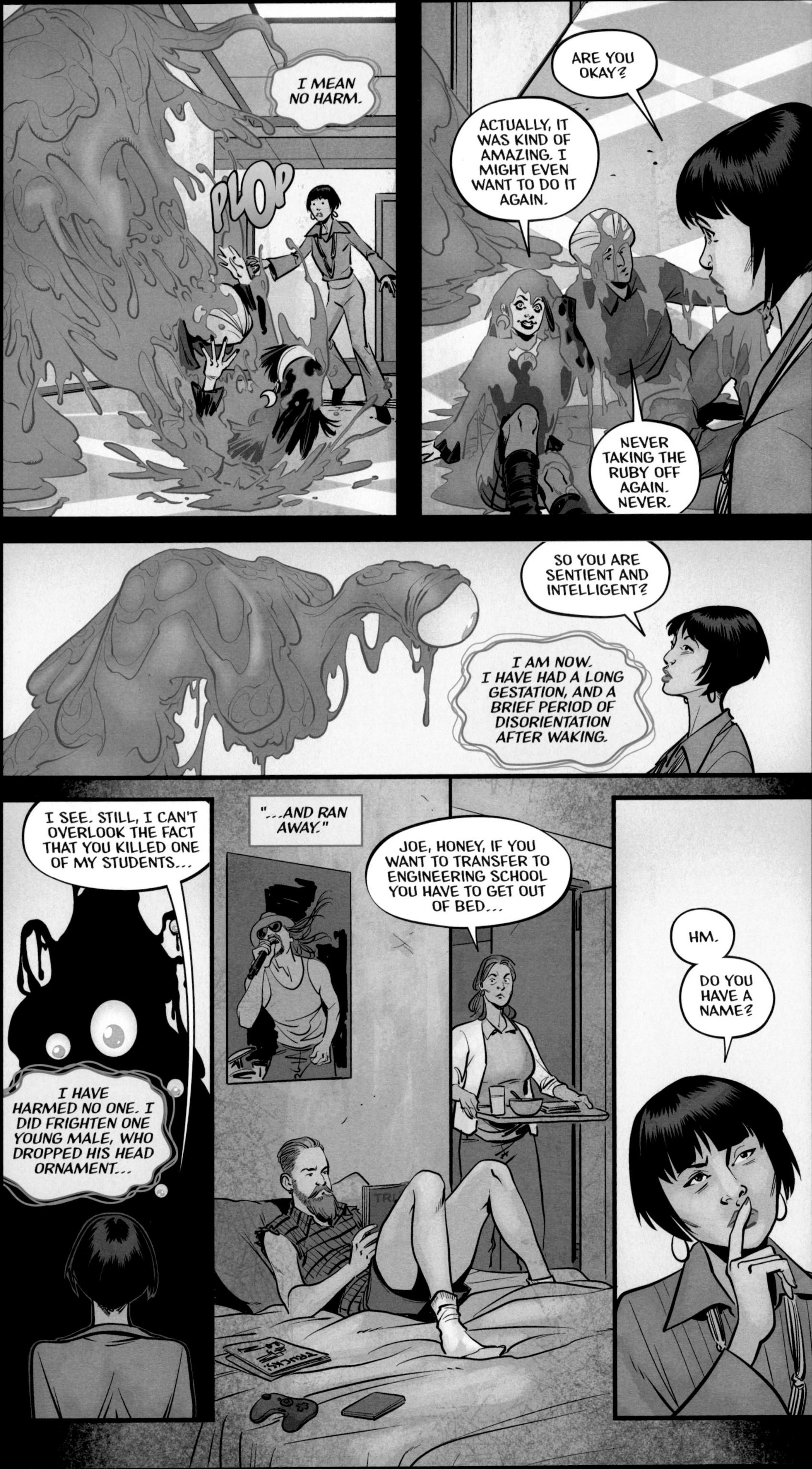
I MEAN NO HARM.
PLOP
ARE YOU OKAY?
ACTUALLY, IT WAS KIND OF AMAZING. I MIGHT EVEN WANT TO DO IT AGAIN.
NEVER TAKING THE RUBY OFF AGAIN. NEVER.
SO YOU ARE SENTIENT AND INTELLIGENT?
I AM NOW. I HAVE HAD A LONG GESTATION, AND A BRIEF PERIOD OF DISORIENTATION AFTER WAKING.
I SEE. STILL, I CAN'T OVERLOOK THE FACT THAT YOU KILLED ONE OF MY STUDENTS...
I HAVE HARMED NO ONE. I DID FRIGHTEN ONE YOUNG MALE, WHO DROPPED HIS HEAD ORNAMENT...
"...AND RAN AWAY."
JOE, HONEY, IF YOU WANT TO TRANSFER TO ENGINEERING SCHOOL YOU HAVE TO GET OUT OF BED...
HM.
DO YOU HAVE A NAME?

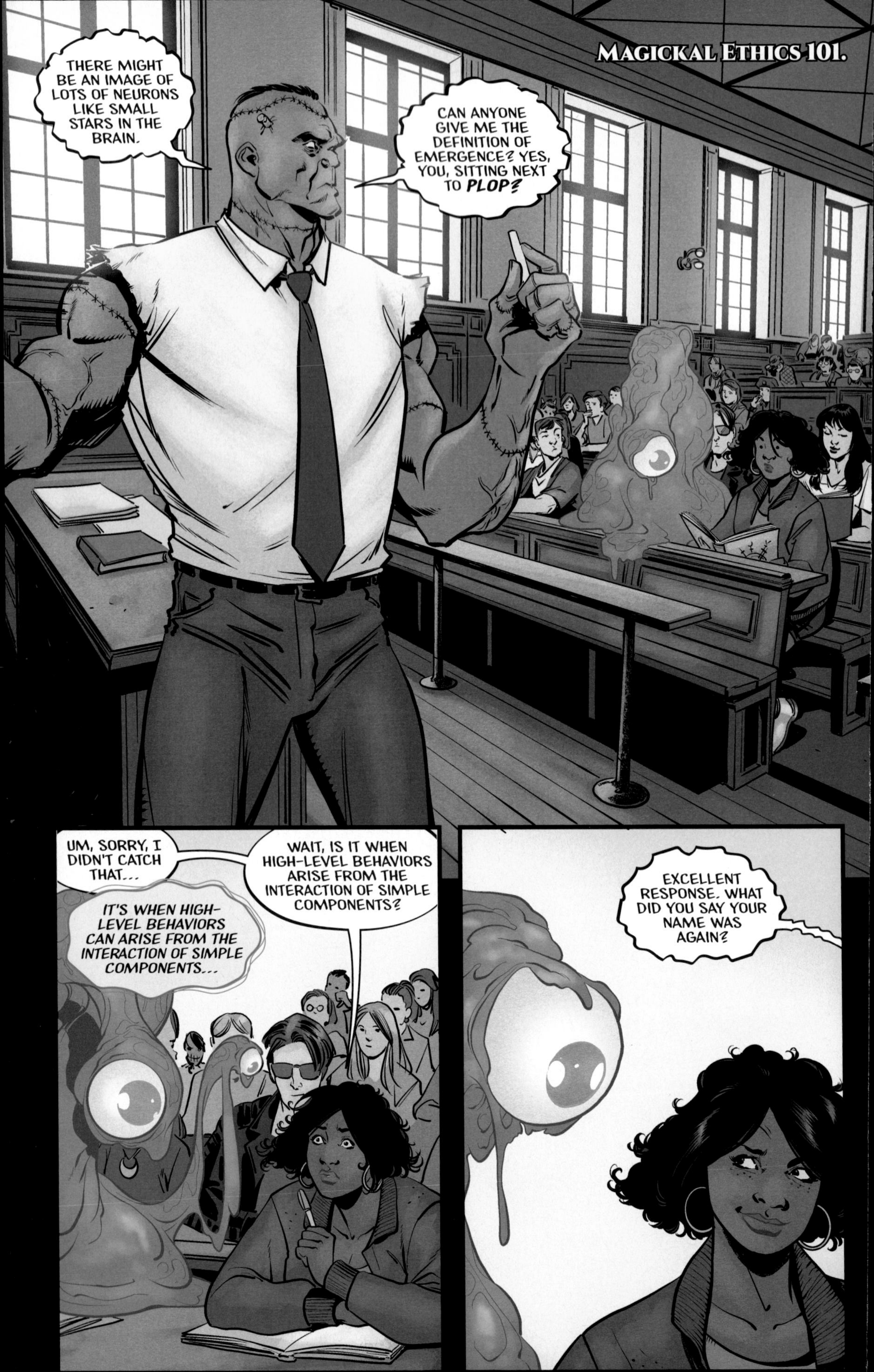
MAGICKAL ETHICS 101.
THERE MIGHT BE AN IMAGE OF LOTS OF NEURONS LIKE SMALL STARS IN THE BRAIN.
CAN ANYONE GIVE ME THE DEFINITION OF EMERGENCE? YES, YOU, SITTING NEXT TO PLOP?
UM, SORRY, I DIDN'T CATCH THAT...
IT'S WHEN HIGH-LEVEL BEHAVIORS CAN ARISE FROM THE INTERACTION OF SIMPLE COMPONENTS...
WAIT, IS IT WHEN HIGH-LEVEL BEHAVIORS ARISE FROM THE INTERACTION OF SIMPLE COMPONENTS?
EXCELLENT RESPONSE. WHAT DID YOU SAY YOUR NAME WAS AGAIN?

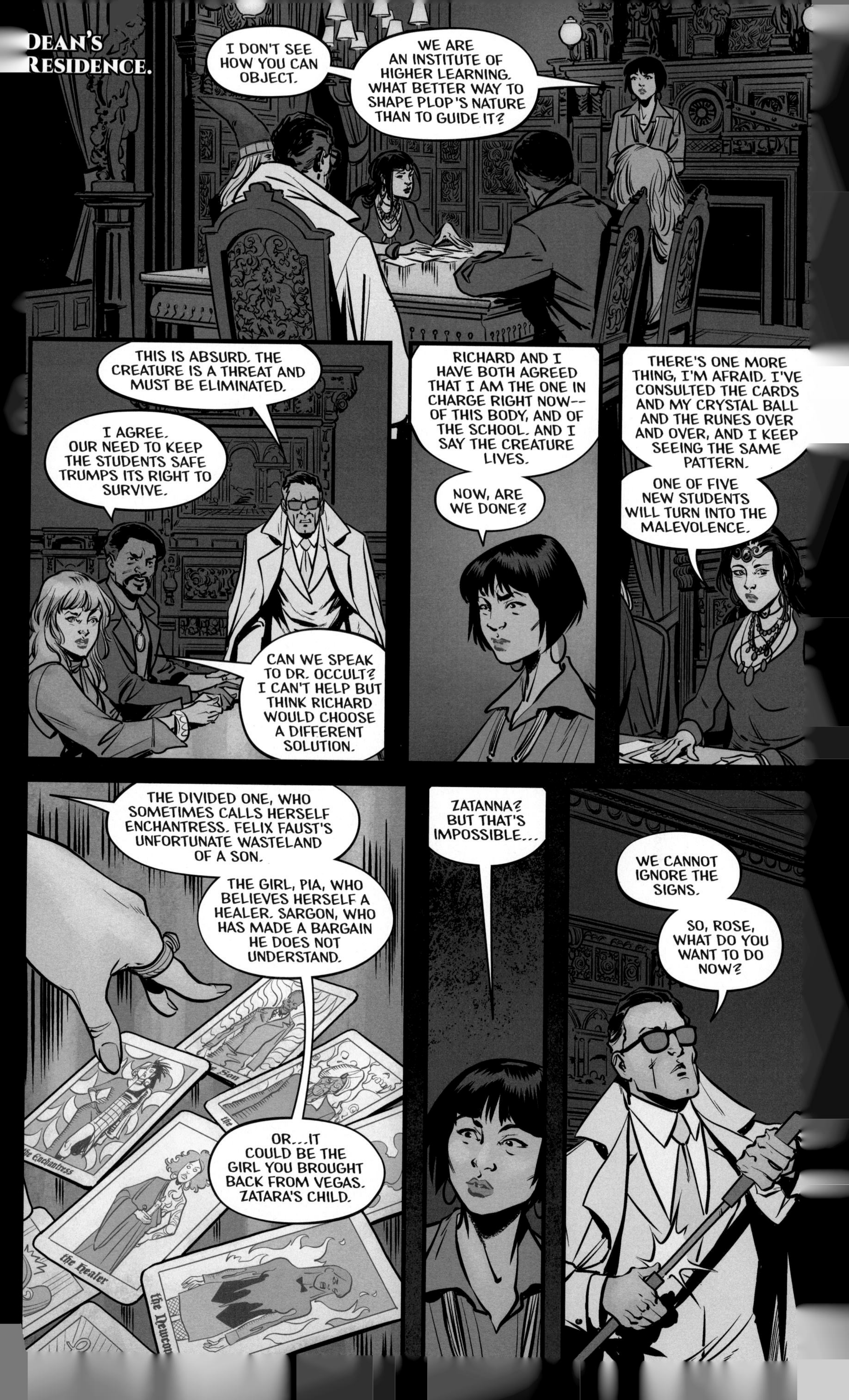
DEAN'S RESIDENCE.
I DON'T SEE HOW YOU CAN OBJECT.
WE ARE AN INSTITUTE OF HIGHER LEARNING. WHAT BETTER WAY TO SHAPE PLOP'S NATURE THAN TO GUIDE IT?
THIS IS ABSURD. THE CREATURE IS A THREAT AND MUST BE ELIMINATED.
I AGREE. OUR NEED TO KEEP THE STUDENTS SAFE TRUMPS ITS RIGHT TO SURVIVE.
CAN WE SPEAK TO DR. OCCULT? I CAN'T HELP BUT THINK RICHARD WOULD CHOOSE A DIFFERENT SOLUTION.
RICHARD AND I HAVE BOTH AGREED THAT I AM THE ONE IN CHARGE RIGHT NOW-- OF THIS BODY, AND OF THE SCHOOL. AND I SAY THE CREATURE LIVES.
NOW, ARE WE DONE?
THERE'S ONE MORE THING, I'M AFRAID. I'VE CONSULTED THE CARDS AND MY CRYSTAL BALL AND THE RUNES OVER AND OVER, AND I KEEP SEEING THE SAME PATTERN.
ONE OF FIVE NEW STUDENTS WILL TURN INTO THE MALEVOLENCE.
THE DIVIDED ONE, WHO SOMETIMES CALLS HERSELF ENCHANTRESS. FELIX FAUST'S UNFORTUNATE WASTELAND OF A SON.
THE GIRL, PIA, WHO BELIEVES HERSELF A HEALER. SARGON, WHO HAS MADE A BARGAIN HE DOES NOT UNDERSTAND.
OR...IT COULD BE THE GIRL YOU BROUGHT BACK FROM VEGAS. ZATARA'S CHILD.
the Enchantress
the Healer
ZATANNA? BUT THAT'S IMPOSSIBLE...
WE CANNOT IGNORE THE SIGNS.
SO, ROSE, WHAT DO YOU WANT TO DO NOW?

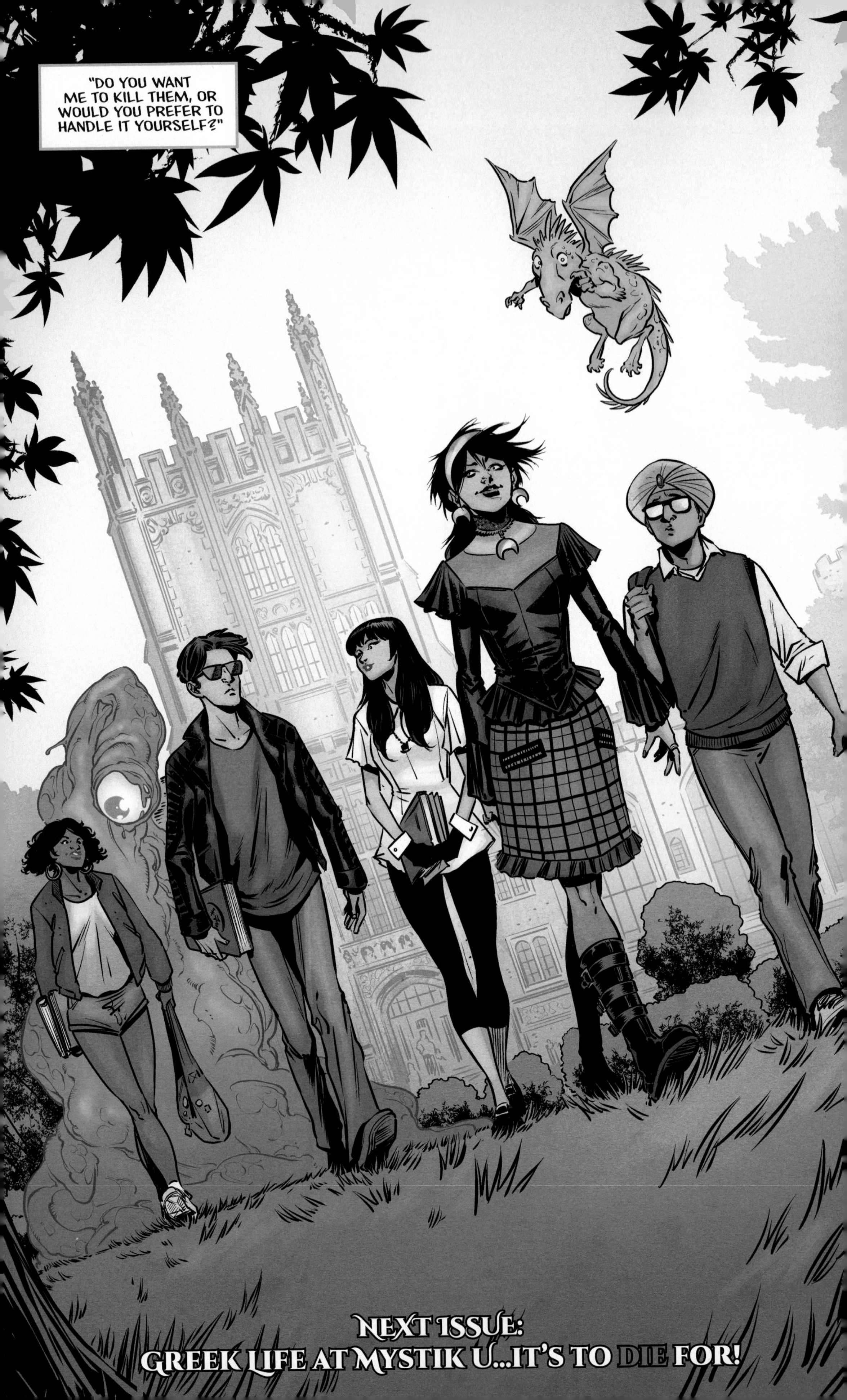
"DO YOU WANT ME TO KILL THEM, OR WOULD YOU PREFER TO HANDLE IT YOURSELF?"
NEXT ISSUE:
GREEK LIFE AT MYSTIK U...IT'S TO DIE FOR!

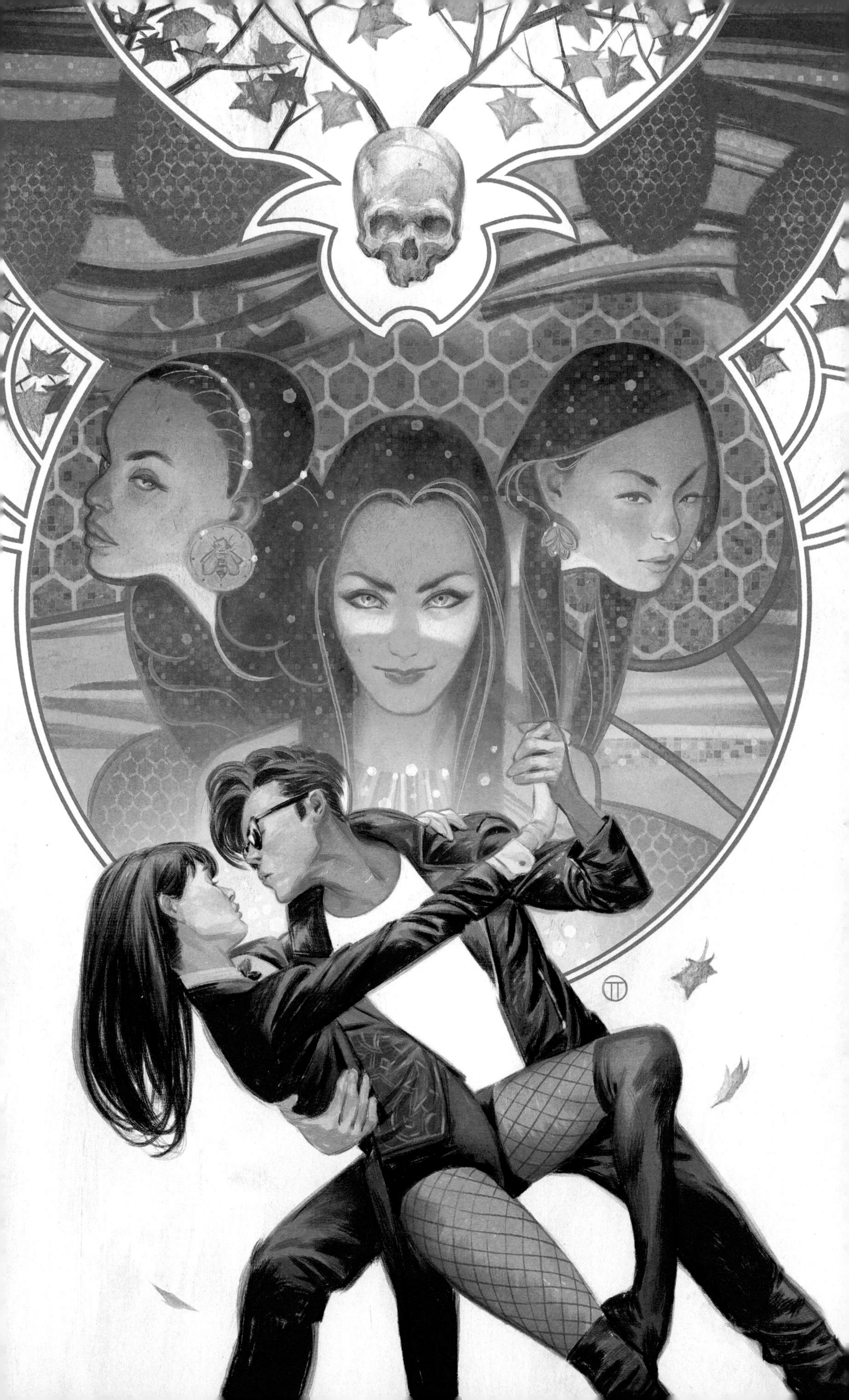

"Magick doesn't like effort.
It doesn't respond well to
desperation or frustration or need."

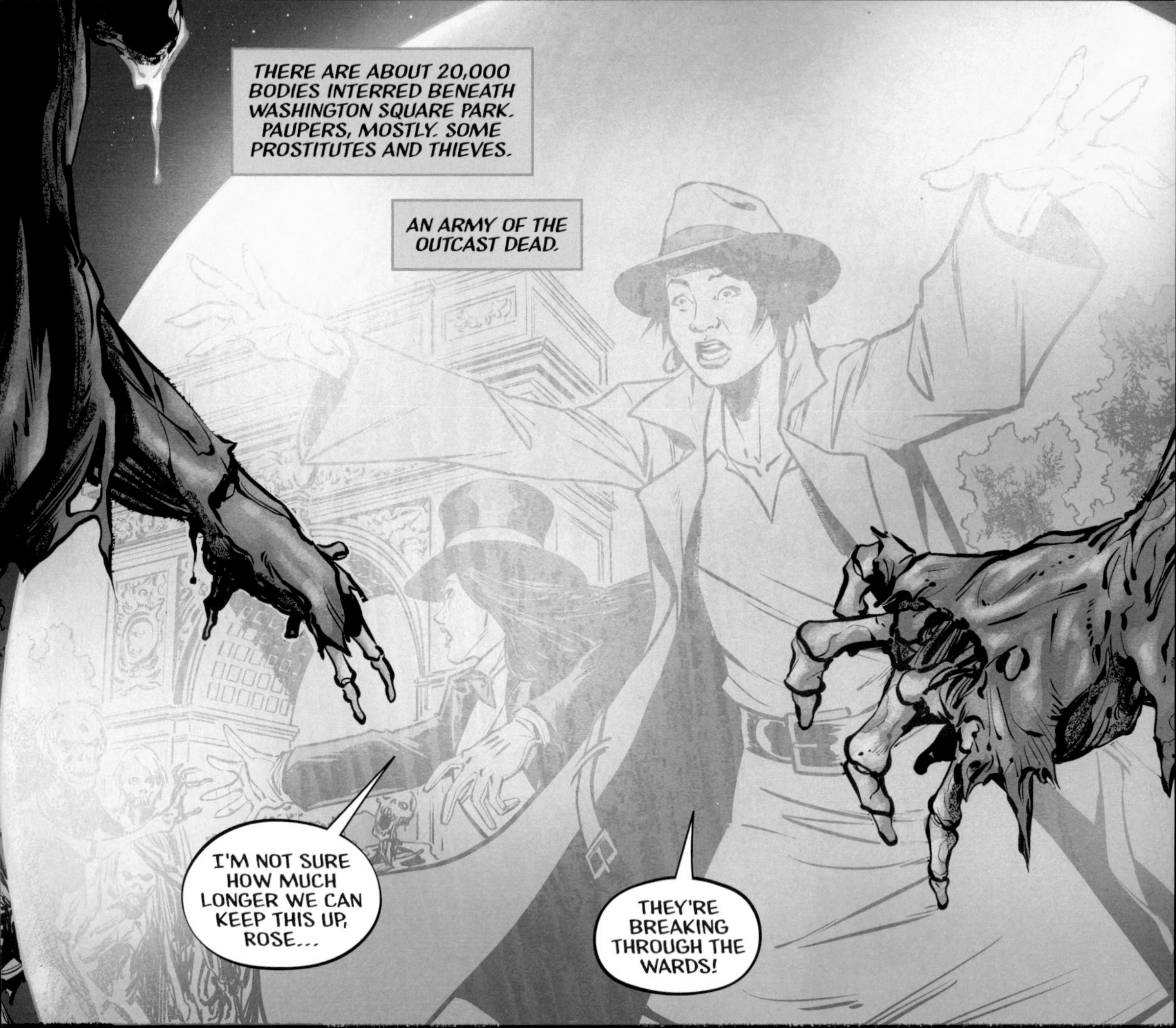
THERE ARE ABOUT 20,000 BODIES INTERRED BENEATH WASHINGTON SQUARE PARK. PAUPERS, MOSTLY. SOME PROSTITUTES AND THIEVES.
AN ARMY OF THE OUTCAST DEAD.
I'M NOT SURE HOW MUCH LONGER WE CAN KEEP THIS UP, ROSE...
THEY'RE BREAKING THROUGH THE WARDS!

Prologue.

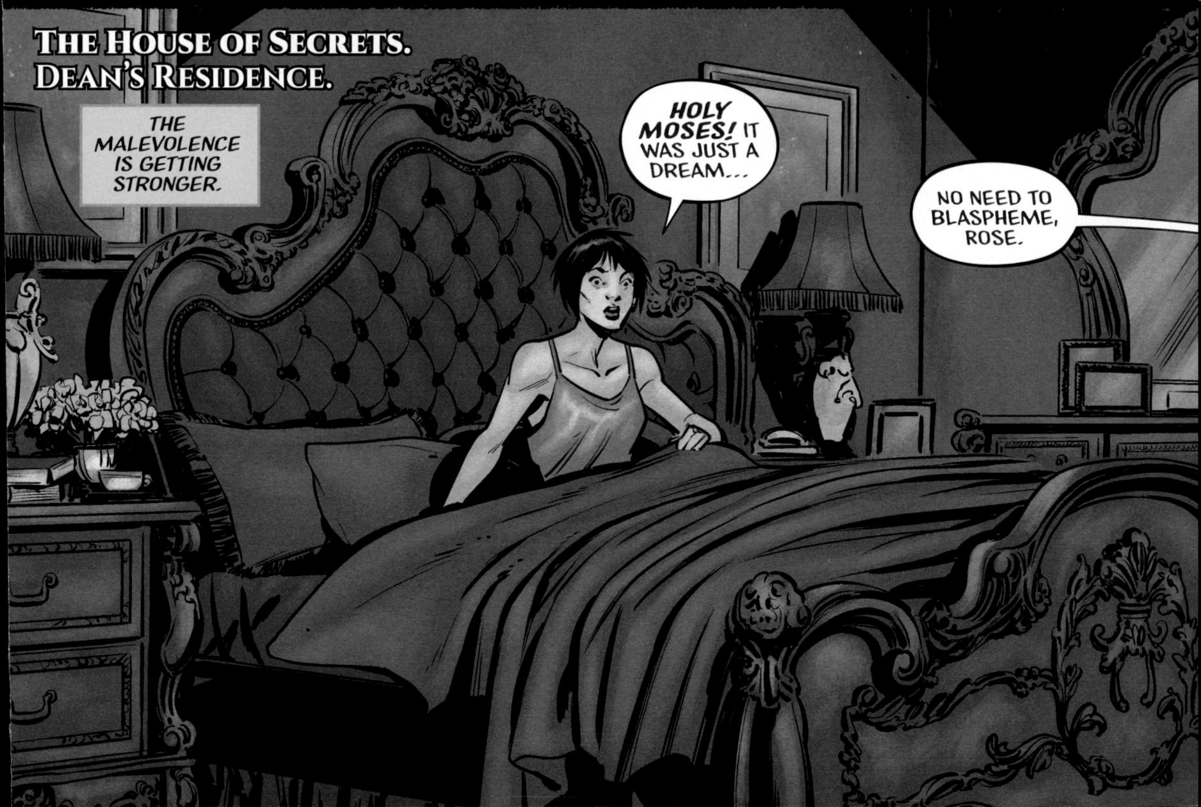
THE HOUSE OF SECRETS. DEAN'S RESIDENCE.
THE MALEVOLENCE IS GETTING STRONGER.
HOLY MOSES! IT WAS JUST A DREAM...
NO NEED TO BLASPHEME, ROSE.

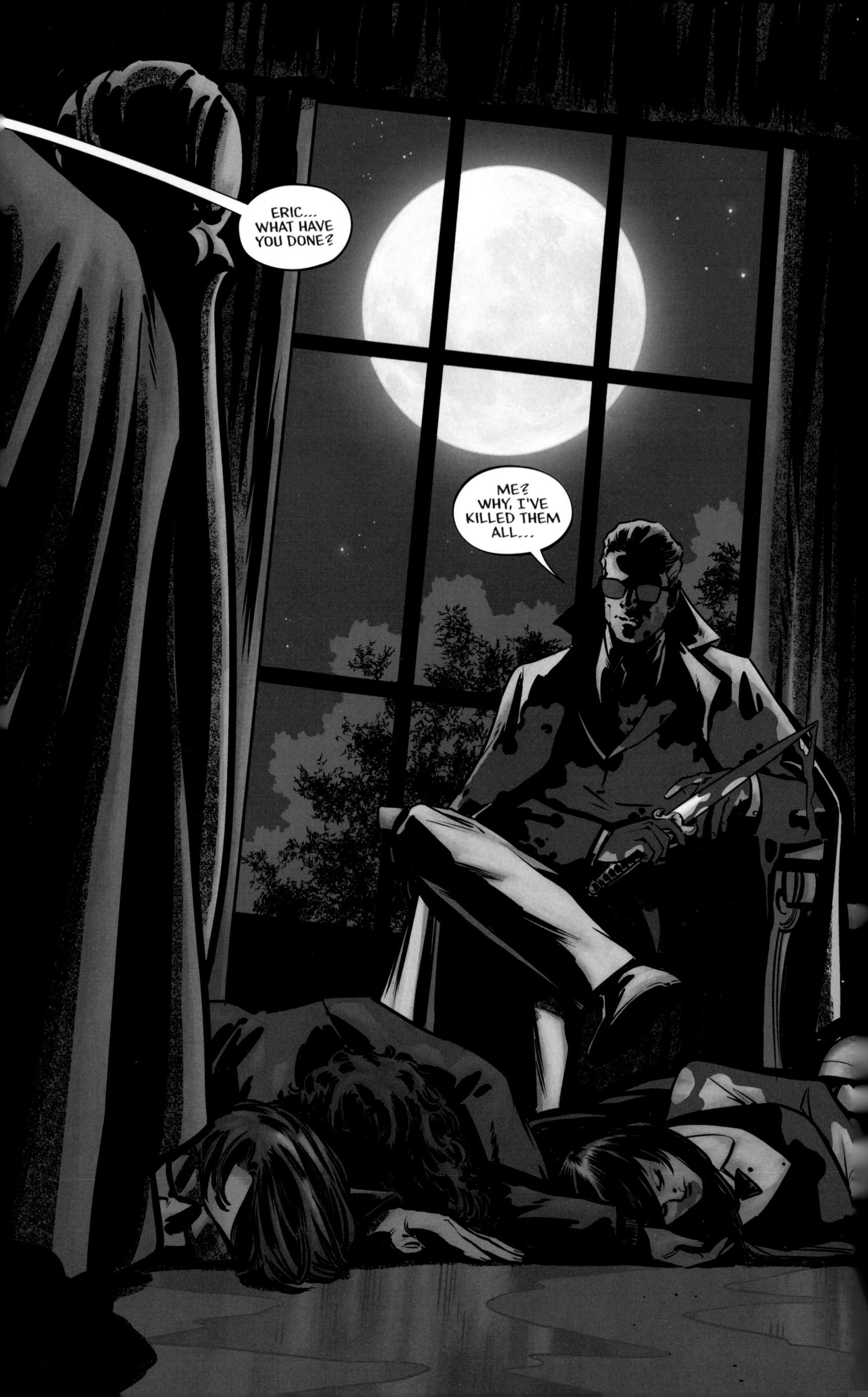
ERIC... WHAT HAVE YOU DONE?
ME? WHY, I'VE KILLED THEM ALL...

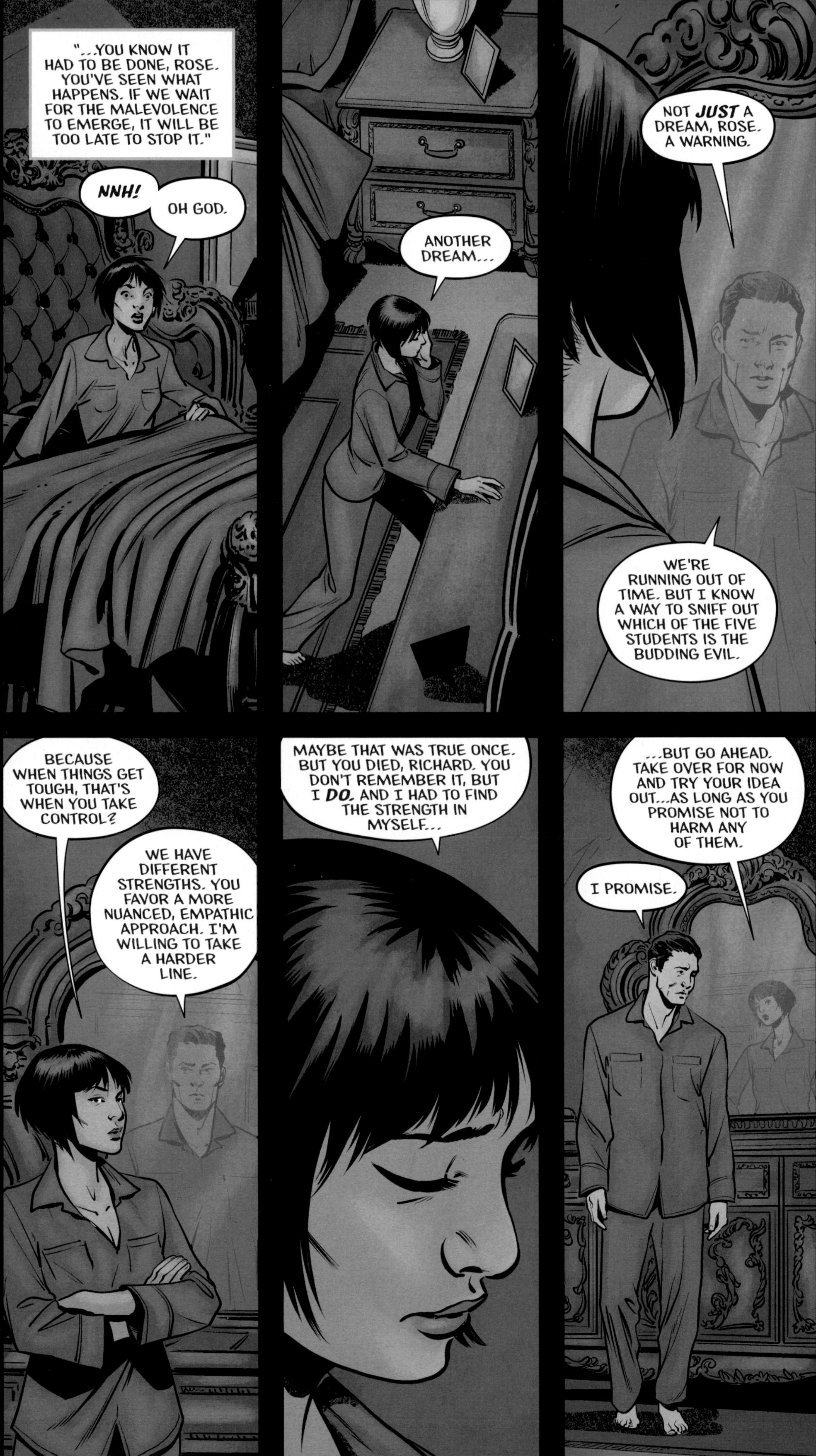
"...YOU KNOW IT HAD TO BE DONE, ROSE. YOU'VE SEEN WHAT HAPPENS. IF WE WAIT FOR THE MALEVOLENCE TO EMERGE, IT WILL BE TOO LATE TO STOP IT."
NNH!
OH GOD.
ANOTHER DREAM...
NOT JUST A DREAM, ROSE. A WARNING.
WE'RE RUNNING OUT OF TIME. BUT I KNOW A WAY TO SNIFF OUT WHICH OF THE FIVE STUDENTS IS THE BUDDING EVIL.
BECAUSE WHEN THINGS GET TOUGH, THAT'S WHEN YOU TAKE CONTROL?
WE HAVE DIFFERENT STRENGTHS. YOU FAVOR A MORE NUANCED, EMPATHIC APPROACH. I'M WILLING TO TAKE A HARDER LINE.
MAYBE THAT WAS TRUE ONCE. BUT YOU DIED, RICHARD. YOU DON'T REMEMBER IT, BUT I DO. AND I HAD TO FIND THE STRENGTH IN MYSELF...
...BUT GO AHEAD. TAKE OVER FOR NOW AND TRY YOUR IDEA OUT...AS LONG AS YOU PROMISE NOT TO HARM ANY OF THEM.
I PROMISE.

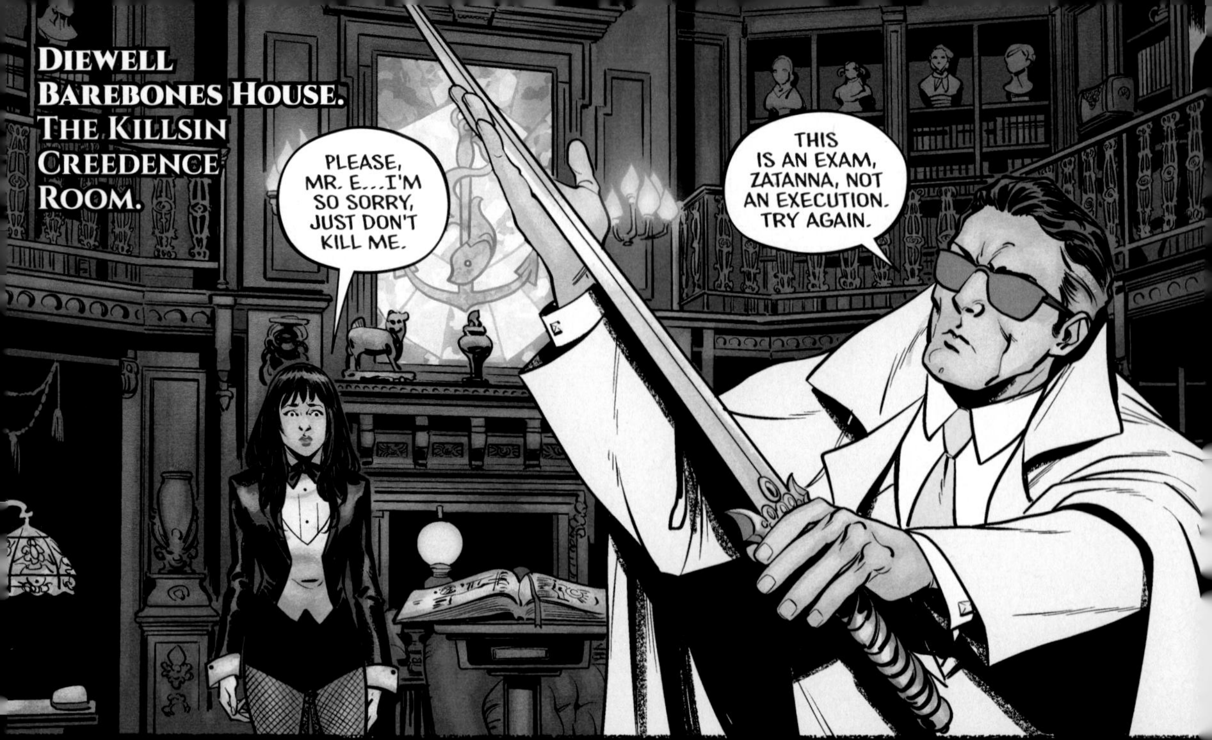
DIEWELL BAREBONES HOUSE. THE KILLSIN CREEDENCE ROOM.
PLEASE, MR. E...I'M SO SORRY, JUST DON'T KILL ME.
THIS IS AN EXAM, ZATANNA, NOT AN EXECUTION. TRY AGAIN.

Chapter One: Magick 101

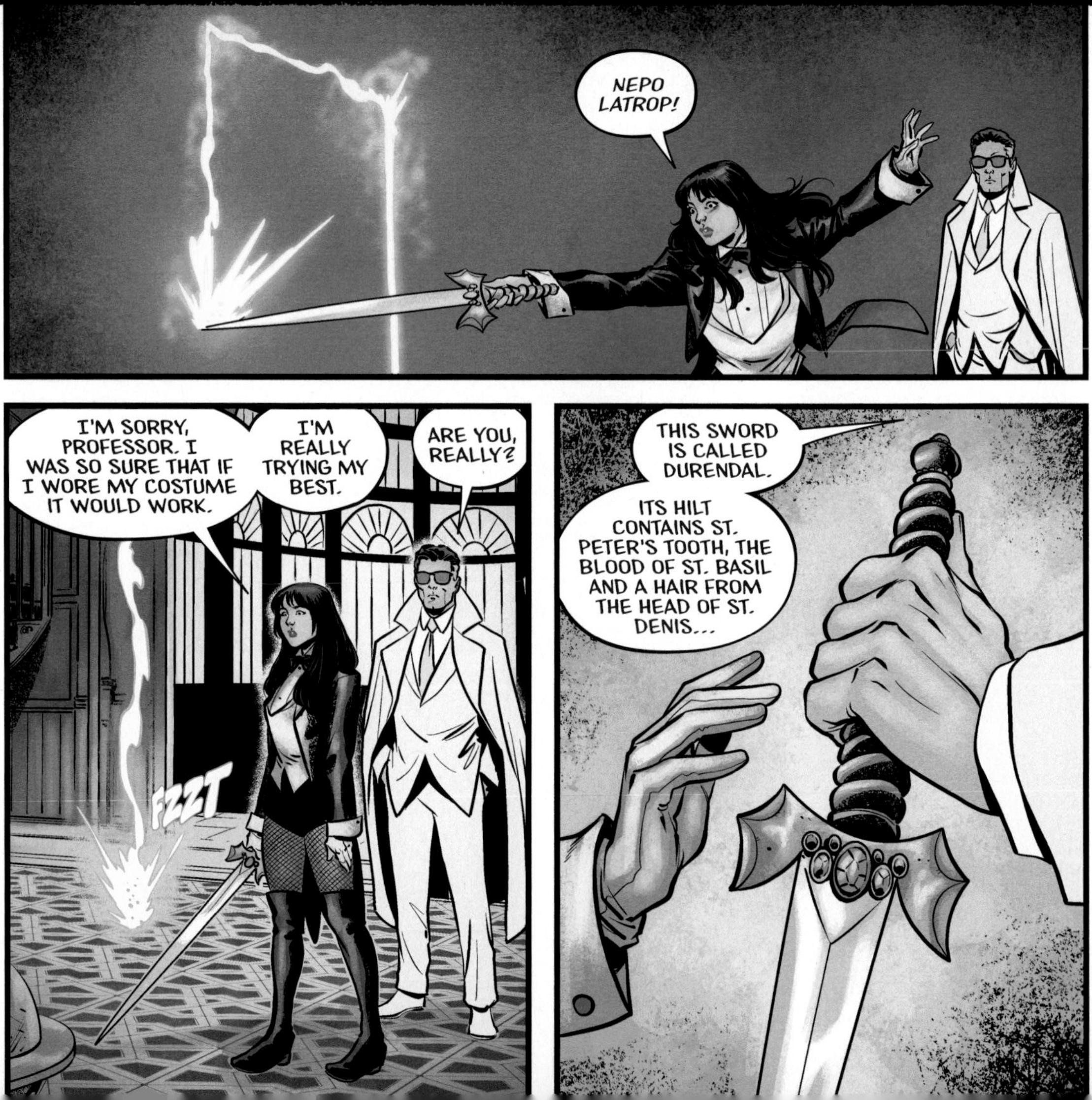
NEPO LATROP!
I'M SORRY, PROFESSOR. I WAS SO SURE THAT IF I WORE MY COSTUME IT WOULD WORK.
I'M REALLY TRYING MY BEST.
ARE YOU, REALLY?
FZZT
THIS SWORD IS CALLED DURENDAL.
ITS HILT CONTAINS ST. PETER'S TOOTH, THE BLOOD OF ST. BASIL AND A HAIR FROM THE HEAD OF ST. DENIS...

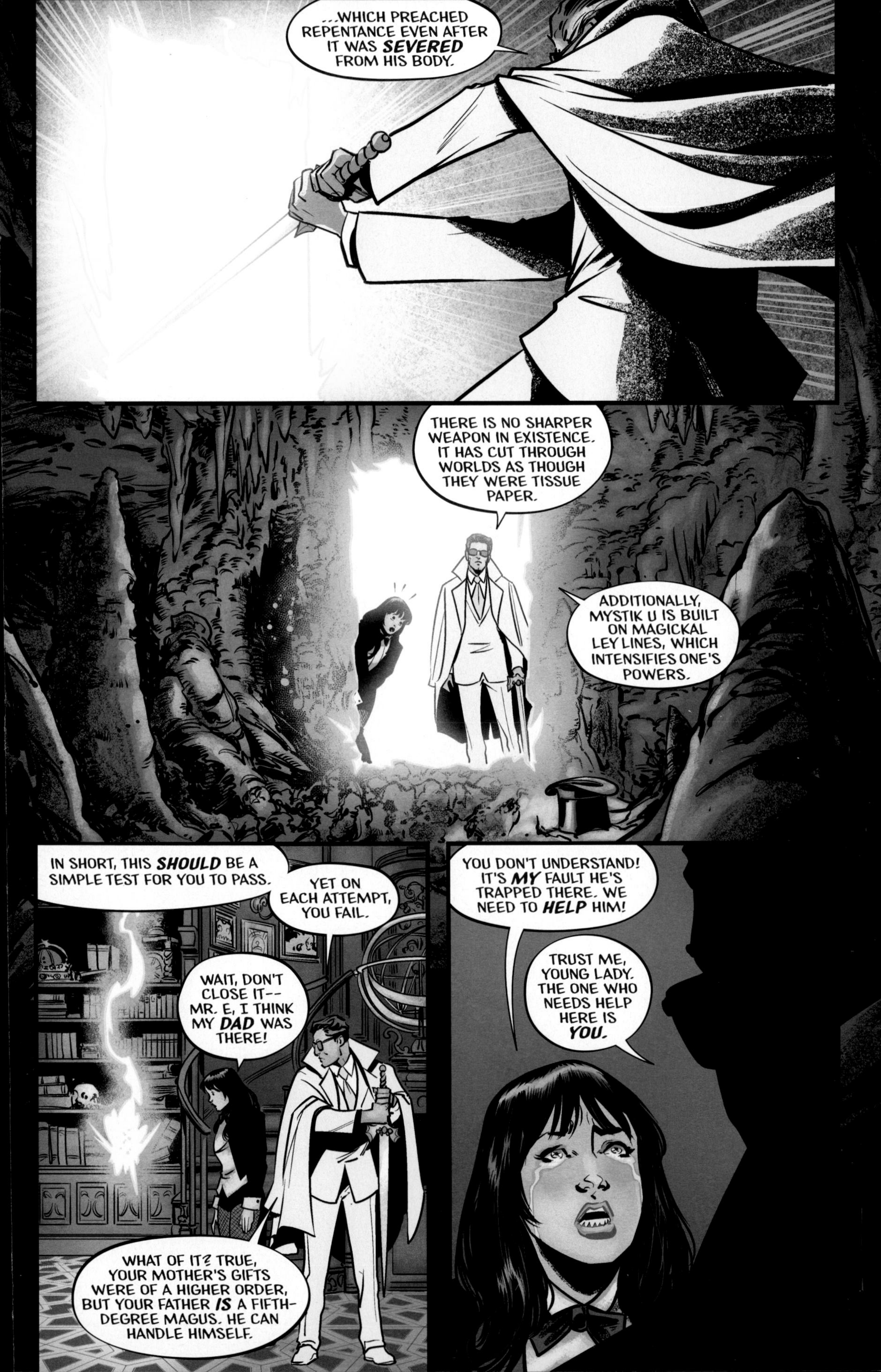
...WHICH PREACHED REPENTANCE EVEN AFTER IT WAS SEVERED FROM HIS BODY.
THERE IS NO SHARPER WEAPON IN EXISTENCE. IT HAS CUT THROUGH WORLDS AS THOUGH THEY WERE TISSUE PAPER.
ADDITIONALLY, MYSTIK U IS BUILT ON MAGICKAL LEY LINES, WHICH INTENSIFIES ONE'S POWERS.
IN SHORT, THIS SHOULD BE A SIMPLE TEST FOR YOU TO PASS.
YET ON EACH ATTEMPT, YOU FAIL.
WAIT, DON'T CLOSE IT-- MR. E, I THINK MY DAD WAS THERE!
WHAT OF IT? TRUE, YOUR MOTHER'S GIFTS WERE OF A HIGHER ORDER, BUT YOUR FATHER IS A FIFTH-DEGREE MAGUS. HE CAN HANDLE HIMSELF.
YOU DON'T UNDERSTAND! IT'S MY FAULT HE'S TRAPPED THERE. WE NEED TO HELP HIM!
TRUST ME, YOUNG LADY. THE ONE WHO NEEDS HELP HERE IS YOU.

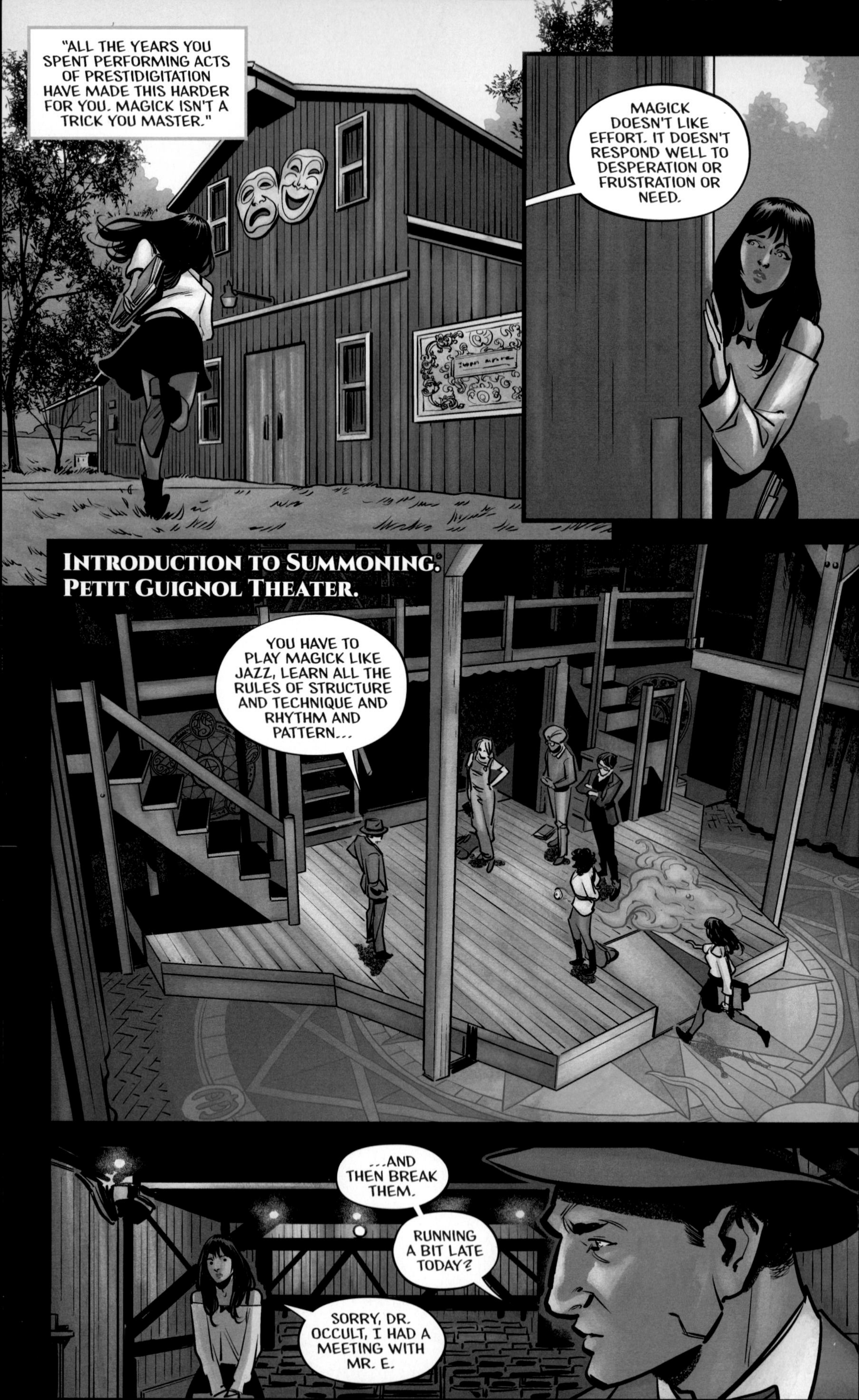
"ALL THE YEARS YOU SPENT PERFORMING ACTS OF PRESTIDIGITATION HAVE MADE THIS HARDER FOR YOU. MAGICK ISN'T A TRICK YOU MASTER."
MAGICK DOESN'T LIKE EFFORT. IT DOESN'T RESPOND WELL TO DESPERATION OR FRUSTRATION OR NEED.
INTRODUCTION TO SUMMONING. PETIT GUIGNOL THEATER.
YOU HAVE TO PLAY MAGICK LIKE JAZZ, LEARN ALL THE RULES OF STRUCTURE AND TECHNIQUE AND RHYTHM AND PATTERN...
...AND THEN BREAK THEM.
RUNNING A BIT LATE TODAY?
SORRY, DR. OCCULT, I HAD A MEETING WITH MR. E.

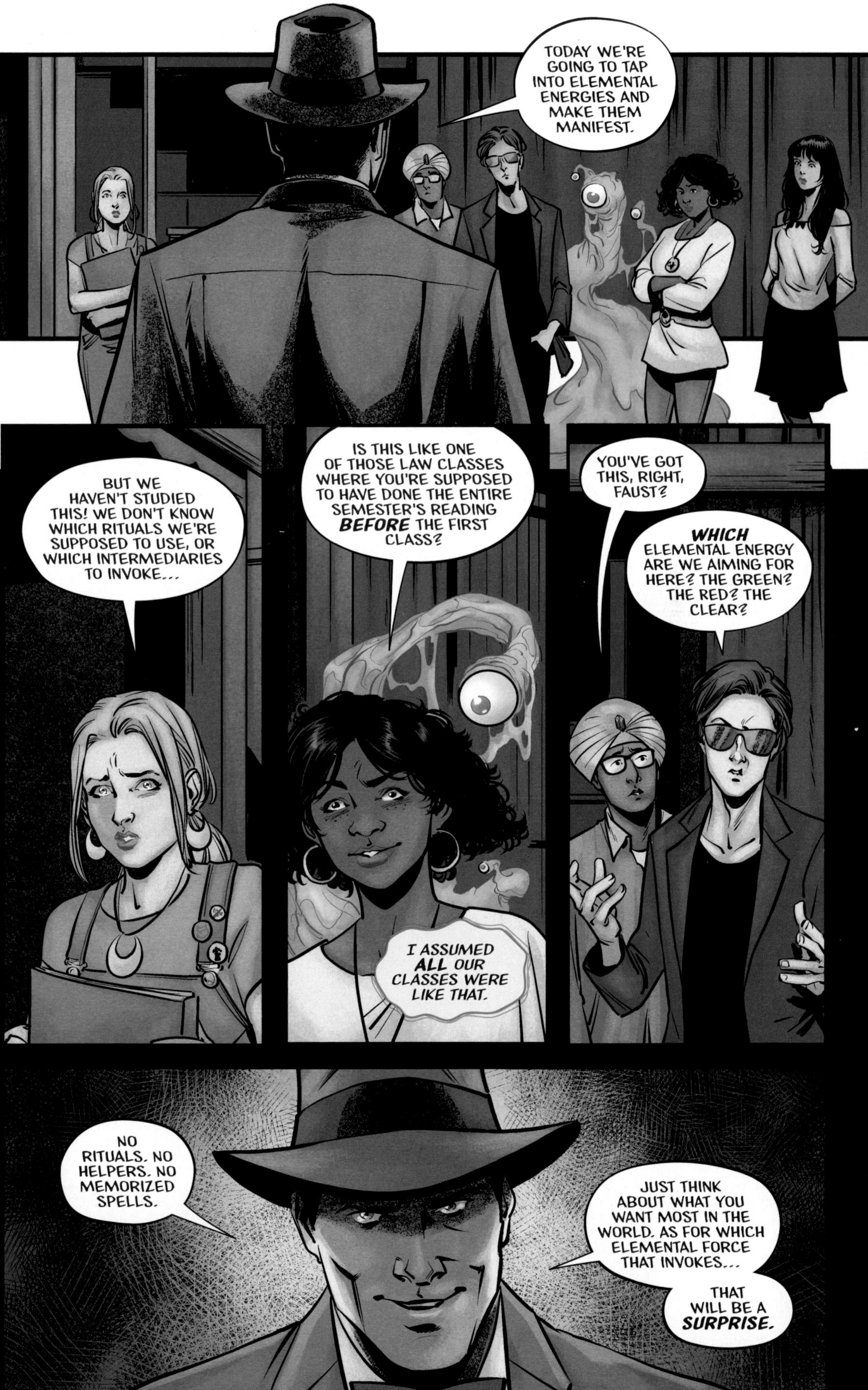
TODAY WE'RE GOING TO TAP INTO ELEMENTAL ENERGIES AND MAKE THEM MANIFEST.
BUT WE HAVEN'T STUDIED THIS! WE DON'T KNOW WHICH RITUALS WE'RE SUPPOSED TO USE, OR WHICH INTERMEDIARIES TO INVOKE...
IS THIS LIKE ONE OF THOSE LAW CLASSES WHERE YOU'RE SUPPOSED TO HAVE DONE THE ENTIRE SEMESTER'S READING BEFORE THE FIRST CLASS?
I ASSUMED ALL OUR CLASSES WERE LIKE THAT.
YOU'VE GOT THIS, RIGHT, FAUST?
WHICH ELEMENTAL ENERGY ARE WE AIMING FOR HERE? THE GREEN? THE RED? THE CLEAR?
NO RITUALS. NO HELPERS. NO MEMORIZED SPELLS.
JUST THINK ABOUT WHAT YOU WANT MOST IN THE WORLD. AS FOR WHICH ELEMENTAL FORCE THAT INVOKES...
THAT WILL BE A SURPRISE.

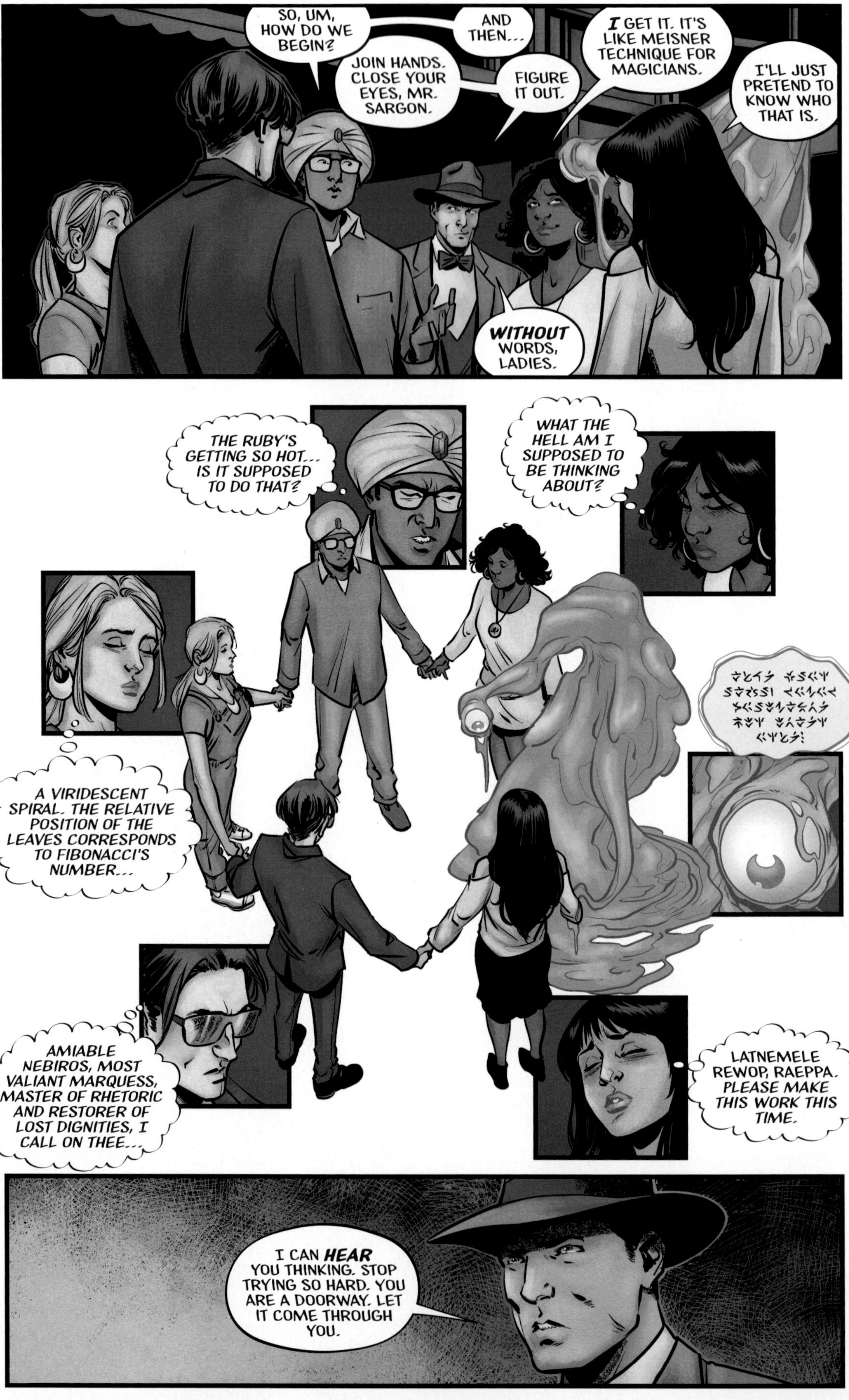
SO, UM, HOW DO WE BEGIN?
JOIN HANDS. CLOSE YOUR EYES, MR. SARGON.
AND THEN...
FIGURE IT OUT.
I GET IT. IT'S LIKE MEISNER TECHNIQUE FOR MAGICIANS.
I'LL JUST PRETEND TO KNOW WHO THAT IS.
WITHOUT WORDS, LADIES.
THE RUBY'S GETTING SO HOT... IS IT SUPPOSED TO DO THAT?
WHAT THE HELL AM I SUPPOSED TO BE THINKING ABOUT?
A VIRIDESCENT SPIRAL. THE RELATIVE POSITION OF THE LEAVES CORRESPONDS TO FIBONACCI'S NUMBER...
AMIABLE NEBIROS, MOST VALIANT MARQUESS, MASTER OF RHETORIC AND RESTORER OF LOST DIGNITIES, I CALL ON THEE...
LATNEMELE REWOP, RAEPPA. PLEASE MAKE THIS WORK THIS TIME.
I CAN HEAR YOU THINKING. STOP TRYING SO HARD. YOU ARE A DOORWAY. LET IT COME THROUGH YOU.

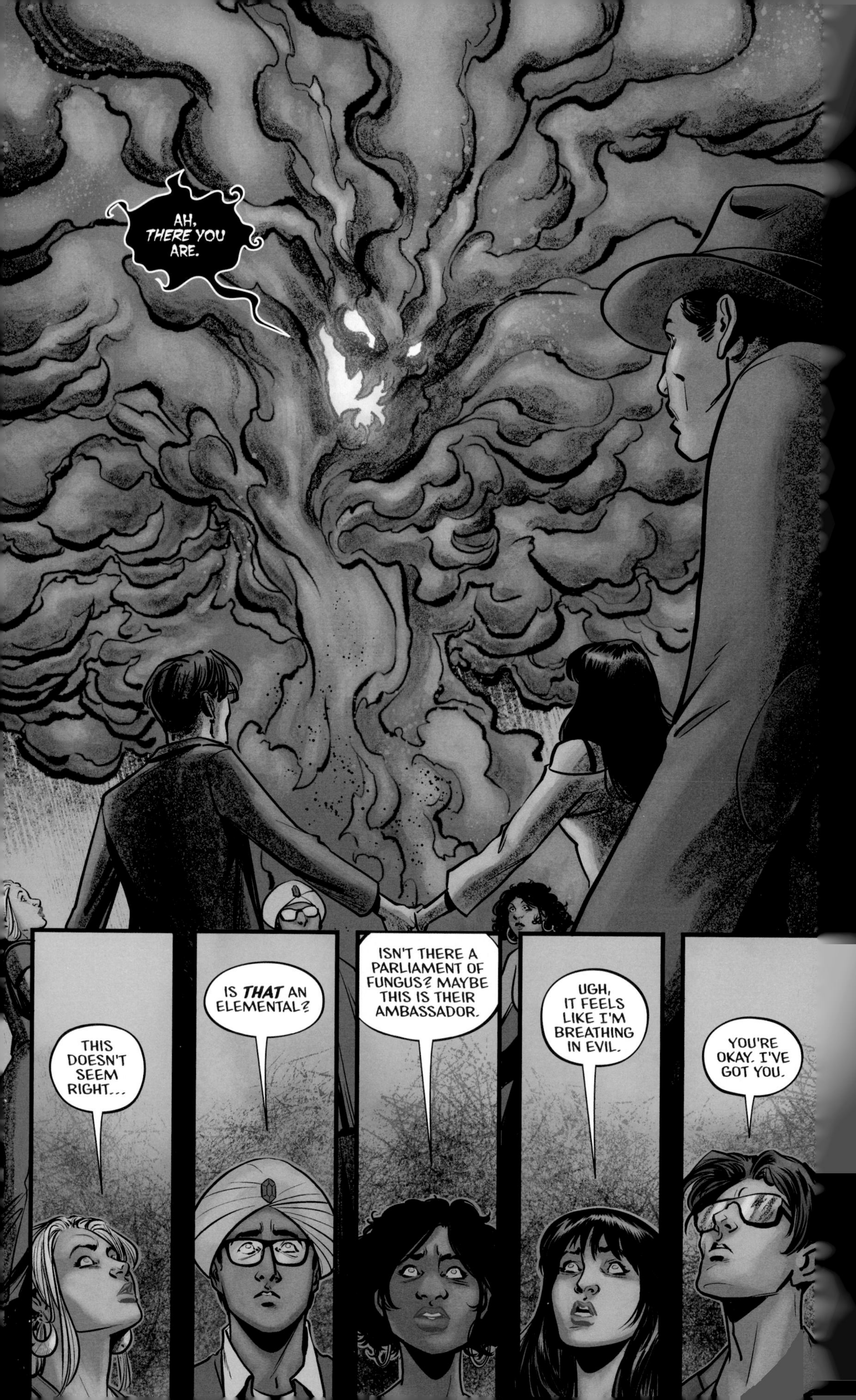
AH, THERE YOU ARE.
THIS DOESN'T SEEM RIGHT...
IS THAT AN ELEMENTAL?
ISN'T THERE A PARLIAMENT OF FUNGUS? MAYBE THIS IS THEIR AMBASSADOR.
UGH, IT FEELS LIKE I'M BREATHING IN EVIL.
YOU'RE OKAY. I'VE GOT YOU.

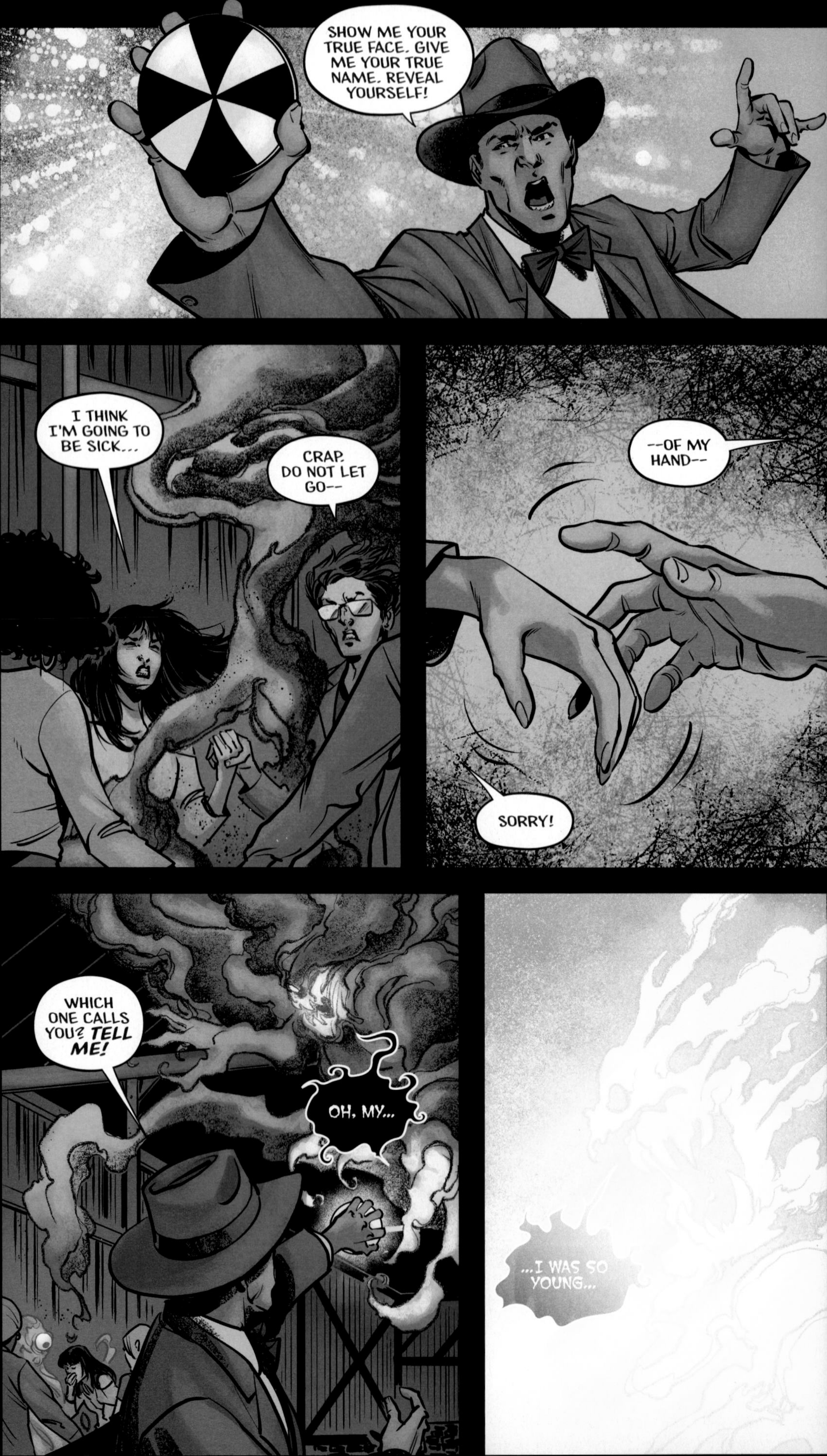
SHOW ME YOUR TRUE FACE. GIVE ME YOUR TRUE NAME. REVEAL YOURSELF!
I THINK I'M GOING TO BE SICK...
CRAP. DO NOT LET GO--
--OF MY HAND--
SORRY!
WHICH ONE CALLS YOU? *TELL ME!*
OH, MY...
...I WAS SO YOUNG...

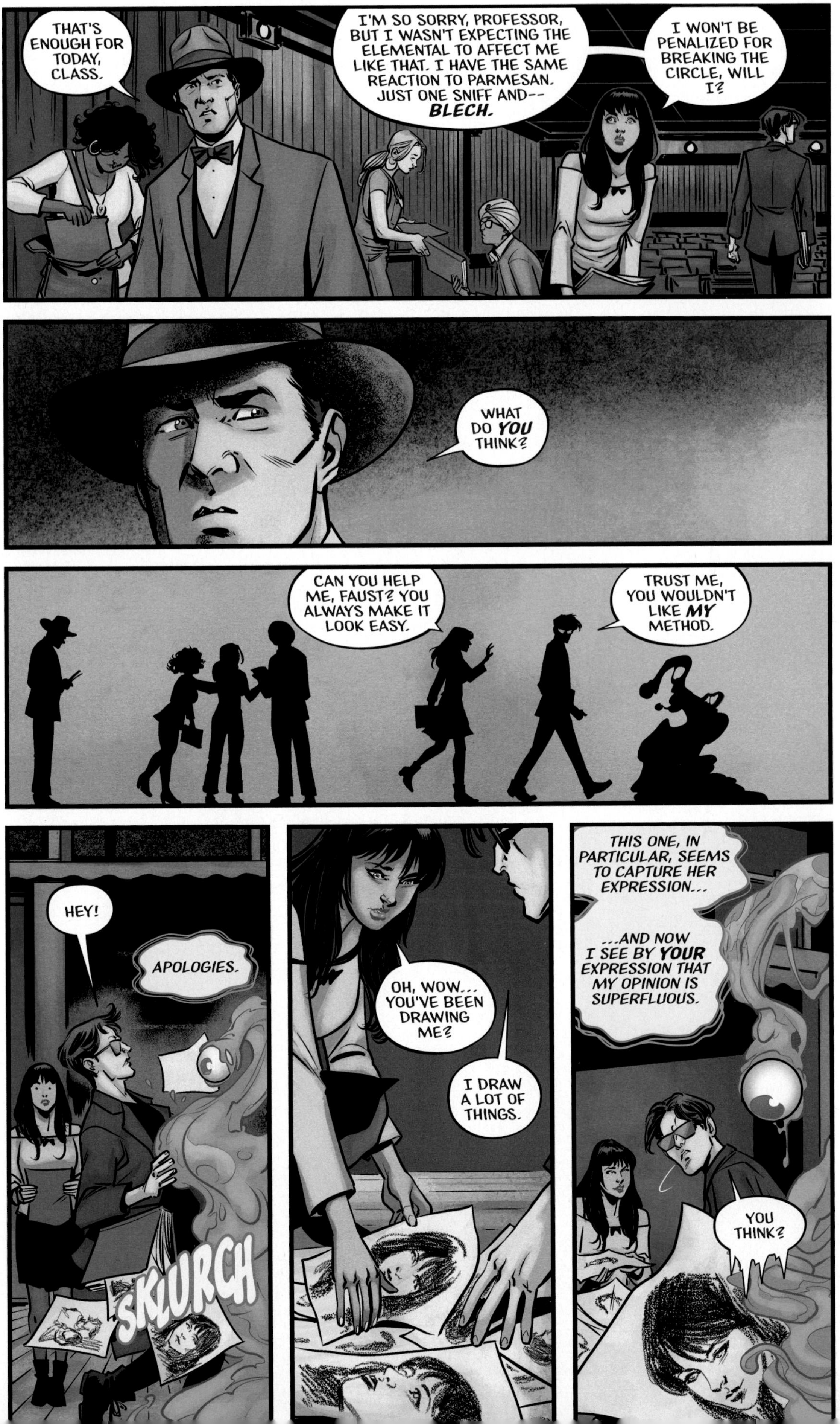
THAT'S ENOUGH FOR TODAY, CLASS.
I'M SO SORRY, PROFESSOR, BUT I WASN'T EXPECTING THE ELEMENTAL TO AFFECT ME LIKE THAT. I HAVE THE SAME REACTION TO PARMESAN. JUST ONE SNIFF AND-- BLECH.
I WON'T BE PENALIZED FOR BREAKING THE CIRCLE, WILL I?
WHAT DO YOU THINK?
CAN YOU HELP ME, FAUST? YOU ALWAYS MAKE IT LOOK EASY.
TRUST ME, YOU WOULDN'T LIKE MY METHOD.
HEY!
APOLOGIES.
SKLURCH
OH, WOW... YOU'VE BEEN DRAWING ME?
I DRAW A LOT OF THINGS.
THIS ONE, IN PARTICULAR, SEEMS TO CAPTURE HER EXPRESSION...
...AND NOW I SEE BY YOUR EXPRESSION THAT MY OPINION IS SUPERFLUOUS.
YOU THINK?

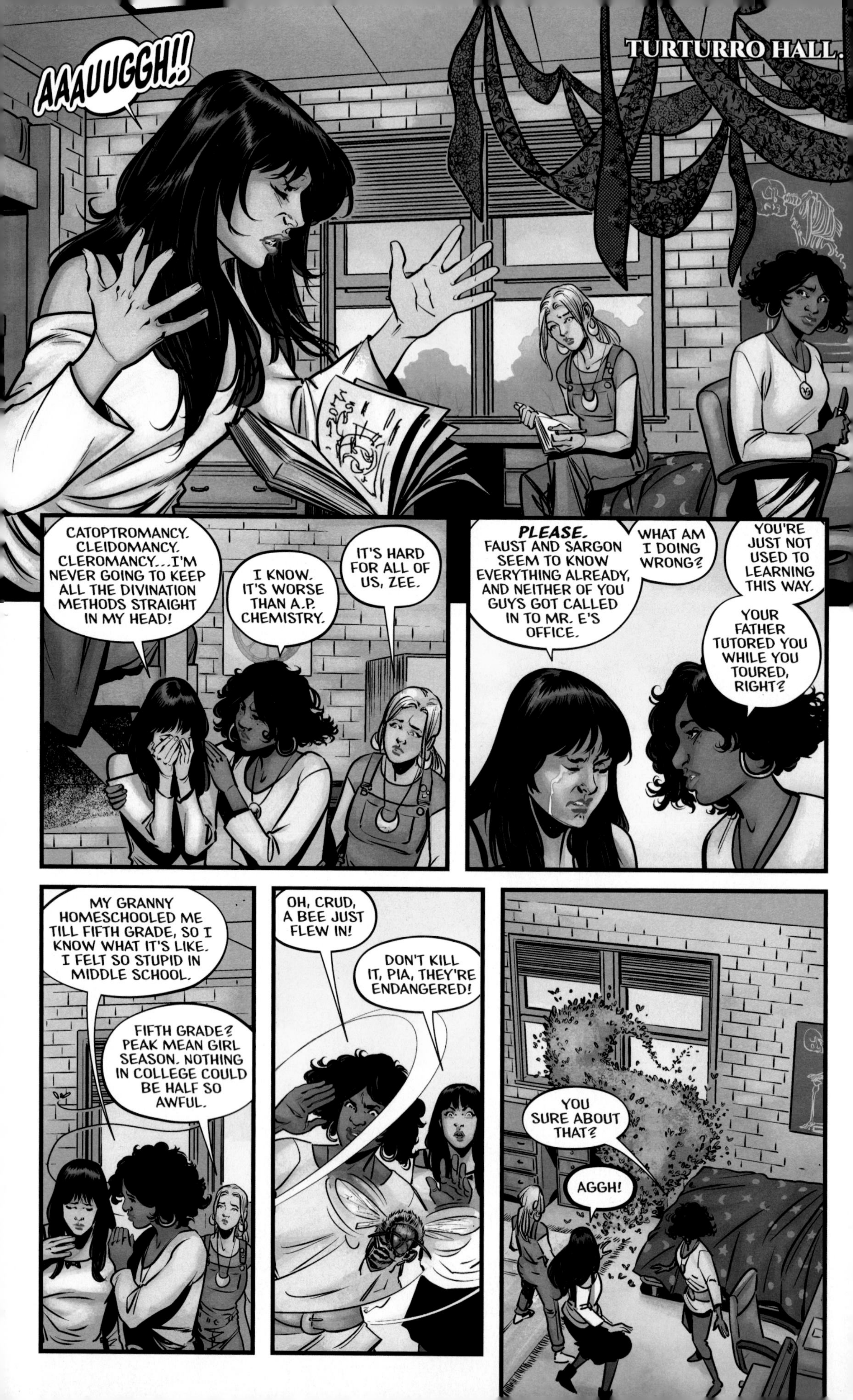
TURTURRO HALL.
AAAUUGGH!!
CATOPTROMANCY. CLEIDOMANCY. CLEROMANCY...I'M NEVER GOING TO KEEP ALL THE DIVINATION METHODS STRAIGHT IN MY HEAD!
I KNOW. IT'S WORSE THAN A.P. CHEMISTRY.
IT'S HARD FOR ALL OF US, ZEE.
PLEASE. FAUST AND SARGON SEEM TO KNOW EVERYTHING ALREADY, AND NEITHER OF YOU GUYS GOT CALLED IN TO MR. E'S OFFICE.
WHAT AM I DOING WRONG?
YOU'RE JUST NOT USED TO LEARNING THIS WAY.
YOUR FATHER TUTORED YOU WHILE YOU TOURED, RIGHT?
MY GRANNY HOMESCHOOLED ME TILL FIFTH GRADE, SO I KNOW WHAT IT'S LIKE. I FELT SO STUPID IN MIDDLE SCHOOL.
FIFTH GRADE? PEAK MEAN GIRL SEASON. NOTHING IN COLLEGE COULD BE HALF SO AWFUL.
OH, CRUD, A BEE JUST FLEW IN!
DON'T KILL IT, PIA, THEY'RE ENDANGERED!
YOU SURE ABOUT THAT?
AGGH!

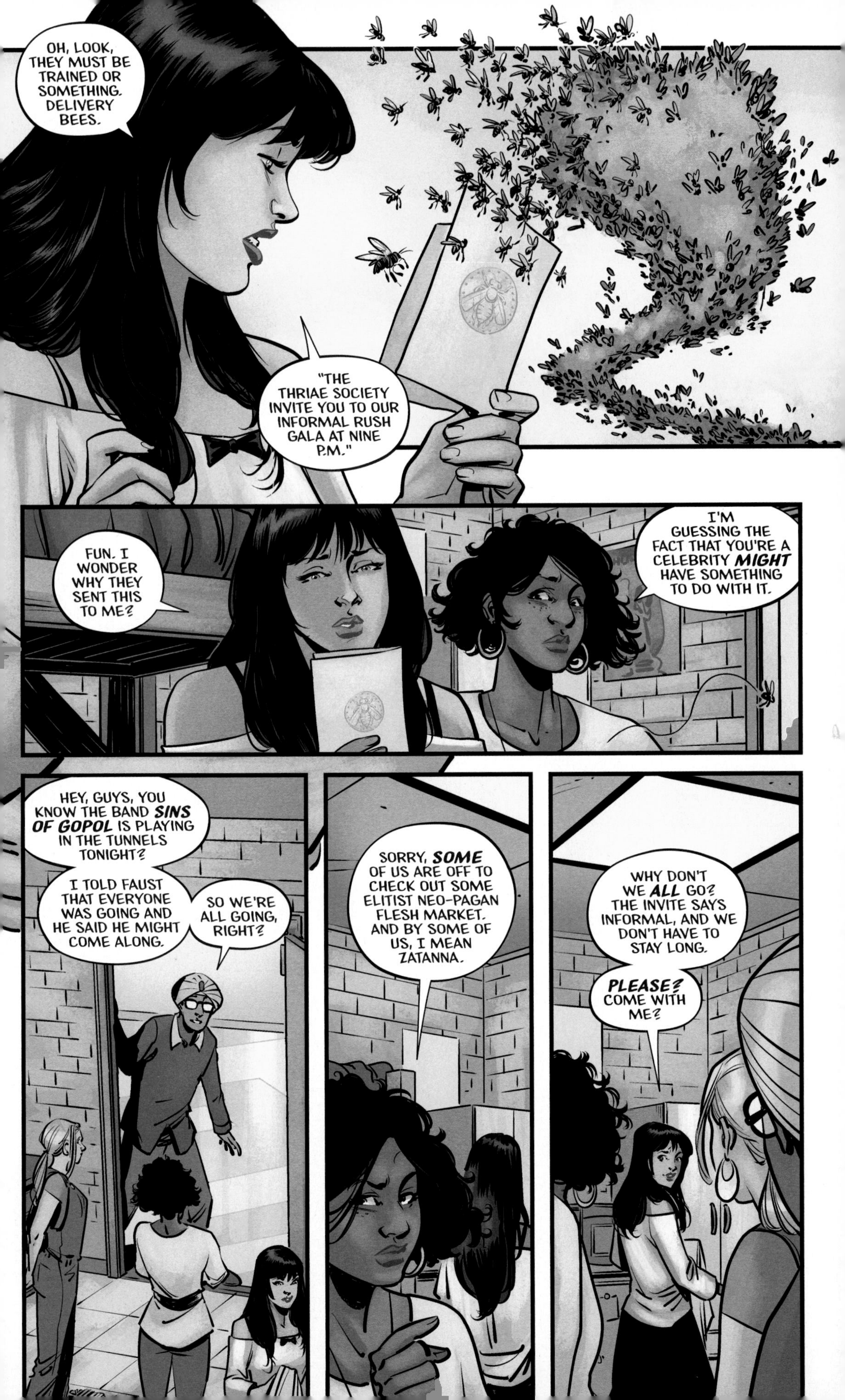
OH, LOOK, THEY MUST BE TRAINED OR SOMETHING. DELIVERY BEES.
"THE THRIAE SOCIETY INVITE YOU TO OUR INFORMAL RUSH GALA AT NINE P.M."
FUN. I WONDER WHY THEY SENT THIS TO ME?
I'M GUESSING THE FACT THAT YOU'RE A CELEBRITY MIGHT HAVE SOMETHING TO DO WITH IT.
HEY, GUYS, YOU KNOW THE BAND SINS OF GOPOL IS PLAYING IN THE TUNNELS TONIGHT?
I TOLD FAUST THAT EVERYONE WAS GOING AND HE SAID HE MIGHT COME ALONG.
SO WE'RE ALL GOING, RIGHT?
SORRY, SOME OF US ARE OFF TO CHECK OUT SOME ELITIST NEO-PAGAN FLESH MARKET. AND BY SOME OF US, I MEAN ZATANNA.
WHY DON'T WE ALL GO? THE INVITE SAYS INFORMAL, AND WE DON'T HAVE TO STAY LONG.
PLEASE? COME WITH ME?

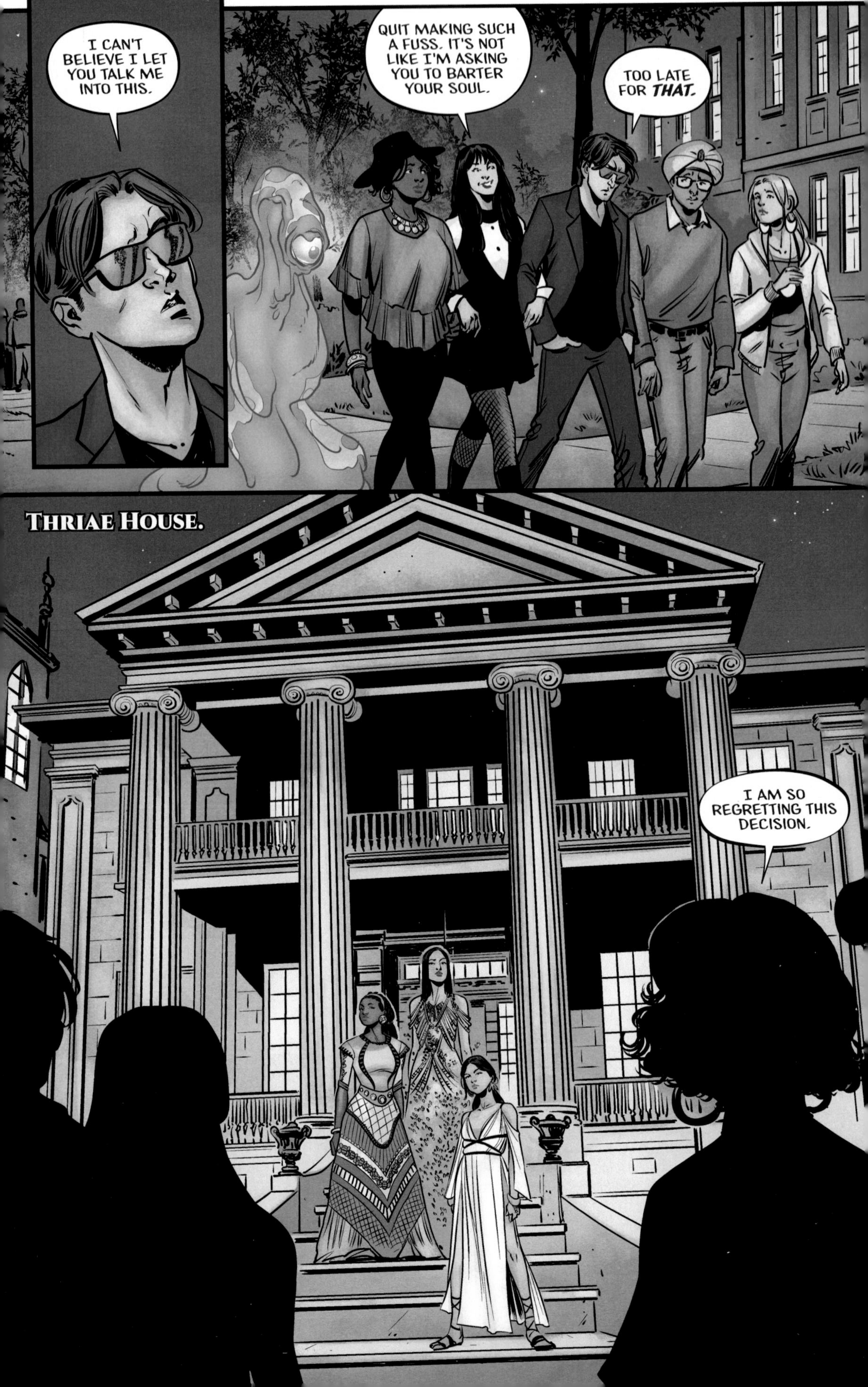
I CAN'T BELIEVE I LET YOU TALK ME INTO THIS.
QUIT MAKING SUCH A FUSS. IT'S NOT LIKE I'M ASKING YOU TO BARTER YOUR SOUL.
TOO LATE FOR *THAT.*
THRIAE HOUSE.
I AM SO REGRETTING THIS DECISION.

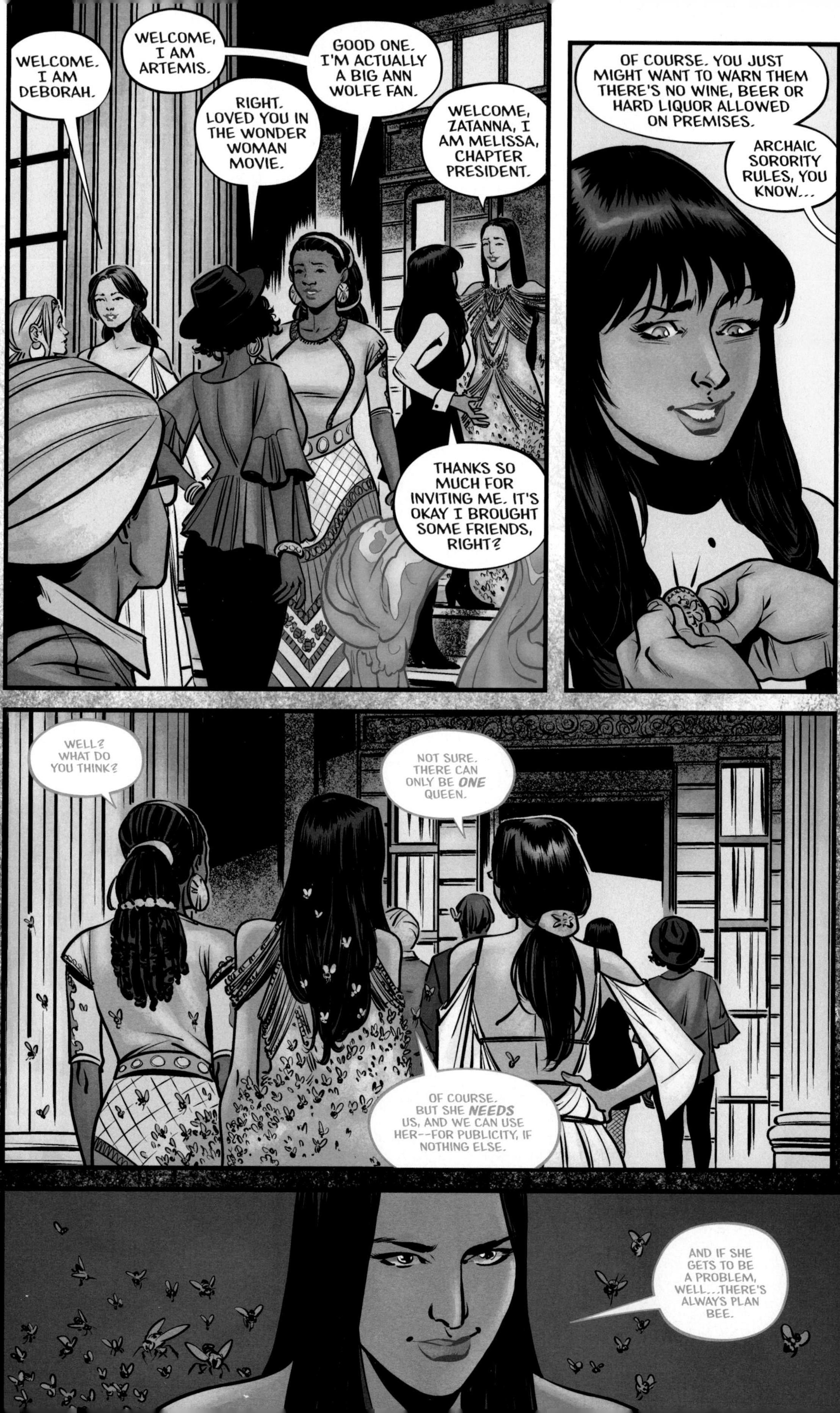
WELCOME. I AM DEBORAH.
WELCOME, I AM ARTEMIS.
RIGHT. LOVED YOU IN THE WONDER WOMAN MOVIE.
GOOD ONE. I'M ACTUALLY A BIG ANN WOLFE FAN.
WELCOME, ZATANNA, I AM MELISSA, CHAPTER PRESIDENT.
THANKS SO MUCH FOR INVITING ME. IT'S OKAY I BROUGHT SOME FRIENDS, RIGHT?
OF COURSE. YOU JUST MIGHT WANT TO WARN THEM THERE'S NO WINE, BEER OR HARD LIQUOR ALLOWED ON PREMISES.
ARCHAIC SORORITY RULES, YOU KNOW...
WELL? WHAT DO YOU THINK?
NOT SURE. THERE CAN ONLY BE ONE QUEEN.
OF COURSE. BUT SHE NEEDS US, AND WE CAN USE HER--FOR PUBLICITY, IF NOTHING ELSE.
AND IF SHE GETS TO BE A PROBLEM, WELL...THERE'S ALWAYS PLAN BEE.

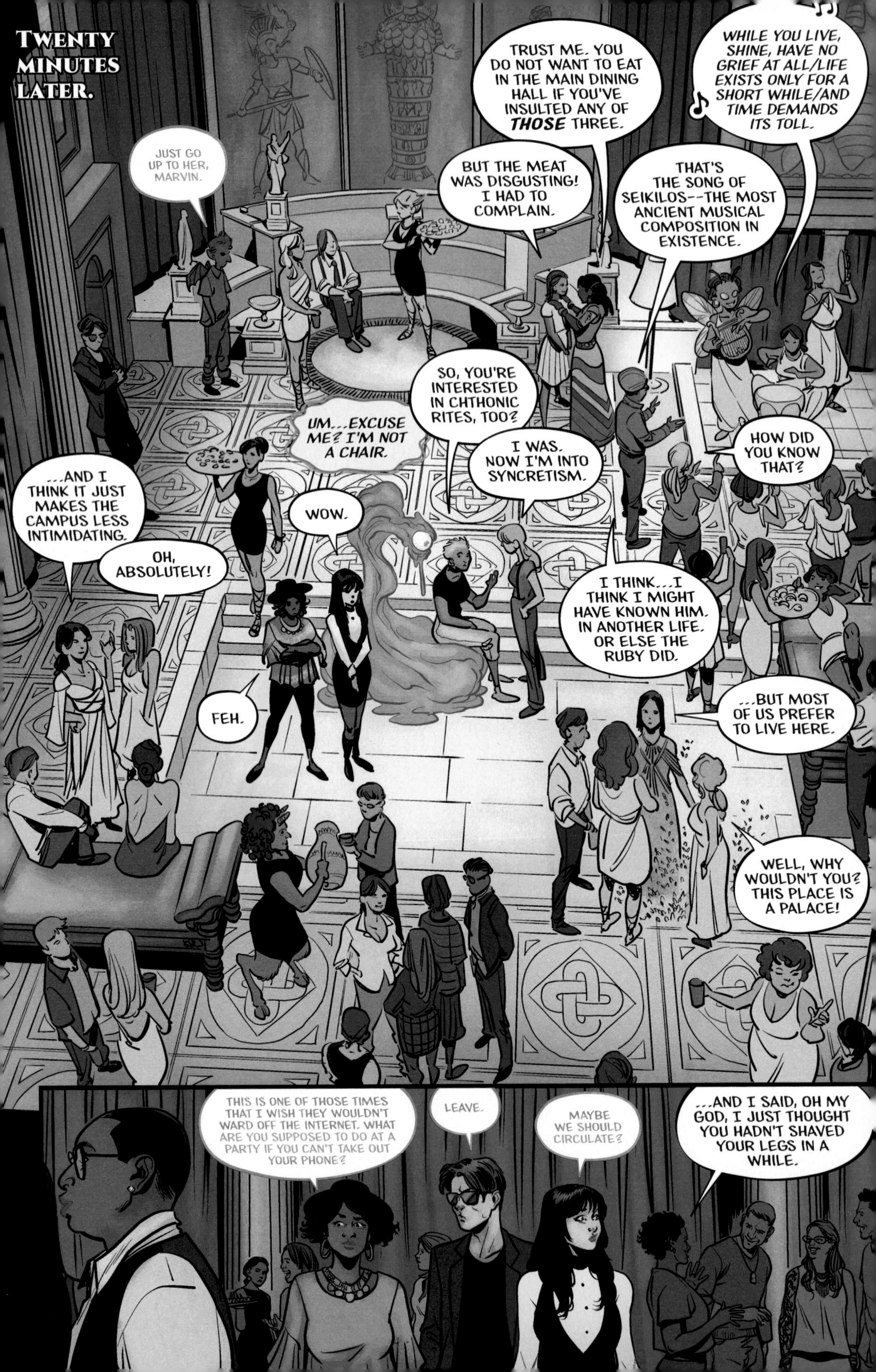
TWENTY MINUTES LATER.
JUST GO UP TO HER, MARVIN.
TRUST ME. YOU DO NOT WANT TO EAT IN THE MAIN DINING HALL IF YOU'VE INSULTED ANY OF *THOSE* THREE.
BUT THE MEAT WAS DISGUSTING! I HAD TO COMPLAIN.
WHILE YOU LIVE, SHINE, HAVE NO GRIEF AT ALL/LIFE EXISTS ONLY FOR A SHORT WHILE/AND TIME DEMANDS ITS TOLL.
THAT'S THE SONG OF SEIKILOS--THE MOST ANCIENT MUSICAL COMPOSITION IN EXISTENCE.
SO, YOU'RE INTERESTED IN CHTHONIC RITES, TOO?
UM...EXCUSE ME? I'M NOT A CHAIR.
I WAS. NOW I'M INTO SYNCRETISM.
HOW DID YOU KNOW THAT?
...AND I THINK IT JUST MAKES THE CAMPUS LESS INTIMIDATING.
WOW.
OH, ABSOLUTELY!
I THINK...I THINK I MIGHT HAVE KNOWN HIM. IN ANOTHER LIFE. OR ELSE THE RUBY DID.
FEH.
...BUT MOST OF US PREFER TO LIVE HERE.
WELL, WHY WOULDN'T YOU? THIS PLACE IS A PALACE!
THIS IS ONE OF THOSE TIMES THAT I WISH THEY WOULDN'T WARD OFF THE INTERNET. WHAT ARE YOU SUPPOSED TO DO AT A PARTY IF YOU CAN'T TAKE OUT YOUR PHONE?
LEAVE.
MAYBE WE SHOULD CIRCULATE?
...AND I SAID, OH MY GOD, I JUST THOUGHT YOU HADN'T SHAVED YOUR LEGS IN A WHILE.

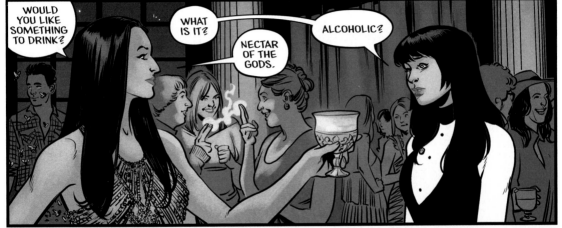

WOULD YOU LIKE SOMETHING TO DRINK?

WHAT IS IT?

NECTAR OF THE GODS.

ALCOHOLIC?

BETTER. ALCOHOL GIVES YOU FALSE CONFIDENCE.

THIS GIVES YOU THE REAL DEAL.

IT'S NOT A DRUG, IS IT?

ABSOLUTELY NOT. *RAKMELION* IS BREWED FROM AN ANCIENT RECIPE... ENHANCED BY A LITTLE MAGICK.

ALL IT DOES IS UNLOCK YOUR POTENTIAL.

HMM.... TASTES LIKE CEREAL WITH HONEY. AND SPICE.

IS IT SUPPOSED TO DO SOMETHING? I DON'T THINK IT WORKED.

JUST GIVE IT A MOMENT.

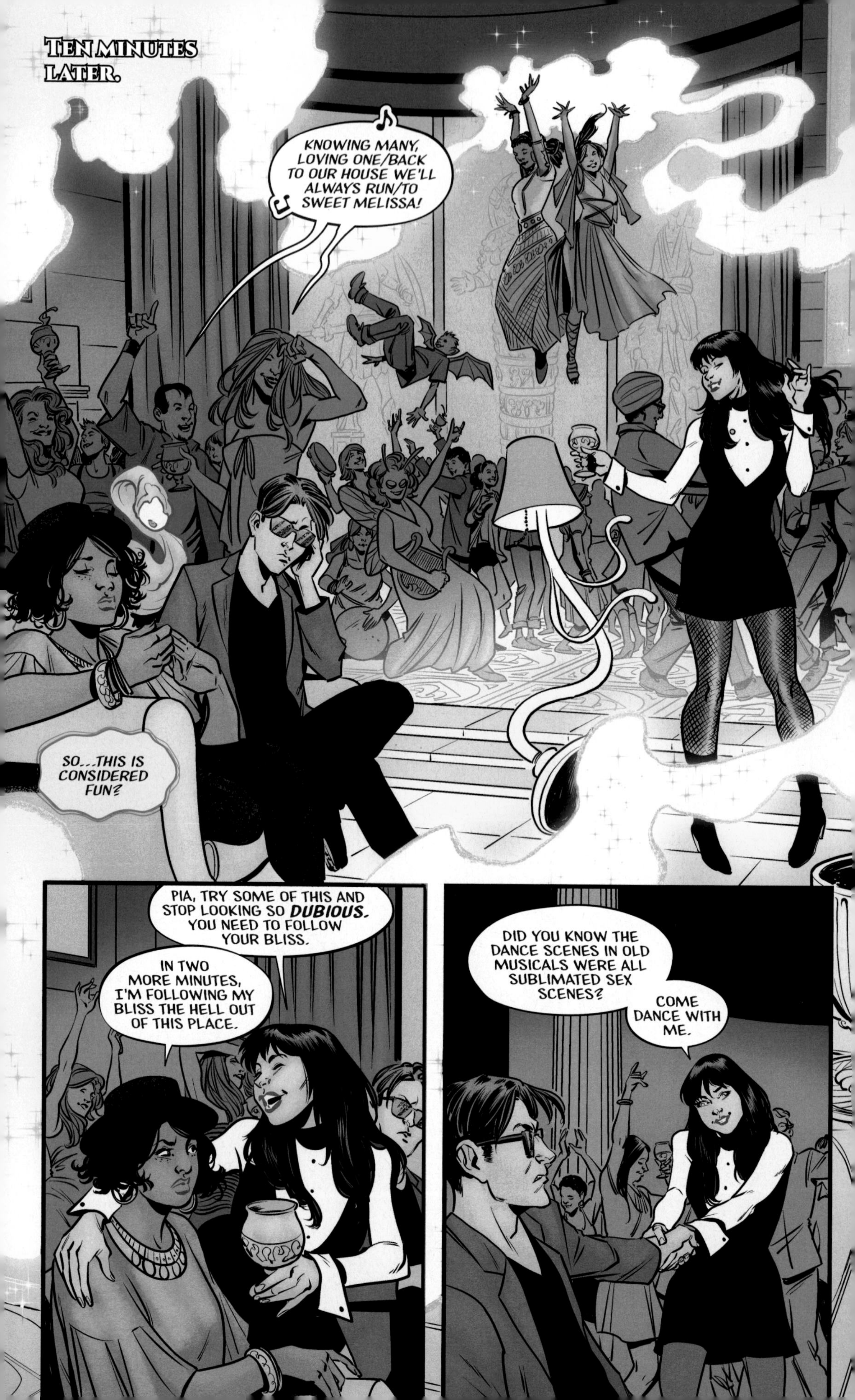

TEN MINUTES LATER.
KNOWING MANY, LOVING ONE/BACK TO OUR HOUSE WE'LL ALWAYS RUN/TO SWEET MELISSA!
SO...THIS IS CONSIDERED FUN?
PIA, TRY SOME OF THIS AND STOP LOOKING SO DUBIOUS. YOU NEED TO FOLLOW YOUR BLISS.
IN TWO MORE MINUTES, I'M FOLLOWING MY BLISS THE HELL OUT OF THIS PLACE.
DID YOU KNOW THE DANCE SCENES IN OLD MUSICALS WERE ALL SUBLIMATED SEX SCENES?
COME DANCE WITH ME.

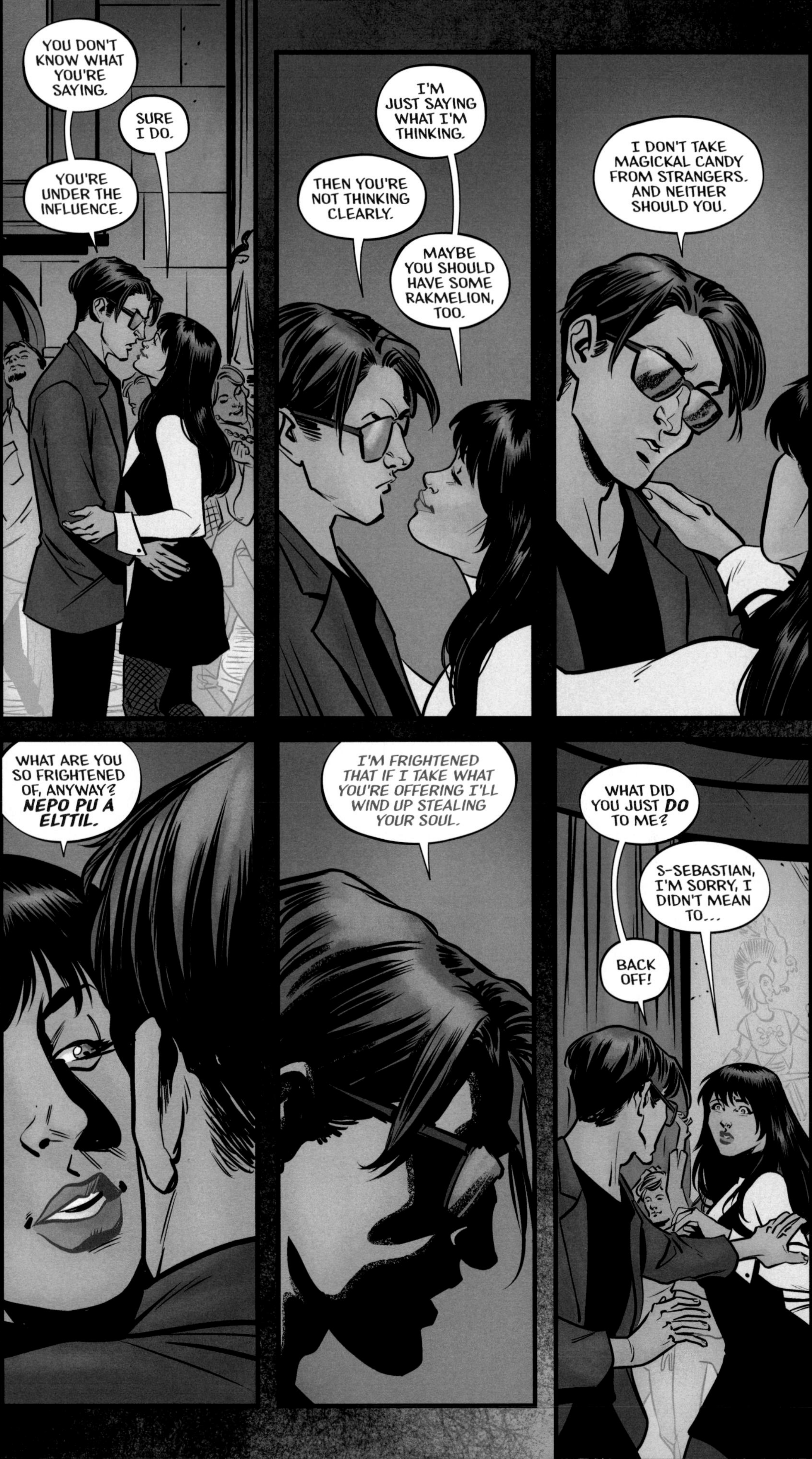
YOU DON'T KNOW WHAT YOU'RE SAYING.
SURE I DO.
YOU'RE UNDER THE INFLUENCE.
I'M JUST SAYING WHAT I'M THINKING.
THEN YOU'RE NOT THINKING CLEARLY.
MAYBE YOU SHOULD HAVE SOME RAKMELION, TOO.
I DON'T TAKE MAGICKAL CANDY FROM STRANGERS. AND NEITHER SHOULD YOU.
WHAT ARE YOU SO FRIGHTENED OF, ANYWAY? NEPO PU A ELTTIL.
I'M FRIGHTENED THAT IF I TAKE WHAT YOU'RE OFFERING I'LL WIND UP STEALING YOUR SOUL.
WHAT DID YOU JUST DO TO ME?
S-SEBASTIAN, I'M SORRY, I DIDN'T MEAN TO...
BACK OFF!

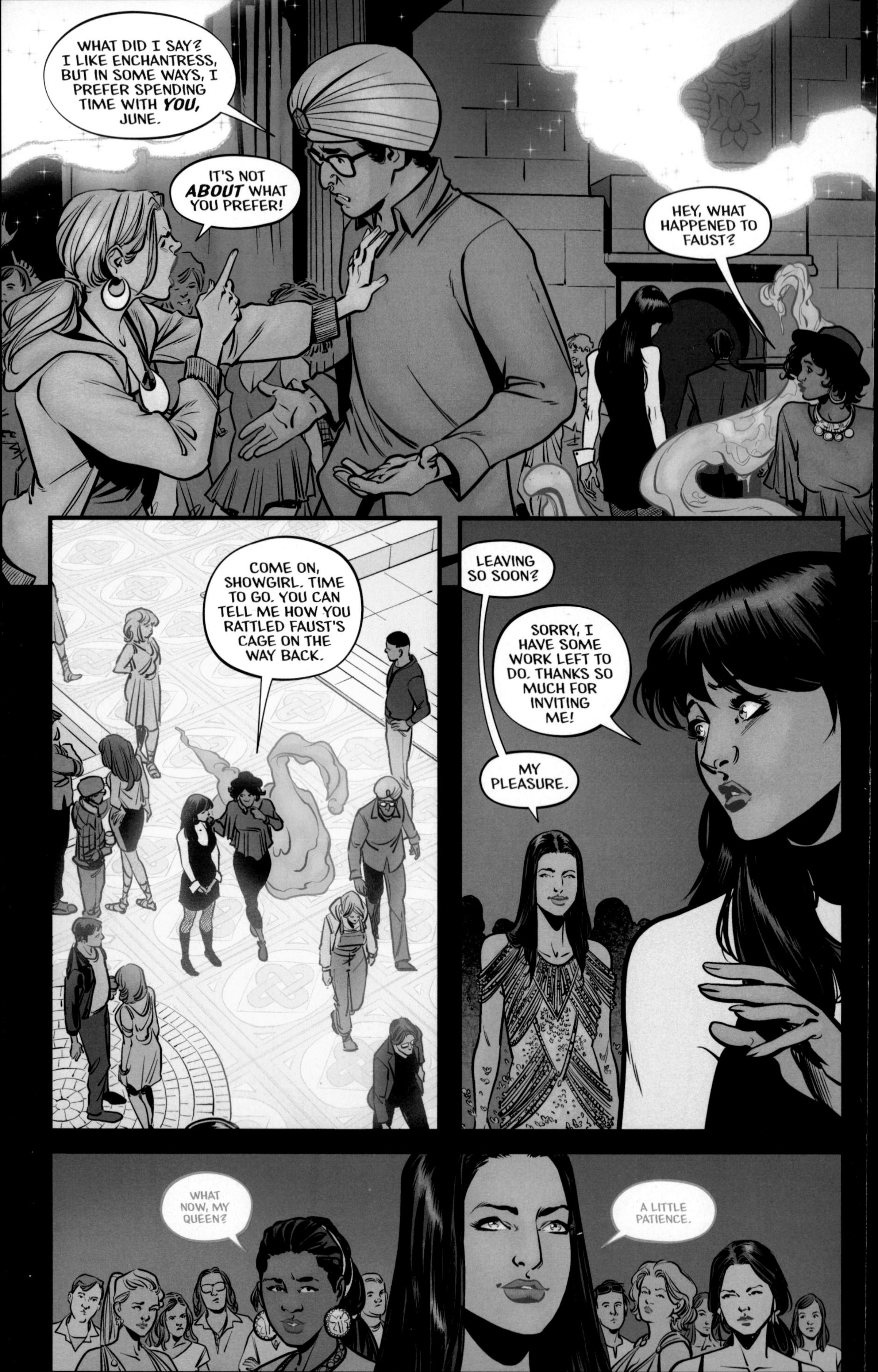
WHAT DID I SAY? I LIKE ENCHANTRESS, BUT IN SOME WAYS, I PREFER SPENDING TIME WITH YOU, JUNE.
IT'S NOT ABOUT WHAT YOU PREFER!
HEY, WHAT HAPPENED TO FAUST?
COME ON, SHOWGIRL. TIME TO GO. YOU CAN TELL ME HOW YOU RATTLED FAUST'S CAGE ON THE WAY BACK.
LEAVING SO SOON?
SORRY, I HAVE SOME WORK LEFT TO DO. THANKS SO MUCH FOR INVITING ME!
MY PLEASURE.
WHAT NOW, MY QUEEN?
A LITTLE PATIENCE.

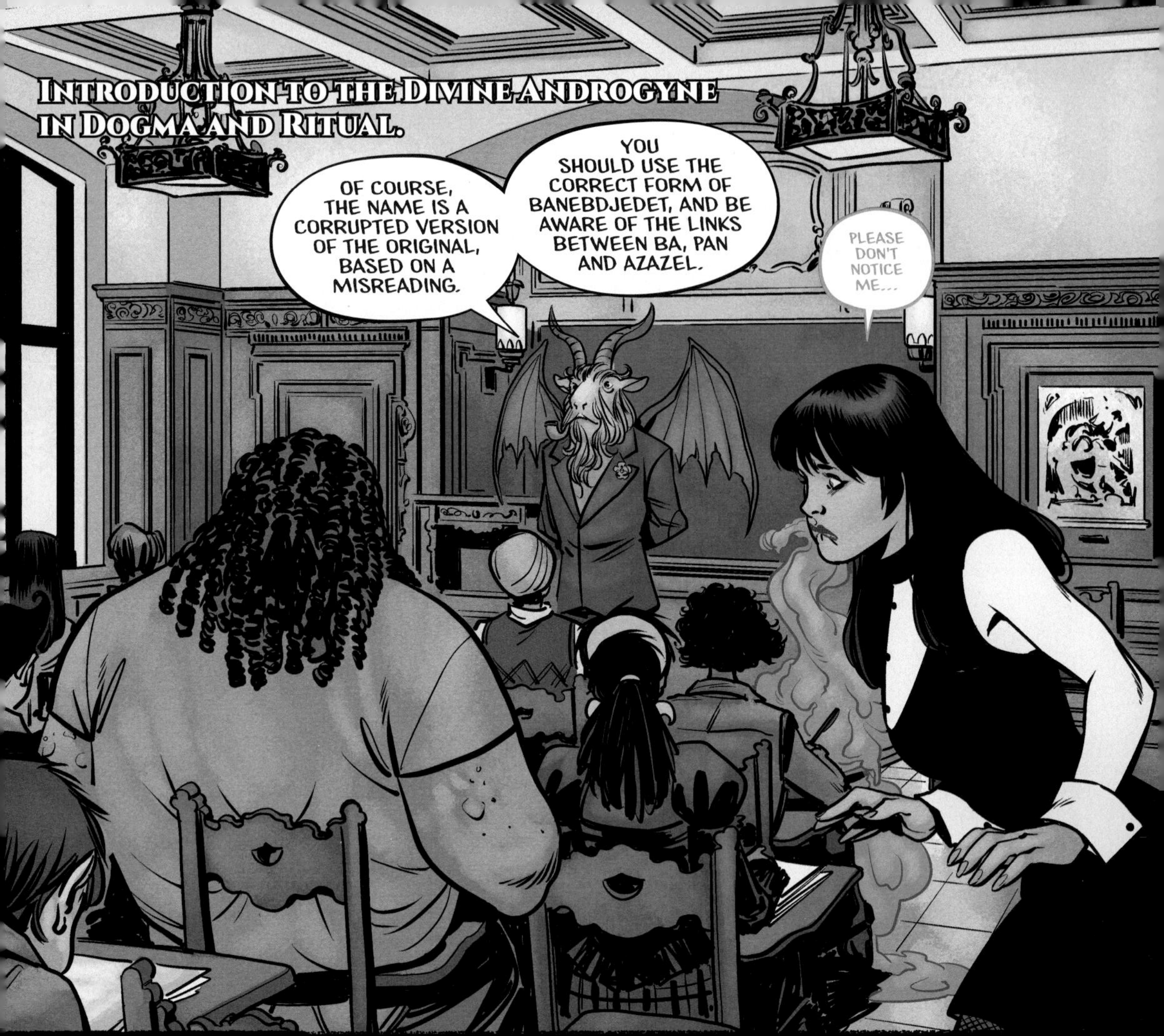
INTRODUCTION TO THE DIVINE ANDROGYNE IN DOGMA AND RITUAL.
OF COURSE, THE NAME IS A CORRUPTED VERSION OF THE ORIGINAL, BASED ON A MISREADING.
YOU SHOULD USE THE CORRECT FORM OF BANEBDJEDET, AND BE AWARE OF THE LINKS BETWEEN BA, PAN AND AZAZEL.
PLEASE DON'T NOTICE ME...

Chapter Two: Blood and Honey

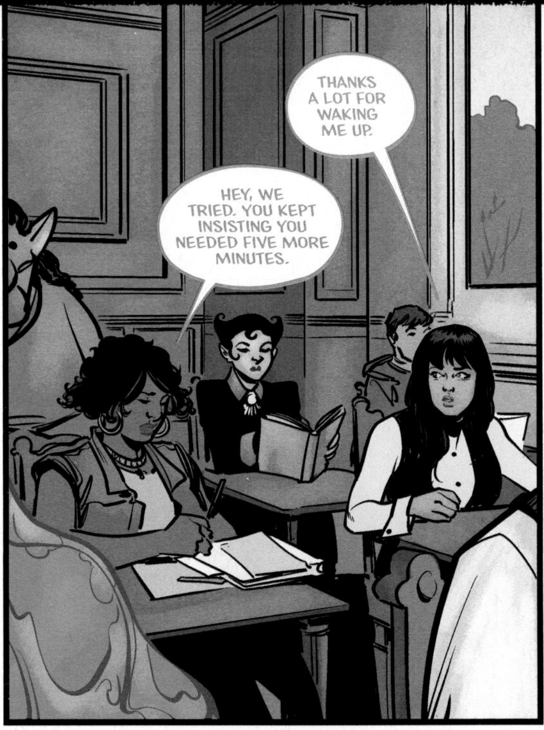
THANKS A LOT FOR WAKING ME UP.
HEY, WE TRIED. YOU KEPT INSISTING YOU NEEDED FIVE MORE MINUTES.

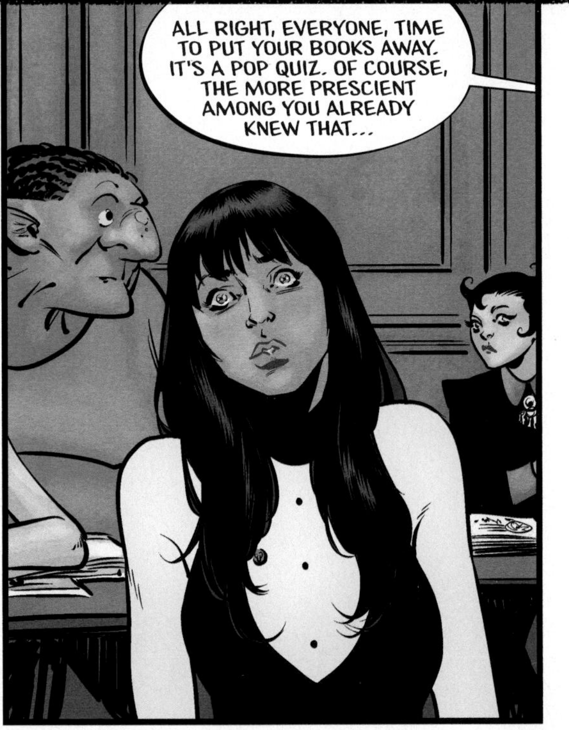
ALL RIGHT, EVERYONE, TIME TO PUT YOUR BOOKS AWAY. IT'S A POP QUIZ. OF COURSE, THE MORE PRESCIENT AMONG YOU ALREADY KNEW THAT...

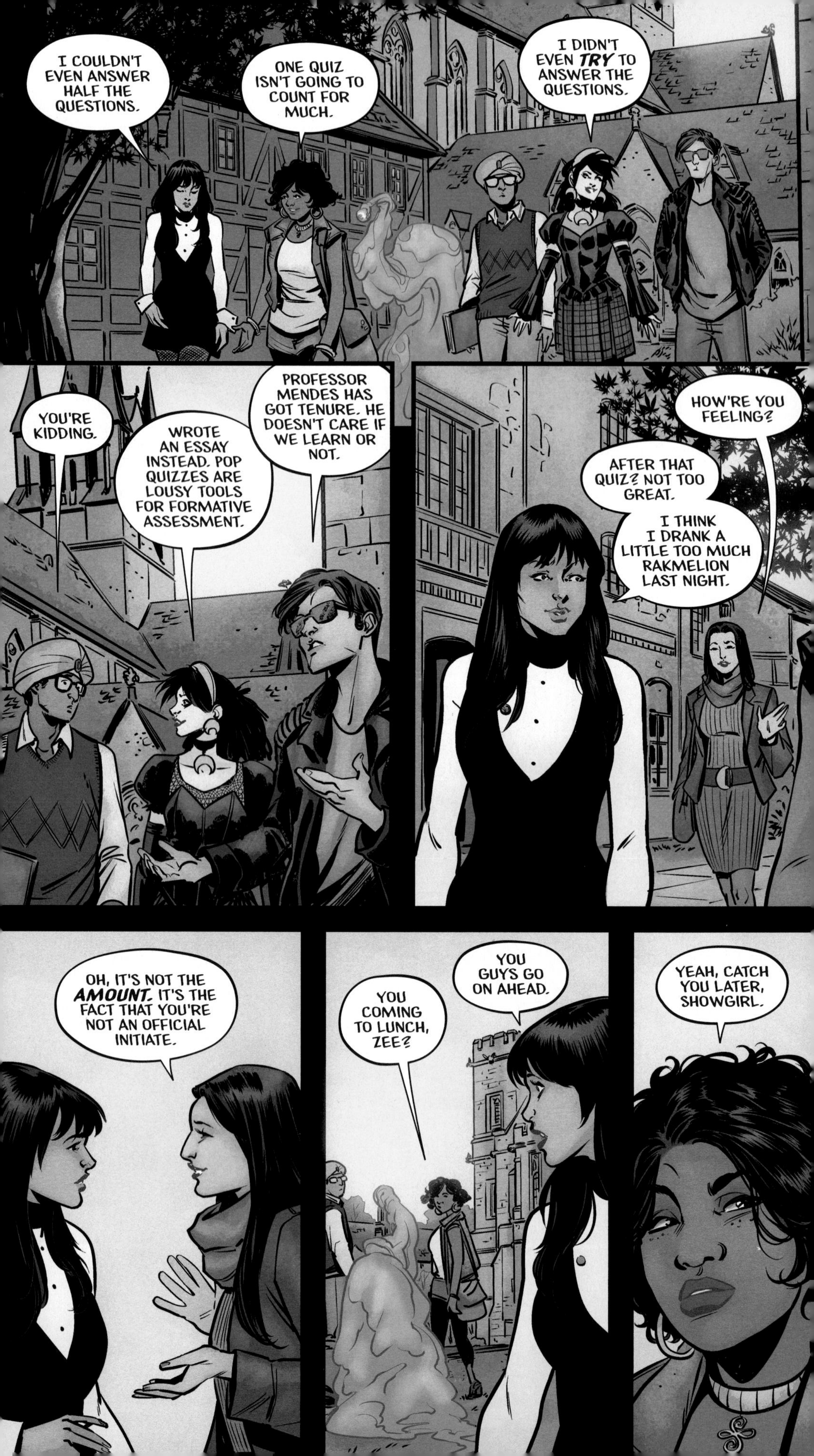
I COULDN'T EVEN ANSWER HALF THE QUESTIONS.
ONE QUIZ ISN'T GOING TO COUNT FOR MUCH.
I DIDN'T EVEN *TRY* TO ANSWER THE QUESTIONS.
YOU'RE KIDDING.
WROTE AN ESSAY INSTEAD. POP QUIZZES ARE LOUSY TOOLS FOR FORMATIVE ASSESSMENT.
PROFESSOR MENDES HAS GOT TENURE. HE DOESN'T CARE IF WE LEARN OR NOT.
HOW'RE YOU FEELING?
AFTER THAT QUIZ? NOT TOO GREAT.
I THINK I DRANK A LITTLE TOO MUCH RAKMELION LAST NIGHT.
OH, IT'S NOT THE *AMOUNT*. IT'S THE FACT THAT YOU'RE NOT AN OFFICIAL INITIATE.
YOU COMING TO LUNCH, ZEE?
YOU GUYS GO ON AHEAD.
YEAH, CATCH YOU LATER, SHOWGIRL.

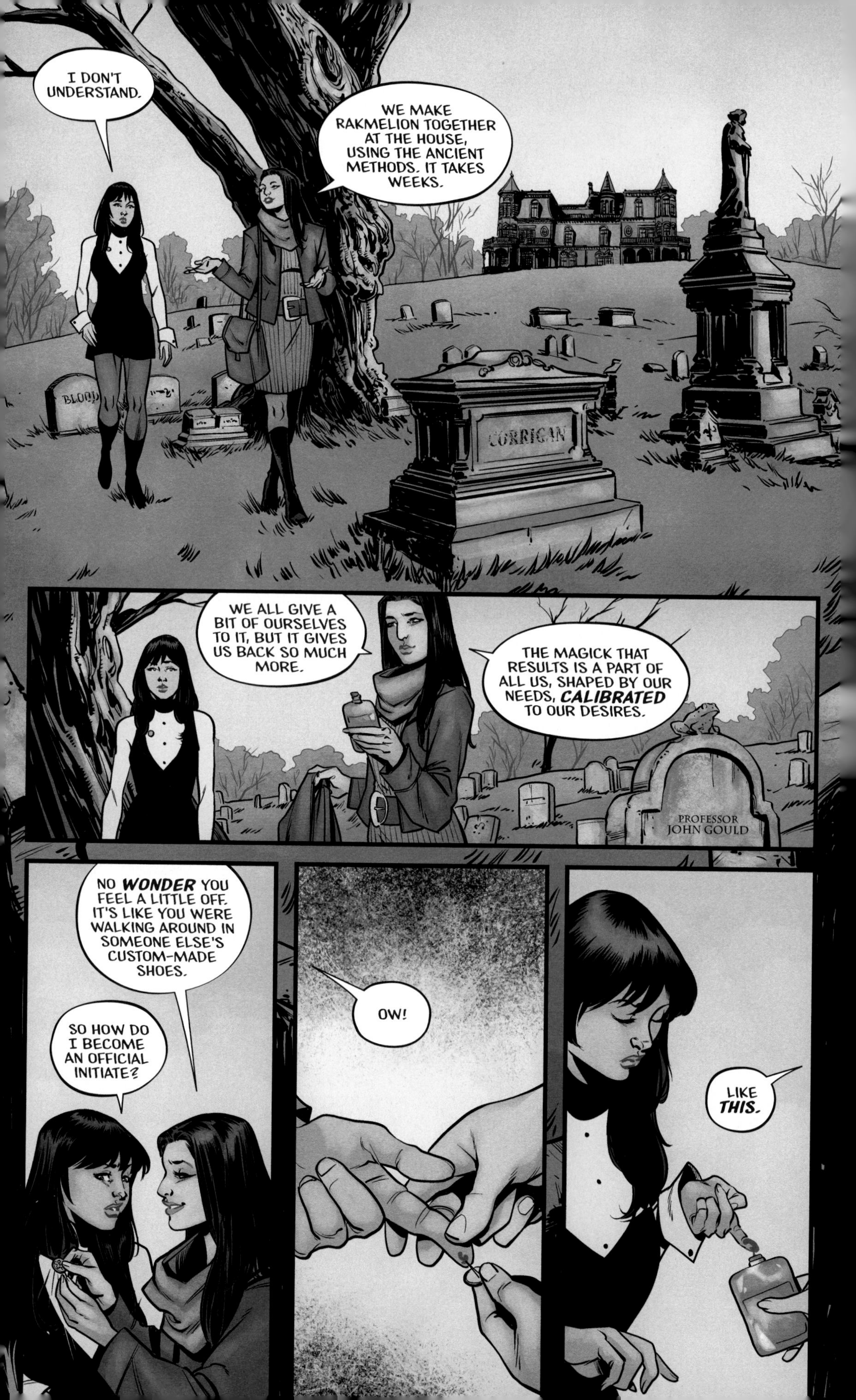
I DON'T UNDERSTAND.
WE MAKE RAKMELION TOGETHER AT THE HOUSE, USING THE ANCIENT METHODS. IT TAKES WEEKS.
BLOOD
CORRIGAN
WE ALL GIVE A BIT OF OURSELVES TO IT, BUT IT GIVES US BACK SO MUCH MORE.
THE MAGICK THAT RESULTS IS A PART OF ALL US, SHAPED BY OUR NEEDS, CALIBRATED TO OUR DESIRES.
PROFESSOR JOHN GOULD
NO WONDER YOU FEEL A LITTLE OFF. IT'S LIKE YOU WERE WALKING AROUND IN SOMEONE ELSE'S CUSTOM-MADE SHOES.
SO HOW DO I BECOME AN OFFICIAL INITIATE?
OW!
LIKE THIS.

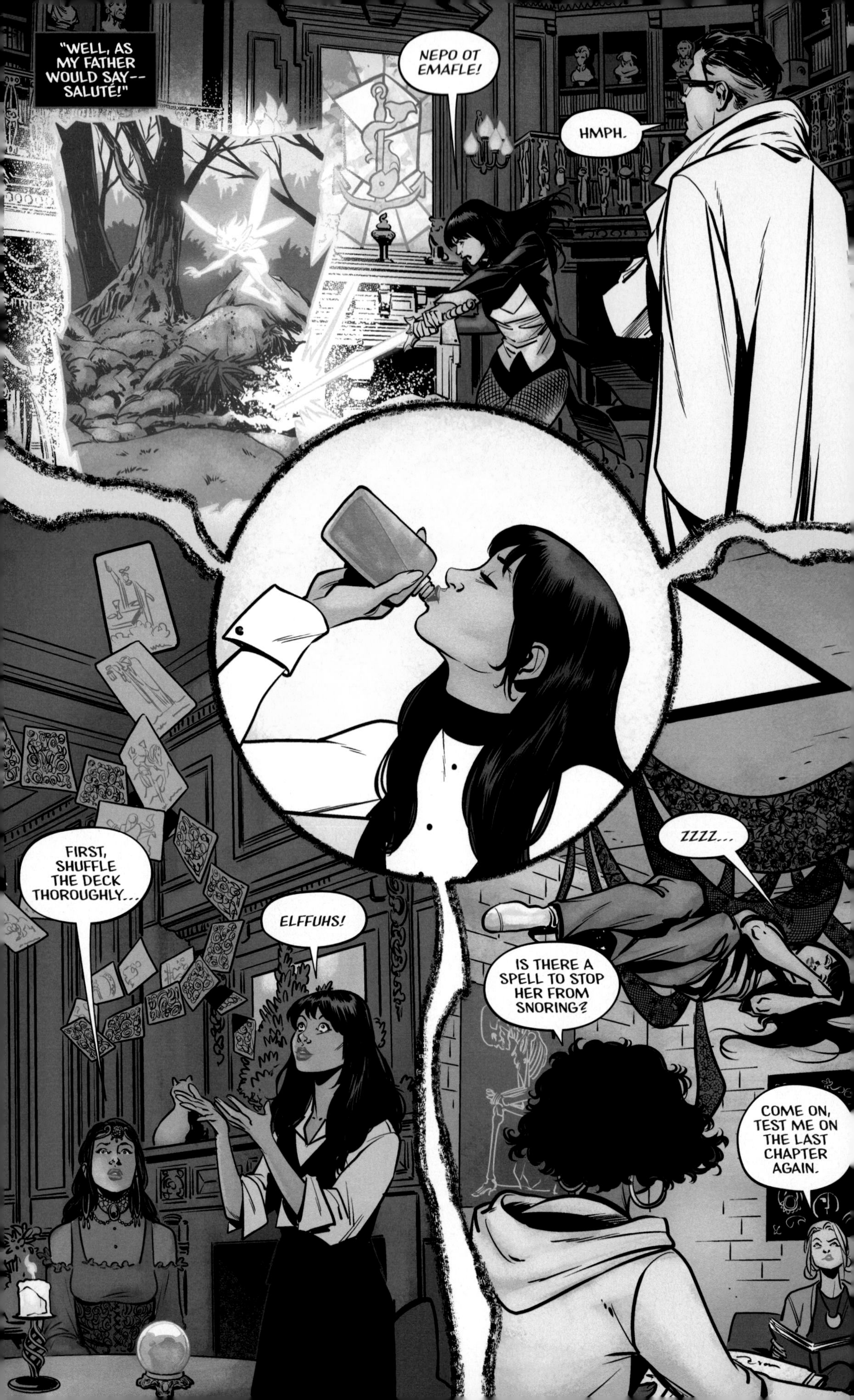
"WELL, AS MY FATHER WOULD SAY-- SALUTÉ!"
NEPO OT EMAFLE!
HMPH.
ZZZZ...
FIRST, SHUFFLE THE DECK THOROUGHLY...
ELFFUHS!
IS THERE A SPELL TO STOP HER FROM SNORING?
COME ON, TEST ME ON THE LAST CHAPTER AGAIN.

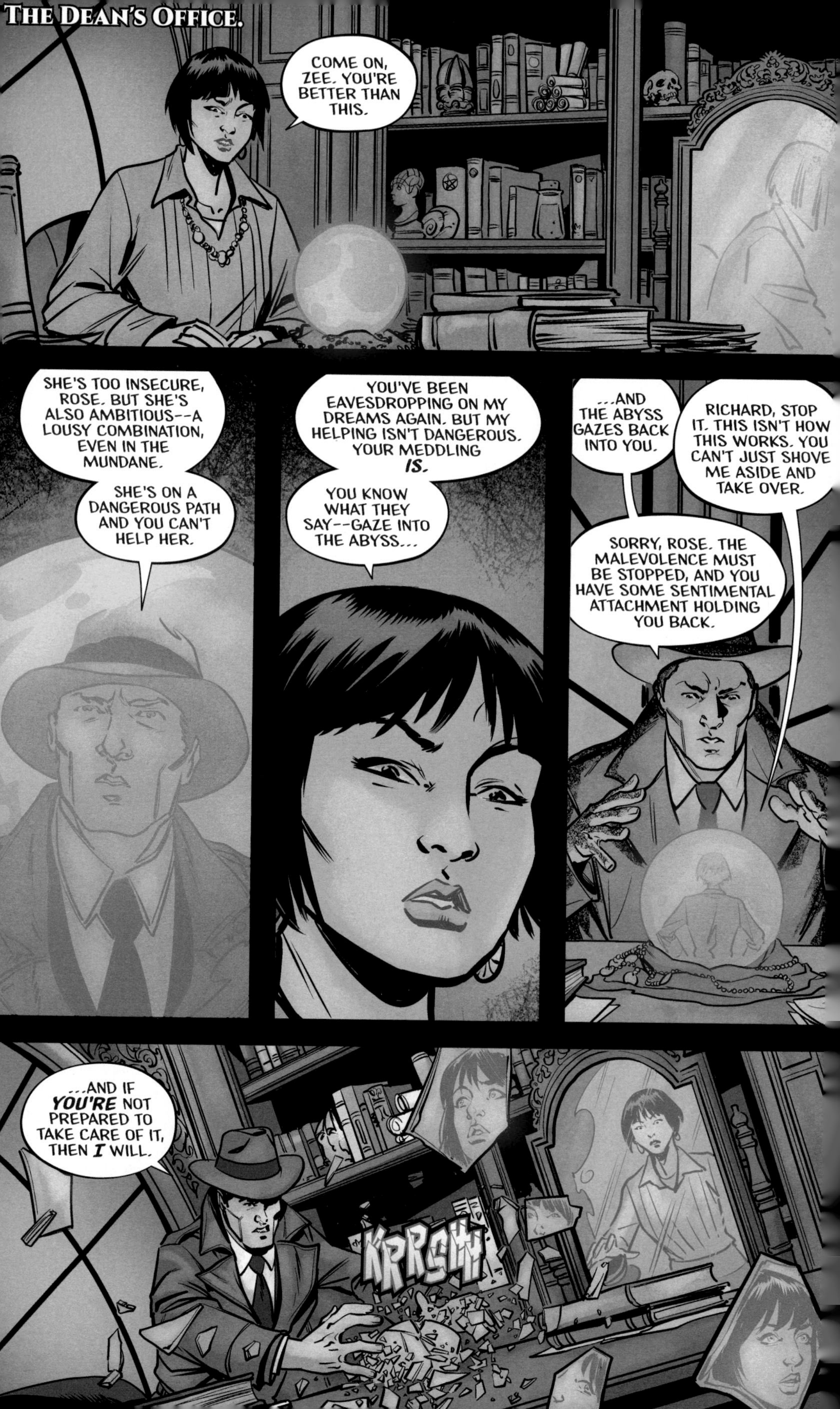
THE DEAN'S OFFICE.
COME ON, ZEE. YOU'RE BETTER THAN THIS.
SHE'S TOO INSECURE, ROSE. BUT SHE'S ALSO AMBITIOUS--A LOUSY COMBINATION, EVEN IN THE MUNDANE.
SHE'S ON A DANGEROUS PATH AND YOU CAN'T HELP HER.
YOU'VE BEEN EAVESDROPPING ON MY DREAMS AGAIN. BUT MY HELPING ISN'T DANGEROUS. YOUR MEDDLING *IS*.
YOU KNOW WHAT THEY SAY--GAZE INTO THE ABYSS...
...AND THE ABYSS GAZES BACK INTO YOU.
RICHARD, STOP IT. THIS ISN'T HOW THIS WORKS. YOU CAN'T JUST SHOVE ME ASIDE AND TAKE OVER.
SORRY, ROSE. THE MALEVOLENCE MUST BE STOPPED, AND YOU HAVE SOME SENTIMENTAL ATTACHMENT HOLDING YOU BACK.
...AND IF *YOU'RE* NOT PREPARED TO TAKE CARE OF IT, THEN *I* WILL.
KRRSHH

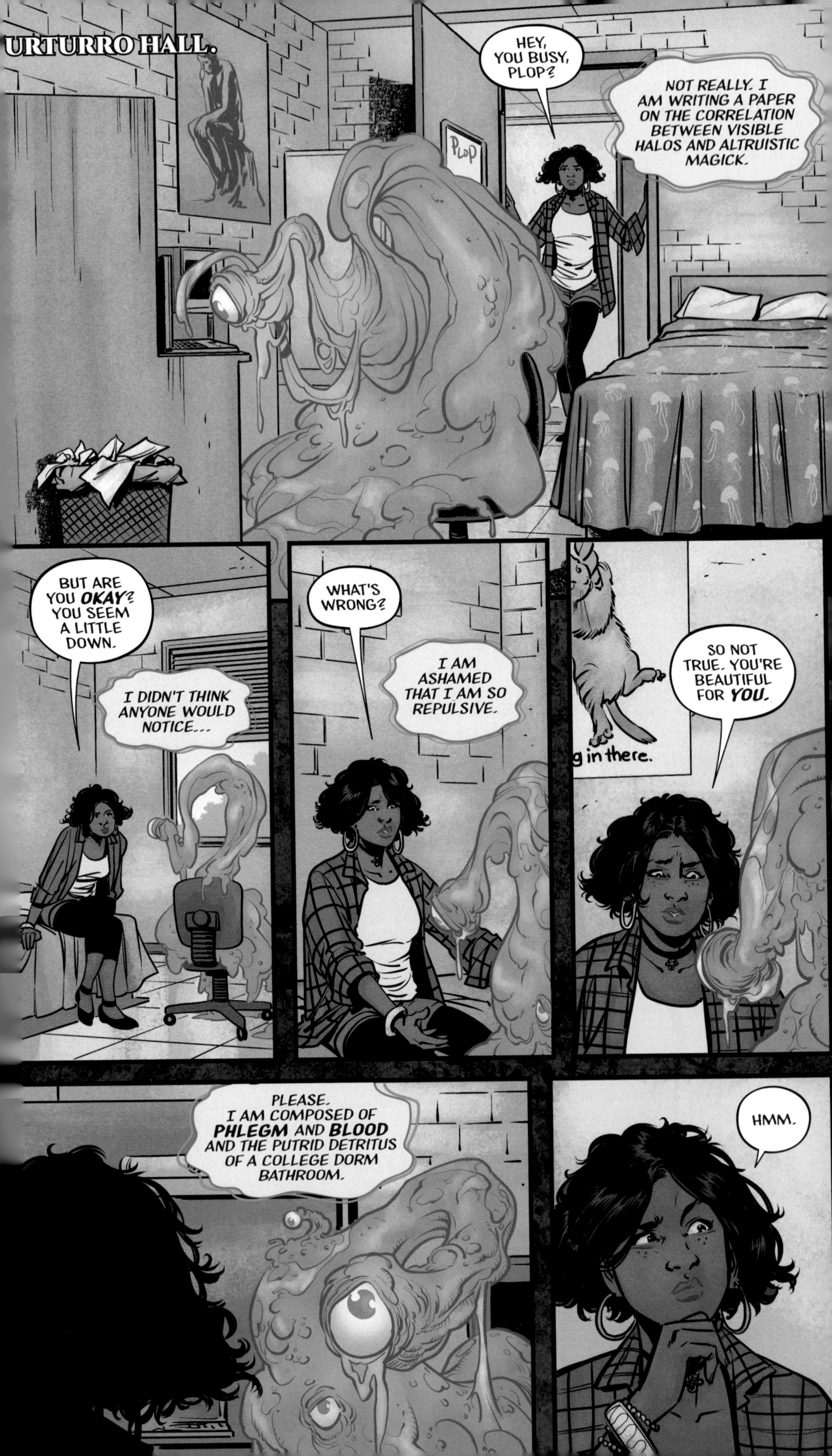
URTURRO HALL.
HEY, YOU BUSY, PLOP?
NOT REALLY. I AM WRITING A PAPER ON THE CORRELATION BETWEEN VISIBLE HALOS AND ALTRUISTIC MAGICK.
PLOP
BUT ARE YOU OKAY? YOU SEEM A LITTLE DOWN.
I DIDN'T THINK ANYONE WOULD NOTICE...
WHAT'S WRONG?
I AM ASHAMED THAT I AM SO REPULSIVE.
g in there.
SO NOT TRUE. YOU'RE BEAUTIFUL FOR YOU.
PLEASE. I AM COMPOSED OF PHLEGM AND BLOOD AND THE PUTRID DETRITUS OF A COLLEGE DORM BATHROOM.
HMM.

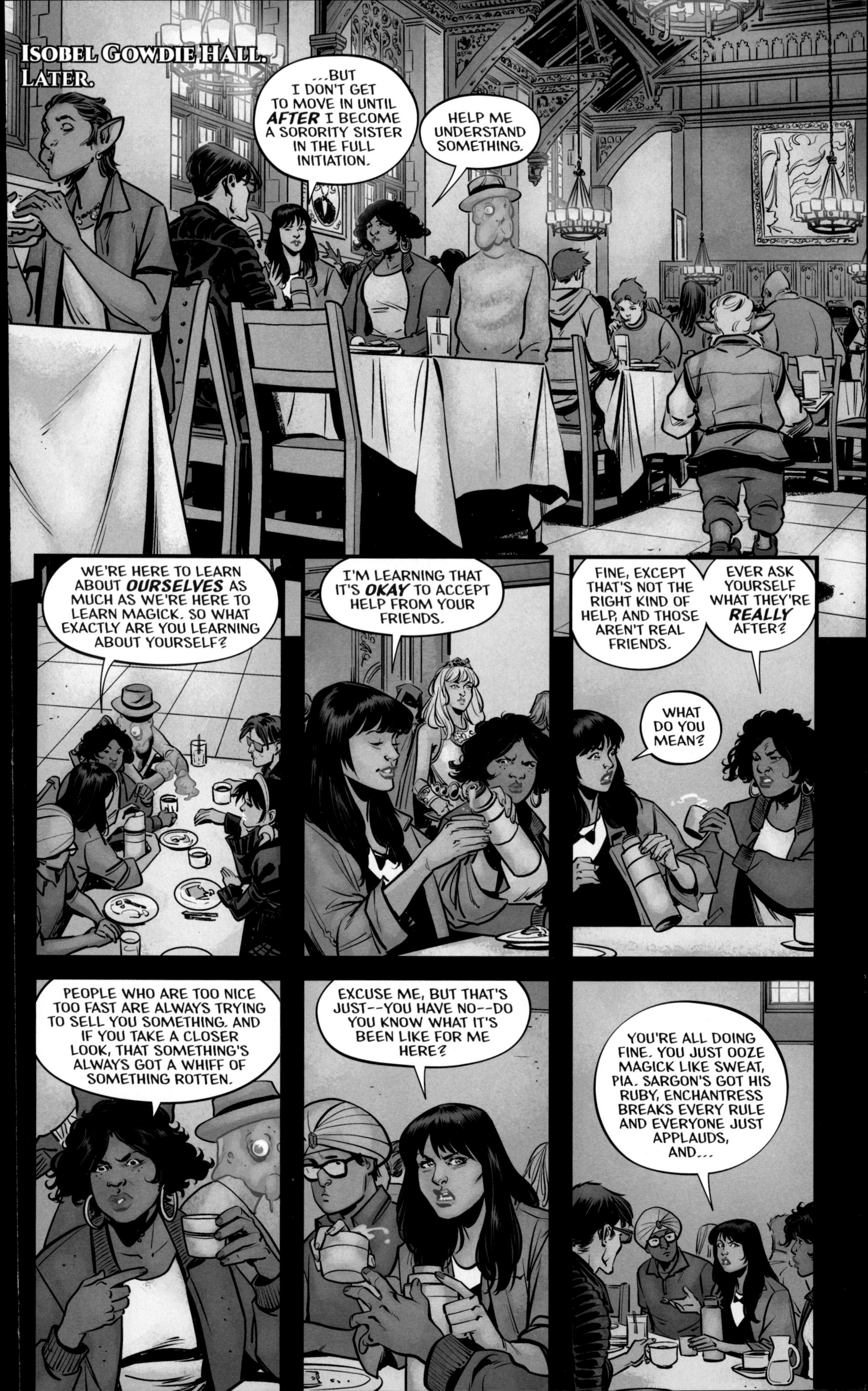
ISOBEL GOWDIE HALL. LATER.
...BUT I DON'T GET TO MOVE IN UNTIL AFTER I BECOME A SORORITY SISTER IN THE FULL INITIATION.
HELP ME UNDERSTAND SOMETHING.
WE'RE HERE TO LEARN ABOUT OURSELVES AS MUCH AS WE'RE HERE TO LEARN MAGICK. SO WHAT EXACTLY ARE YOU LEARNING ABOUT YOURSELF?
I'M LEARNING THAT IT'S OKAY TO ACCEPT HELP FROM YOUR FRIENDS.
FINE, EXCEPT THAT'S NOT THE RIGHT KIND OF HELP, AND THOSE AREN'T REAL FRIENDS.
EVER ASK YOURSELF WHAT THEY'RE REALLY AFTER?
WHAT DO YOU MEAN?
PEOPLE WHO ARE TOO NICE TOO FAST ARE ALWAYS TRYING TO SELL YOU SOMETHING. AND IF YOU TAKE A CLOSER LOOK, THAT SOMETHING'S ALWAYS GOT A WHIFF OF SOMETHING ROTTEN.
EXCUSE ME, BUT THAT'S JUST--YOU HAVE NO--DO YOU KNOW WHAT IT'S BEEN LIKE FOR ME HERE?
YOU'RE ALL DOING FINE. YOU JUST OOZE MAGICK LIKE SWEAT, PIA. SARGON'S GOT HIS RUBY, ENCHANTRESS BREAKS EVERY RULE AND EVERYONE JUST APPLAUDS, AND...

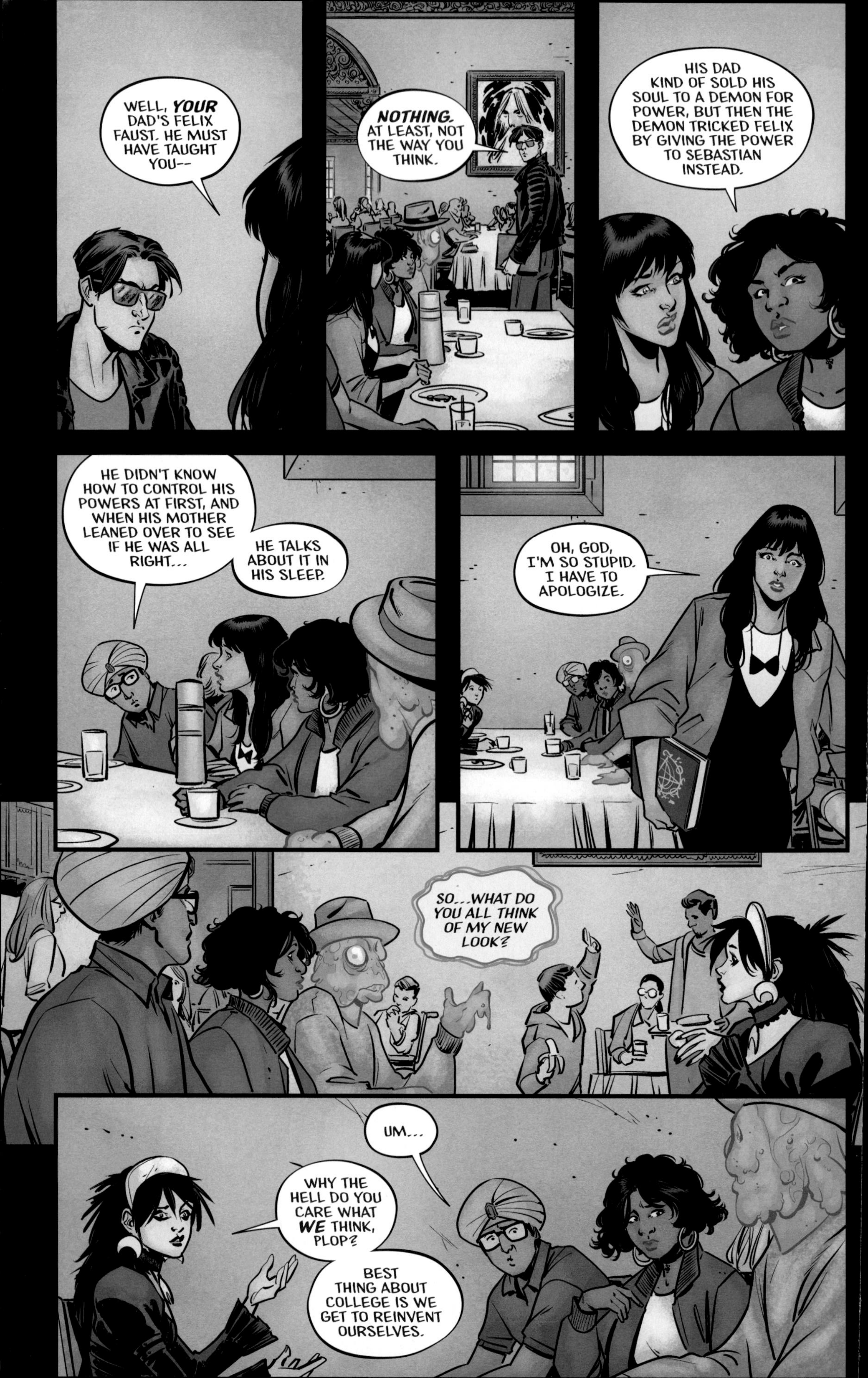
WELL, YOUR DAD'S FELIX FAUST. HE MUST HAVE TAUGHT YOU--
NOTHING. AT LEAST, NOT THE WAY YOU THINK.
HIS DAD KIND OF SOLD HIS SOUL TO A DEMON FOR POWER, BUT THEN THE DEMON TRICKED FELIX BY GIVING THE POWER TO SEBASTIAN INSTEAD.
HE DIDN'T KNOW HOW TO CONTROL HIS POWERS AT FIRST, AND WHEN HIS MOTHER LEANED OVER TO SEE IF HE WAS ALL RIGHT...
HE TALKS ABOUT IT IN HIS SLEEP.
OH, GOD, I'M SO STUPID. I HAVE TO APOLOGIZE.
SO...WHAT DO YOU ALL THINK OF MY NEW LOOK?
UM...
WHY THE HELL DO YOU CARE WHAT WE THINK, PLOP?
BEST THING ABOUT COLLEGE IS WE GET TO REINVENT OURSELVES.

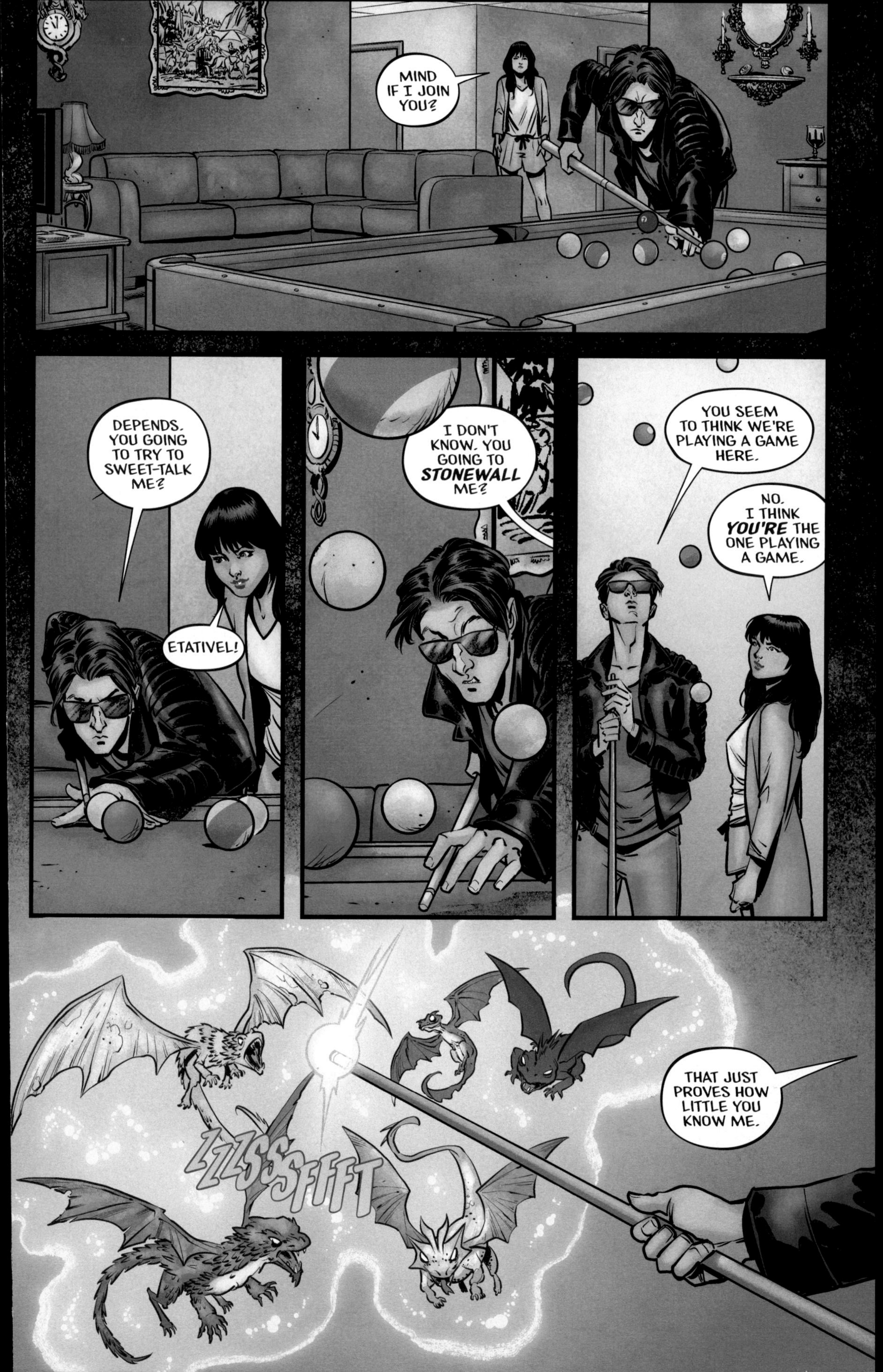
MIND IF I JOIN YOU?
DEPENDS. YOU GOING TO TRY TO SWEET-TALK ME?
ETATIVEL!
I DON'T KNOW. YOU GOING TO STONEWALL ME?
YOU SEEM TO THINK WE'RE PLAYING A GAME HERE.
NO. I THINK YOU'RE THE ONE PLAYING A GAME.
ZZZSSSFFFT
THAT JUST PROVES HOW LITTLE YOU KNOW ME.

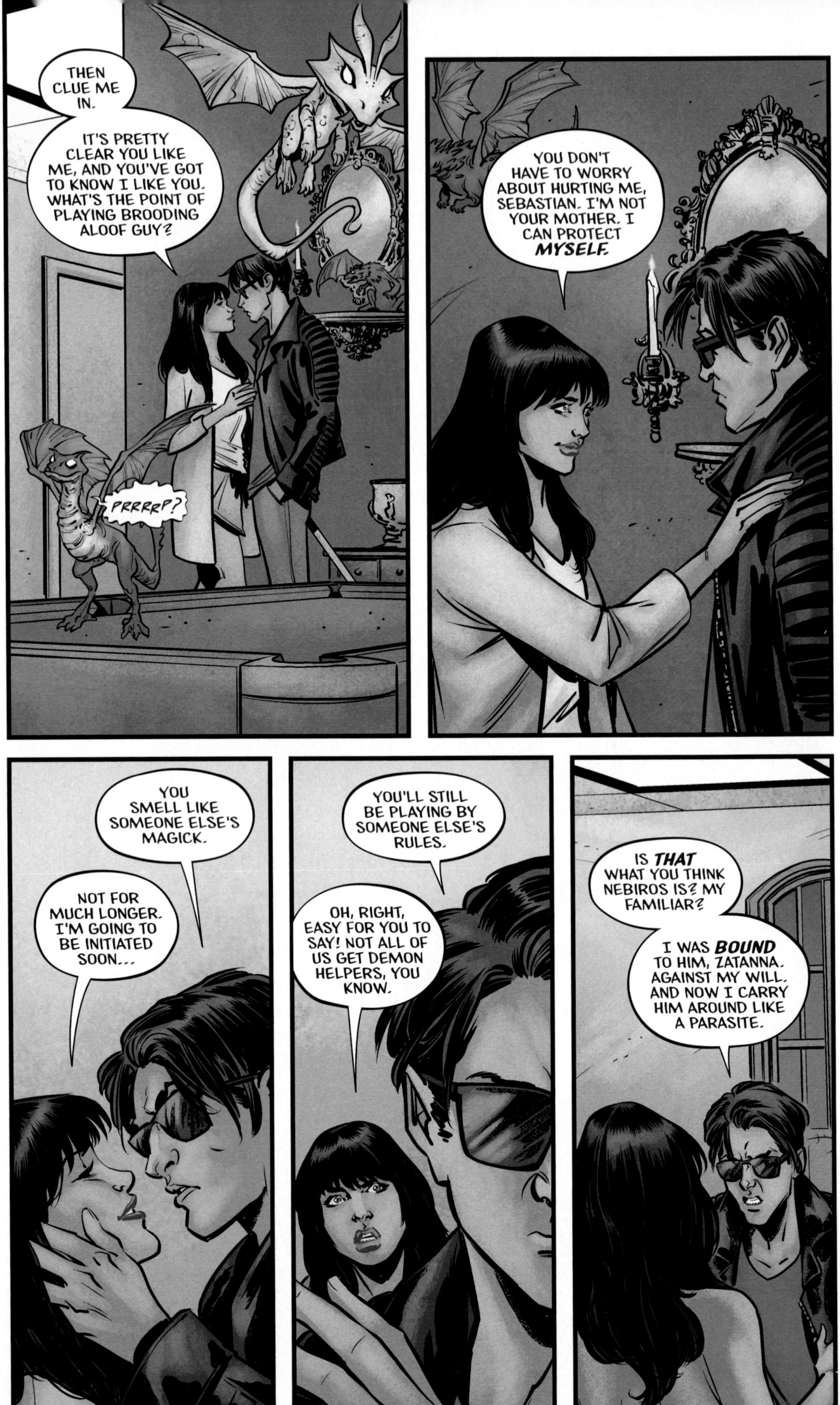
THEN CLUE ME IN.
IT'S PRETTY CLEAR YOU LIKE ME, AND YOU'VE GOT TO KNOW I LIKE YOU. WHAT'S THE POINT OF PLAYING BROODING ALOOF GUY?
PRRRRP?
YOU DON'T HAVE TO WORRY ABOUT HURTING ME, SEBASTIAN. I'M NOT YOUR MOTHER. I CAN PROTECT MYSELF.
YOU SMELL LIKE SOMEONE ELSE'S MAGICK.
NOT FOR MUCH LONGER. I'M GOING TO BE INITIATED SOON...
YOU'LL STILL BE PLAYING BY SOMEONE ELSE'S RULES.
OH, RIGHT, EASY FOR YOU TO SAY! NOT ALL OF US GET DEMON HELPERS, YOU KNOW.
IS THAT WHAT YOU THINK NEBIROS IS? MY FAMILIAR?
I WAS BOUND TO HIM, ZATANNA. AGAINST MY WILL. AND NOW I CARRY HIM AROUND LIKE A PARASITE.

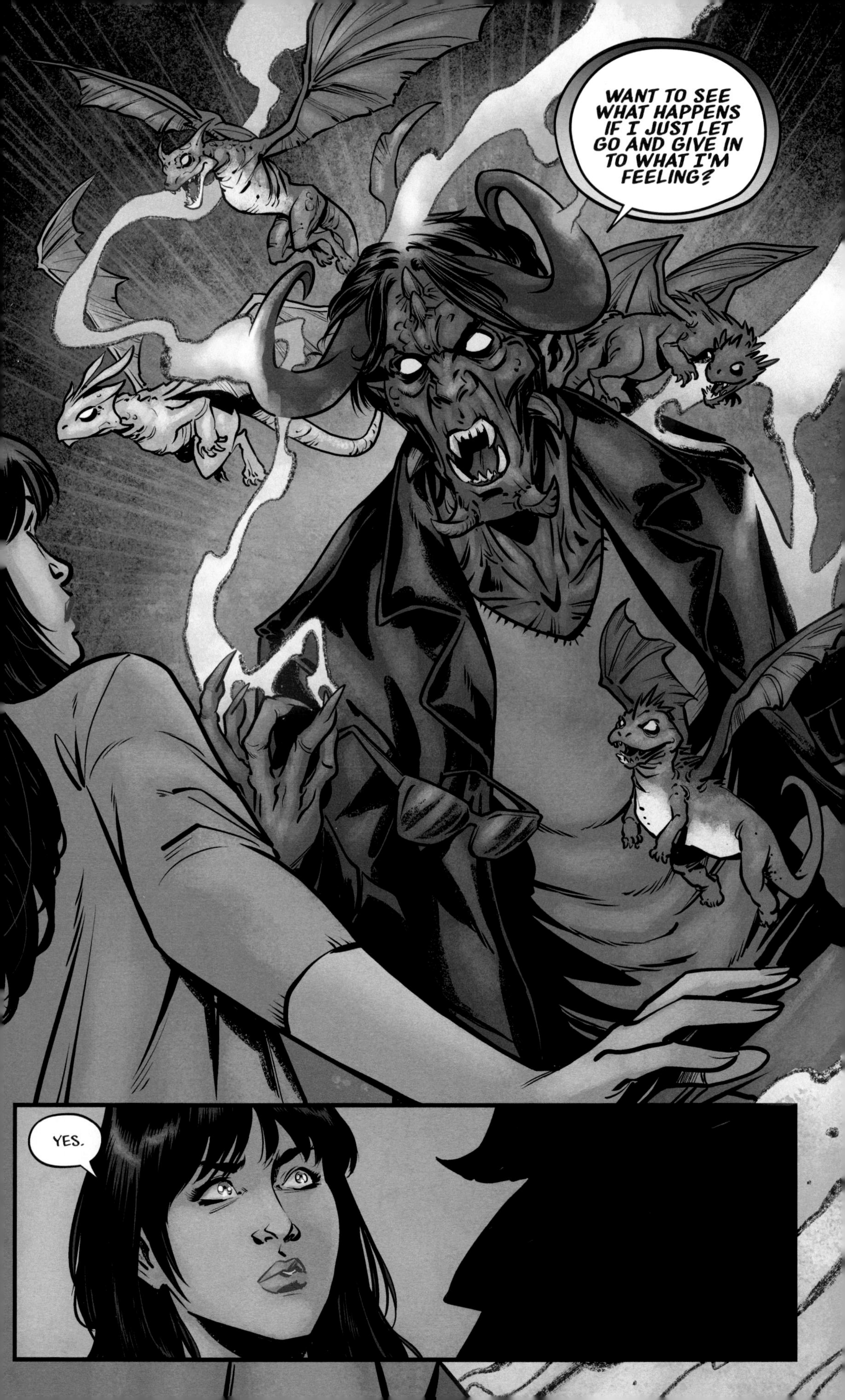
WANT TO SEE WHAT HAPPENS IF I JUST LET GO AND GIVE IN TO WHAT I'M FEELING?
YES.

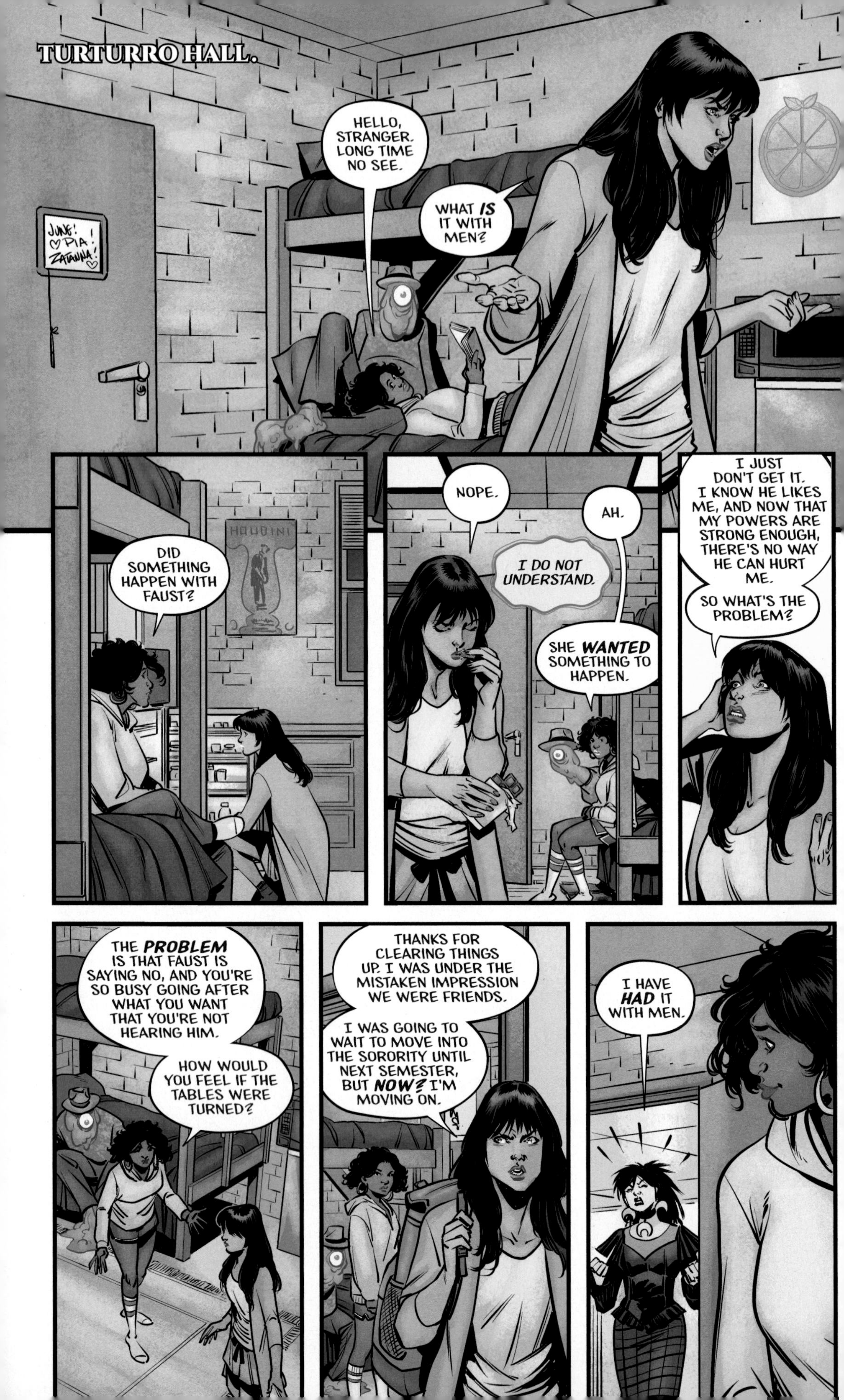
TURTURRO HALL.
JUNE! ♡ PIA! ZATANNA! ♡
HELLO, STRANGER. LONG TIME NO SEE.
WHAT IS IT WITH MEN?
DID SOMETHING HAPPEN WITH FAUST?
HOUDINI
NOPE.
I DO NOT UNDERSTAND.
AH.
SHE WANTED SOMETHING TO HAPPEN.
I JUST DON'T GET IT. I KNOW HE LIKES ME, AND NOW THAT MY POWERS ARE STRONG ENOUGH, THERE'S NO WAY HE CAN HURT ME.
SO WHAT'S THE PROBLEM?
THE PROBLEM IS THAT FAUST IS SAYING NO, AND YOU'RE SO BUSY GOING AFTER WHAT YOU WANT THAT YOU'RE NOT HEARING HIM.
HOW WOULD YOU FEEL IF THE TABLES WERE TURNED?
THANKS FOR CLEARING THINGS UP. I WAS UNDER THE MISTAKEN IMPRESSION WE WERE FRIENDS.
I WAS GOING TO WAIT TO MOVE INTO THE SORORITY UNTIL NEXT SEMESTER, BUT NOW? I'M MOVING ON.
I HAVE HAD IT WITH MEN.

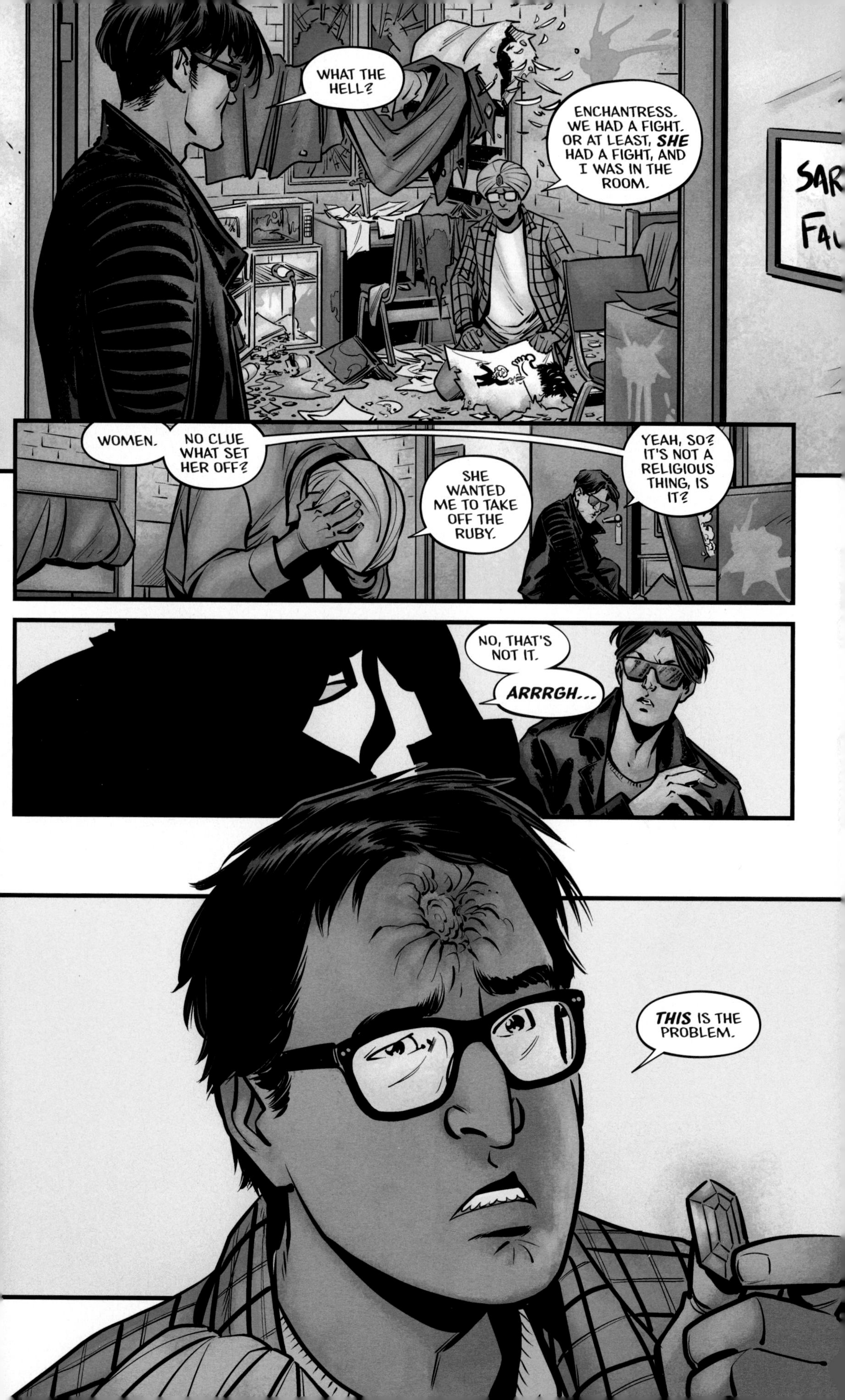
WHAT THE HELL?
ENCHANTRESS. WE HAD A FIGHT. OR AT LEAST, *SHE* HAD A FIGHT, AND I WAS IN THE ROOM.
WOMEN.
NO CLUE WHAT SET HER OFF?
SHE WANTED ME TO TAKE OFF THE RUBY.
YEAH, SO? IT'S NOT A RELIGIOUS THING, IS IT?
NO, THAT'S NOT IT.
ARRRGH...
THIS IS THE PROBLEM.

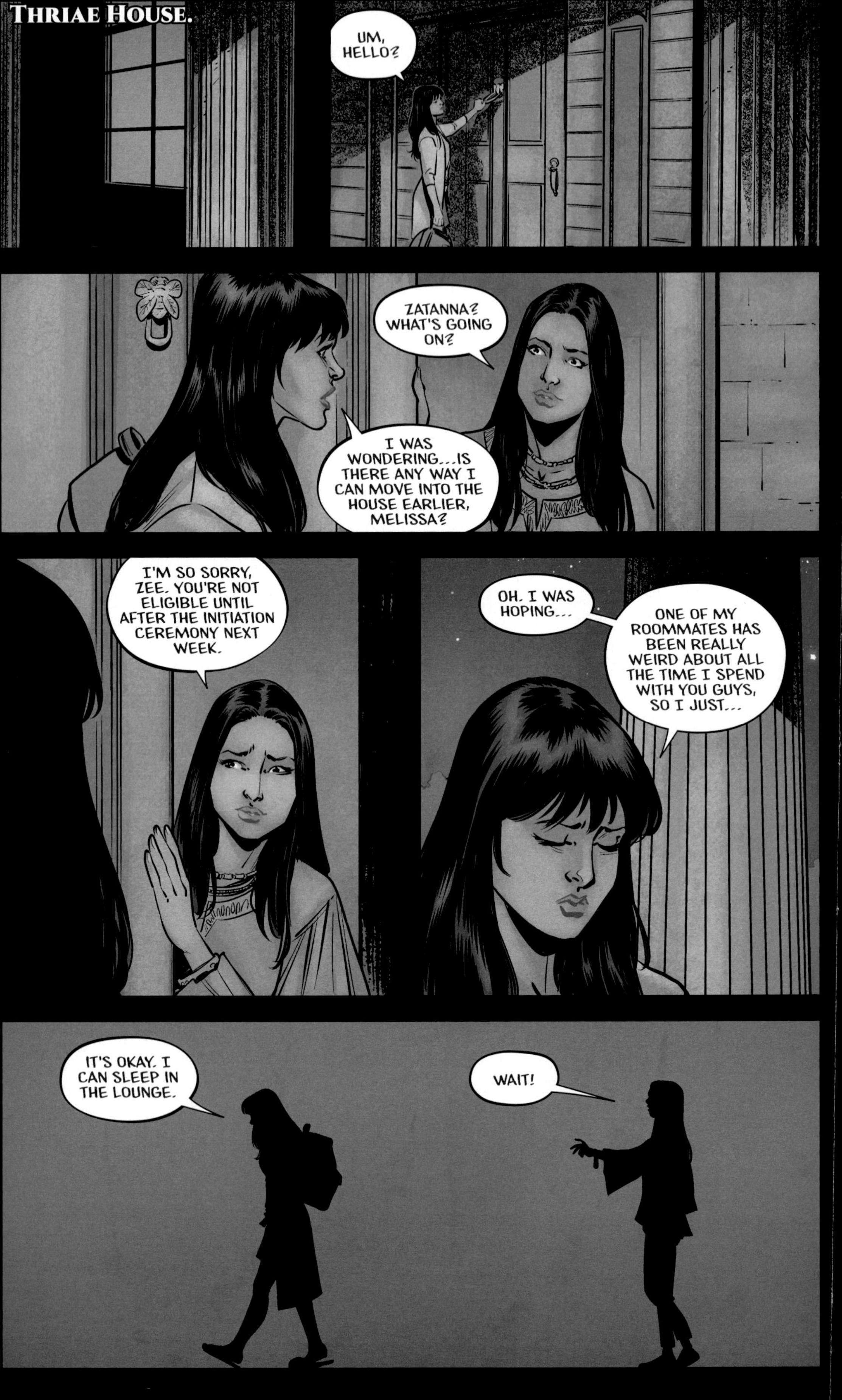
THRIAE HOUSE.
UM, HELLO?
ZATANNA? WHAT'S GOING ON?
I WAS WONDERING...IS THERE ANY WAY I CAN MOVE INTO THE HOUSE EARLIER, MELISSA?
I'M SO SORRY, ZEE. YOU'RE NOT ELIGIBLE UNTIL AFTER THE INITIATION CEREMONY NEXT WEEK.
OH. I WAS HOPING...
ONE OF MY ROOMMATES HAS BEEN REALLY WEIRD ABOUT ALL THE TIME I SPEND WITH YOU GUYS, SO I JUST...
IT'S OKAY. I CAN SLEEP IN THE LOUNGE.
WAIT!

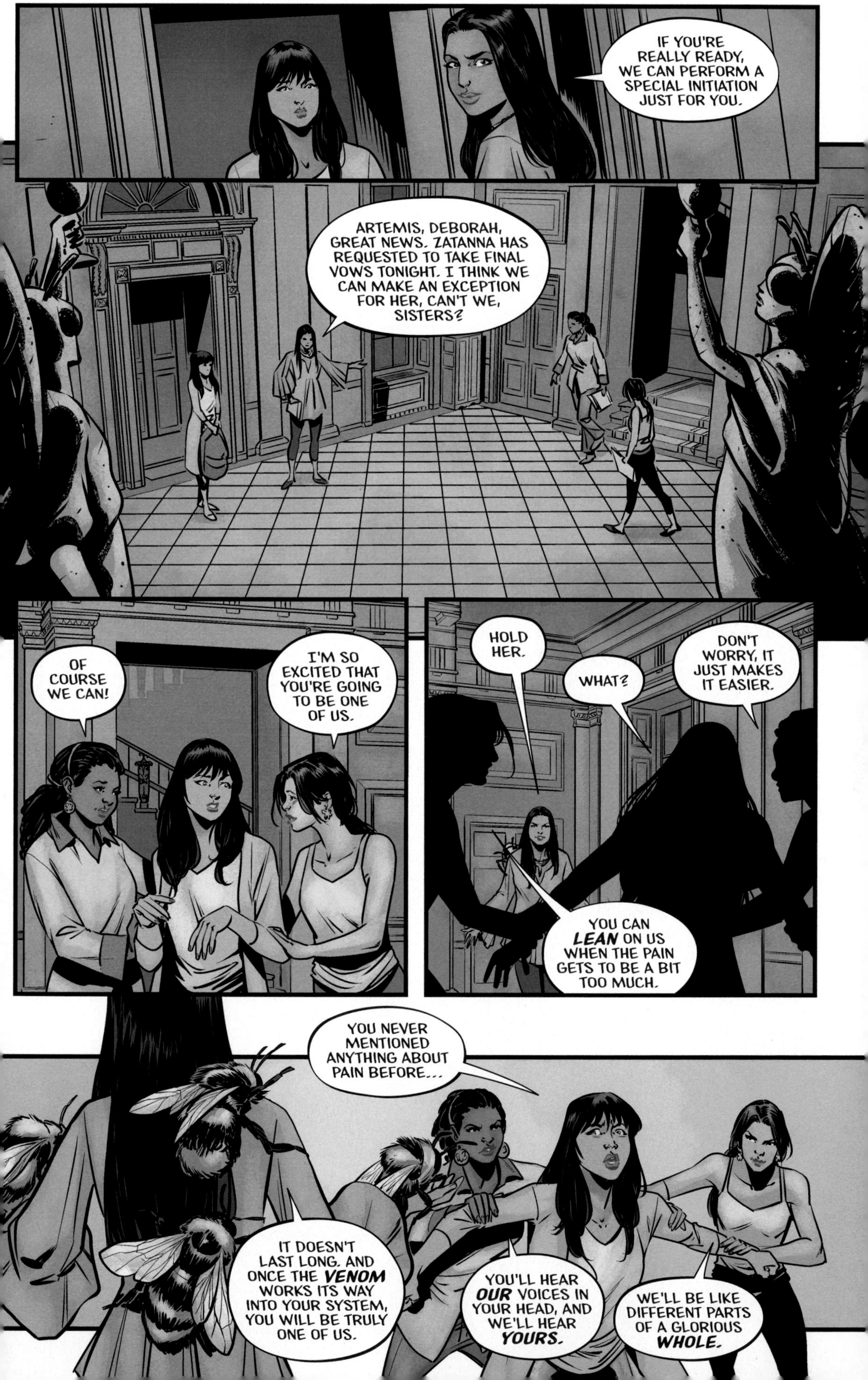
IF YOU'RE REALLY READY, WE CAN PERFORM A SPECIAL INITIATION JUST FOR YOU.
ARTEMIS, DEBORAH, GREAT NEWS. ZATANNA HAS REQUESTED TO TAKE FINAL VOWS TONIGHT. I THINK WE CAN MAKE AN EXCEPTION FOR HER, CAN'T WE, SISTERS?
OF COURSE WE CAN!
I'M SO EXCITED THAT YOU'RE GOING TO BE ONE OF US.
HOLD HER.
WHAT?
DON'T WORRY, IT JUST MAKES IT EASIER.
YOU CAN *LEAN* ON US WHEN THE PAIN GETS TO BE A BIT TOO MUCH.
YOU NEVER MENTIONED ANYTHING ABOUT PAIN BEFORE...
IT DOESN'T LAST LONG. AND ONCE THE *VENOM* WORKS ITS WAY INTO YOUR SYSTEM, YOU WILL BE TRULY ONE OF US.
YOU'LL HEAR *OUR* VOICES IN YOUR HEAD, AND WE'LL HEAR *YOURS.*
WE'LL BE LIKE DIFFERENT PARTS OF A GLORIOUS *WHOLE.*

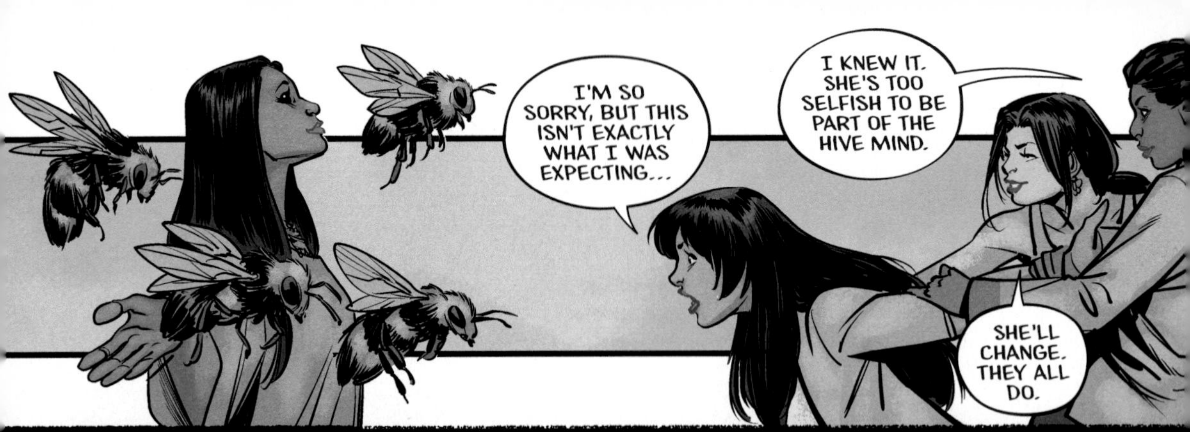
I'M SO SORRY, BUT THIS ISN'T EXACTLY WHAT I WAS EXPECTING...
I KNEW IT. SHE'S TOO SELFISH TO BE PART OF THE HIVE MIND.
SHE'LL CHANGE. THEY ALL DO.

Chapter Three: Wyrding Words

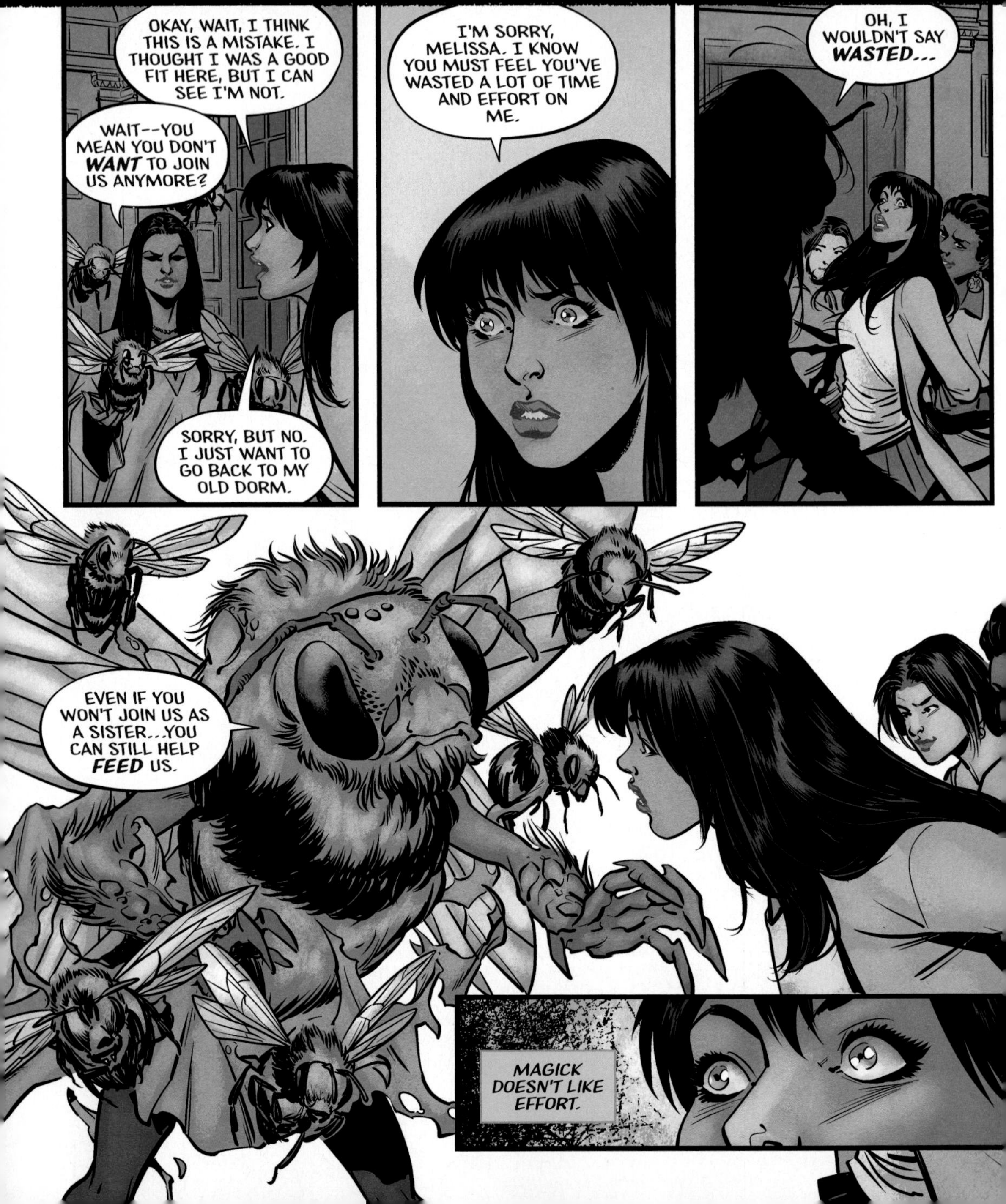
OKAY, WAIT, I THINK THIS IS A MISTAKE. I THOUGHT I WAS A GOOD FIT HERE, BUT I CAN SEE I'M NOT.
WAIT--YOU MEAN YOU DON'T ***WANT*** TO JOIN US ANYMORE?
SORRY, BUT NO. I JUST WANT TO GO BACK TO MY OLD DORM.
I'M SORRY, MELISSA. I KNOW YOU MUST FEEL YOU'VE WASTED A LOT OF TIME AND EFFORT ON ME.
OH, I WOULDN'T SAY ***WASTED...***
EVEN IF YOU WON'T JOIN US AS A SISTER...YOU CAN STILL HELP ***FEED*** US.
MAGICK DOESN'T LIKE EFFORT.

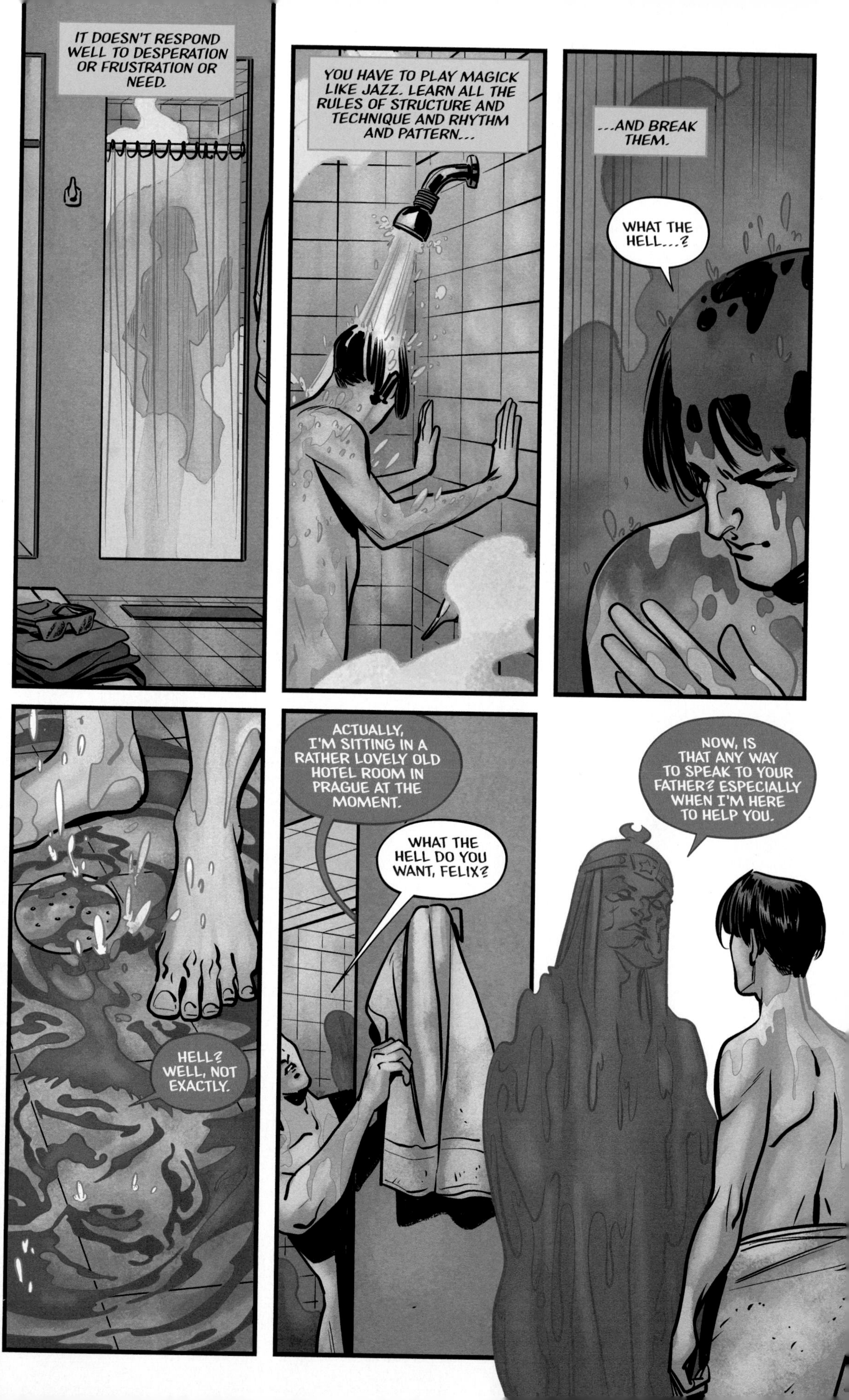
IT DOESN'T RESPOND WELL TO DESPERATION OR FRUSTRATION OR NEED.
YOU HAVE TO PLAY MAGICK LIKE JAZZ. LEARN ALL THE RULES OF STRUCTURE AND TECHNIQUE AND RHYTHM AND PATTERN...
...AND BREAK THEM.
WHAT THE HELL...?
HELL? WELL, NOT EXACTLY.
ACTUALLY, I'M SITTING IN A RATHER LOVELY OLD HOTEL ROOM IN PRAGUE AT THE MOMENT.
WHAT THE HELL DO YOU WANT, FELIX?
NOW, IS THAT ANY WAY TO SPEAK TO YOUR FATHER? ESPECIALLY WHEN I'M HERE TO HELP YOU.

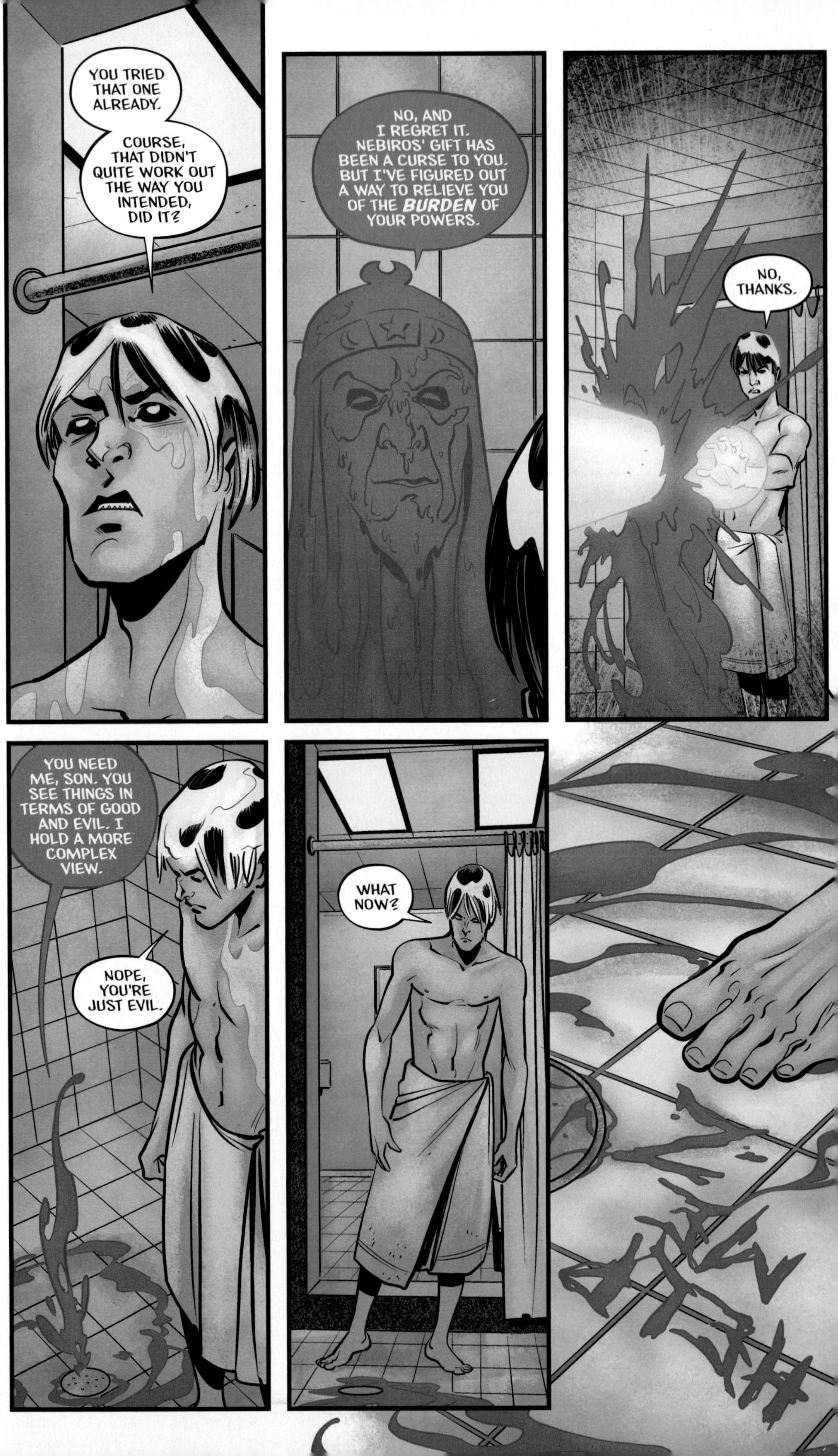
YOU TRIED THAT ONE ALREADY.
COURSE, THAT DIDN'T QUITE WORK OUT THE WAY YOU INTENDED, DID IT?
NO, AND I REGRET IT. NEBIROS' GIFT HAS BEEN A CURSE TO YOU. BUT I'VE FIGURED OUT A WAY TO RELIEVE YOU OF THE *BURDEN* OF YOUR POWERS.
NO, THANKS.
YOU NEED ME, SON. YOU SEE THINGS IN TERMS OF GOOD AND EVIL. I HOLD A MORE COMPLEX VIEW.
NOPE, YOU'RE JUST EVIL.
WHAT NOW?

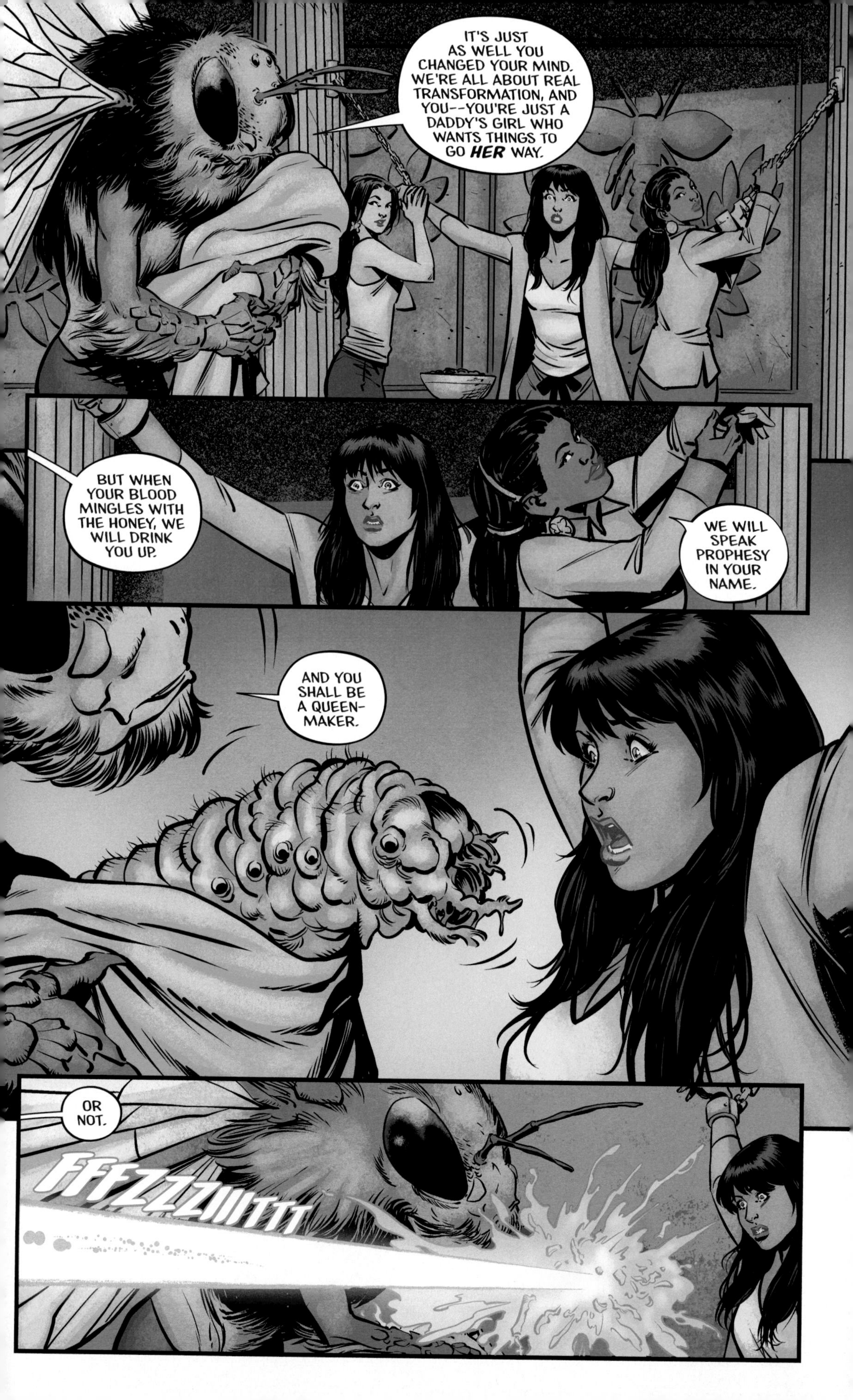
IT'S JUST AS WELL YOU CHANGED YOUR MIND. WE'RE ALL ABOUT REAL TRANSFORMATION, AND YOU--YOU'RE JUST A DADDY'S GIRL WHO WANTS THINGS TO GO HER WAY.
BUT WHEN YOUR BLOOD MINGLES WITH THE HONEY, WE WILL DRINK YOU UP.
WE WILL SPEAK PROPHESY IN YOUR NAME.
AND YOU SHALL BE A QUEEN-MAKER.
OR NOT.
FFFZZZIIITTT

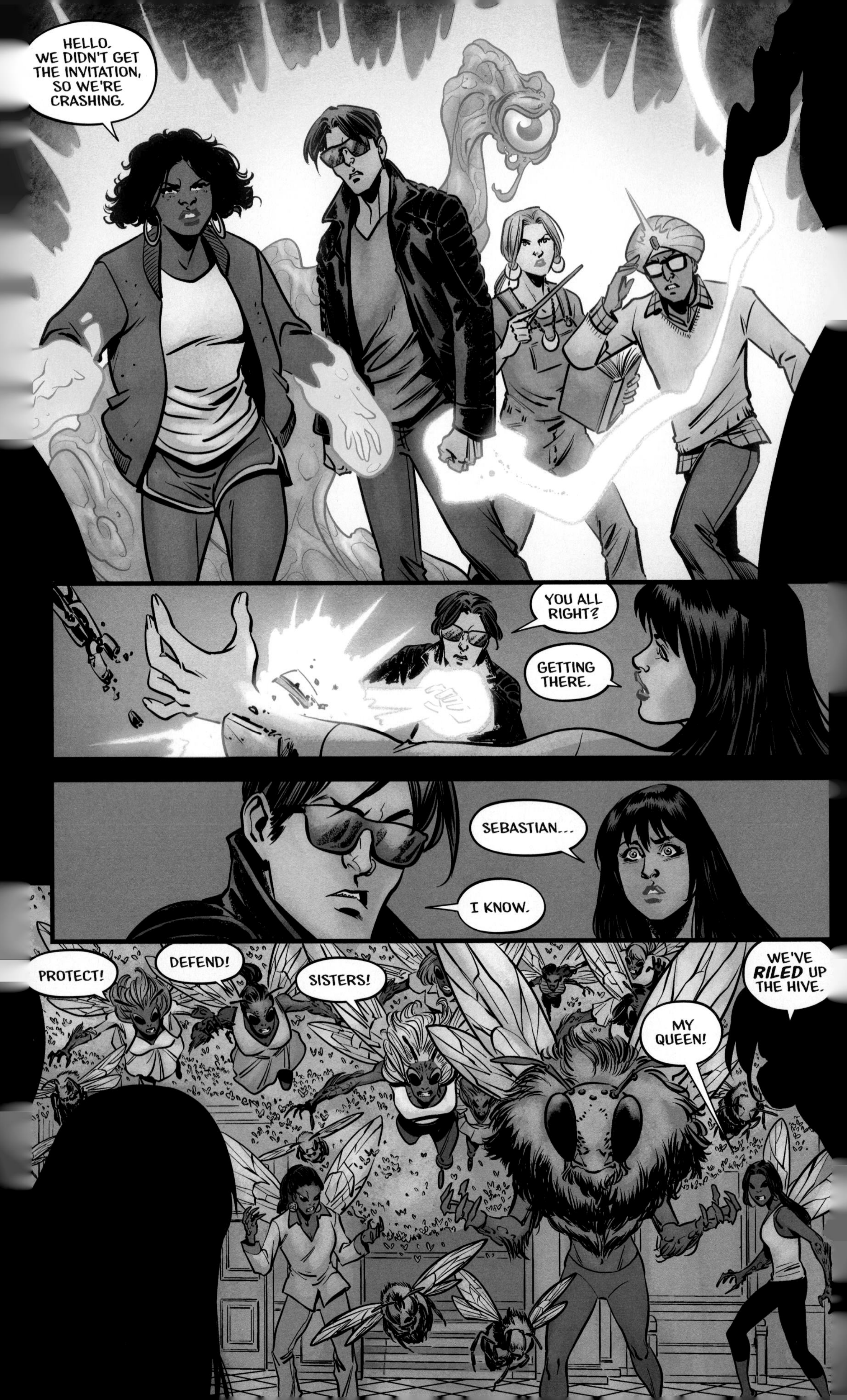
HELLO. WE DIDN'T GET THE INVITATION, SO WE'RE CRASHING.
YOU ALL RIGHT?
GETTING THERE.
SEBASTIAN...
I KNOW.
PROTECT!
DEFEND!
SISTERS!
WE'VE *RILED* UP THE HIVE.
MY QUEEN!

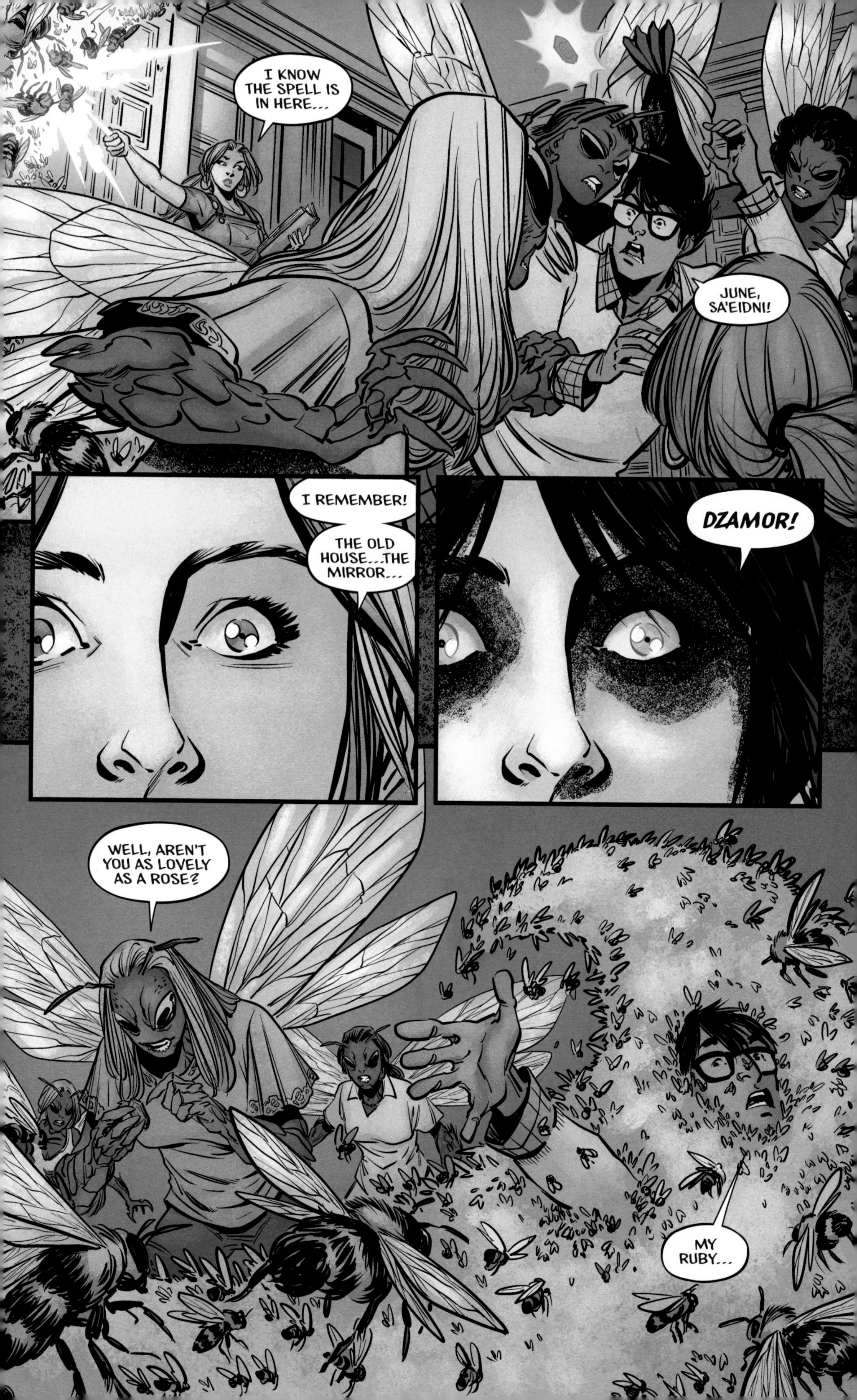
I KNOW THE SPELL IS IN HERE...
JUNE, SA'EIDNI!
I REMEMBER!
THE OLD HOUSE...THE MIRROR...
DZAMOR!
WELL, AREN'T YOU AS LOVELY AS A ROSE?
MY RUBY...

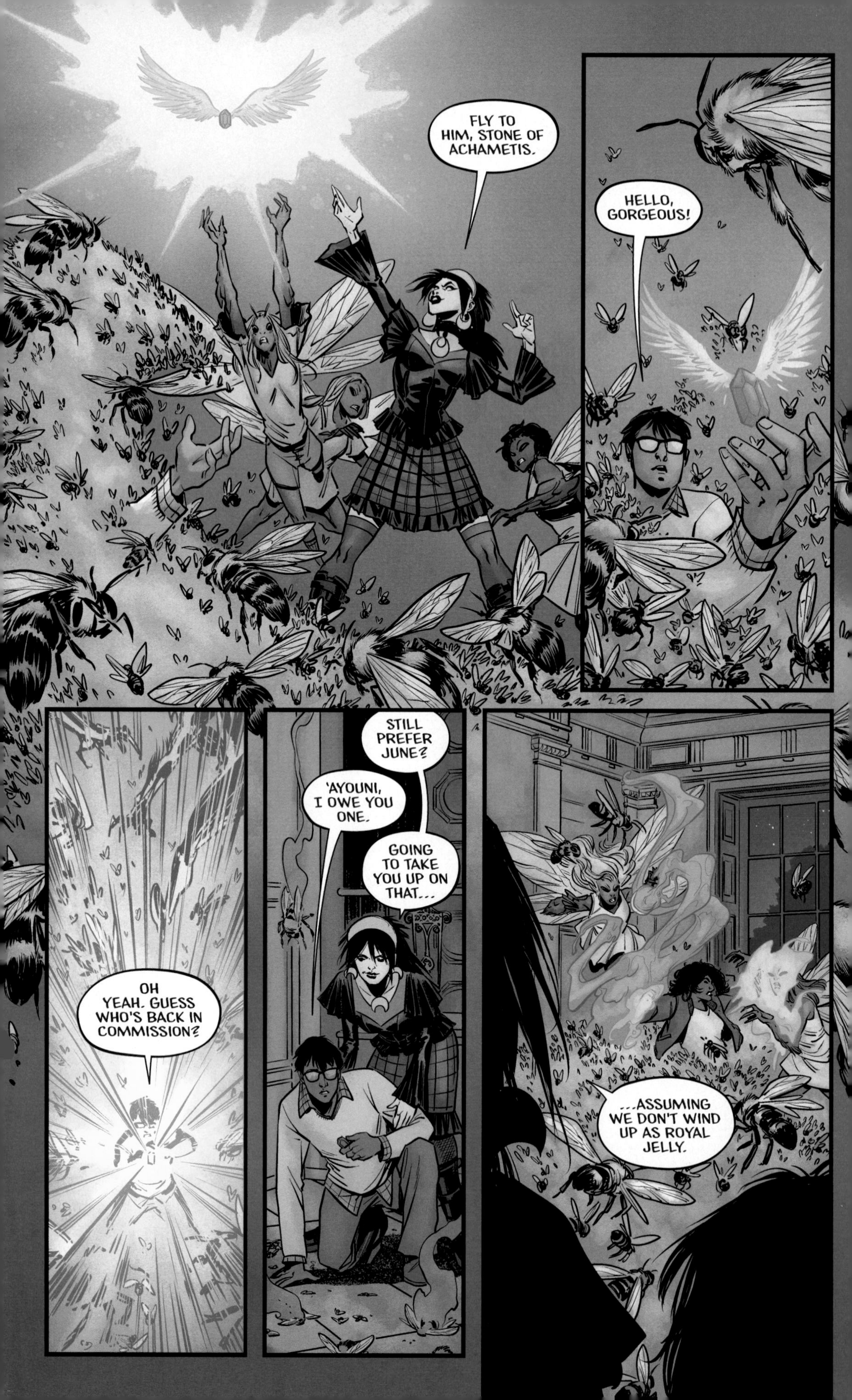
FLY TO
HIM, STONE OF
ACHAMETIS.
HELLO,
GORGEOUS!
OH
YEAH. GUESS
WHO'S BACK IN
COMMISSION?
STILL
PREFER
JUNE?
'AYOUNI,
I OWE YOU
ONE.
GOING
TO TAKE
YOU UP ON
THAT...
...ASSUMING
WE DON'T WIND
UP AS ROYAL
JELLY.

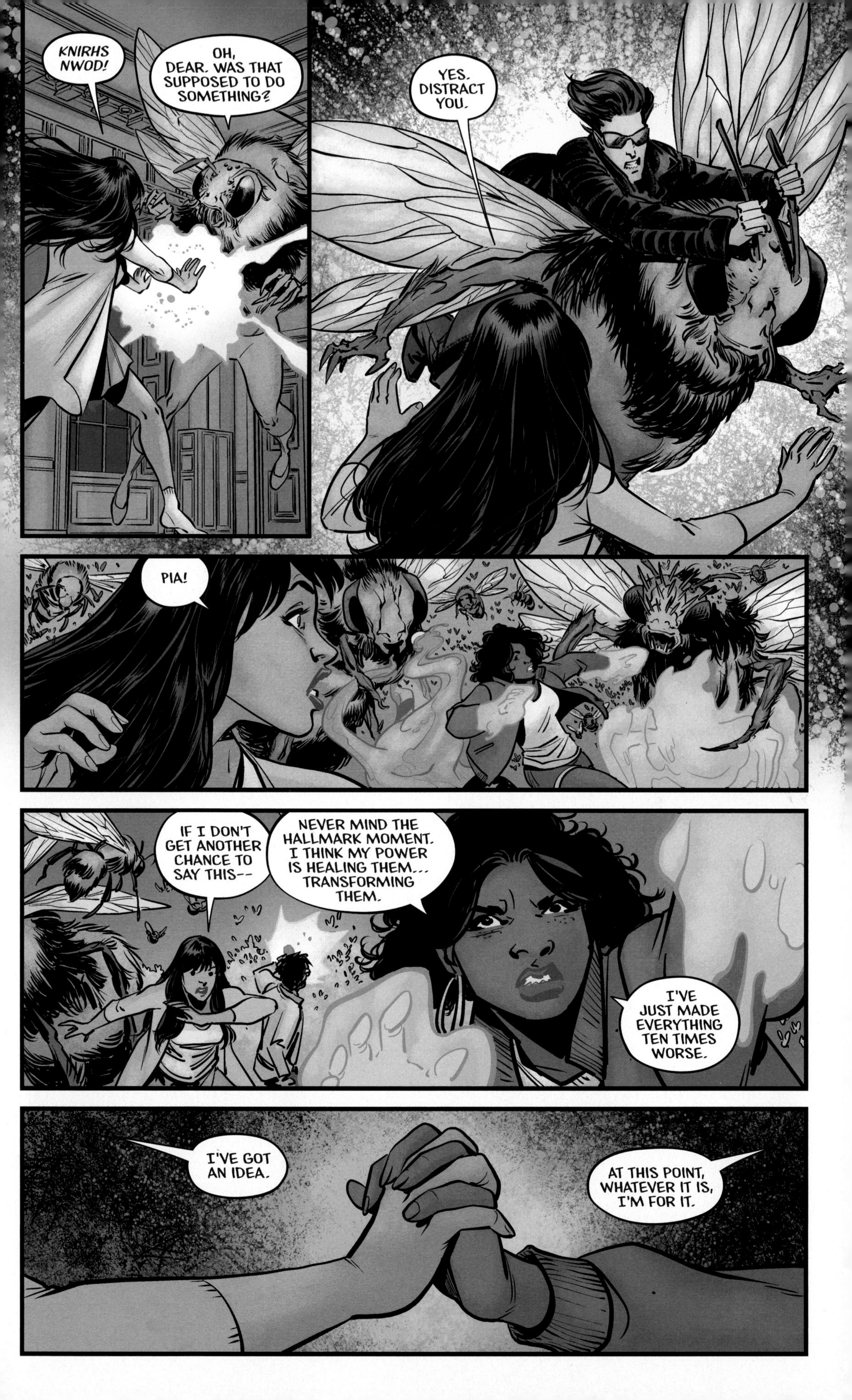
KNIRHS NWOD!
OH, DEAR. WAS THAT SUPPOSED TO DO SOMETHING?
YES. DISTRACT YOU.
PIA!
IF I DON'T GET ANOTHER CHANCE TO SAY THIS--
NEVER MIND THE HALLMARK MOMENT. I THINK MY POWER IS HEALING THEM... TRANSFORMING THEM.
I'VE JUST MADE EVERYTHING TEN TIMES WORSE.
I'VE GOT AN IDEA.
AT THIS POINT, WHATEVER IT IS, I'M FOR IT.

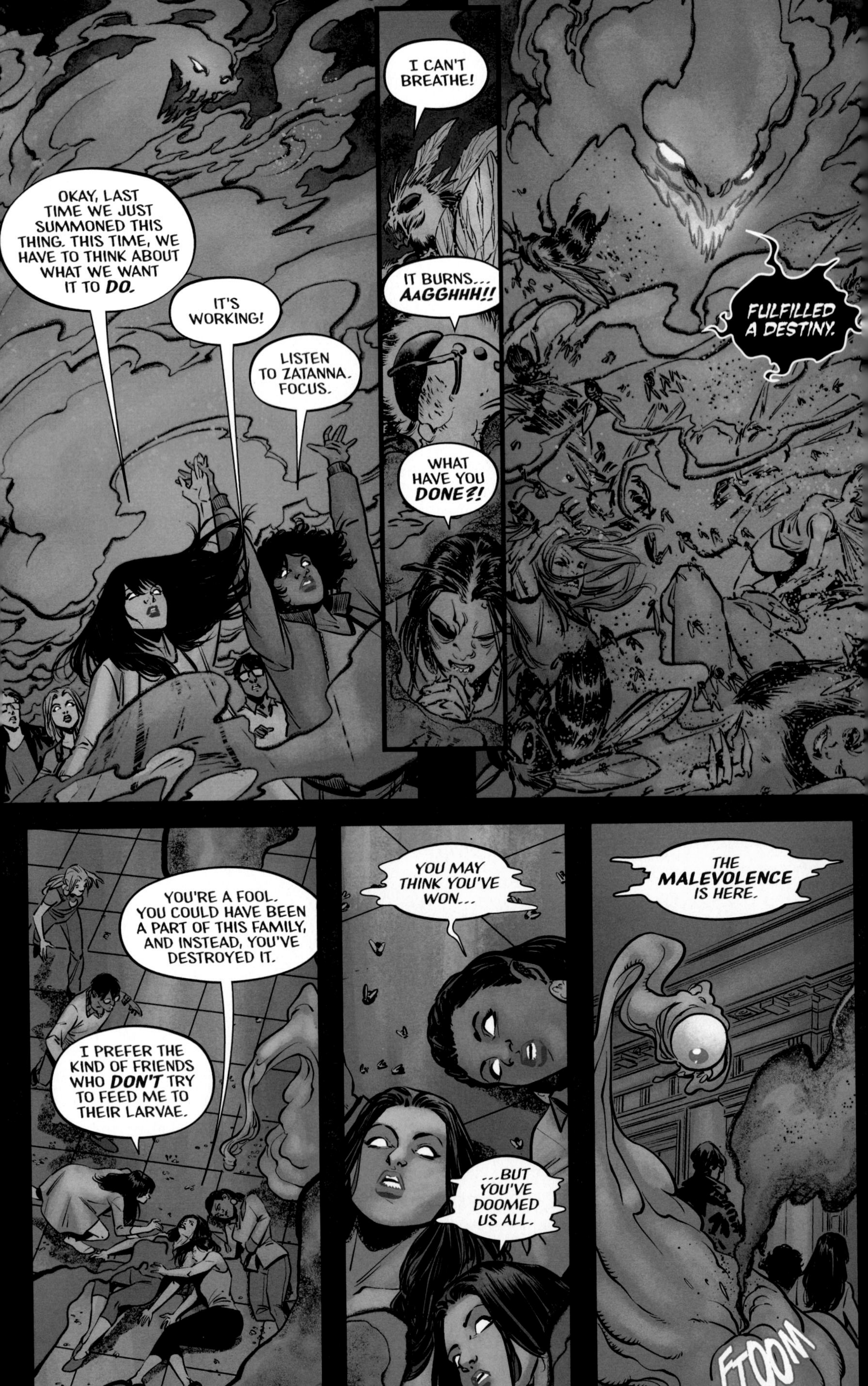
OKAY, LAST TIME WE JUST SUMMONED THIS THING. THIS TIME, WE HAVE TO THINK ABOUT WHAT WE WANT IT TO DO.
IT'S WORKING!
LISTEN TO ZATANNA. FOCUS.
I CAN'T BREATHE!
IT BURNS... AAGGHHH!!
WHAT HAVE YOU DONE?!
FULFILLED A DESTINY.
YOU'RE A FOOL. YOU COULD HAVE BEEN A PART OF THIS FAMILY, AND INSTEAD, YOU'VE DESTROYED IT.
I PREFER THE KIND OF FRIENDS WHO DON'T TRY TO FEED ME TO THEIR LARVAE.
YOU MAY THINK YOU'VE WON...
...BUT YOU'VE DOOMED US ALL.
THE MALEVOLENCE IS HERE.
FTOOM

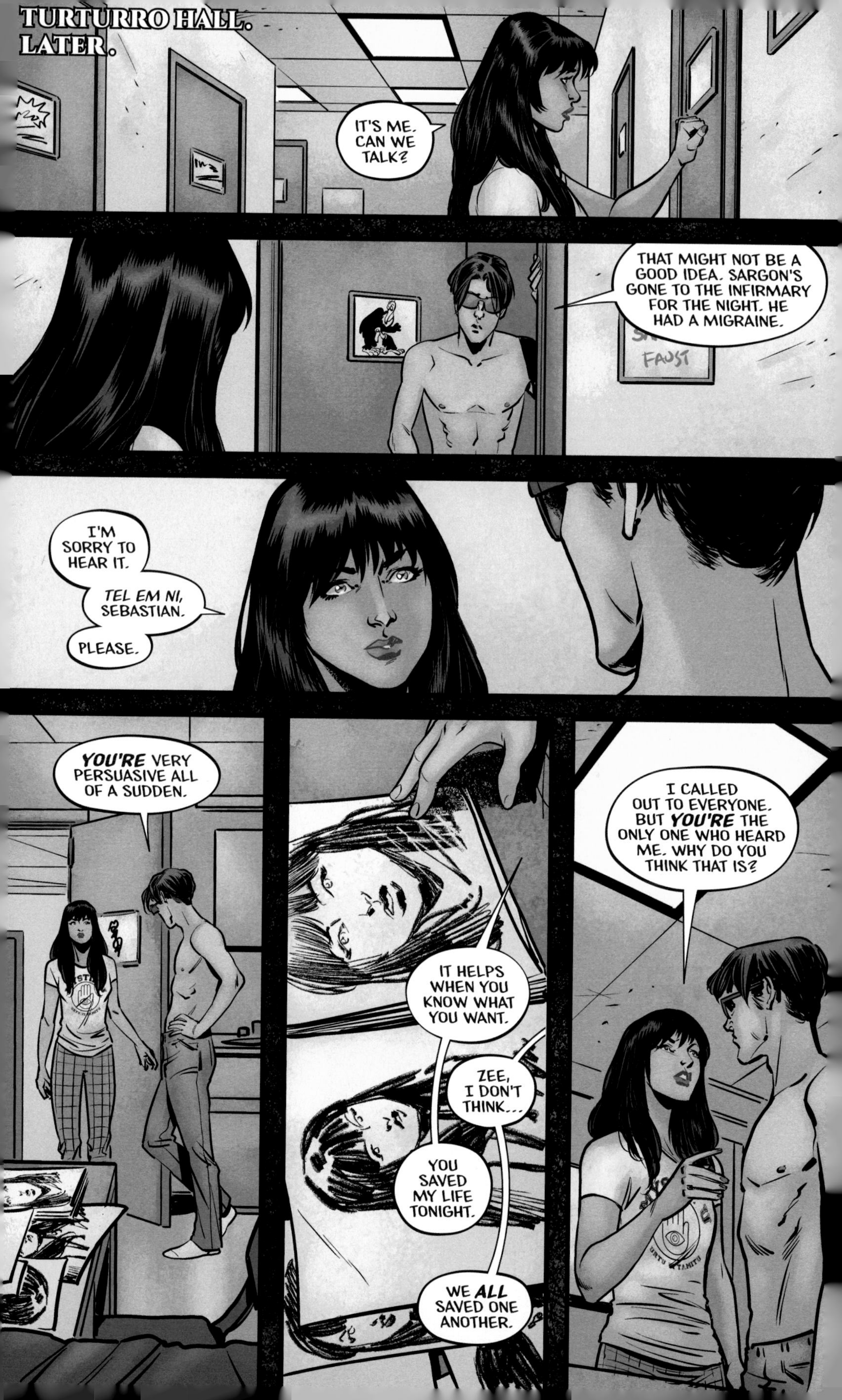
TURTURRO HALL.
LATER.
IT'S ME. CAN WE TALK?
THAT MIGHT NOT BE A GOOD IDEA. SARGON'S GONE TO THE INFIRMARY FOR THE NIGHT. HE HAD A MIGRAINE.
FAUST
I'M SORRY TO HEAR IT.
TEL EM NI, SEBASTIAN.
PLEASE.
YOU'RE VERY PERSUASIVE ALL OF A SUDDEN.
IT HELPS WHEN YOU KNOW WHAT YOU WANT.
ZEE, I DON'T THINK...
YOU SAVED MY LIFE TONIGHT.
WE ALL SAVED ONE ANOTHER.
I CALLED OUT TO EVERYONE. BUT YOU'RE THE ONLY ONE WHO HEARD ME. WHY DO YOU THINK THAT IS?

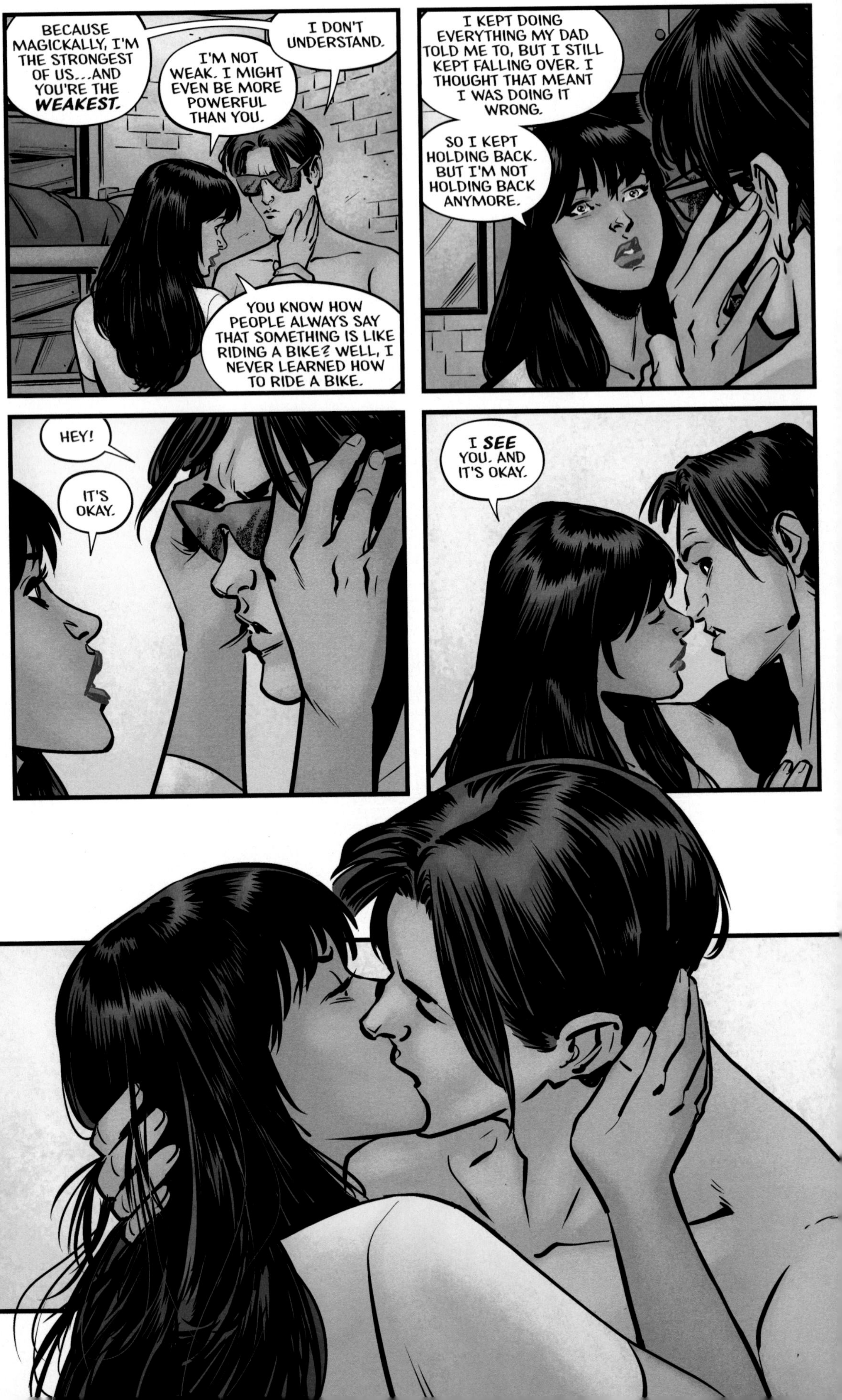
BECAUSE MAGICKALLY, I'M THE STRONGEST OF US...AND YOU'RE THE WEAKEST.
I DON'T UNDERSTAND.
I'M NOT WEAK. I MIGHT EVEN BE MORE POWERFUL THAN YOU.
YOU KNOW HOW PEOPLE ALWAYS SAY THAT SOMETHING IS LIKE RIDING A BIKE? WELL, I NEVER LEARNED HOW TO RIDE A BIKE.
I KEPT DOING EVERYTHING MY DAD TOLD ME TO, BUT I STILL KEPT FALLING OVER. I THOUGHT THAT MEANT I WAS DOING IT WRONG.
SO I KEPT HOLDING BACK. BUT I'M NOT HOLDING BACK ANYMORE.
HEY!
IT'S OKAY.
I SEE YOU. AND IT'S OKAY.

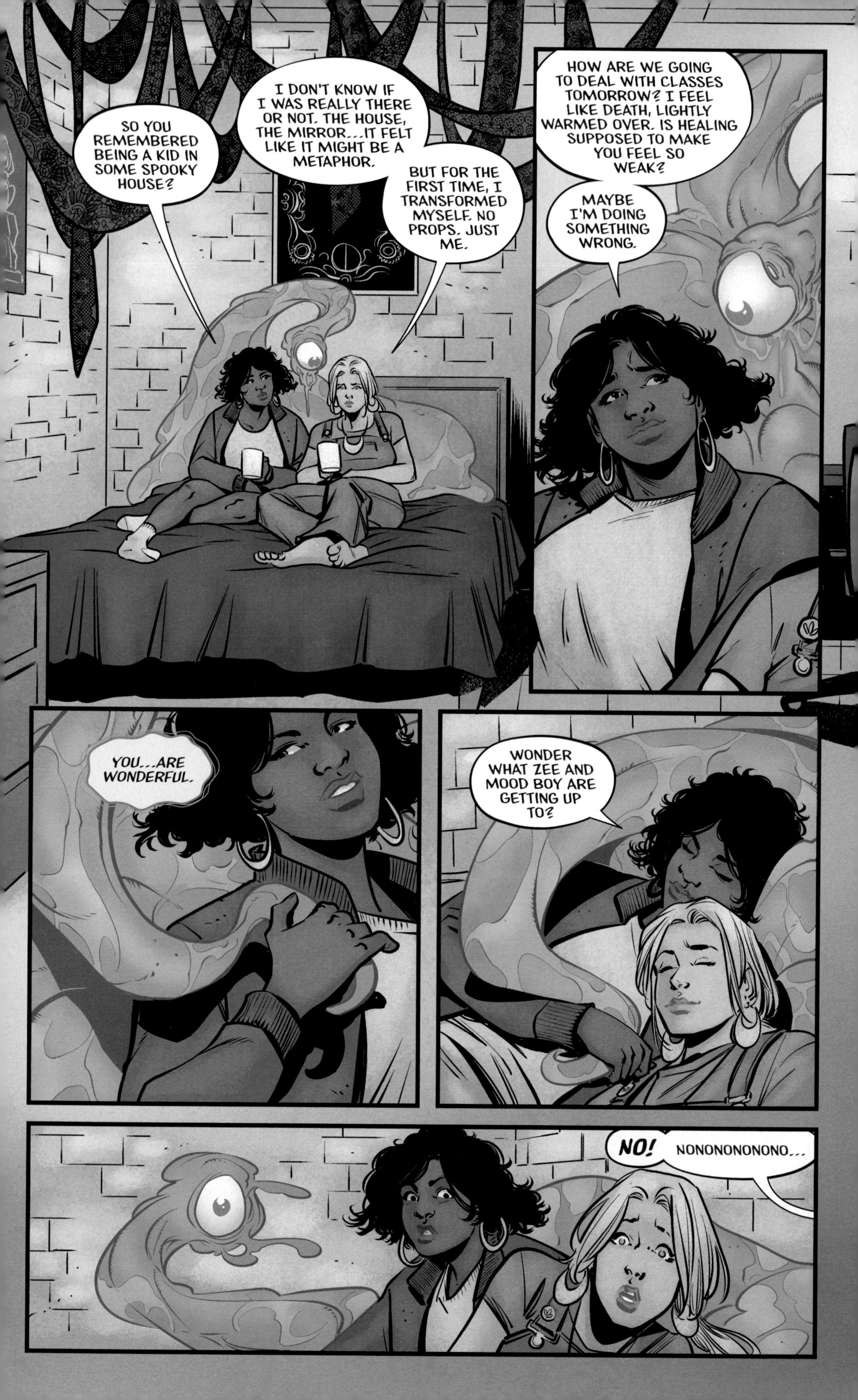
SO YOU REMEMBERED BEING A KID IN SOME SPOOKY HOUSE?
I DON'T KNOW IF I WAS REALLY THERE OR NOT. THE HOUSE, THE MIRROR...IT FELT LIKE IT MIGHT BE A METAPHOR.
BUT FOR THE FIRST TIME, I TRANSFORMED MYSELF. NO PROPS. JUST ME.
HOW ARE WE GOING TO DEAL WITH CLASSES TOMORROW? I FEEL LIKE DEATH, LIGHTLY WARMED OVER. IS HEALING SUPPOSED TO MAKE YOU FEEL SO WEAK?
MAYBE I'M DOING SOMETHING WRONG.
YOU...ARE WONDERFUL.
WONDER WHAT ZEE AND MOOD BOY ARE GETTING UP TO?
NO! NONONONONONO...

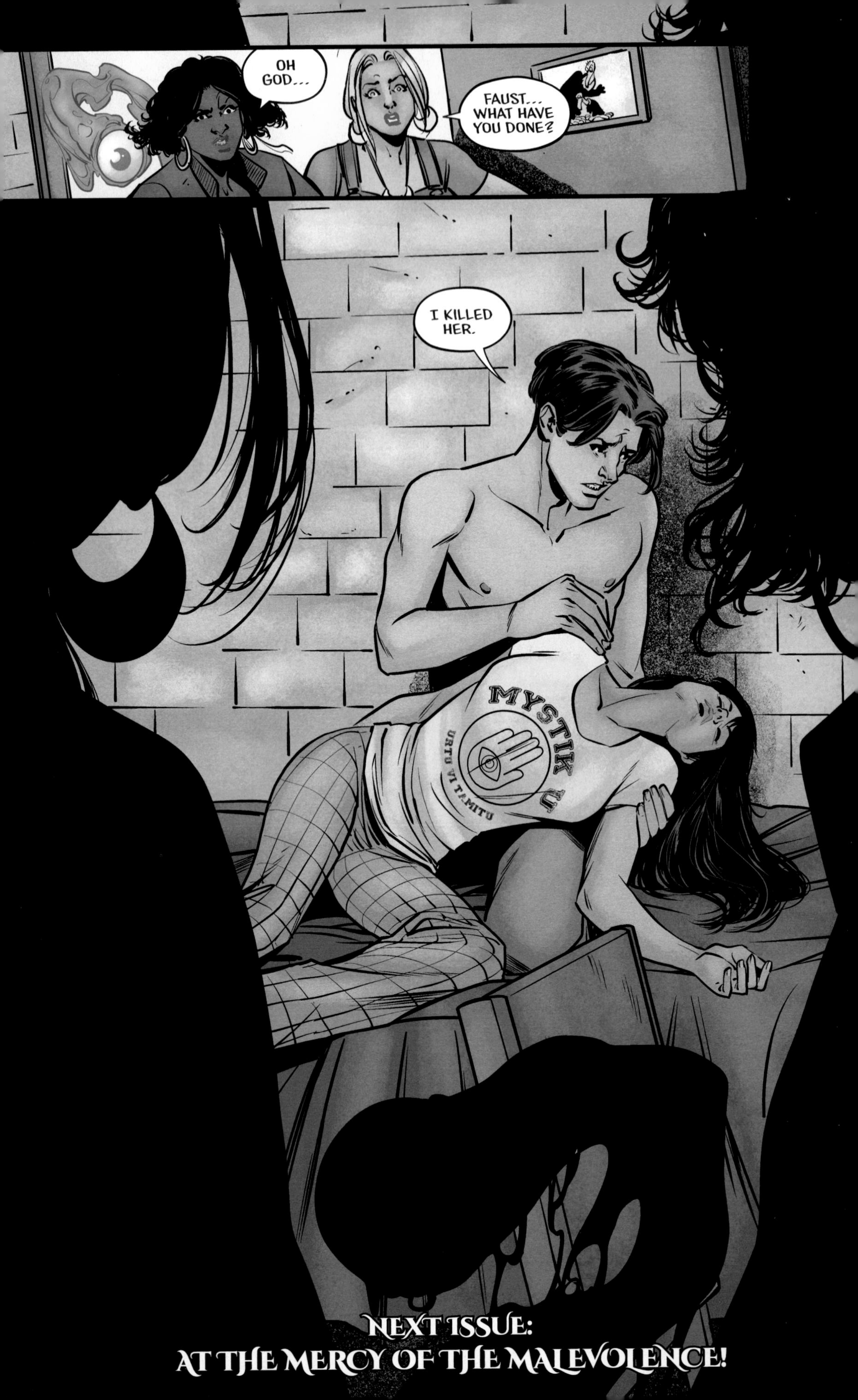
OH GOD...
FAUST... WHAT HAVE YOU DONE?
I KILLED HER.
MYSTIK U
URTU VI TAMITU
NEXT ISSUE:
AT THE MERCY OF THE MALEVOLENCE!

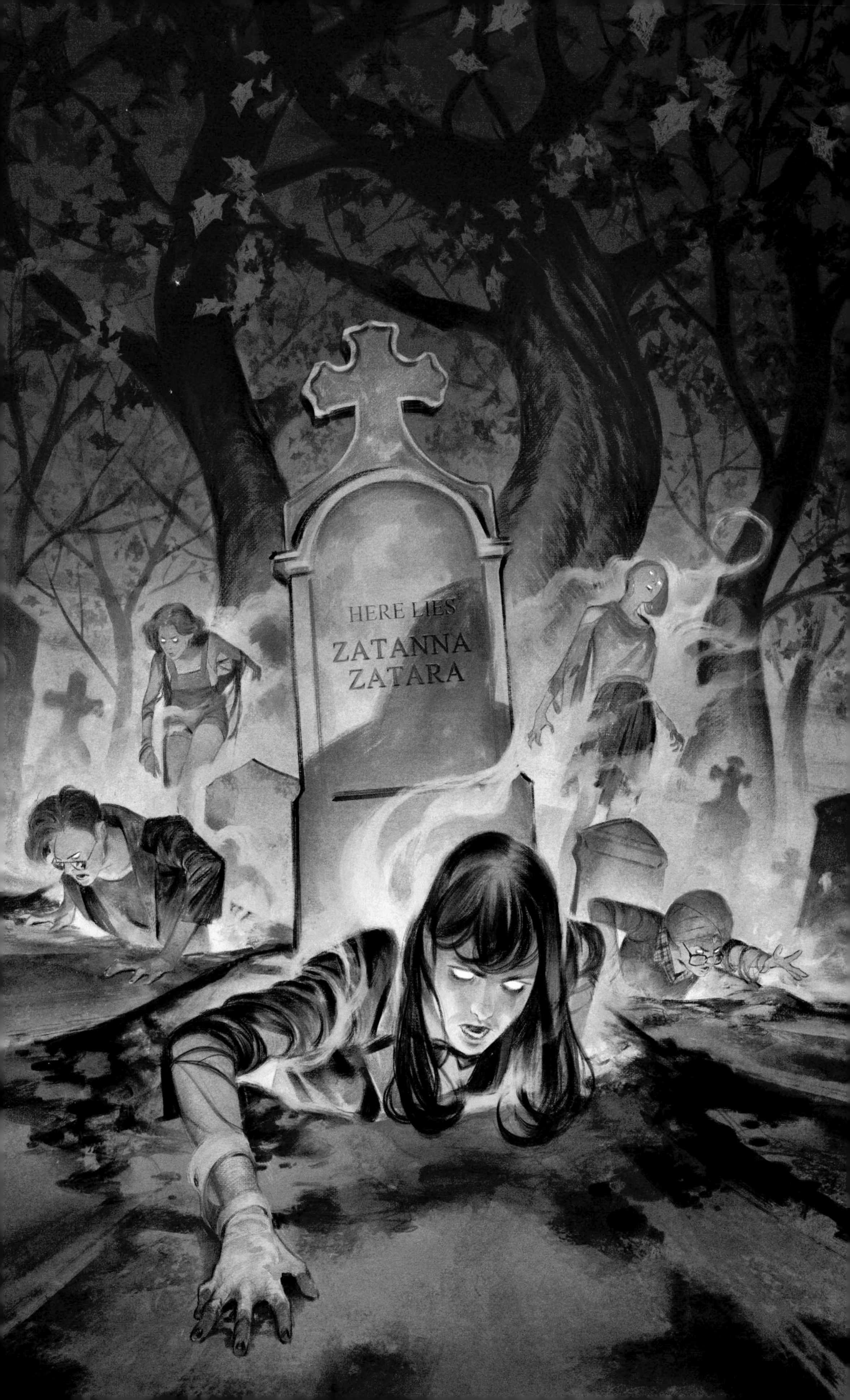
HERE LIES
ZATANNA
ZATARA

"Like all endings,
it's also a beginning."

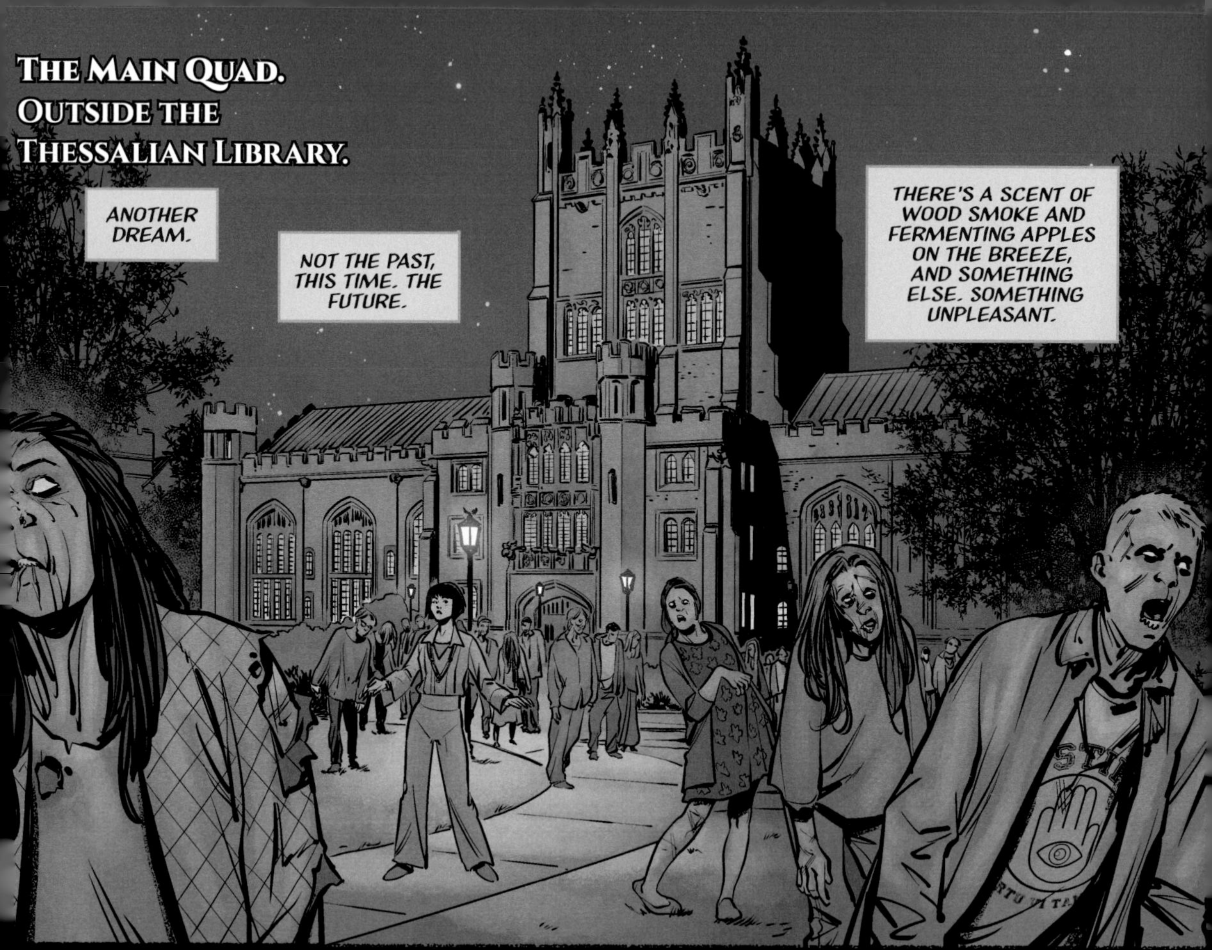
THE MAIN QUAD.
OUTSIDE THE
THESSALIAN LIBRARY.
ANOTHER DREAM.
NOT THE PAST, THIS TIME. THE FUTURE.
THERE'S A SCENT OF WOOD SMOKE AND FERMENTING APPLES ON THE BREEZE, AND SOMETHING ELSE. SOMETHING UNPLEASANT.

Prologue.

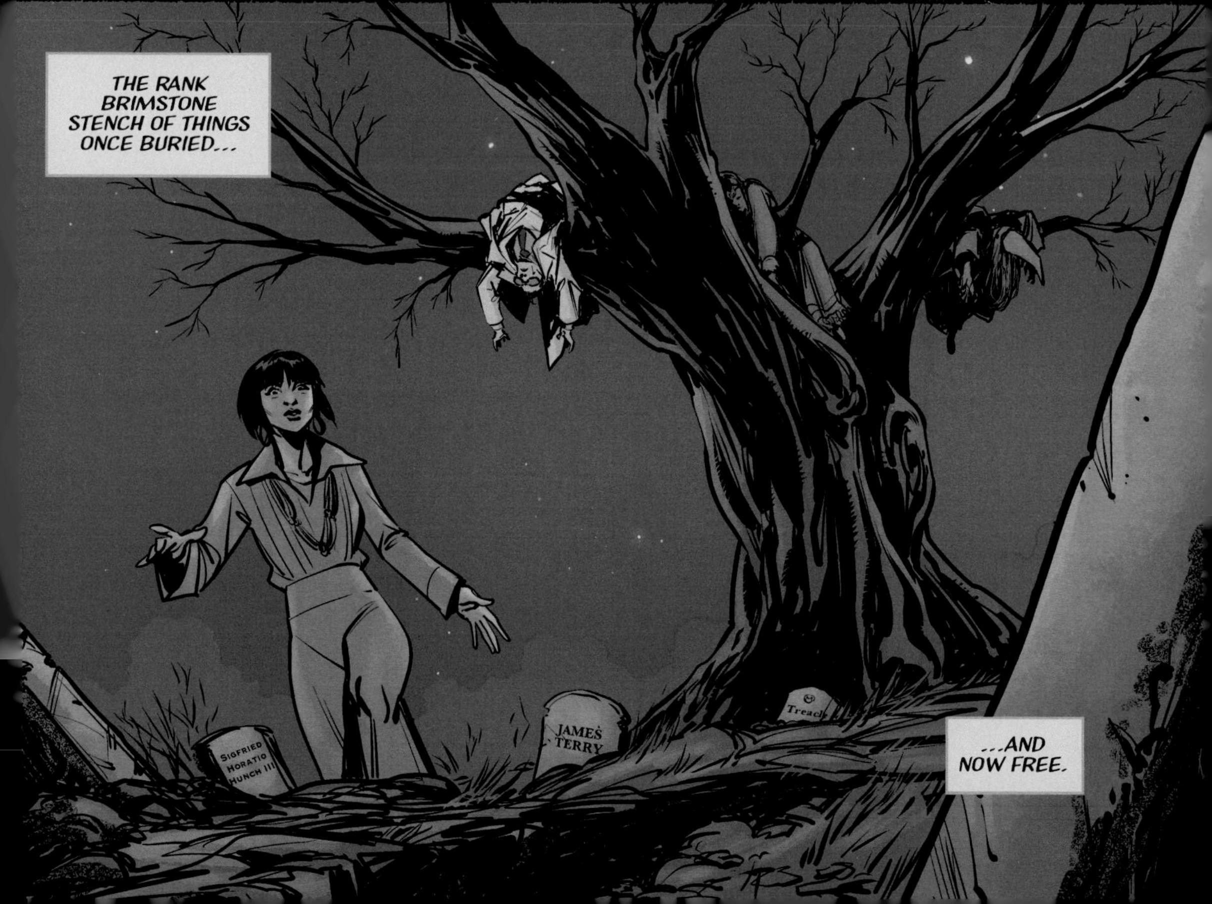
THE RANK BRIMSTONE STENCH OF THINGS ONCE BURIED...
SIGFRIED HORATIO HUNCH III
JAMES TERRY
...AND NOW FREE.

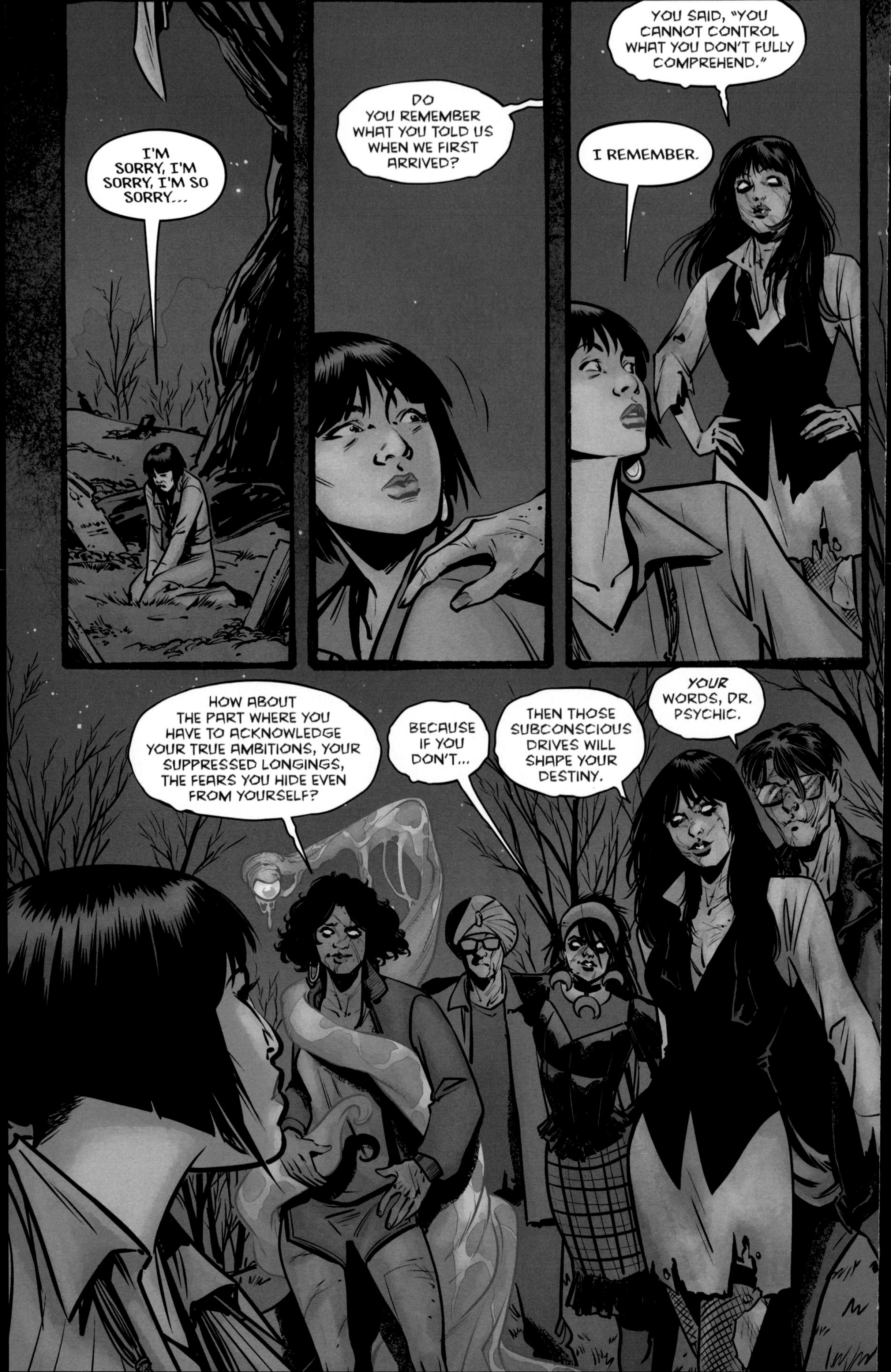
I'M SORRY, I'M SORRY, I'M SO SORRY...
DO YOU REMEMBER WHAT YOU TOLD US WHEN WE FIRST ARRIVED?
YOU SAID, "YOU CANNOT CONTROL WHAT YOU DON'T FULLY COMPREHEND."
I REMEMBER.
HOW ABOUT THE PART WHERE YOU HAVE TO ACKNOWLEDGE YOUR TRUE AMBITIONS, YOUR SUPPRESSED LONGINGS, THE FEARS YOU HIDE EVEN FROM YOURSELF?
BECAUSE IF YOU DON'T...
THEN THOSE SUBCONSCIOUS DRIVES WILL SHAPE YOUR DESTINY.
YOUR WORDS, DR. PSYCHIC.

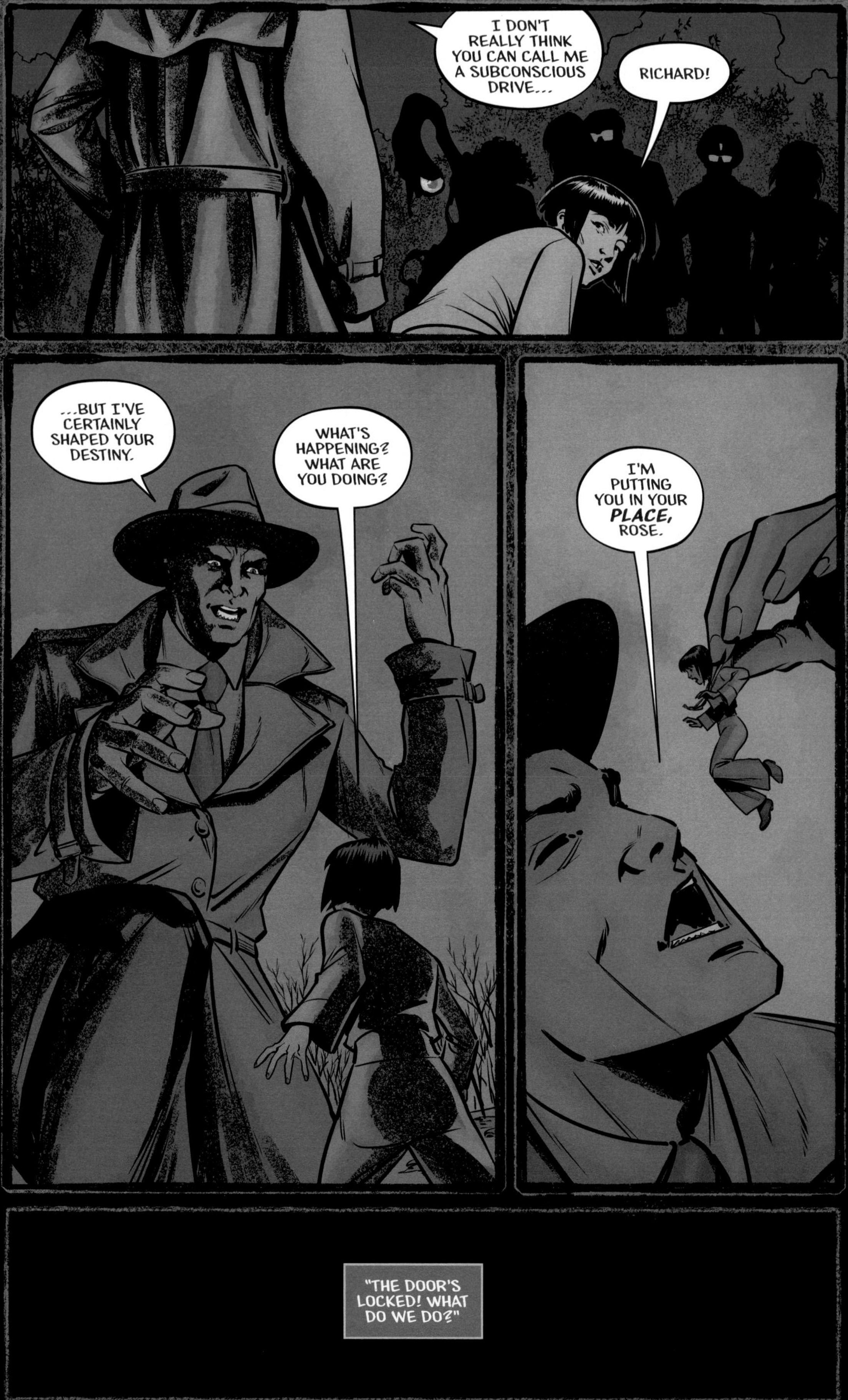
I DON'T REALLY THINK YOU CAN CALL ME A SUBCONSCIOUS DRIVE...
RICHARD!
...BUT I'VE CERTAINLY SHAPED YOUR DESTINY.
WHAT'S HAPPENING? WHAT ARE YOU DOING?
I'M PUTTING YOU IN YOUR *PLACE,* ROSE.
"THE DOOR'S LOCKED! WHAT DO WE DO?"

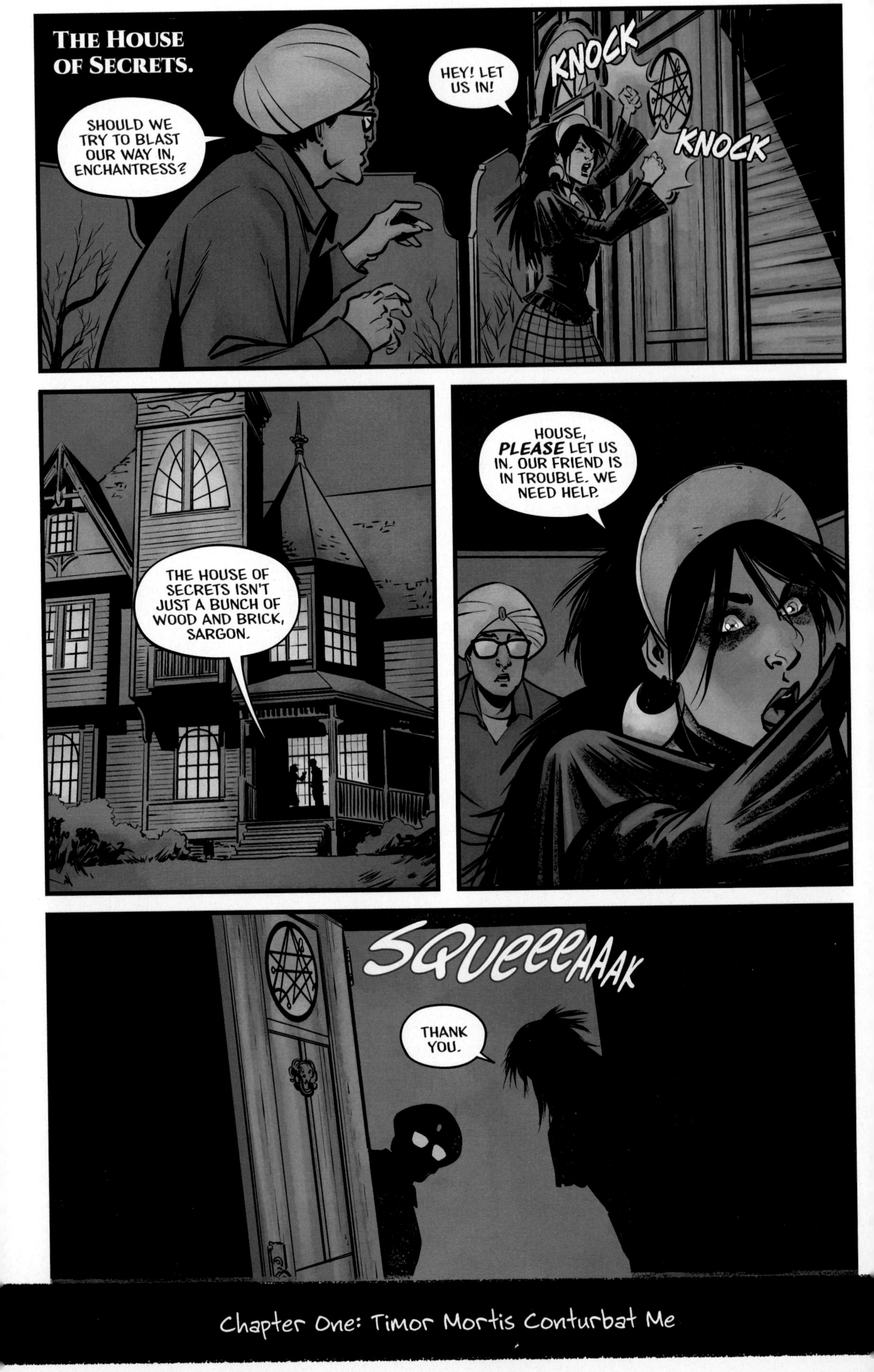
THE HOUSE OF SECRETS.
SHOULD WE TRY TO BLAST OUR WAY IN, ENCHANTRESS?
HEY! LET US IN!
KNOCK
KNOCK
THE HOUSE OF SECRETS ISN'T JUST A BUNCH OF WOOD AND BRICK, SARGON.
HOUSE, PLEASE LET US IN. OUR FRIEND IS IN TROUBLE. WE NEED HELP.
SQUEEEAAAK
THANK YOU.

Chapter One: Timor Mortis Conturbat Me

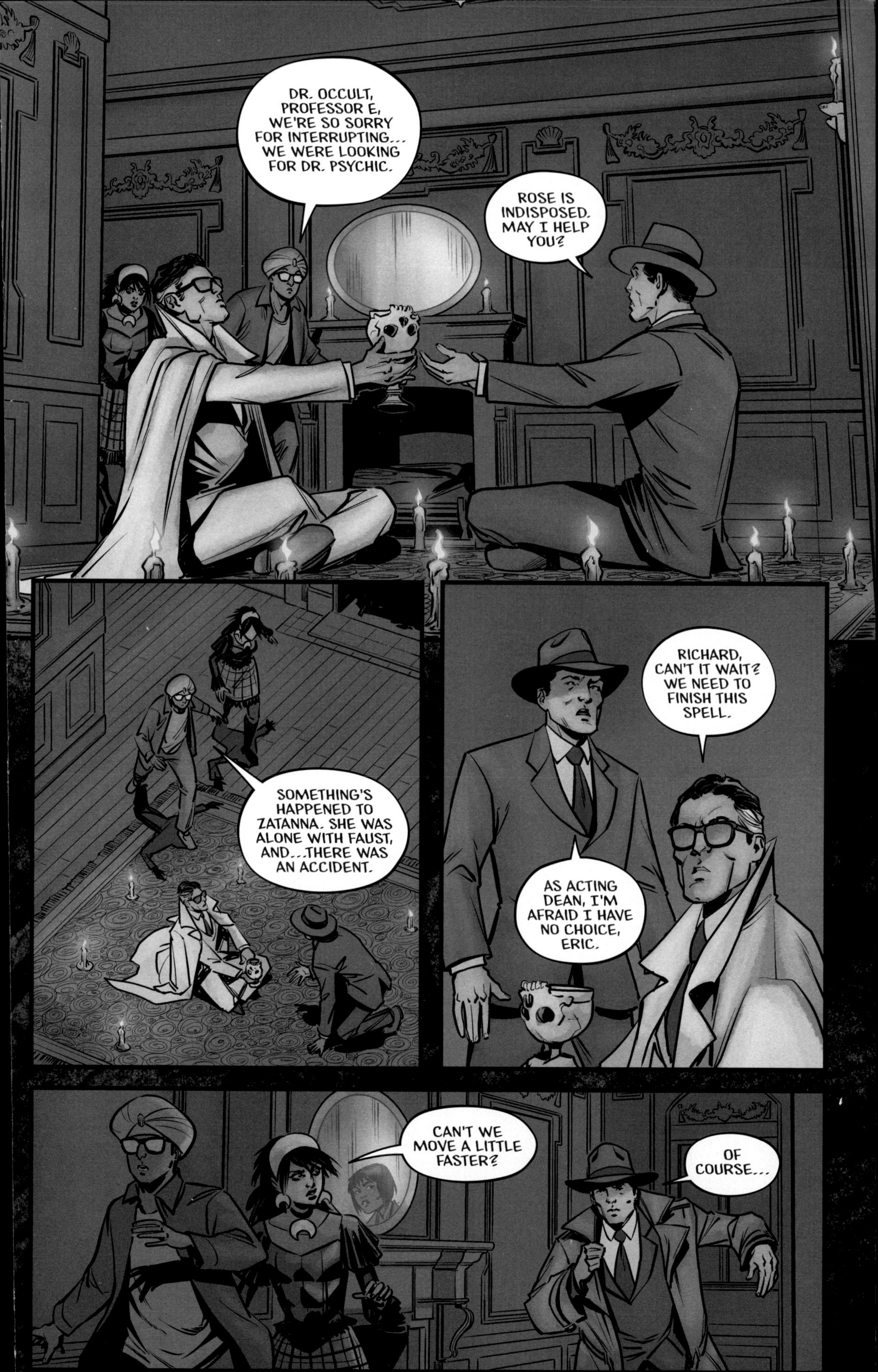
DR. OCCULT, PROFESSOR E, WE'RE SO SORRY FOR INTERRUPTING... WE WERE LOOKING FOR DR. PSYCHIC.
ROSE IS INDISPOSED. MAY I HELP YOU?
SOMETHING'S HAPPENED TO ZATANNA. SHE WAS ALONE WITH FAUST, AND...THERE WAS AN ACCIDENT.
RICHARD, CAN'T IT WAIT? WE NEED TO FINISH THIS SPELL.
AS ACTING DEAN, I'M AFRAID I HAVE NO CHOICE, ERIC.
CAN'T WE MOVE A LITTLE FASTER?
OF COURSE...

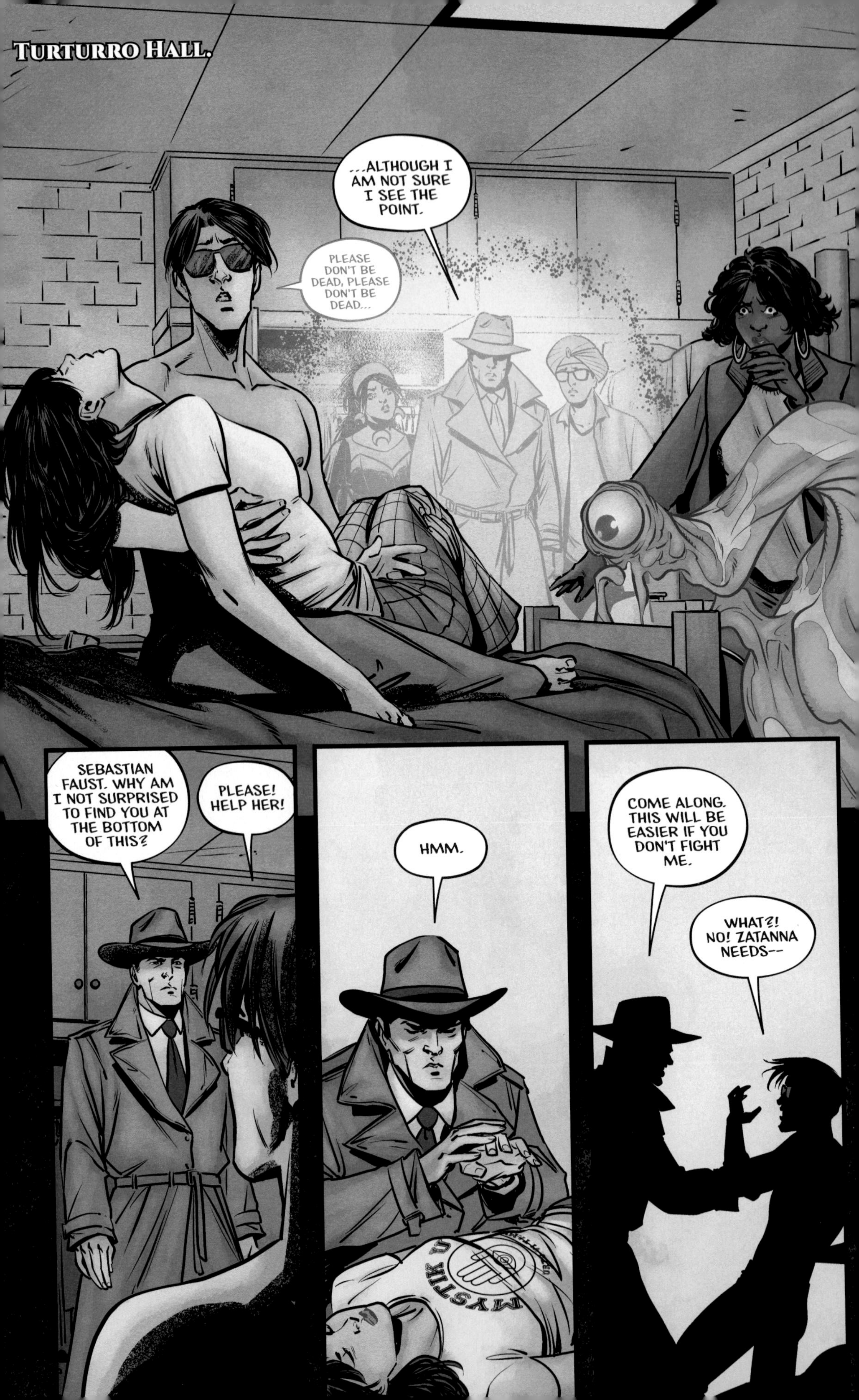
TURTURRO HALL.
PLEASE DON'T BE DEAD, PLEASE DON'T BE DEAD...
...ALTHOUGH I AM NOT SURE I SEE THE POINT.
SEBASTIAN FAUST. WHY AM I NOT SURPRISED TO FIND YOU AT THE BOTTOM OF THIS?
PLEASE! HELP HER!
HMM.
MYSTIK U
COME ALONG. THIS WILL BE EASIER IF YOU DON'T FIGHT ME.
WHAT?! NO! ZATANNA NEEDS--

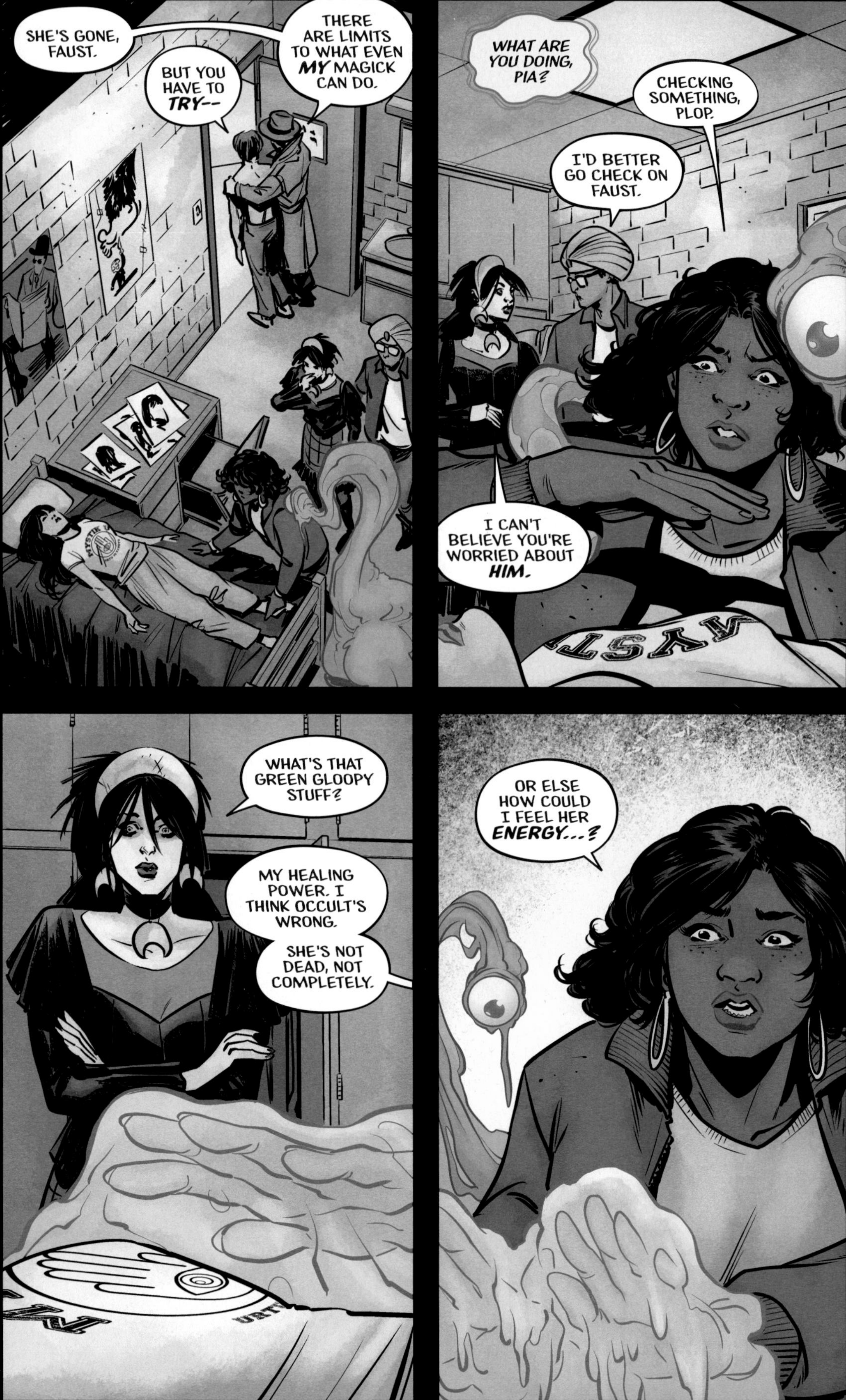
SHE'S GONE, FAUST.
BUT YOU HAVE TO TRY--
THERE ARE LIMITS TO WHAT EVEN MY MAGICK CAN DO.
WHAT ARE YOU DOING, PIA?
CHECKING SOMETHING, PLOP.
I'D BETTER GO CHECK ON FAUST.
I CAN'T BELIEVE YOU'RE WORRIED ABOUT HIM.
WHAT'S THAT GREEN GLOOPY STUFF?
MY HEALING POWER. I THINK OCCULT'S WRONG.
SHE'S NOT DEAD, NOT COMPLETELY.
OR ELSE HOW COULD I FEEL HER ENERGY...?

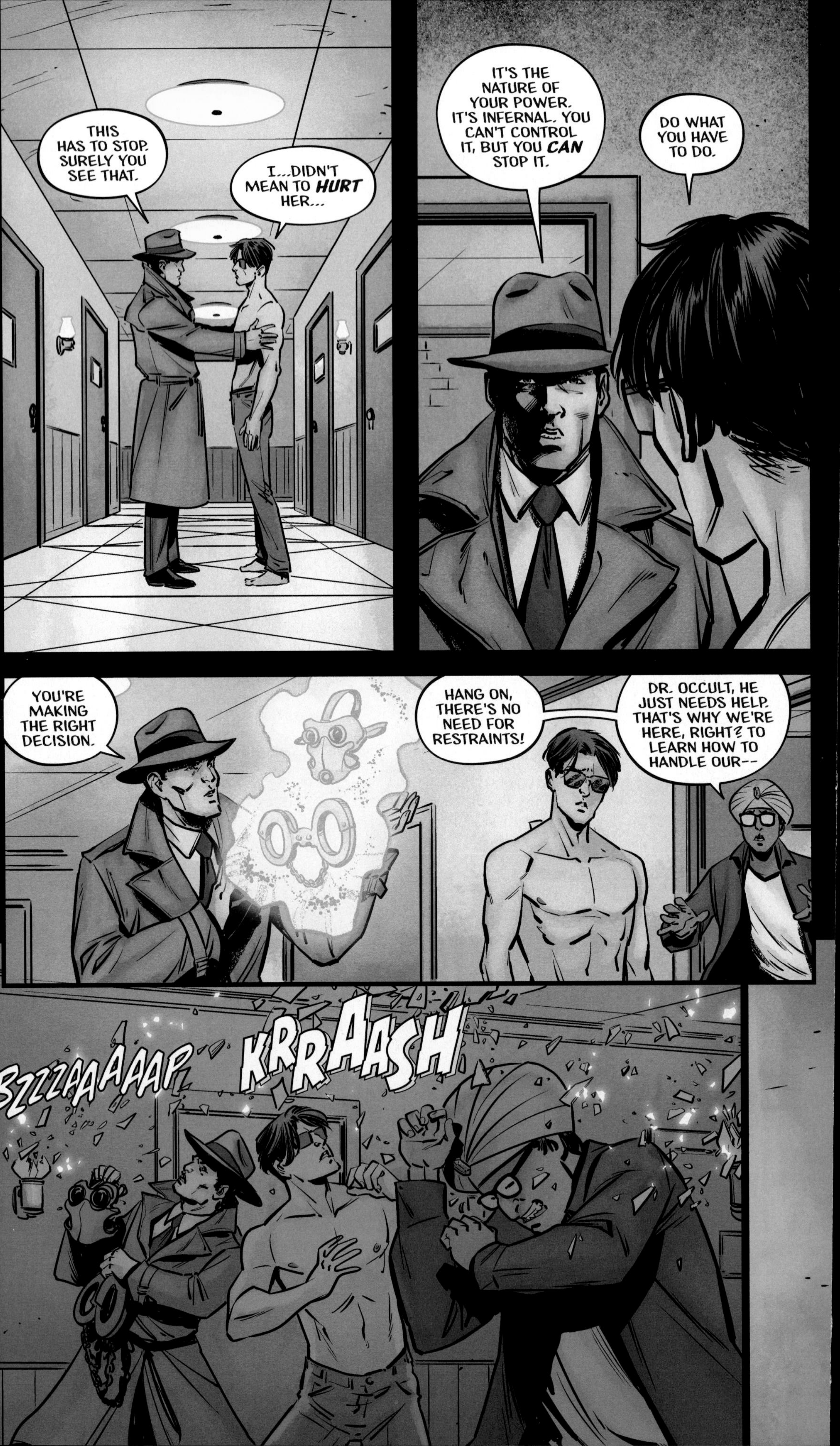
THIS HAS TO STOP. SURELY YOU SEE THAT.
I...DIDN'T MEAN TO HURT HER...
IT'S THE NATURE OF YOUR POWER. IT'S INFERNAL. YOU CAN'T CONTROL IT, BUT YOU CAN STOP IT.
DO WHAT YOU HAVE TO DO.
YOU'RE MAKING THE RIGHT DECISION.
HANG ON, THERE'S NO NEED FOR RESTRAINTS!
DR. OCCULT, HE JUST NEEDS HELP. THAT'S WHY WE'RE HERE, RIGHT? TO LEARN HOW TO HANDLE OUR--
BZZZAAAAAP
KRRAASH

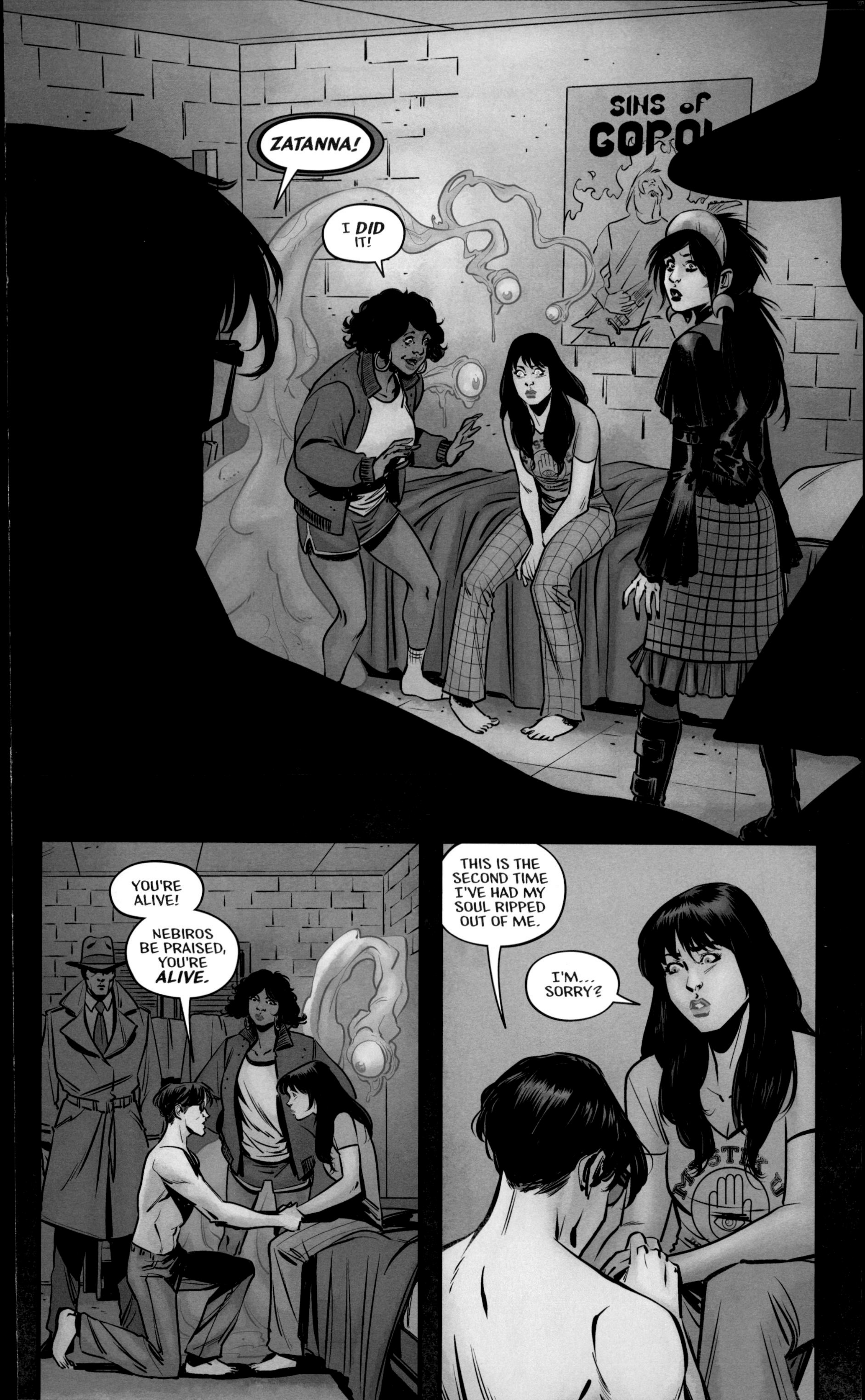
SINS of
GORO
ZATANNA!
I DID IT!
YOU'RE ALIVE!
NEBIROS BE PRAISED, YOU'RE ALIVE.
THIS IS THE SECOND TIME I'VE HAD MY SOUL RIPPED OUT OF ME.
I'M... SORRY?

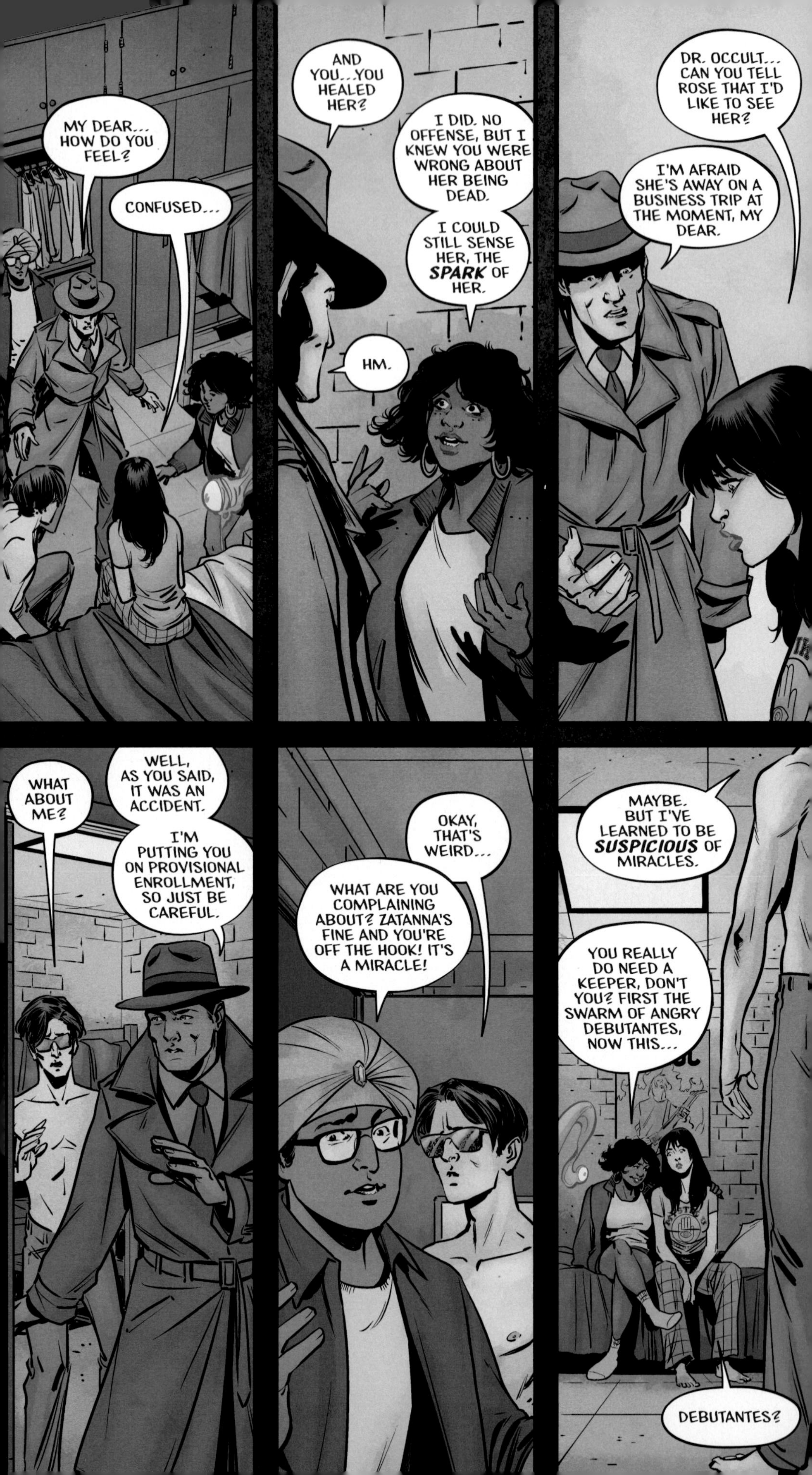
MY DEAR... HOW DO YOU FEEL?
CONFUSED...
AND YOU...YOU HEALED HER?
I DID. NO OFFENSE, BUT I KNEW YOU WERE WRONG ABOUT HER BEING DEAD.
I COULD STILL SENSE HER, THE SPARK OF HER.
HM.
DR. OCCULT... CAN YOU TELL ROSE THAT I'D LIKE TO SEE HER?
I'M AFRAID SHE'S AWAY ON A BUSINESS TRIP AT THE MOMENT, MY DEAR.
WHAT ABOUT ME?
WELL, AS YOU SAID, IT WAS AN ACCIDENT.
I'M PUTTING YOU ON PROVISIONAL ENROLLMENT, SO JUST BE CAREFUL.
OKAY, THAT'S WEIRD...
WHAT ARE YOU COMPLAINING ABOUT? ZATANNA'S FINE AND YOU'RE OFF THE HOOK! IT'S A MIRACLE!
MAYBE. BUT I'VE LEARNED TO BE SUSPICIOUS OF MIRACLES.
YOU REALLY DO NEED A KEEPER, DON'T YOU? FIRST THE SWARM OF ANGRY DEBUTANTES, NOW THIS...
DEBUTANTES?

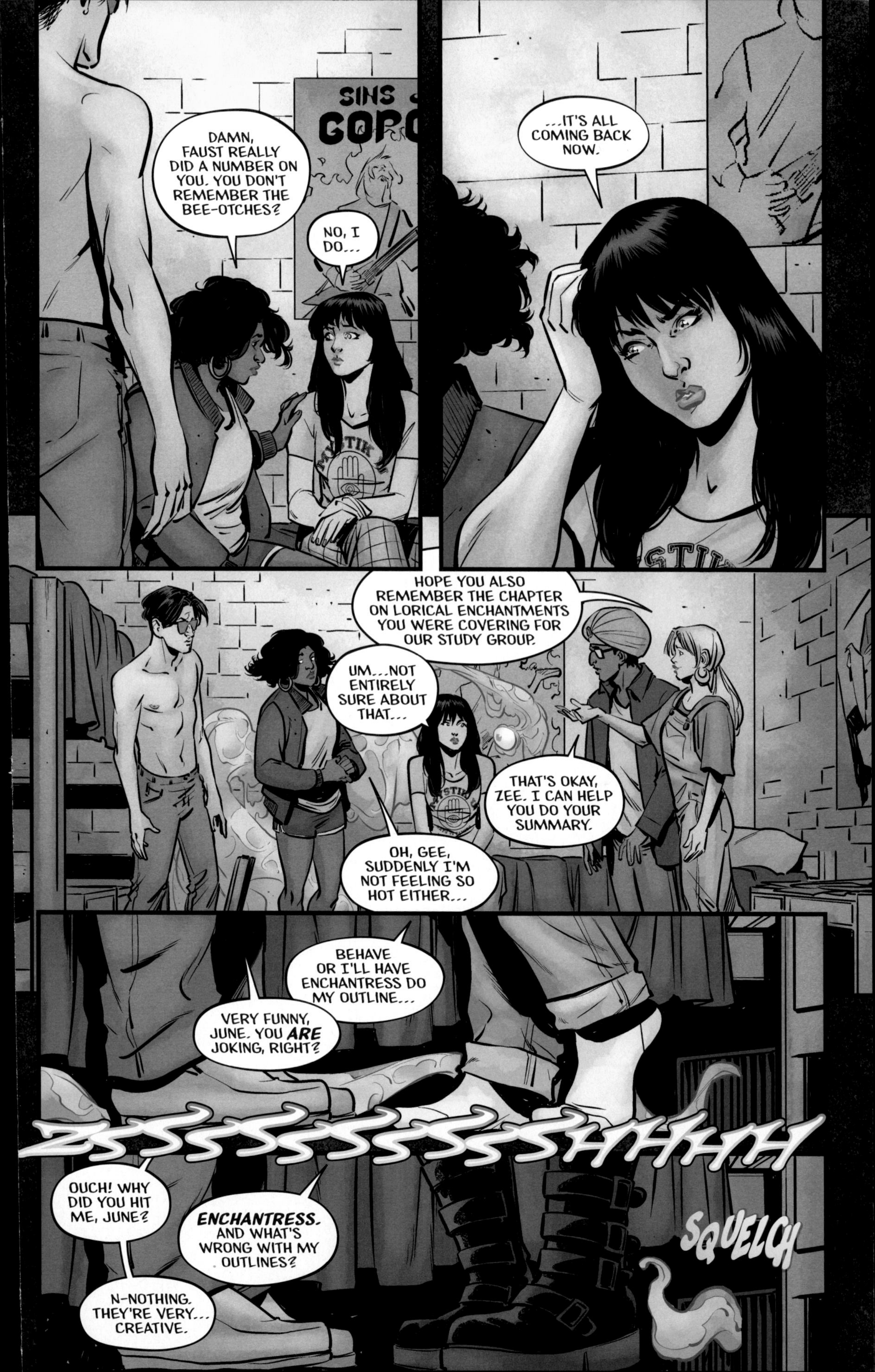
SINS
GOPO
DAMN, FAUST REALLY DID A NUMBER ON YOU. YOU DON'T REMEMBER THE BEE-OTCHES?
NO, I DO...
...IT'S ALL COMING BACK NOW.
HOPE YOU ALSO REMEMBER THE CHAPTER ON LORICAL ENCHANTMENTS YOU WERE COVERING FOR OUR STUDY GROUP.
UM...NOT ENTIRELY SURE ABOUT THAT...
THAT'S OKAY, ZEE. I CAN HELP YOU DO YOUR SUMMARY.
OH, GEE, SUDDENLY I'M NOT FEELING SO HOT EITHER...
BEHAVE OR I'LL HAVE ENCHANTRESS DO MY OUTLINE...
VERY FUNNY, JUNE. YOU **ARE** JOKING, RIGHT?
ZSSSSSSSSSSSHHHHH
OUCH! WHY DID YOU HIT ME, JUNE?
ENCHANTRESS. AND WHAT'S WRONG WITH MY OUTLINES?
N-NOTHING. THEY'RE VERY... CREATIVE.
SQUELCH

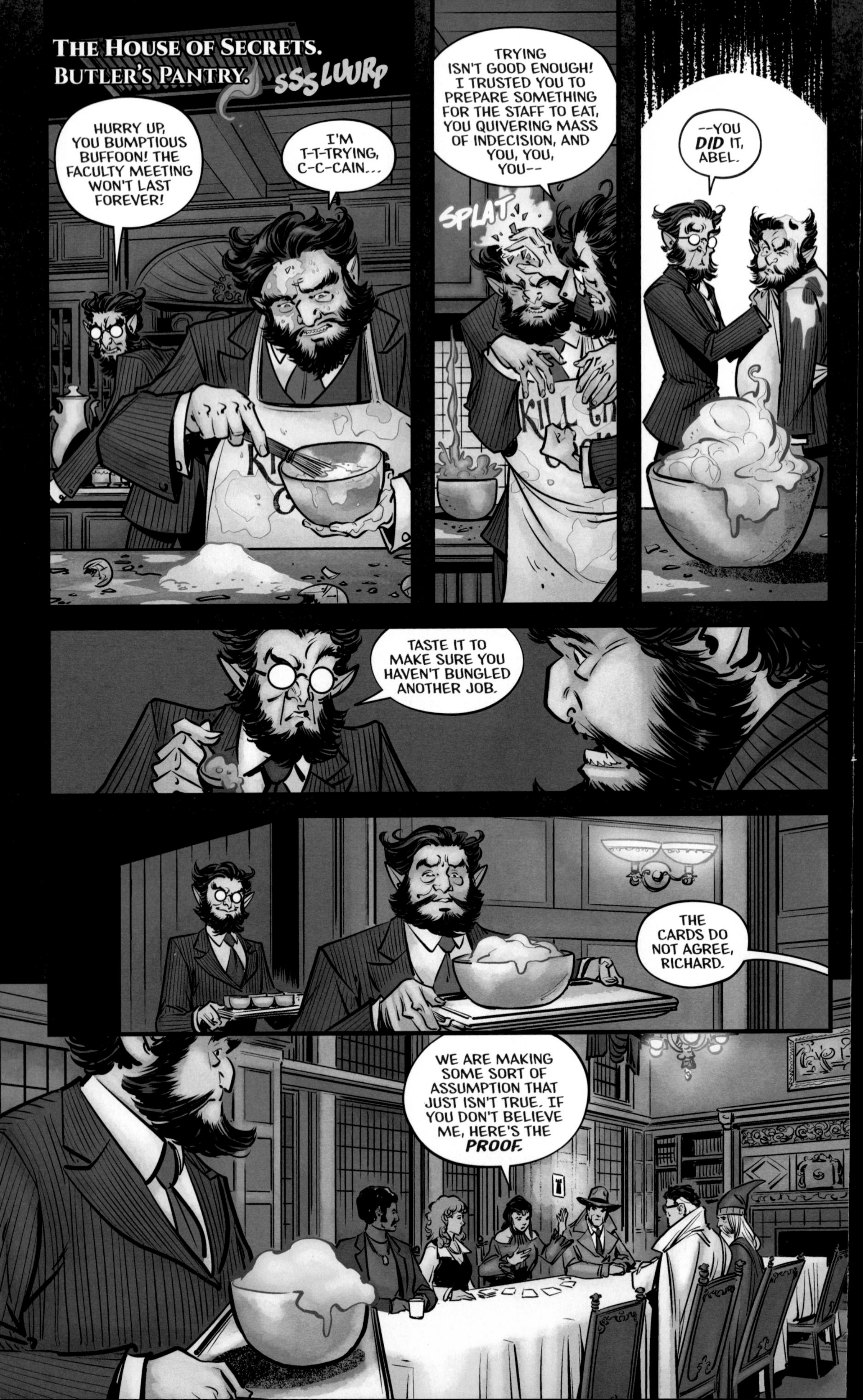
THE HOUSE OF SECRETS. BUTLER'S PANTRY.
SSSLUURP
HURRY UP, YOU BUMPTIOUS BUFFOON! THE FACULTY MEETING WON'T LAST FOREVER!
I'M T-T-TRYING, C-C-CAIN...
TRYING ISN'T GOOD ENOUGH! I TRUSTED YOU TO PREPARE SOMETHING FOR THE STAFF TO EAT, YOU QUIVERING MASS OF INDECISION, AND YOU, YOU, YOU--
SPLAT
--YOU DID IT, ABEL.
TASTE IT TO MAKE SURE YOU HAVEN'T BUNGLED ANOTHER JOB.
THE CARDS DO NOT AGREE, RICHARD.
WE ARE MAKING SOME SORT OF ASSUMPTION THAT JUST ISN'T TRUE. IF YOU DON'T BELIEVE ME, HERE'S THE PROOF.

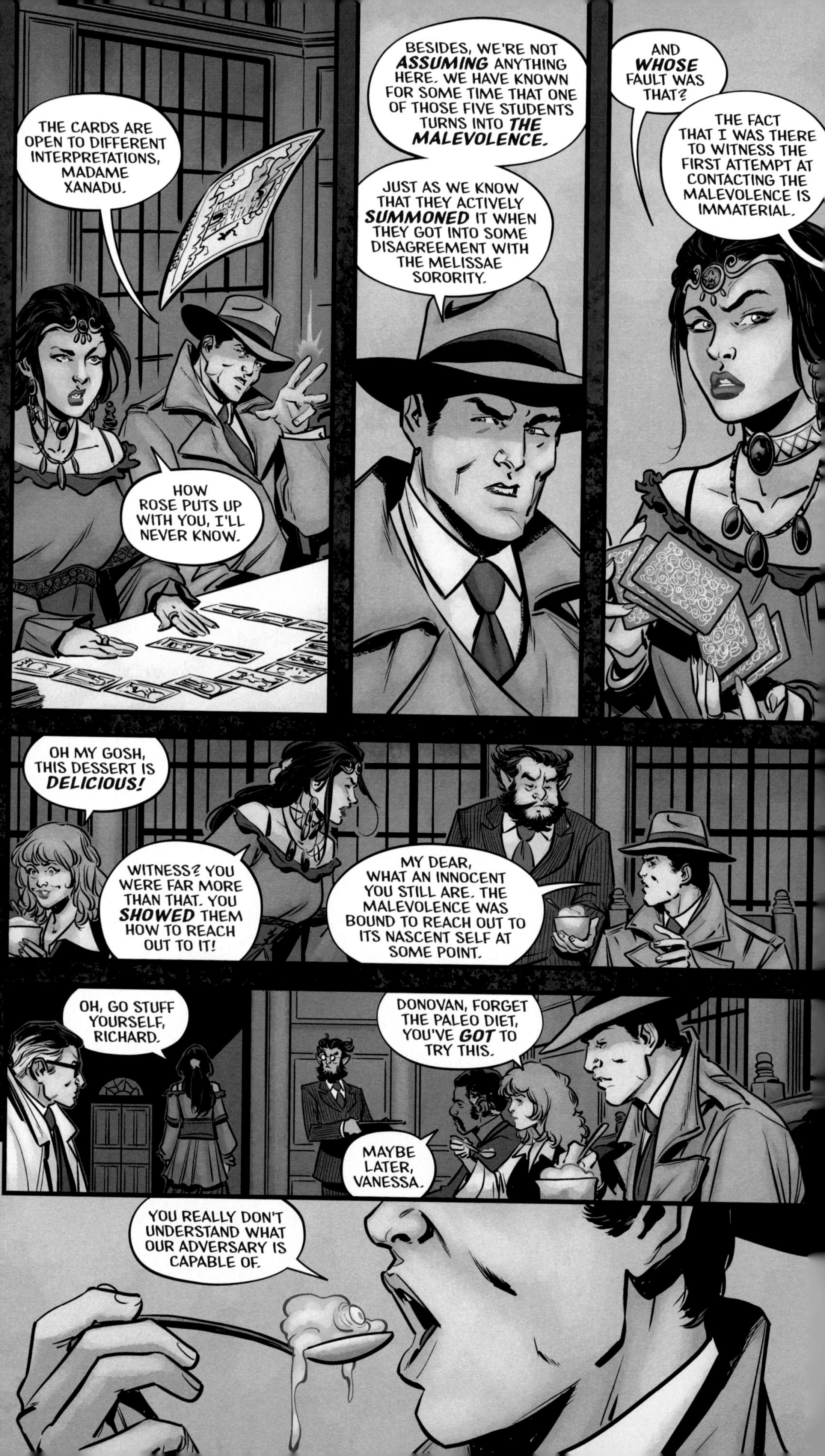
THE CARDS ARE OPEN TO DIFFERENT INTERPRETATIONS, MADAME XANADU.
HOW ROSE PUTS UP WITH YOU, I'LL NEVER KNOW.
BESIDES, WE'RE NOT ASSUMING ANYTHING HERE. WE HAVE KNOWN FOR SOME TIME THAT ONE OF THOSE FIVE STUDENTS TURNS INTO THE MALEVOLENCE.
JUST AS WE KNOW THAT THEY ACTIVELY SUMMONED IT WHEN THEY GOT INTO SOME DISAGREEMENT WITH THE MELISSAE SORORITY.
AND WHOSE FAULT WAS THAT?
THE FACT THAT I WAS THERE TO WITNESS THE FIRST ATTEMPT AT CONTACTING THE MALEVOLENCE IS IMMATERIAL.
OH MY GOSH, THIS DESSERT IS DELICIOUS!
WITNESS? YOU WERE FAR MORE THAN THAT. YOU SHOWED THEM HOW TO REACH OUT TO IT!
MY DEAR, WHAT AN INNOCENT YOU STILL ARE. THE MALEVOLENCE WAS BOUND TO REACH OUT TO ITS NASCENT SELF AT SOME POINT.
OH, GO STUFF YOURSELF, RICHARD.
DONOVAN, FORGET THE PALEO DIET, YOU'VE GOT TO TRY THIS.
MAYBE LATER, VANESSA.
YOU REALLY DON'T UNDERSTAND WHAT OUR ADVERSARY IS CAPABLE OF.

DON'T YOU WANT SOME OF THE DESSERT, MR. E? IT'S DELICIOUS!

YES, YOU *MUST* TRY SOME.

I AM FASTING TO PREPARE MYSELF FOR THE BATTLE TO COME, MERLIN.

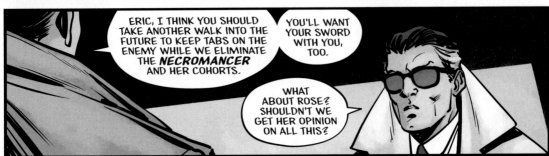

ERIC, I THINK YOU SHOULD TAKE ANOTHER WALK INTO THE FUTURE TO KEEP TABS ON THE ENEMY WHILE WE ELIMINATE THE *NECROMANCER* AND HER COHORTS.

YOU'LL WANT YOUR SWORD WITH YOU, TOO.

WHAT ABOUT ROSE? SHOULDN'T WE GET HER OPINION ON ALL THIS?

DON'T WORRY, I'VE SPOKEN TO HER...

"...AND SHE'S 100 PERCENT ON BOARD."

UNBELIEVABLE! MAY A LONG-HAIRED CARPATHIAN SHE-WOLF SOIL HIS BEDDING.

IT'S ONE THING TO DISREGARD ME, BUT HE'S IGNORING THE CARDS, ROSE!

I KNOW, NIM. HE WANTS A SIMPLE SOLUTION, SO HE'S IGNORING EVERY CLUE THAT TELLS HIM HE CAN'T JUST RESOLVE THIS WITH FORCE.

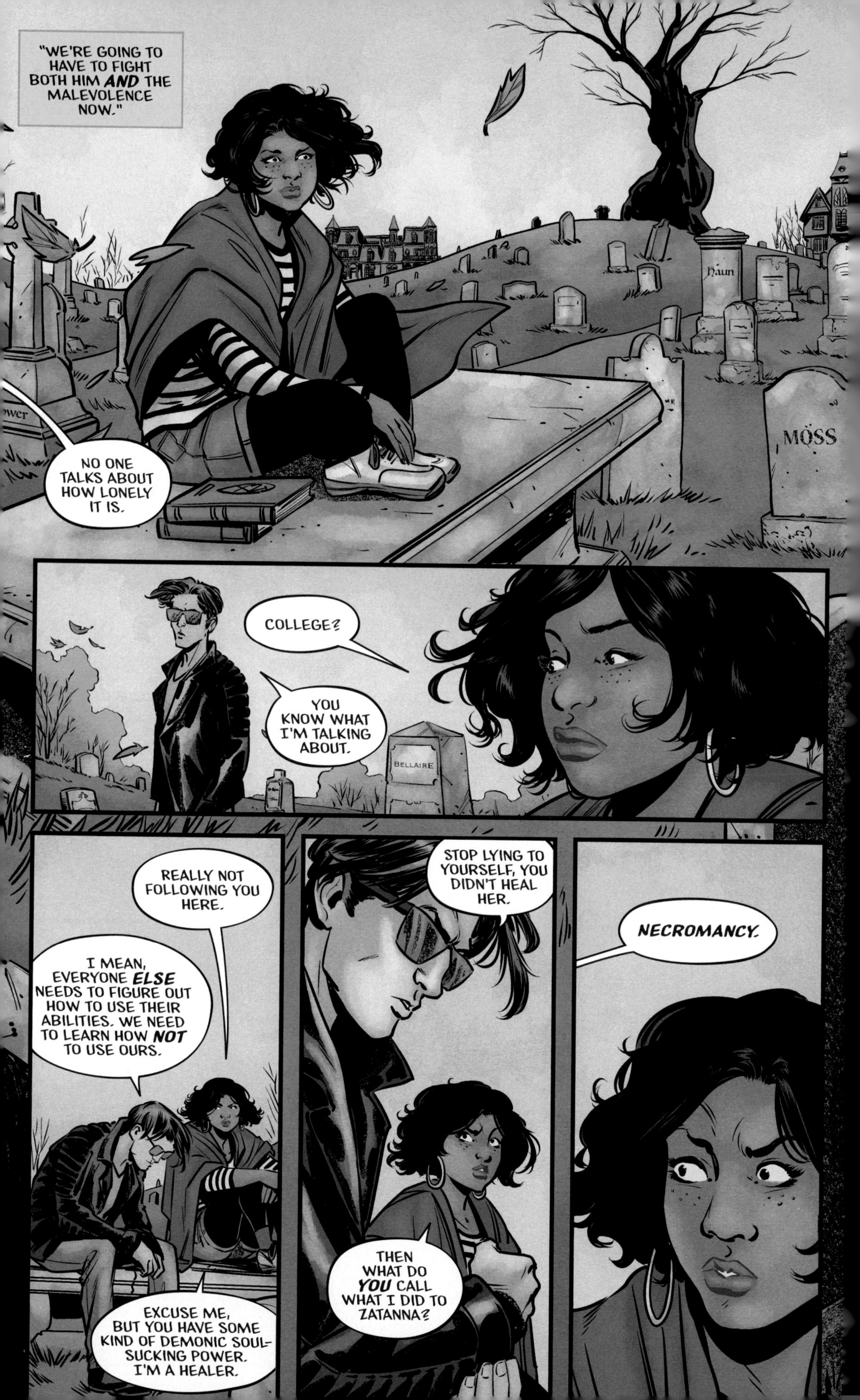
"WE'RE GOING TO HAVE TO FIGHT BOTH HIM AND THE MALEVOLENCE NOW."
NO ONE TALKS ABOUT HOW LONELY IT IS.
Haun
MOSS
COLLEGE?
YOU KNOW WHAT I'M TALKING ABOUT.
BELLAIRE
REALLY NOT FOLLOWING YOU HERE.
I MEAN, EVERYONE ELSE NEEDS TO FIGURE OUT HOW TO USE THEIR ABILITIES. WE NEED TO LEARN HOW NOT TO USE OURS.
EXCUSE ME, BUT YOU HAVE SOME KIND OF DEMONIC SOUL-SUCKING POWER. I'M A HEALER.
STOP LYING TO YOURSELF, YOU DIDN'T HEAL HER.
THEN WHAT DO YOU CALL WHAT I DID TO ZATANNA?
NECROMANCY.

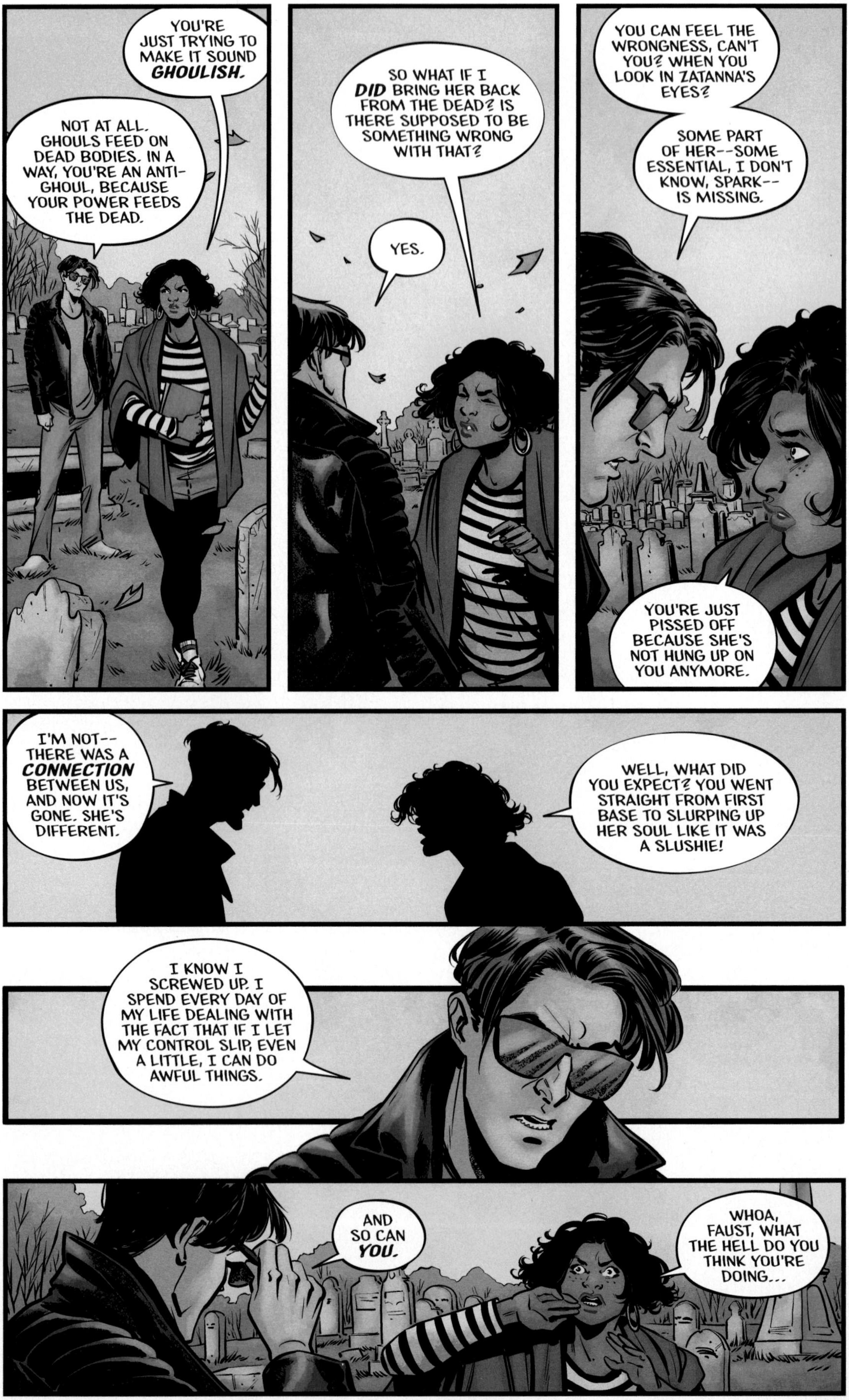
YOU'RE JUST TRYING TO MAKE IT SOUND GHOULISH.
NOT AT ALL. GHOULS FEED ON DEAD BODIES. IN A WAY, YOU'RE AN ANTI-GHOUL, BECAUSE YOUR POWER FEEDS THE DEAD.
SO WHAT IF I DID BRING HER BACK FROM THE DEAD? IS THERE SUPPOSED TO BE SOMETHING WRONG WITH THAT?
YES.
YOU CAN FEEL THE WRONGNESS, CAN'T YOU? WHEN YOU LOOK IN ZATANNA'S EYES?
SOME PART OF HER--SOME ESSENTIAL, I DON'T KNOW, SPARK--IS MISSING.
YOU'RE JUST PISSED OFF BECAUSE SHE'S NOT HUNG UP ON YOU ANYMORE.
I'M NOT--THERE WAS A CONNECTION BETWEEN US, AND NOW IT'S GONE. SHE'S DIFFERENT.
WELL, WHAT DID YOU EXPECT? YOU WENT STRAIGHT FROM FIRST BASE TO SLURPING UP HER SOUL LIKE IT WAS A SLUSHIE!
I KNOW I SCREWED UP. I SPEND EVERY DAY OF MY LIFE DEALING WITH THE FACT THAT IF I LET MY CONTROL SLIP, EVEN A LITTLE, I CAN DO AWFUL THINGS.
AND SO CAN YOU.
WHOA, FAUST, WHAT THE HELL DO YOU THINK YOU'RE DOING...

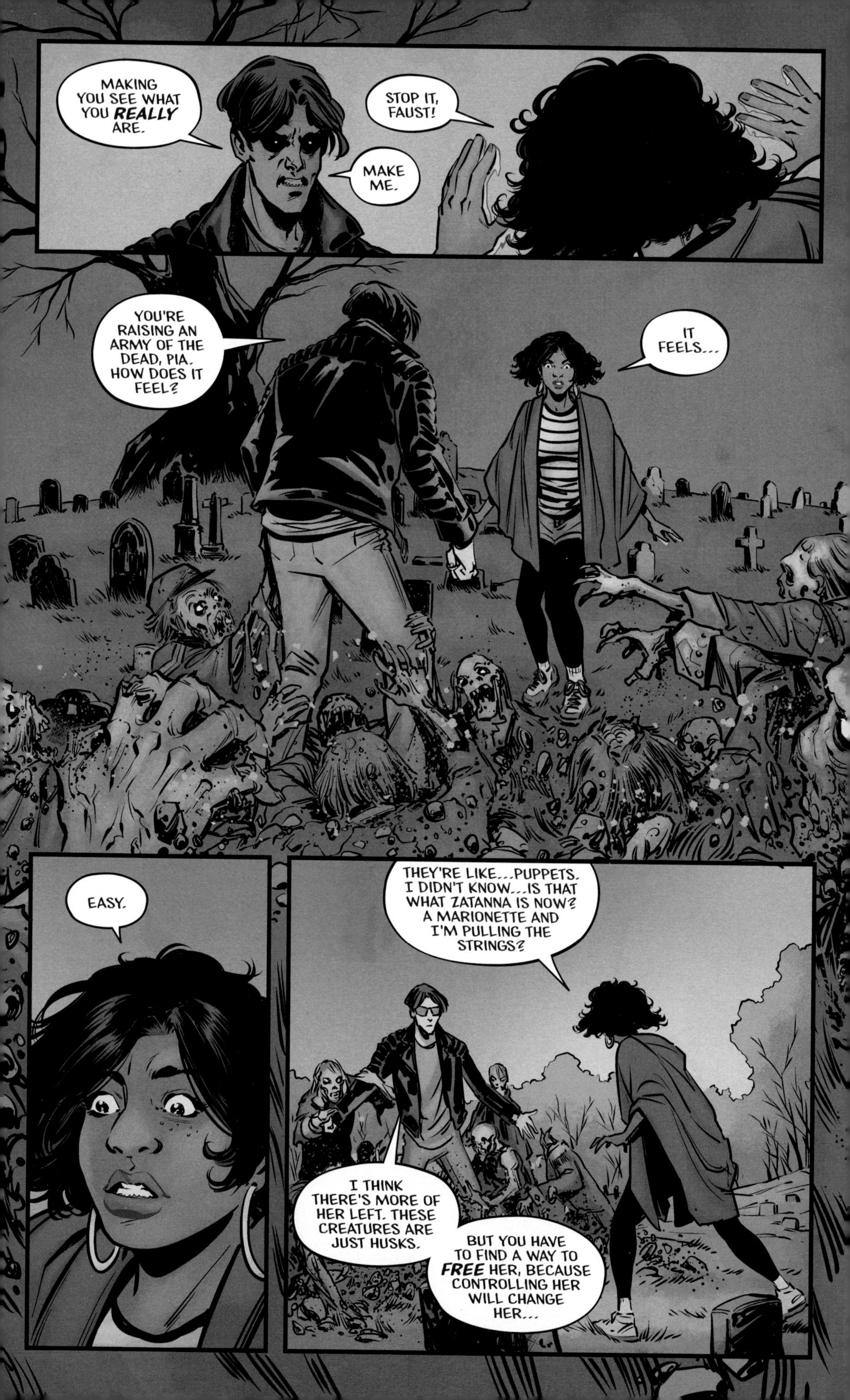
MAKING YOU SEE WHAT YOU REALLY ARE.
STOP IT, FAUST!
MAKE ME.
YOU'RE RAISING AN ARMY OF THE DEAD, PIA. HOW DOES IT FEEL?
IT FEELS...
EASY.
THEY'RE LIKE...PUPPETS. I DIDN'T KNOW...IS THAT WHAT ZATANNA IS NOW? A MARIONETTE AND I'M PULLING THE STRINGS?
I THINK THERE'S MORE OF HER LEFT. THESE CREATURES ARE JUST HUSKS.
BUT YOU HAVE TO FIND A WAY TO FREE HER, BECAUSE CONTROLLING HER WILL CHANGE HER...

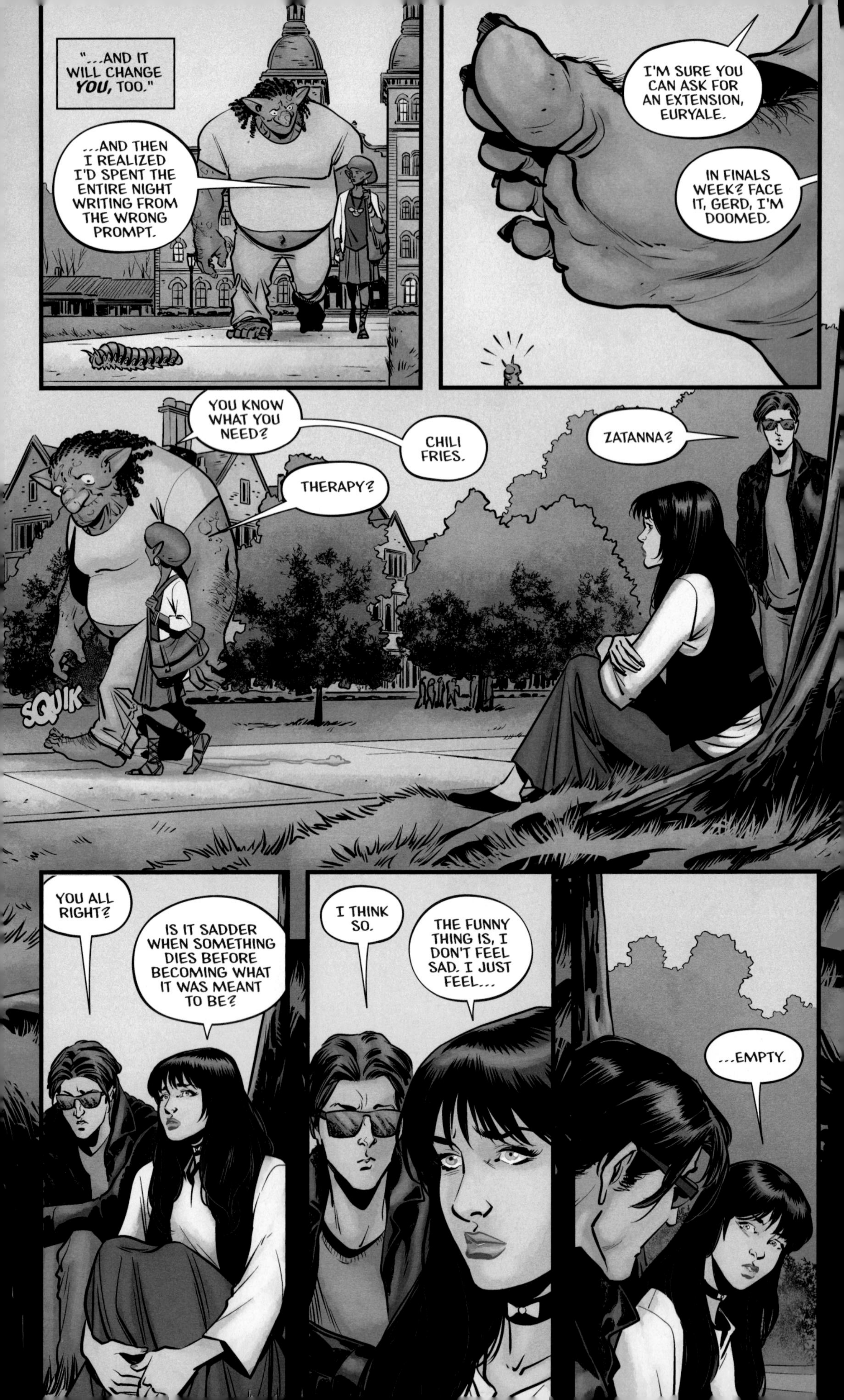
"...AND IT WILL CHANGE YOU, TOO."
...AND THEN I REALIZED I'D SPENT THE ENTIRE NIGHT WRITING FROM THE WRONG PROMPT.
I'M SURE YOU CAN ASK FOR AN EXTENSION, EURYALE.
IN FINALS WEEK? FACE IT, GERD, I'M DOOMED.
YOU KNOW WHAT YOU NEED?
CHILI FRIES.
THERAPY?
SQUIK
ZATANNA?
YOU ALL RIGHT?
IS IT SADDER WHEN SOMETHING DIES BEFORE BECOMING WHAT IT WAS MEANT TO BE?
I THINK SO.
THE FUNNY THING IS, I DON'T FEEL SAD. I JUST FEEL...
...EMPTY.

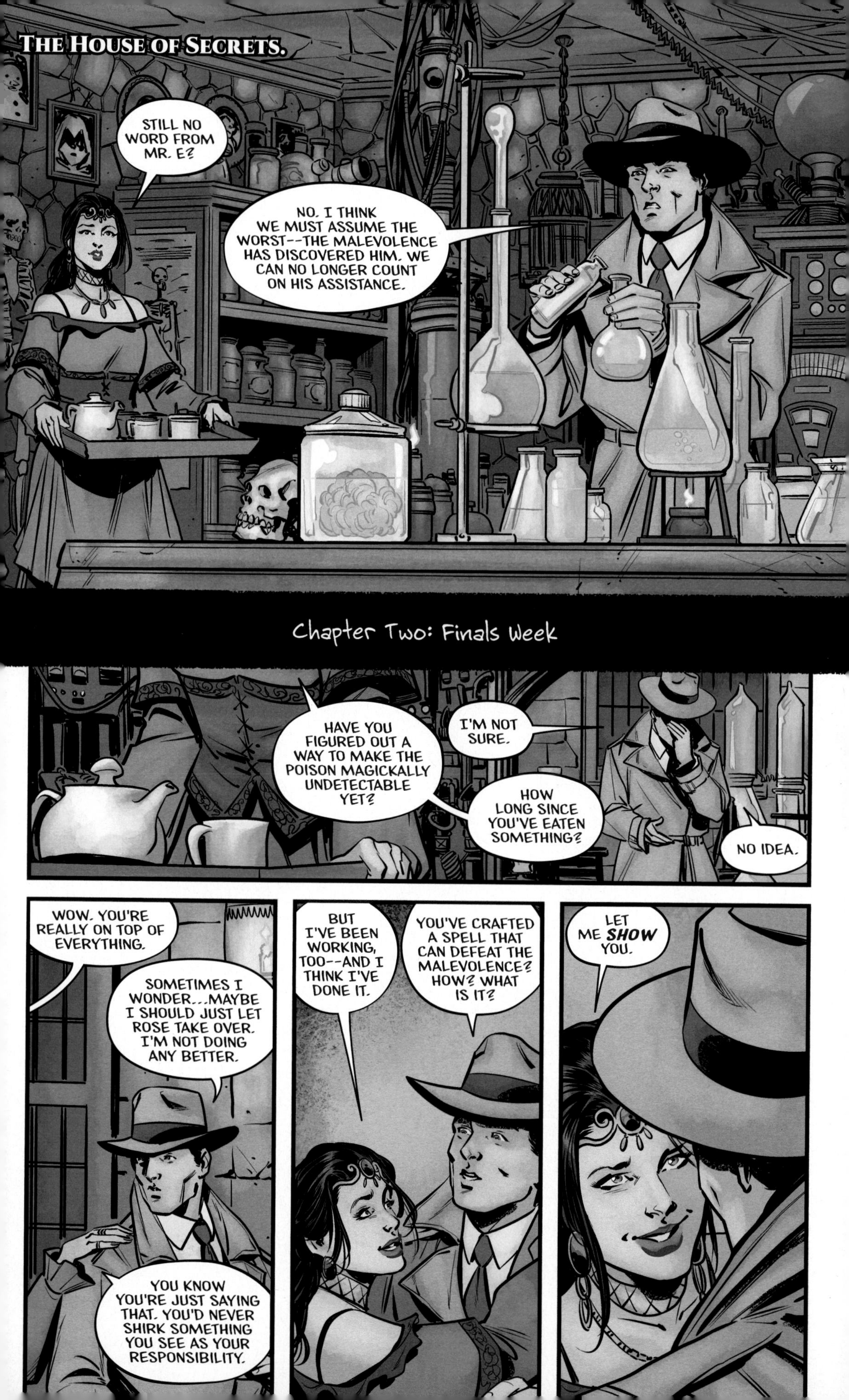
THE HOUSE OF SECRETS.
STILL NO WORD FROM MR. E?
NO. I THINK WE MUST ASSUME THE WORST--THE MALEVOLENCE HAS DISCOVERED HIM. WE CAN NO LONGER COUNT ON HIS ASSISTANCE.
Chapter Two: Finals Week
HAVE YOU FIGURED OUT A WAY TO MAKE THE POISON MAGICKALLY UNDETECTABLE YET?
I'M NOT SURE.
HOW LONG SINCE YOU'VE EATEN SOMETHING?
NO IDEA.
WOW. YOU'RE REALLY ON TOP OF EVERYTHING.
SOMETIMES I WONDER...MAYBE I SHOULD JUST LET ROSE TAKE OVER. I'M NOT DOING ANY BETTER.
YOU KNOW YOU'RE JUST SAYING THAT. YOU'D NEVER SHIRK SOMETHING YOU SEE AS YOUR RESPONSIBILITY.
BUT I'VE BEEN WORKING, TOO--AND I THINK I'VE DONE IT.
YOU'VE CRAFTED A SPELL THAT CAN DEFEAT THE MALEVOLENCE? HOW? WHAT IS IT?
LET ME SHOW YOU.

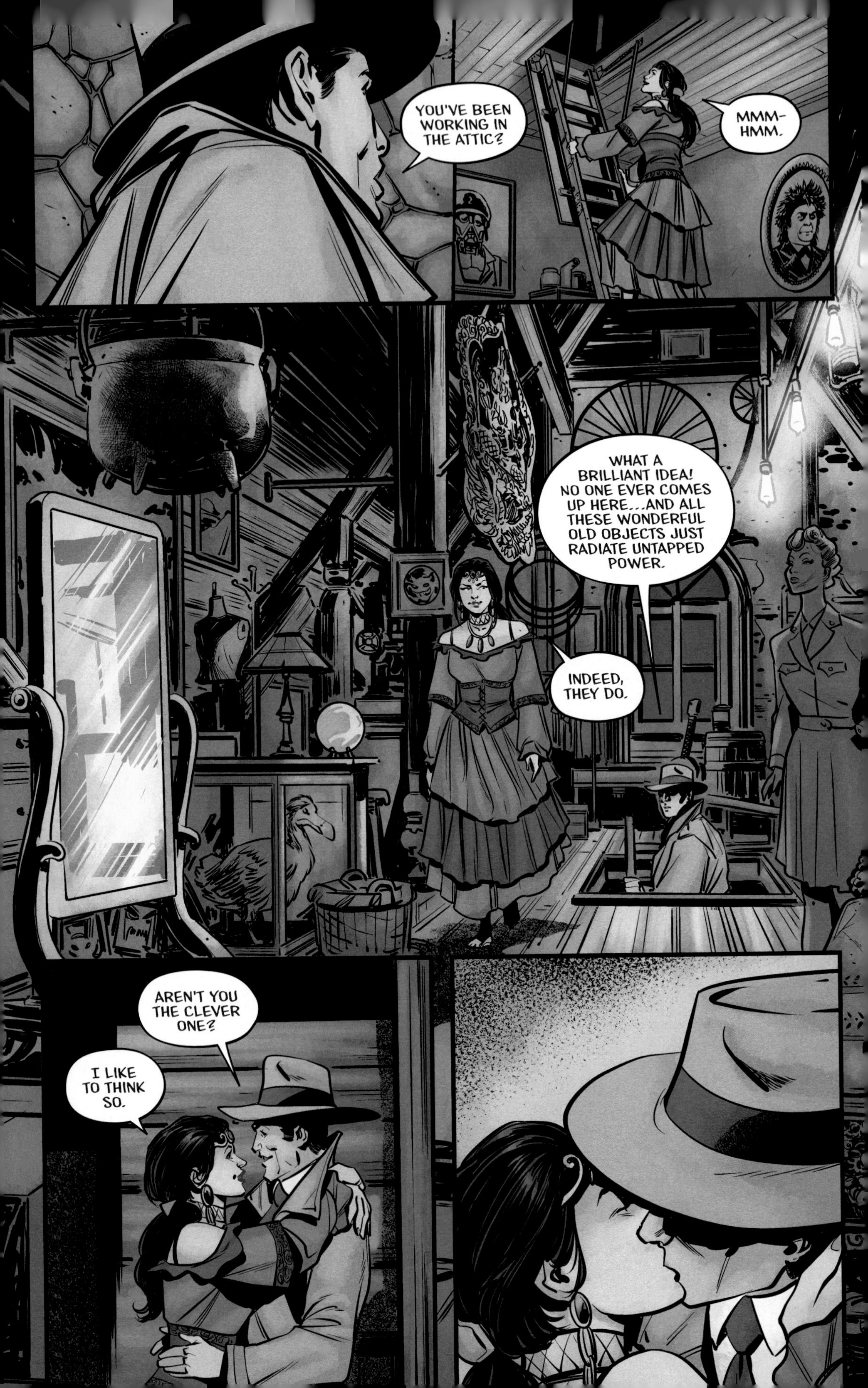
YOU'VE BEEN WORKING IN THE ATTIC?
MMM-HMM.
WHAT A BRILLIANT IDEA! NO ONE EVER COMES UP HERE...AND ALL THESE WONDERFUL OLD OBJECTS JUST RADIATE UNTAPPED POWER.
INDEED, THEY DO.
AREN'T YOU THE CLEVER ONE?
I LIKE TO THINK SO.

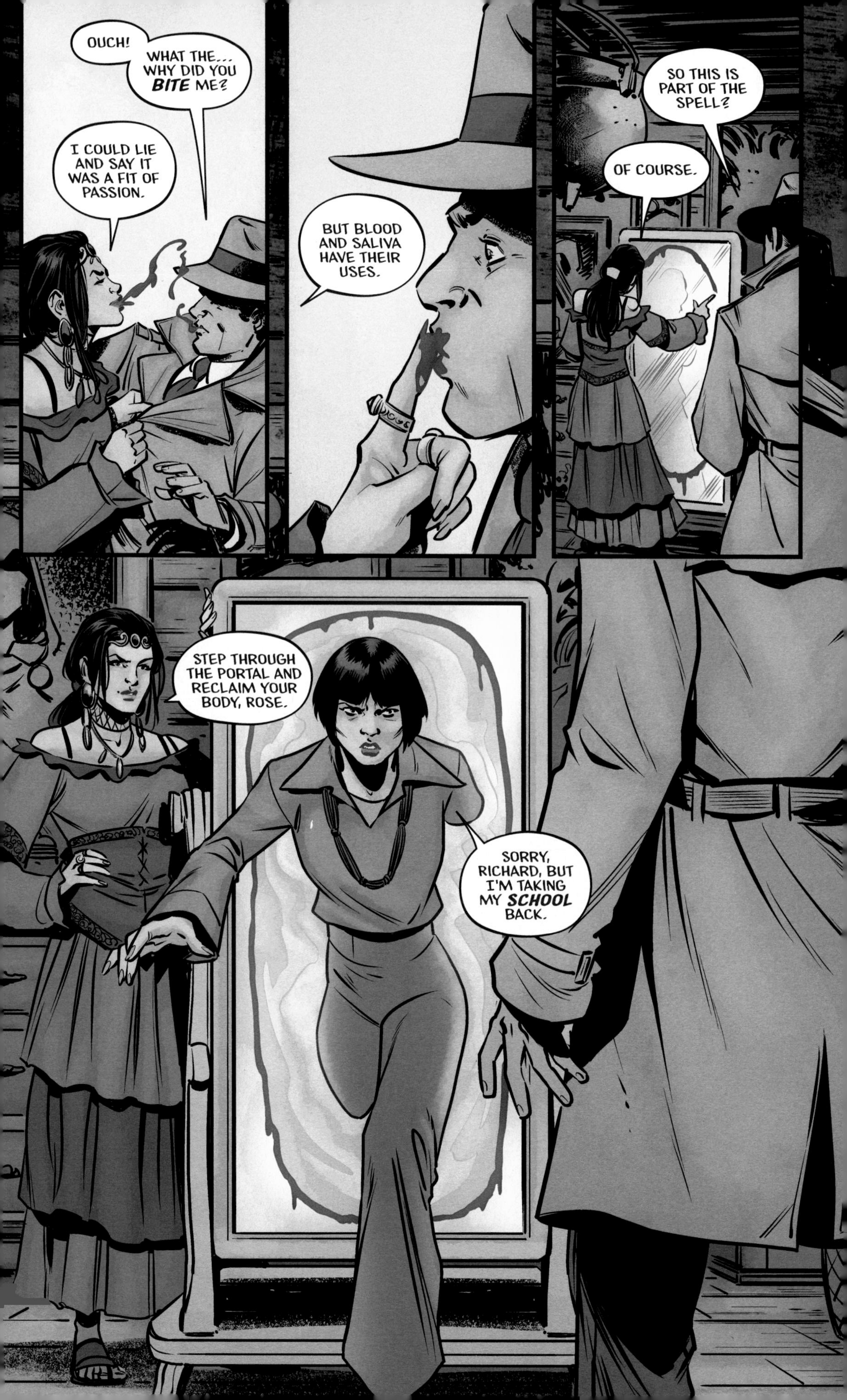
OUCH!
WHAT THE... WHY DID YOU BITE ME?
I COULD LIE AND SAY IT WAS A FIT OF PASSION.
BUT BLOOD AND SALIVA HAVE THEIR USES.
SO THIS IS PART OF THE SPELL?
OF COURSE.
STEP THROUGH THE PORTAL AND RECLAIM YOUR BODY, ROSE.
SORRY, RICHARD, BUT I'M TAKING MY SCHOOL BACK.

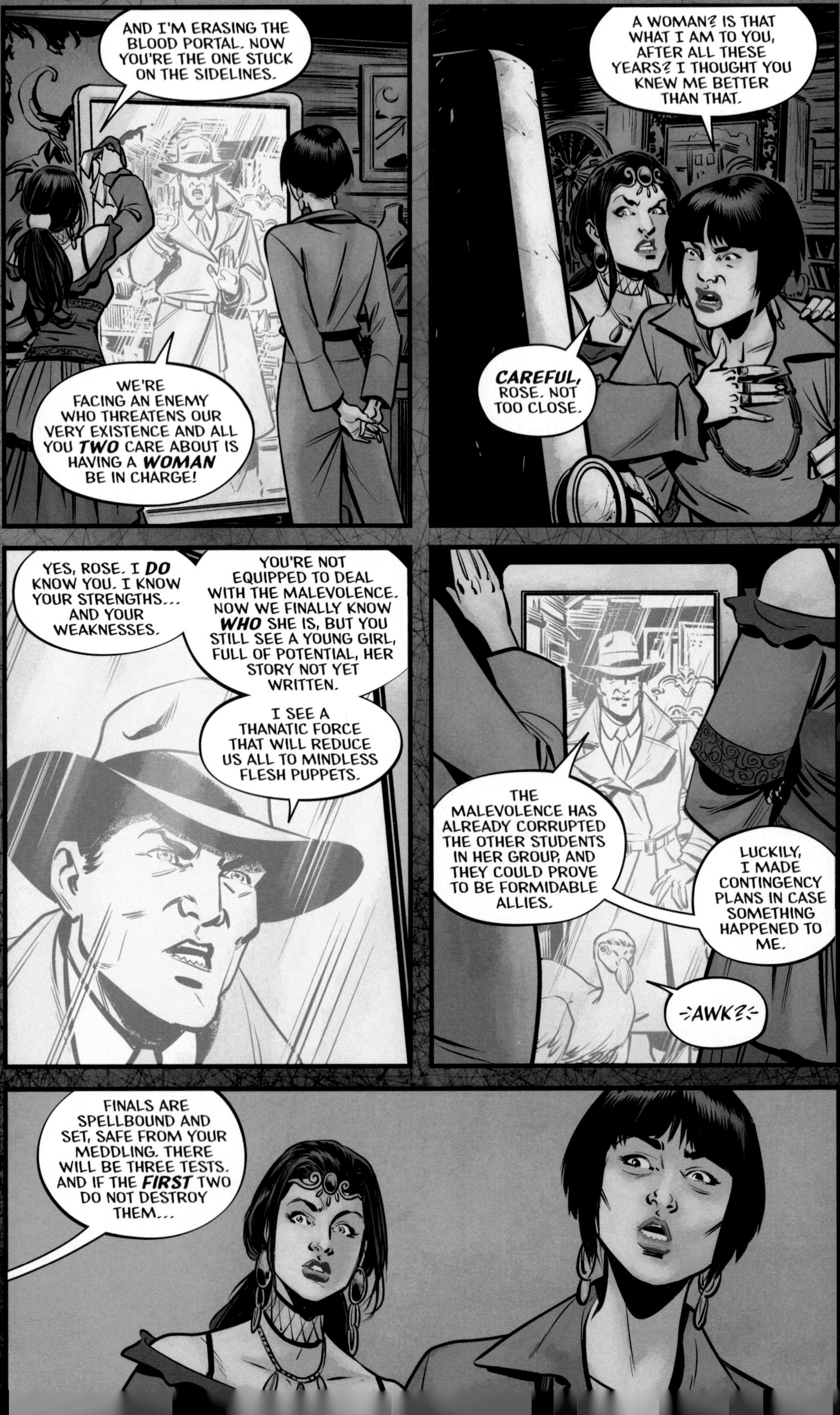
AND I'M ERASING THE BLOOD PORTAL. NOW YOU'RE THE ONE STUCK ON THE SIDELINES.
WE'RE FACING AN ENEMY WHO THREATENS OUR VERY EXISTENCE AND ALL YOU *TWO* CARE ABOUT IS HAVING A *WOMAN* BE IN CHARGE!
A WOMAN? IS THAT WHAT I AM TO YOU, AFTER ALL THESE YEARS? I THOUGHT YOU KNEW ME BETTER THAN THAT.
CAREFUL, ROSE. NOT TOO CLOSE.
YES, ROSE. I *DO* KNOW YOU. I KNOW YOUR STRENGTHS... AND YOUR WEAKNESSES.
YOU'RE NOT EQUIPPED TO DEAL WITH THE MALEVOLENCE. NOW WE FINALLY KNOW *WHO* SHE IS, BUT YOU STILL SEE A YOUNG GIRL, FULL OF POTENTIAL, HER STORY NOT YET WRITTEN.
I SEE A THANATIC FORCE THAT WILL REDUCE US ALL TO MINDLESS FLESH PUPPETS.
THE MALEVOLENCE HAS ALREADY CORRUPTED THE OTHER STUDENTS IN HER GROUP, AND THEY COULD PROVE TO BE FORMIDABLE ALLIES.
LUCKILY, I MADE CONTINGENCY PLANS IN CASE SOMETHING HAPPENED TO ME.
AWK?
FINALS ARE SPELLBOUND AND SET, SAFE FROM YOUR MEDDLING. THERE WILL BE THREE TESTS. AND IF THE *FIRST* TWO DO NOT DESTROY THEM...

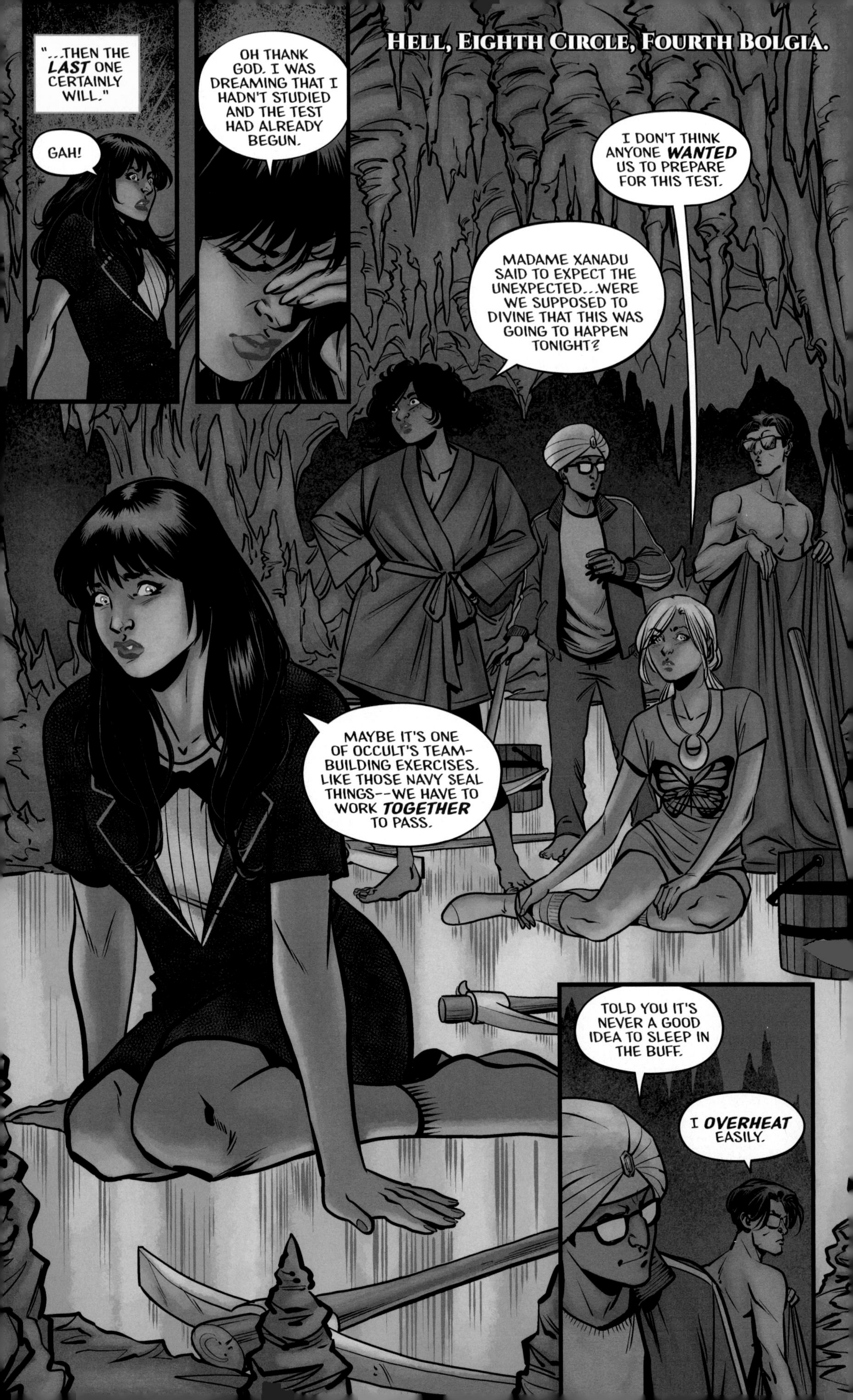
"...THEN THE LAST ONE CERTAINLY WILL."
GAH!
OH THANK GOD. I WAS DREAMING THAT I HADN'T STUDIED AND THE TEST HAD ALREADY BEGUN.
HELL, EIGHTH CIRCLE, FOURTH BOLGIA.
I DON'T THINK ANYONE WANTED US TO PREPARE FOR THIS TEST.
MADAME XANADU SAID TO EXPECT THE UNEXPECTED...WERE WE SUPPOSED TO DIVINE THAT THIS WAS GOING TO HAPPEN TONIGHT?
MAYBE IT'S ONE OF OCCULT'S TEAM-BUILDING EXERCISES. LIKE THOSE NAVY SEAL THINGS--WE HAVE TO WORK TOGETHER TO PASS.
TOLD YOU IT'S NEVER A GOOD IDEA TO SLEEP IN THE BUFF.
I OVERHEAT EASILY.

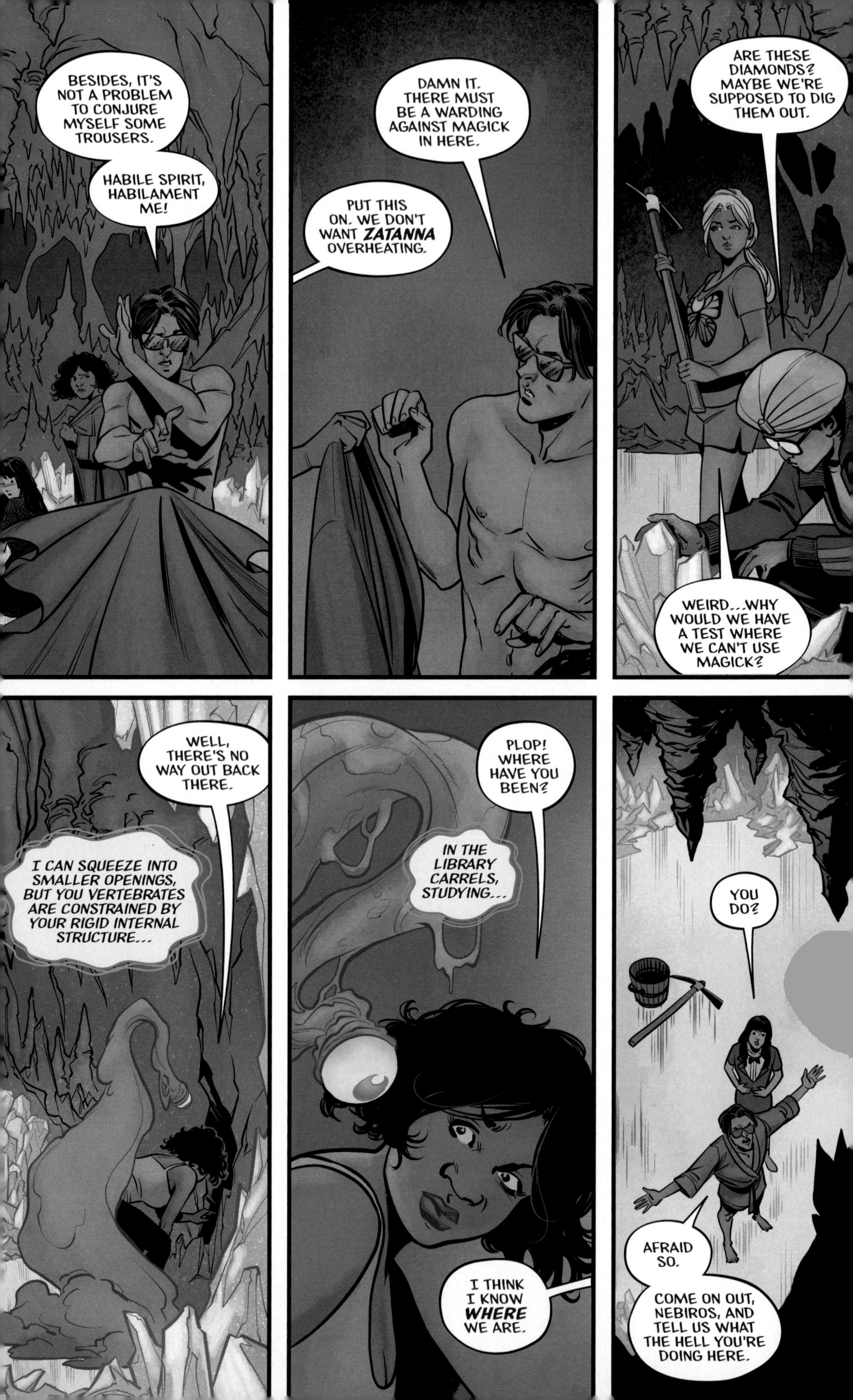
BESIDES, IT'S NOT A PROBLEM TO CONJURE MYSELF SOME TROUSERS.
HABILE SPIRIT, HABILAMENT ME!
DAMN IT. THERE MUST BE A WARDING AGAINST MAGICK IN HERE.
PUT THIS ON. WE DON'T WANT ZATANNA OVERHEATING.
ARE THESE DIAMONDS? MAYBE WE'RE SUPPOSED TO DIG THEM OUT.
WEIRD...WHY WOULD WE HAVE A TEST WHERE WE CAN'T USE MAGICK?
WELL, THERE'S NO WAY OUT BACK THERE.
I CAN SQUEEZE INTO SMALLER OPENINGS, BUT YOU VERTEBRATES ARE CONSTRAINED BY YOUR RIGID INTERNAL STRUCTURE...
PLOP! WHERE HAVE YOU BEEN?
IN THE LIBRARY CARRELS, STUDYING...
I THINK I KNOW WHERE WE ARE.
YOU DO?
AFRAID SO.
COME ON OUT, NEBIROS, AND TELL US WHAT THE HELL YOU'RE DOING HERE.

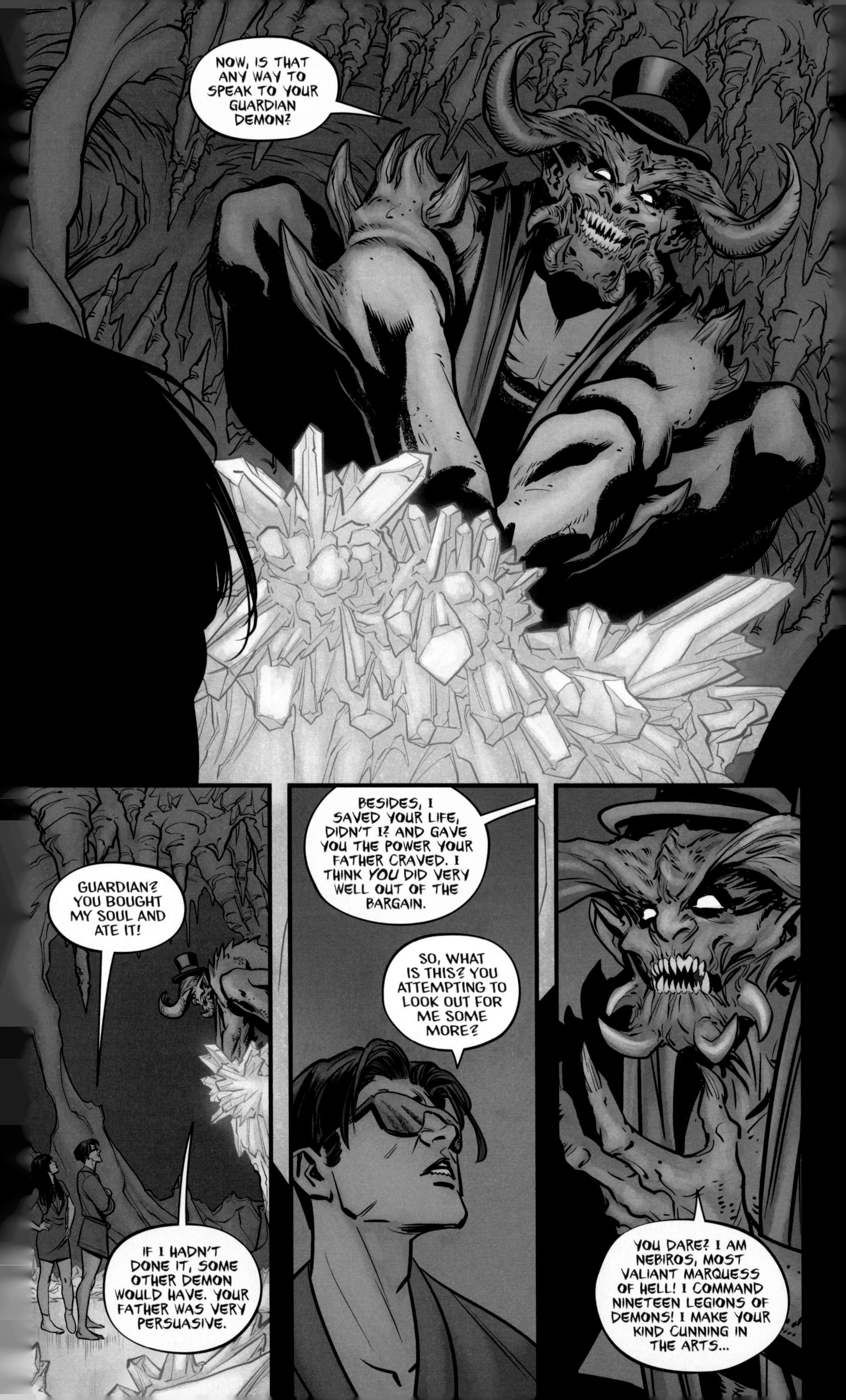
NOW, IS THAT ANY WAY TO SPEAK TO YOUR GUARDIAN DEMON?
GUARDIAN? YOU BOUGHT MY SOUL AND ATE IT!
IF I HADN'T DONE IT, SOME OTHER DEMON WOULD HAVE. YOUR FATHER WAS VERY PERSUASIVE.
BESIDES, I SAVED YOUR LIFE, DIDN'T I? AND GAVE YOU THE POWER YOUR FATHER CRAVED. I THINK YOU DID VERY WELL OUT OF THE BARGAIN.
SO, WHAT IS THIS? YOU ATTEMPTING TO LOOK OUT FOR ME SOME MORE?
YOU DARE? I AM NEBIROS, MOST VALIANT MARQUESS OF HELL! I COMMAND NINETEEN LEGIONS OF DEMONS! I MAKE YOUR KIND CUNNING IN THE ARTS...

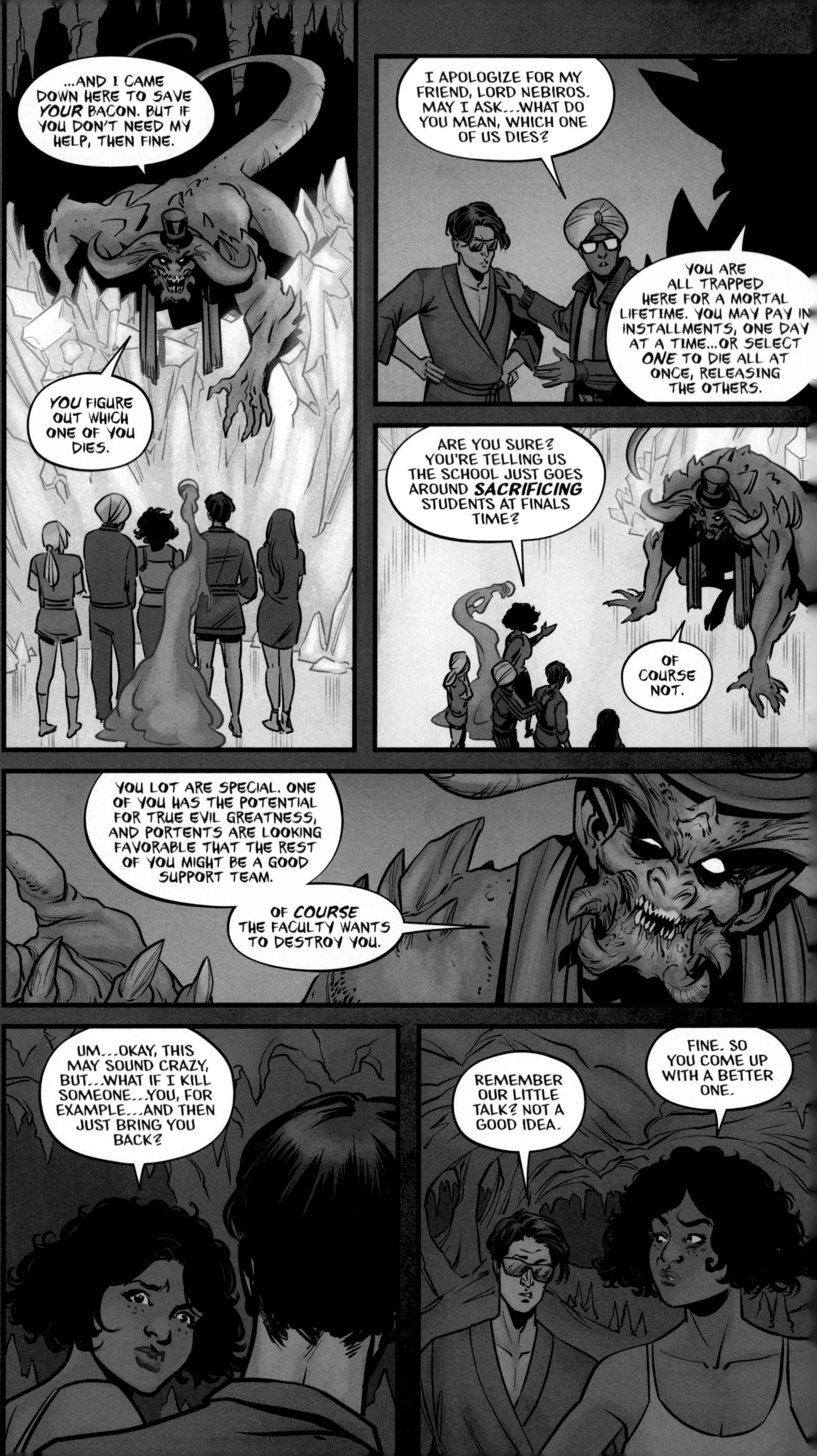
...AND I CAME DOWN HERE TO SAVE YOUR BACON. BUT IF YOU DON'T NEED MY HELP, THEN FINE.
YOU FIGURE OUT WHICH ONE OF YOU DIES.
I APOLOGIZE FOR MY FRIEND, LORD NEBIROS. MAY I ASK...WHAT DO YOU MEAN, WHICH ONE OF US DIES?
YOU ARE ALL TRAPPED HERE FOR A MORTAL LIFETIME. YOU MAY PAY IN INSTALLMENTS, ONE DAY AT A TIME...OR SELECT ONE TO DIE ALL AT ONCE, RELEASING THE OTHERS.
ARE YOU SURE? YOU'RE TELLING US THE SCHOOL JUST GOES AROUND SACRIFICING STUDENTS AT FINALS TIME?
OF COURSE NOT.
YOU LOT ARE SPECIAL. ONE OF YOU HAS THE POTENTIAL FOR TRUE EVIL GREATNESS, AND PORTENTS ARE LOOKING FAVORABLE THAT THE REST OF YOU MIGHT BE A GOOD SUPPORT TEAM.
OF COURSE THE FACULTY WANTS TO DESTROY YOU.
UM...OKAY, THIS MAY SOUND CRAZY, BUT...WHAT IF I KILL SOMEONE...YOU, FOR EXAMPLE...AND THEN JUST BRING YOU BACK?
REMEMBER OUR LITTLE TALK? NOT A GOOD IDEA.
FINE. SO YOU COME UP WITH A BETTER ONE.

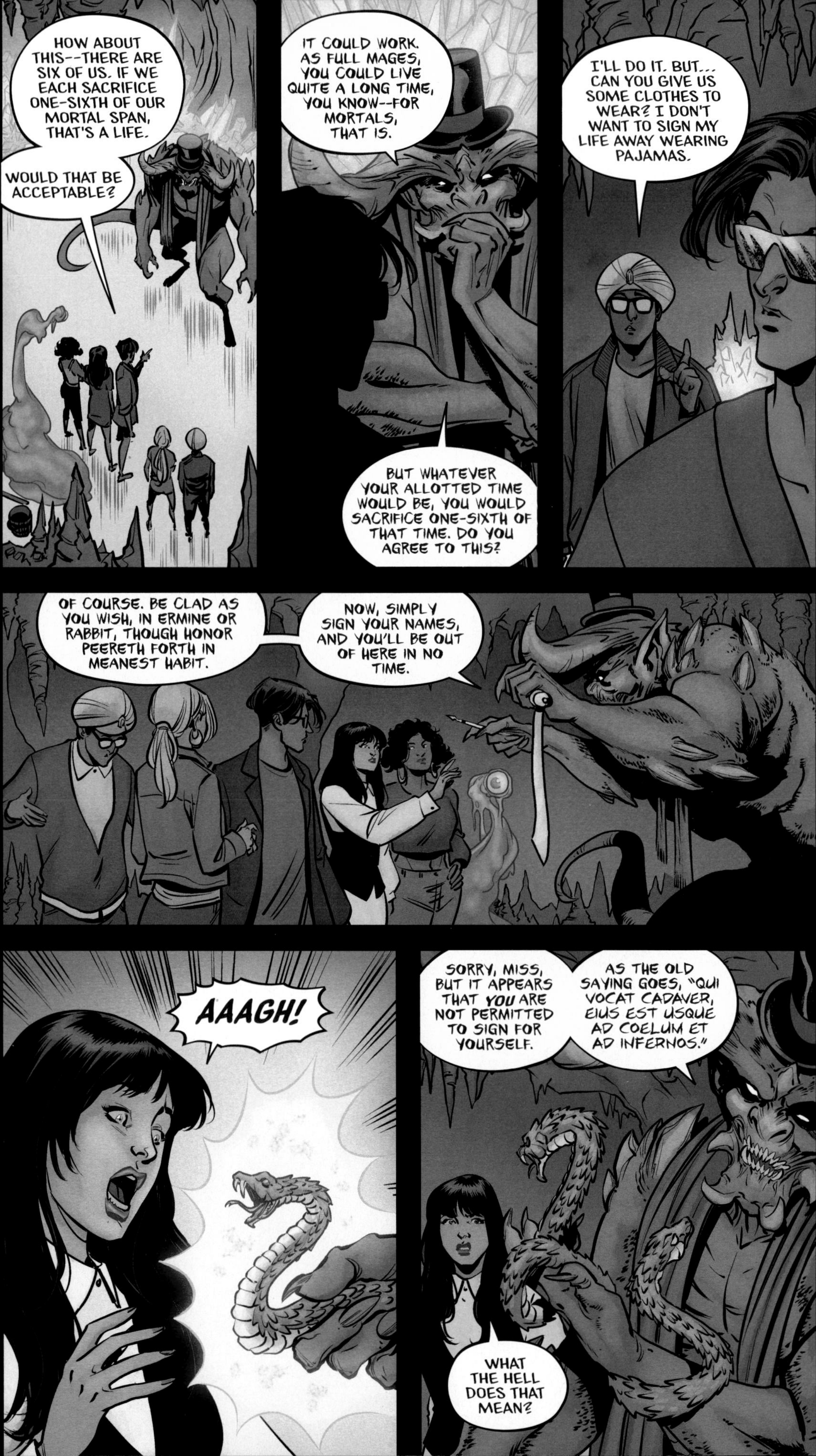
HOW ABOUT THIS--THERE ARE SIX OF US. IF WE EACH SACRIFICE ONE-SIXTH OF OUR MORTAL SPAN, THAT'S A LIFE.
WOULD THAT BE ACCEPTABLE?
IT COULD WORK. AS FULL MAGES, YOU COULD LIVE QUITE A LONG TIME, YOU KNOW--FOR MORTALS, THAT IS.
BUT WHATEVER YOUR ALLOTTED TIME WOULD BE, YOU WOULD SACRIFICE ONE-SIXTH OF THAT TIME. DO YOU AGREE TO THIS?
I'LL DO IT. BUT... CAN YOU GIVE US SOME CLOTHES TO WEAR? I DON'T WANT TO SIGN MY LIFE AWAY WEARING PAJAMAS.
OF COURSE. BE CLAD AS YOU WISH, IN ERMINE OR RABBIT, THOUGH HONOR PEERETH FORTH IN MEANEST HABIT.
NOW, SIMPLY SIGN YOUR NAMES, AND YOU'LL BE OUT OF HERE IN NO TIME.
AAAGH!
SORRY, MISS, BUT IT APPEARS THAT *YOU* ARE NOT PERMITTED TO SIGN FOR YOURSELF.
AS THE OLD SAYING GOES, "QUI VOCAT CADAVER, EIUS EST USQUE AD COELUM ET AD INFERNOS."
WHAT THE HELL DOES THAT MEAN?

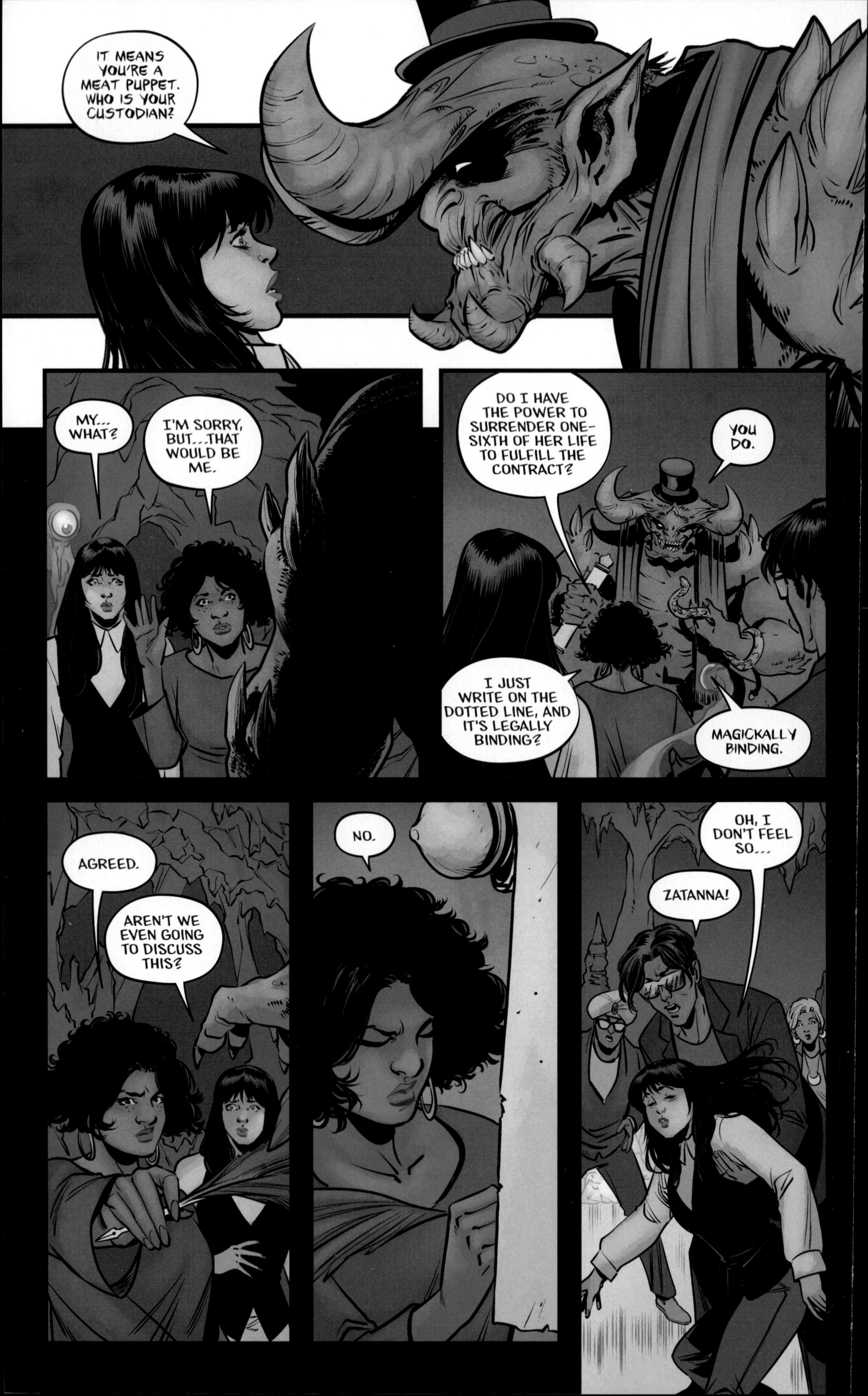
IT MEANS YOU'RE A MEAT PUPPET. WHO IS YOUR CUSTODIAN?
MY... WHAT?
I'M SORRY, BUT...THAT WOULD BE ME.
DO I HAVE THE POWER TO SURRENDER ONE-SIXTH OF HER LIFE TO FULFILL THE CONTRACT?
YOU DO.
I JUST WRITE ON THE DOTTED LINE, AND IT'S LEGALLY BINDING?
MAGICKALLY BINDING.
AGREED.
AREN'T WE EVEN GOING TO DISCUSS THIS?
NO.
OH, I DON'T FEEL SO...
ZATANNA!

HUH.

We, the undersigned, do deed one-sixths part of our mortal tenure on this earth to Nebiros, Most Valiant Marquess of Hell, as a per curiam, in exchange for release from imprisonment in these infernal regions.

Sebastian Faust

David Sargon. Plop

Pia Katrina Morales

June Moone/Enchantress

Zatanna Zatara (As avouched by her legal guardian)

Addendum:
As Zatanna Zatara's legal guardian and custodian, I hereby deed back to her the remaining five-sixths of her existence, free of any liens or hindrance.

WHAT HAPPENED?

YOUR EYES--THEY'RE BLUE AGAIN.

THEY'VE *ALWAYS* BEEN BLUE.

NO. WHEN PIA BROUGHT YOU BACK, THEY WERE DIFFERENT. *YOU* WERE DIFFERENT. TETHERED TO HER POWER--LEASHED.

HMPH.

WHAT DOES HE MEAN? WERE YOU CONTROLLING ME?

NO! NO, I WOULD NEVER--I WASN'T DOING ANYTHING ON PURPOSE. I JUST DIDN'T UNDERSTAND HOW MY POWER WORKED.

AND NOW YOU BELONG TO YOURSELF AGAIN.

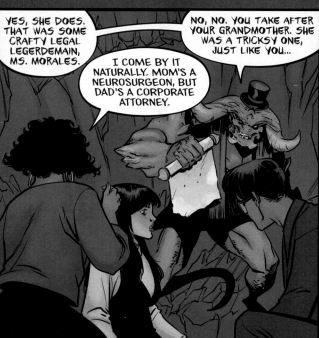

YES, SHE DOES. THAT WAS SOME CRAFTY LEGAL LEGERDEMAIN, MS. MORALES.

I COME BY IT NATURALLY. MOM'S A NEUROSURGEON, BUT DAD'S A CORPORATE ATTORNEY.

NO, NO. YOU TAKE AFTER YOUR GRANDMOTHER. SHE WAS A TRICKSY ONE, JUST LIKE YOU...

...BUT I *TAUGHT* CUNNING TO MORTALS.

YOU MADE A DEAL, NEBIROS...

INDEED. BUT I'M A DEMON...

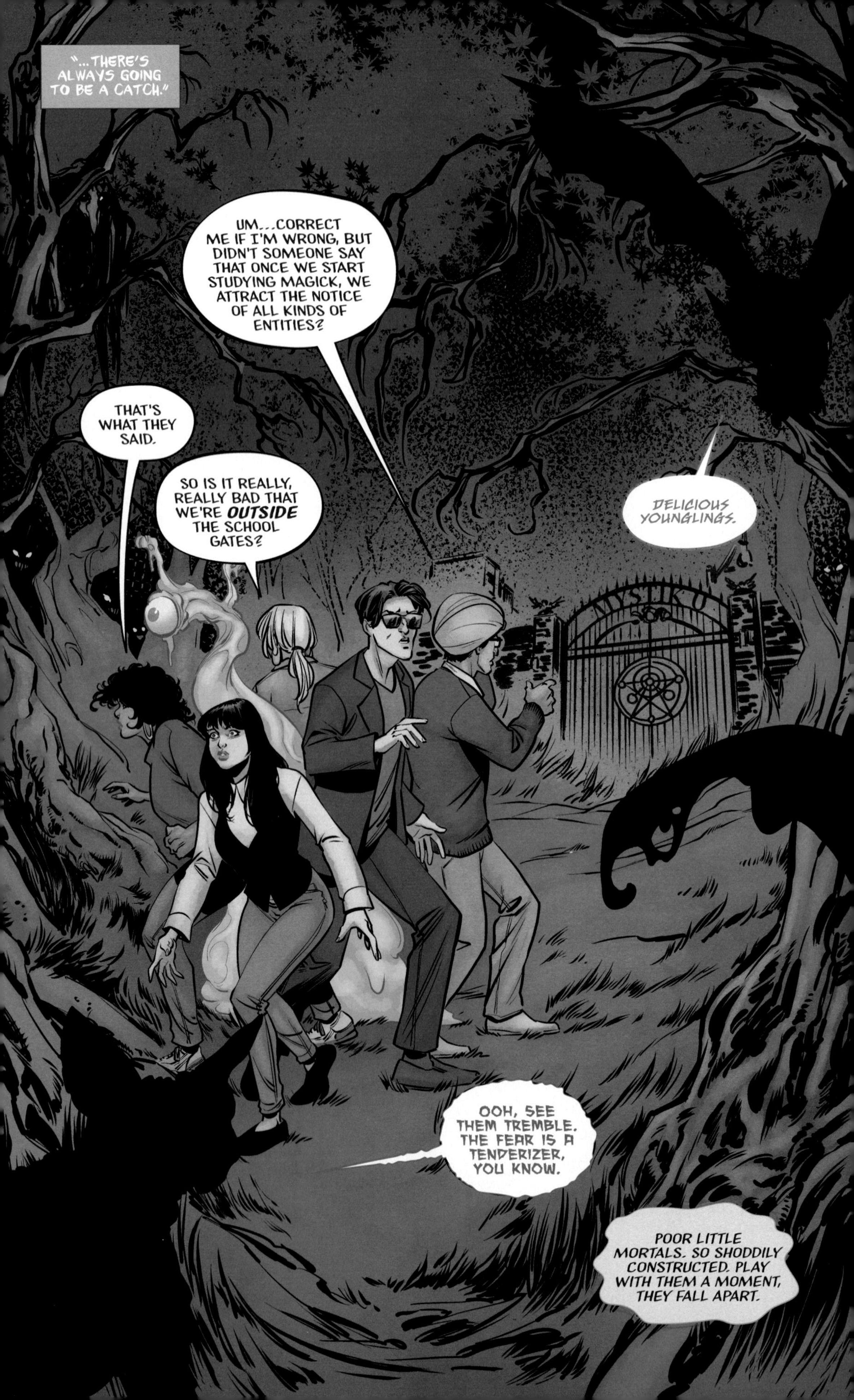
"...THERE'S ALWAYS GOING TO BE A CATCH."
UM...CORRECT ME IF I'M WRONG, BUT DIDN'T SOMEONE SAY THAT ONCE WE START STUDYING MAGICK, WE ATTRACT THE NOTICE OF ALL KINDS OF ENTITIES?
THAT'S WHAT THEY SAID.
SO IS IT REALLY, REALLY BAD THAT WE'RE OUTSIDE THE SCHOOL GATES?
DELICIOUS YOUNGLINGS.
MYSTIKO
OOH, SEE THEM TREMBLE. THE FEAR IS A TENDERIZER, YOU KNOW.
POOR LITTLE MORTALS. SO SHODDILY CONSTRUCTED. PLAY WITH THEM A MOMENT, THEY FALL APART.

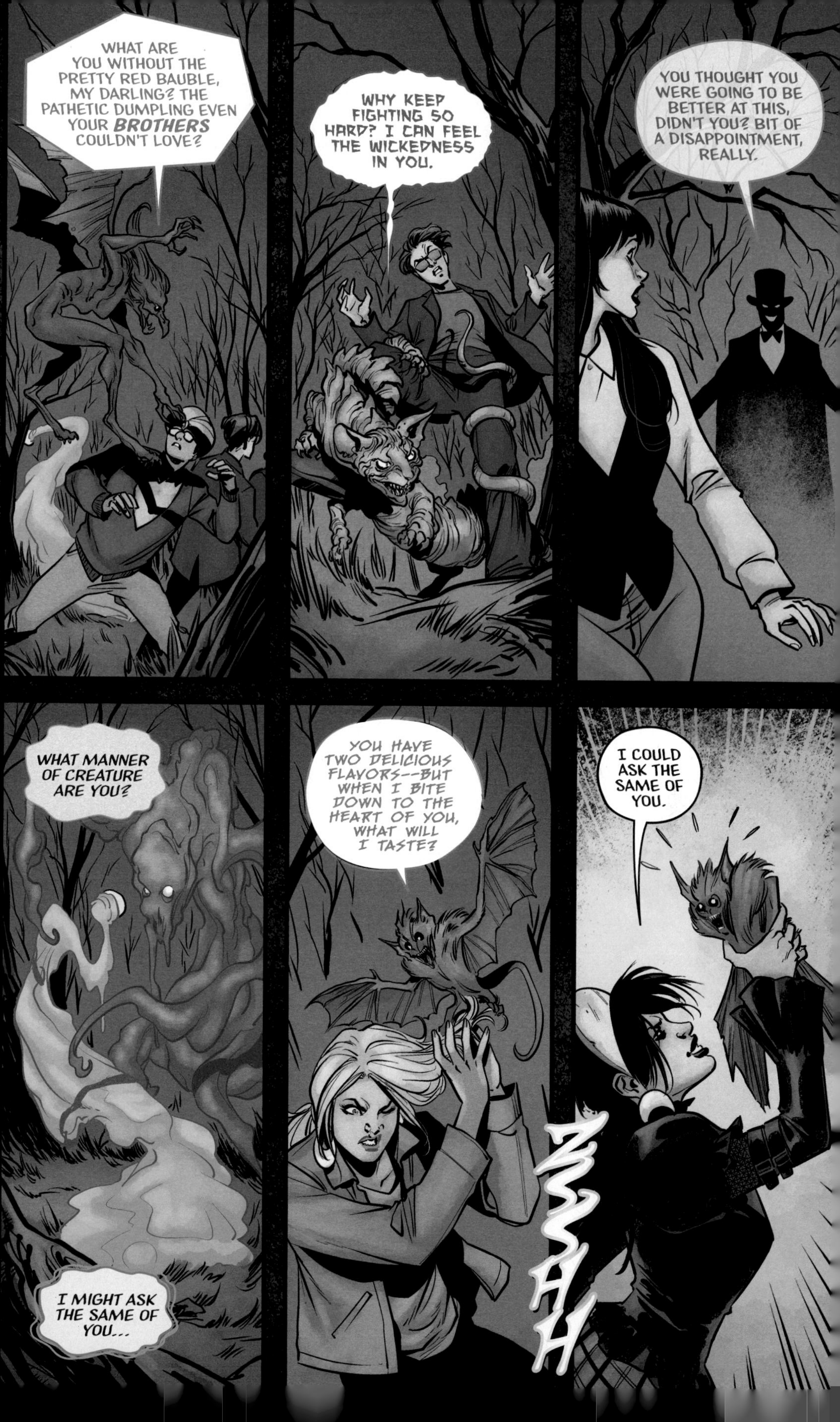
WHAT ARE YOU WITHOUT THE PRETTY RED BAUBLE, MY DARLING? THE PATHETIC DUMPLING EVEN YOUR BROTHERS COULDN'T LOVE?
WHY KEEP FIGHTING SO HARD? I CAN FEEL THE WICKEDNESS IN YOU.
YOU THOUGHT YOU WERE GOING TO BE BETTER AT THIS, DIDN'T YOU? BIT OF A DISAPPOINTMENT, REALLY.
WHAT MANNER OF CREATURE ARE YOU?
I MIGHT ASK THE SAME OF YOU...
YOU HAVE TWO DELICIOUS FLAVORS--BUT WHEN I BITE DOWN TO THE HEART OF YOU, WHAT WILL I TASTE?
I COULD ASK THE SAME OF YOU.
ZWSHH

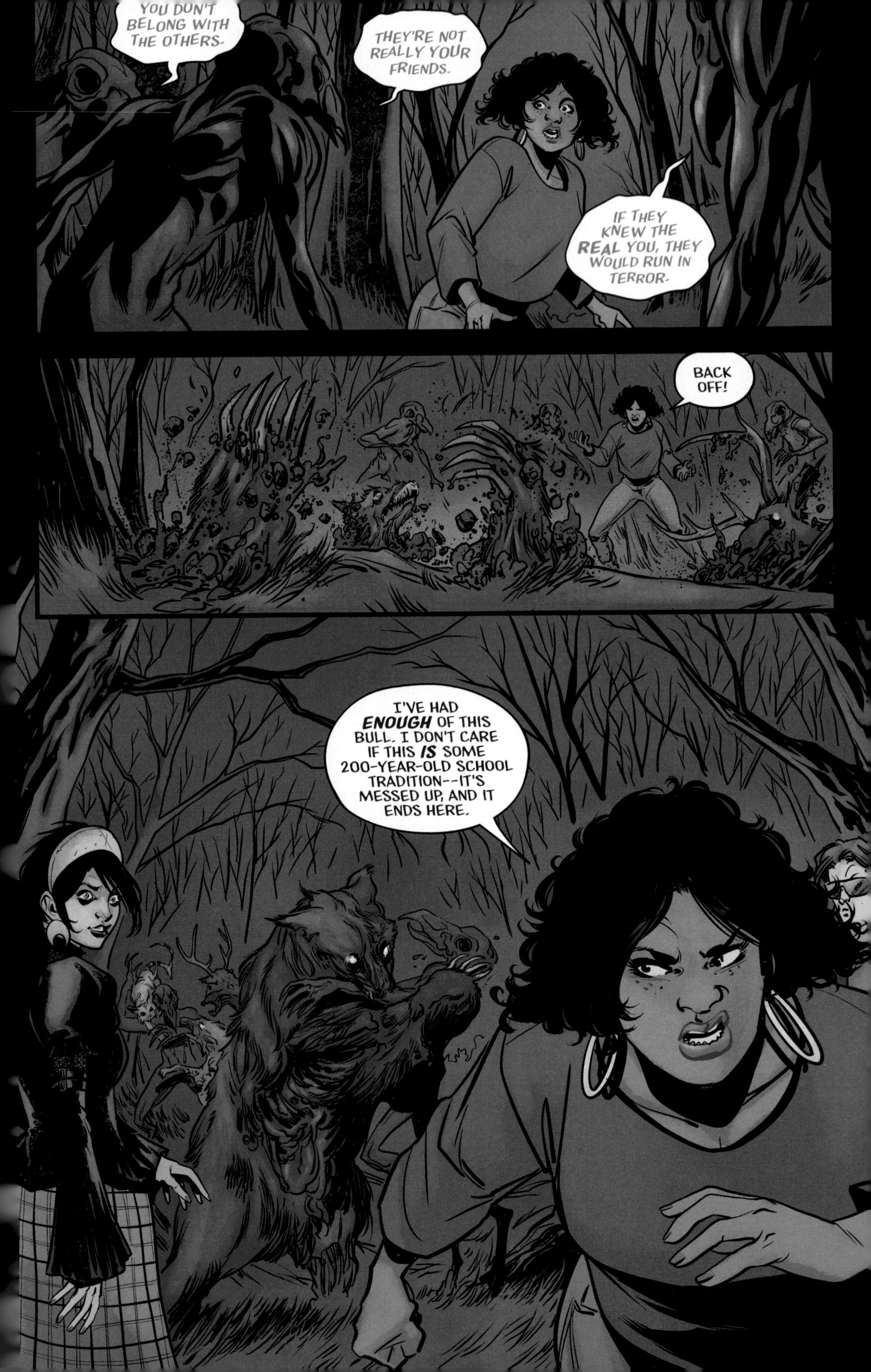
YOU DON'T BELONG WITH THE OTHERS.
THEY'RE NOT REALLY YOUR FRIENDS.
IF THEY KNEW THE REAL YOU, THEY WOULD RUN IN TERROR.
BACK OFF!
I'VE HAD ENOUGH OF THIS BULL. I DON'T CARE IF THIS IS SOME 200-YEAR-OLD SCHOOL TRADITION--IT'S MESSED UP, AND IT ENDS HERE.

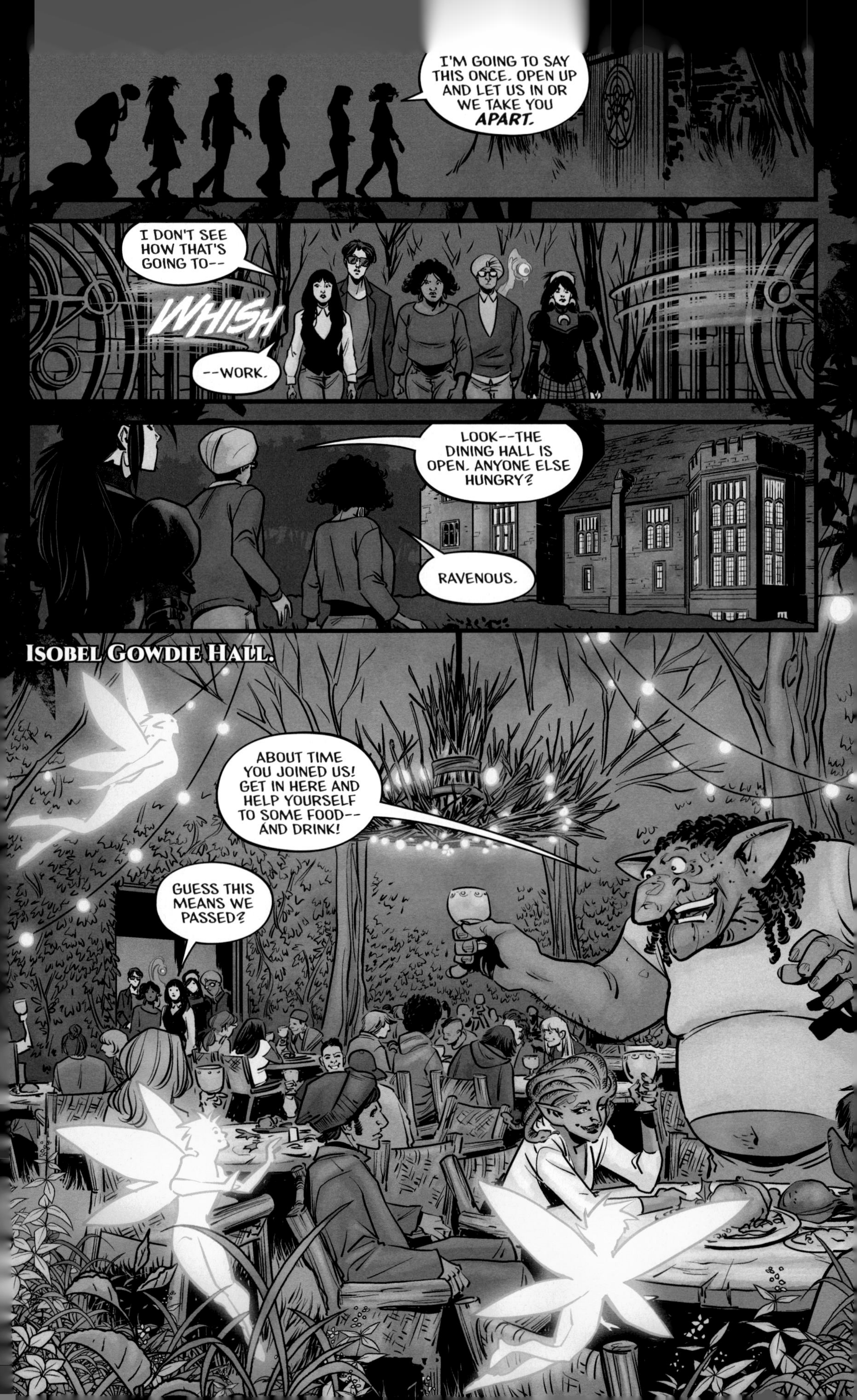
I'M GOING TO SAY THIS ONCE. OPEN UP AND LET US IN OR WE TAKE YOU APART.
I DON'T SEE HOW THAT'S GOING TO--
WHISH
--WORK.
LOOK--THE DINING HALL IS OPEN. ANYONE ELSE HUNGRY?
RAVENOUS.
ISOBEL GOWDIE HALL.
ABOUT TIME YOU JOINED US! GET IN HERE AND HELP YOURSELF TO SOME FOOD--AND DRINK!
GUESS THIS MEANS WE PASSED?

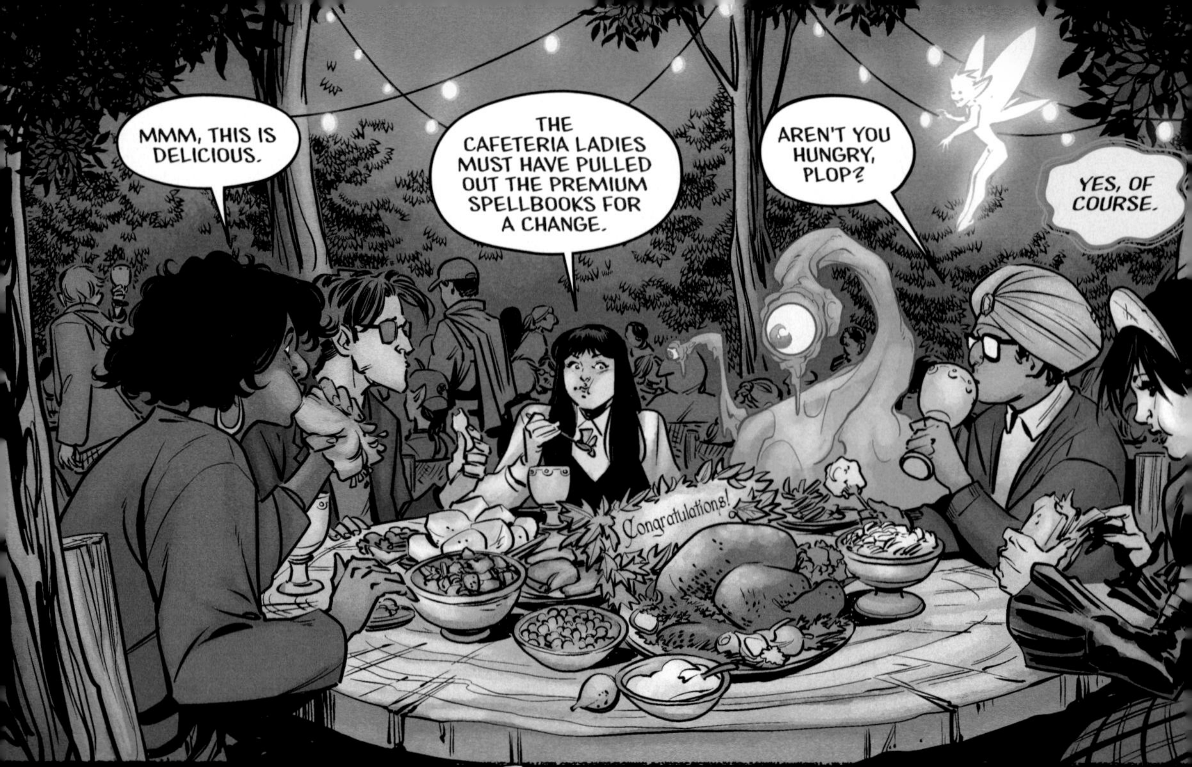
MMM, THIS IS DELICIOUS.
THE CAFETERIA LADIES MUST HAVE PULLED OUT THE PREMIUM SPELLBOOKS FOR A CHANGE.
Congratulations!
AREN'T YOU HUNGRY, PLOP?
YES, OF COURSE.

Chapter Three: The Boneyard Queen

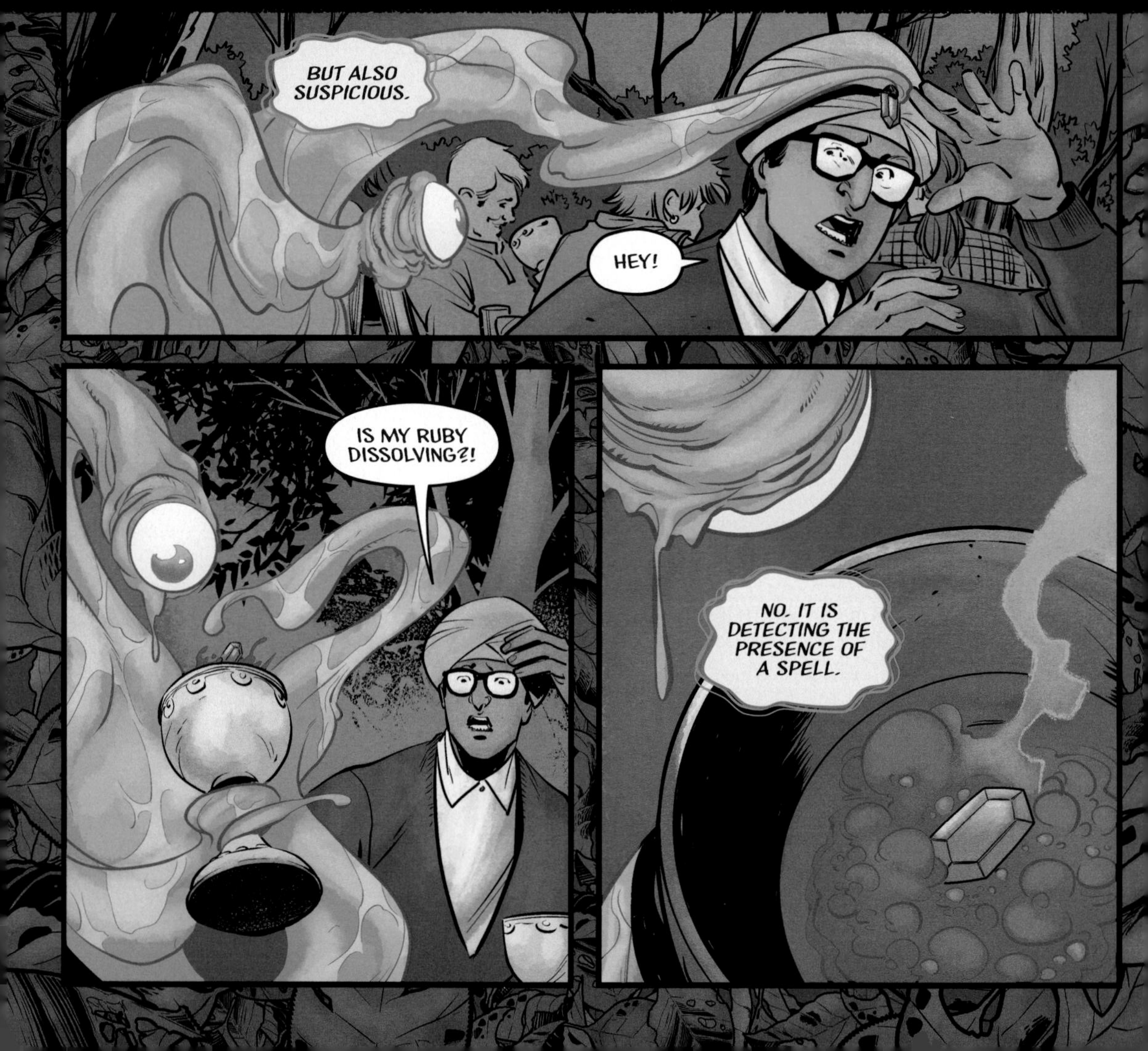
BUT ALSO SUSPICIOUS.
HEY!
IS MY RUBY DISSOLVING?!
NO. IT IS DETECTING THE PRESENCE OF A SPELL.

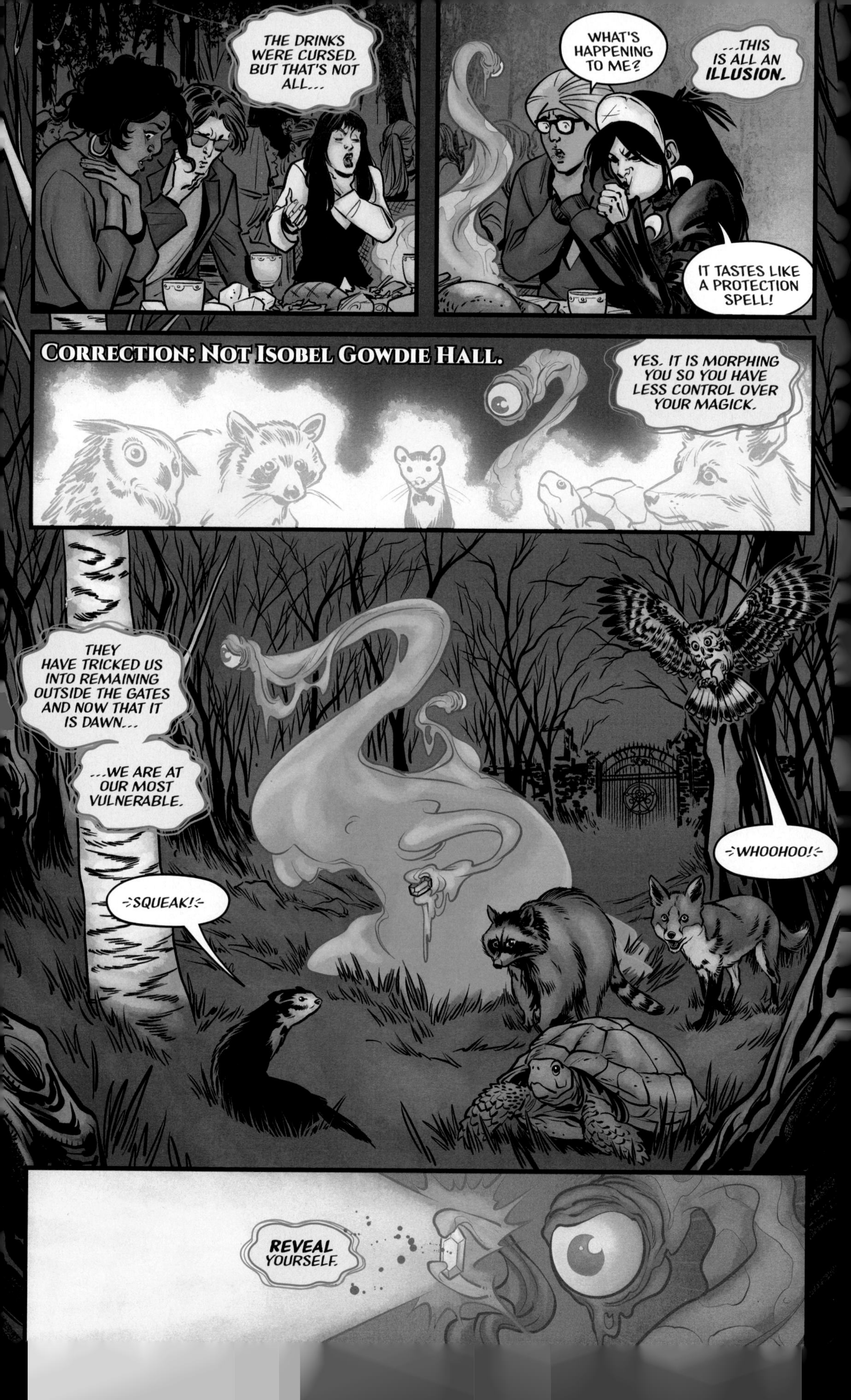
THE DRINKS WERE CURSED. BUT THAT'S NOT ALL...
WHAT'S HAPPENING TO ME?
...THIS IS ALL AN ILLUSION.
IT TASTES LIKE A PROTECTION SPELL!
CORRECTION: NOT ISOBEL GOWDIE HALL.
YES. IT IS MORPHING YOU SO YOU HAVE LESS CONTROL OVER YOUR MAGICK.
THEY HAVE TRICKED US INTO REMAINING OUTSIDE THE GATES AND NOW THAT IT IS DAWN...
...WE ARE AT OUR MOST VULNERABLE.
WHOOHOO!
SQUEAK!
REVEAL YOURSELF.

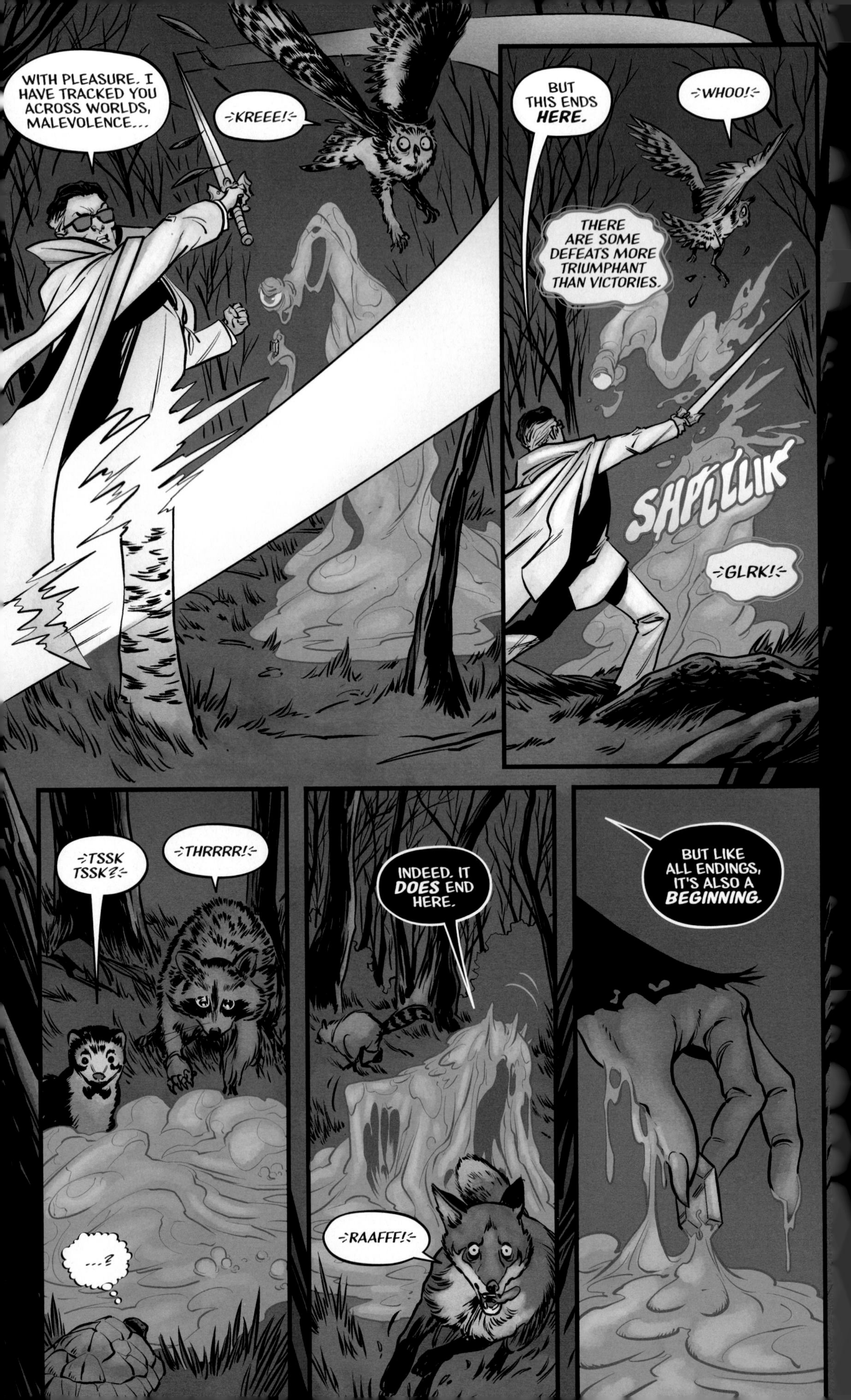
WITH PLEASURE. I HAVE TRACKED YOU ACROSS WORLDS, MALEVOLENCE...
KREEE!
BUT THIS ENDS HERE.
WHOO!
THERE ARE SOME DEFEATS MORE TRIUMPHANT THAN VICTORIES.
SHPLLLIK
GLRK!
TSSK TSSK?
THRRRR!
...?
INDEED. IT DOES END HERE.
RAAFFF!
BUT LIKE ALL ENDINGS, IT'S ALSO A BEGINNING.

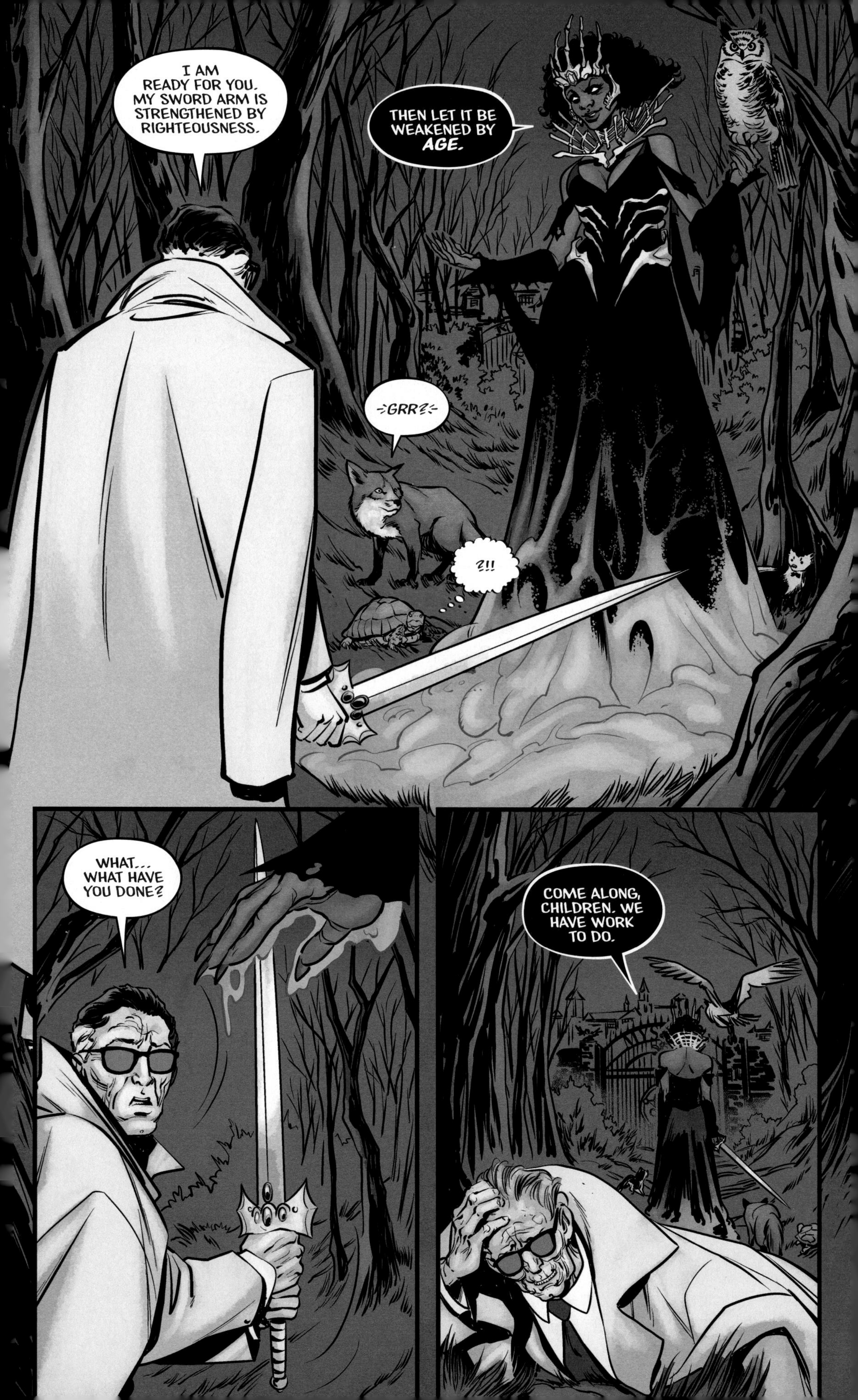
I AM READY FOR YOU. MY SWORD ARM IS STRENGTHENED BY RIGHTEOUSNESS.
THEN LET IT BE WEAKENED BY AGE.
GRR?
?!!
WHAT... WHAT HAVE YOU DONE?
COME ALONG, CHILDREN. WE HAVE WORK TO DO.

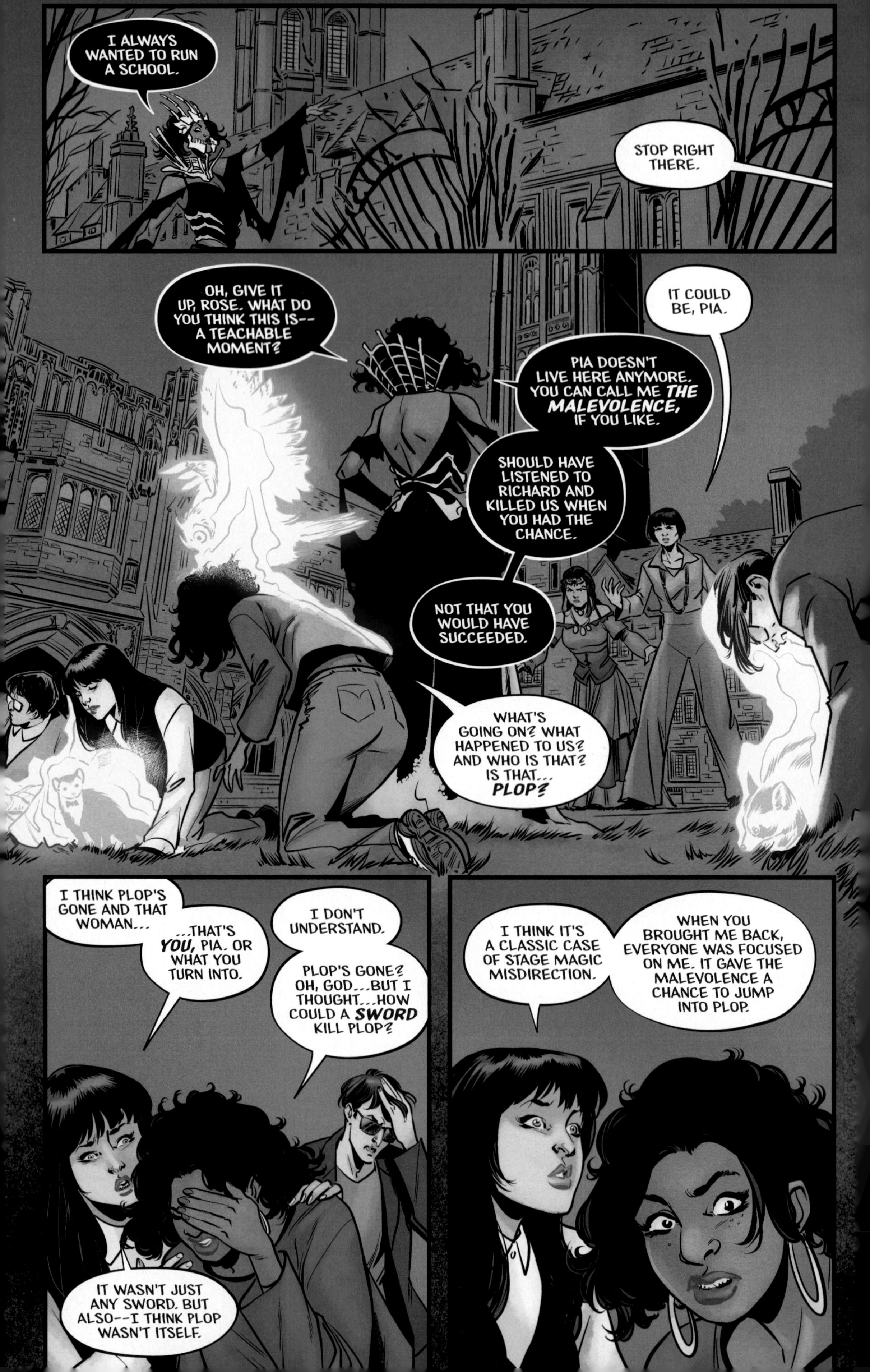
I ALWAYS WANTED TO RUN A SCHOOL.
STOP RIGHT THERE.
OH, GIVE IT UP, ROSE. WHAT DO YOU THINK THIS IS-- A TEACHABLE MOMENT?
IT COULD BE, PIA.
PIA DOESN'T LIVE HERE ANYMORE. YOU CAN CALL ME THE MALEVOLENCE, IF YOU LIKE.
SHOULD HAVE LISTENED TO RICHARD AND KILLED US WHEN YOU HAD THE CHANCE.
NOT THAT YOU WOULD HAVE SUCCEEDED.
WHAT'S GOING ON? WHAT HAPPENED TO US? AND WHO IS THAT? IS THAT... PLOP?
I THINK PLOP'S GONE AND THAT WOMAN...
...THAT'S YOU, PIA. OR WHAT YOU TURN INTO.
I DON'T UNDERSTAND.
PLOP'S GONE? OH, GOD...BUT I THOUGHT...HOW COULD A SWORD KILL PLOP?
IT WASN'T JUST ANY SWORD. BUT ALSO--I THINK PLOP WASN'T ITSELF.
I THINK IT'S A CLASSIC CASE OF STAGE MAGIC MISDIRECTION.
WHEN YOU BROUGHT ME BACK, EVERYONE WAS FOCUSED ON ME. IT GAVE THE MALEVOLENCE A CHANCE TO JUMP INTO PLOP.

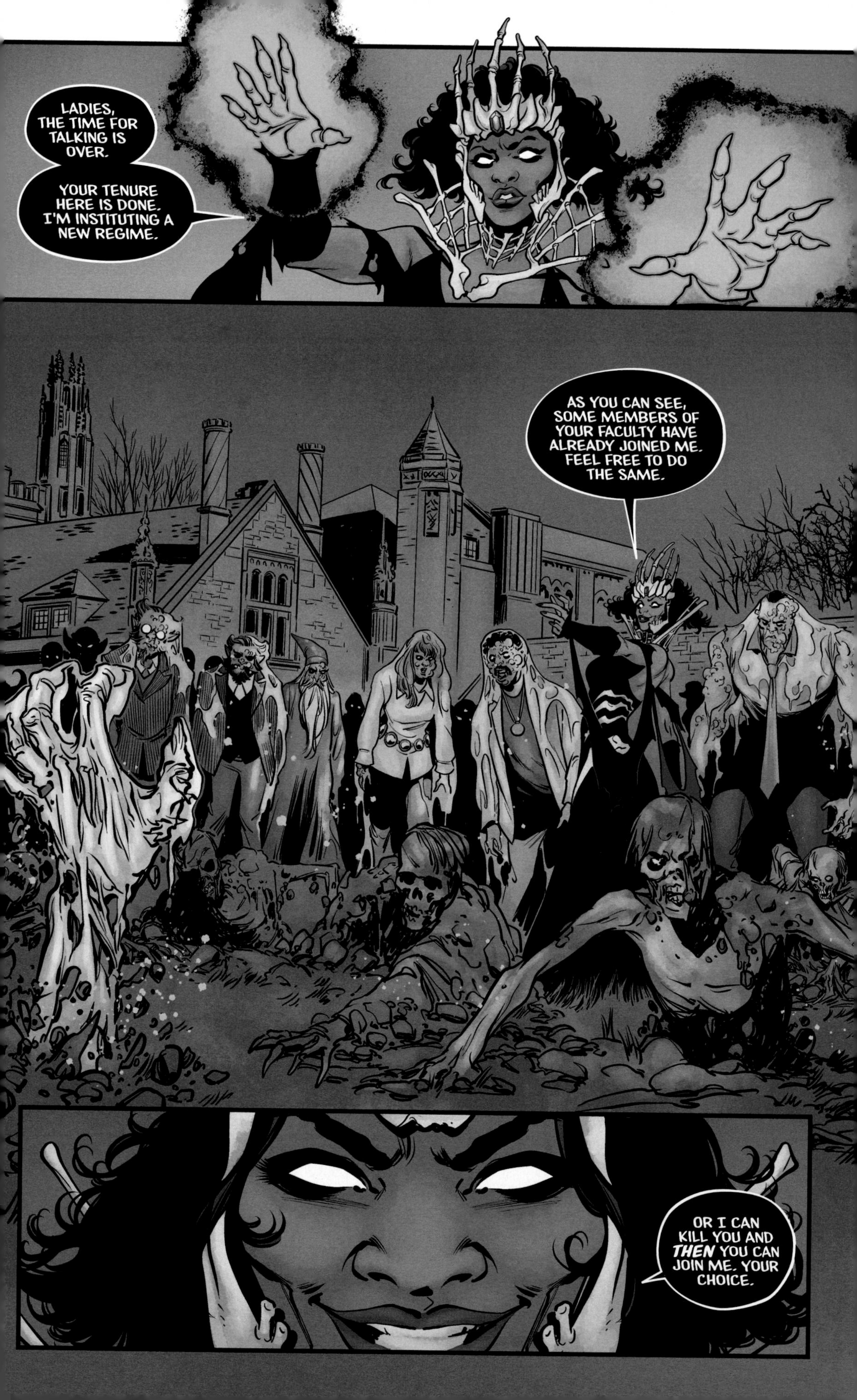
LADIES, THE TIME FOR TALKING IS OVER.
YOUR TENURE HERE IS DONE. I'M INSTITUTING A NEW REGIME.
AS YOU CAN SEE, SOME MEMBERS OF YOUR FACULTY HAVE ALREADY JOINED ME. FEEL FREE TO DO THE SAME.
OR I CAN KILL YOU AND *THEN* YOU CAN JOIN ME. YOUR CHOICE.

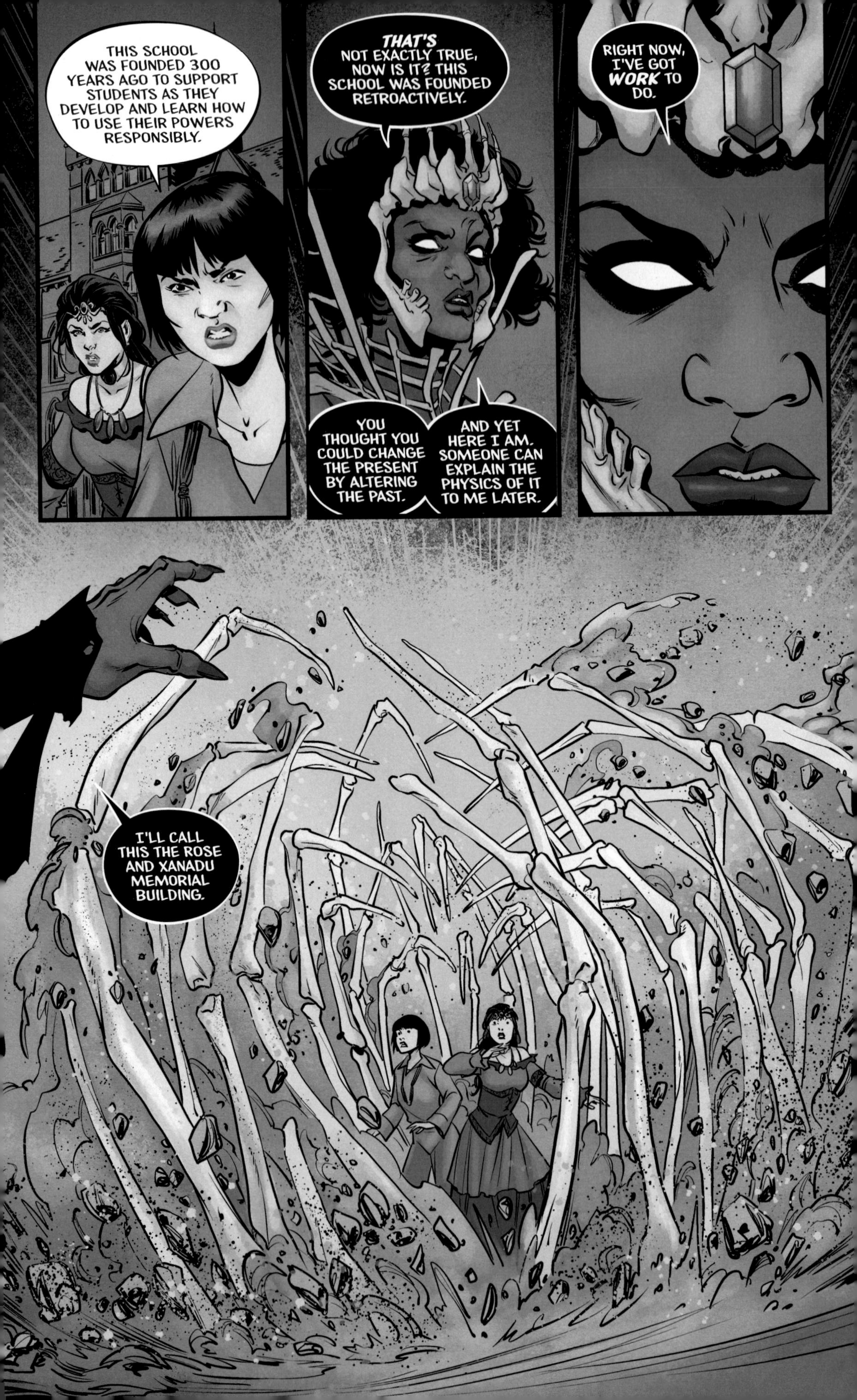
THIS SCHOOL WAS FOUNDED 300 YEARS AGO TO SUPPORT STUDENTS AS THEY DEVELOP AND LEARN HOW TO USE THEIR POWERS RESPONSIBLY.
THAT'S NOT EXACTLY TRUE, NOW IS IT? THIS SCHOOL WAS FOUNDED RETROACTIVELY.
YOU THOUGHT YOU COULD CHANGE THE PRESENT BY ALTERING THE PAST.
AND YET HERE I AM. SOMEONE CAN EXPLAIN THE PHYSICS OF IT TO ME LATER.
RIGHT NOW, I'VE GOT WORK TO DO.
I'LL CALL THIS THE ROSE AND XANADU MEMORIAL BUILDING.

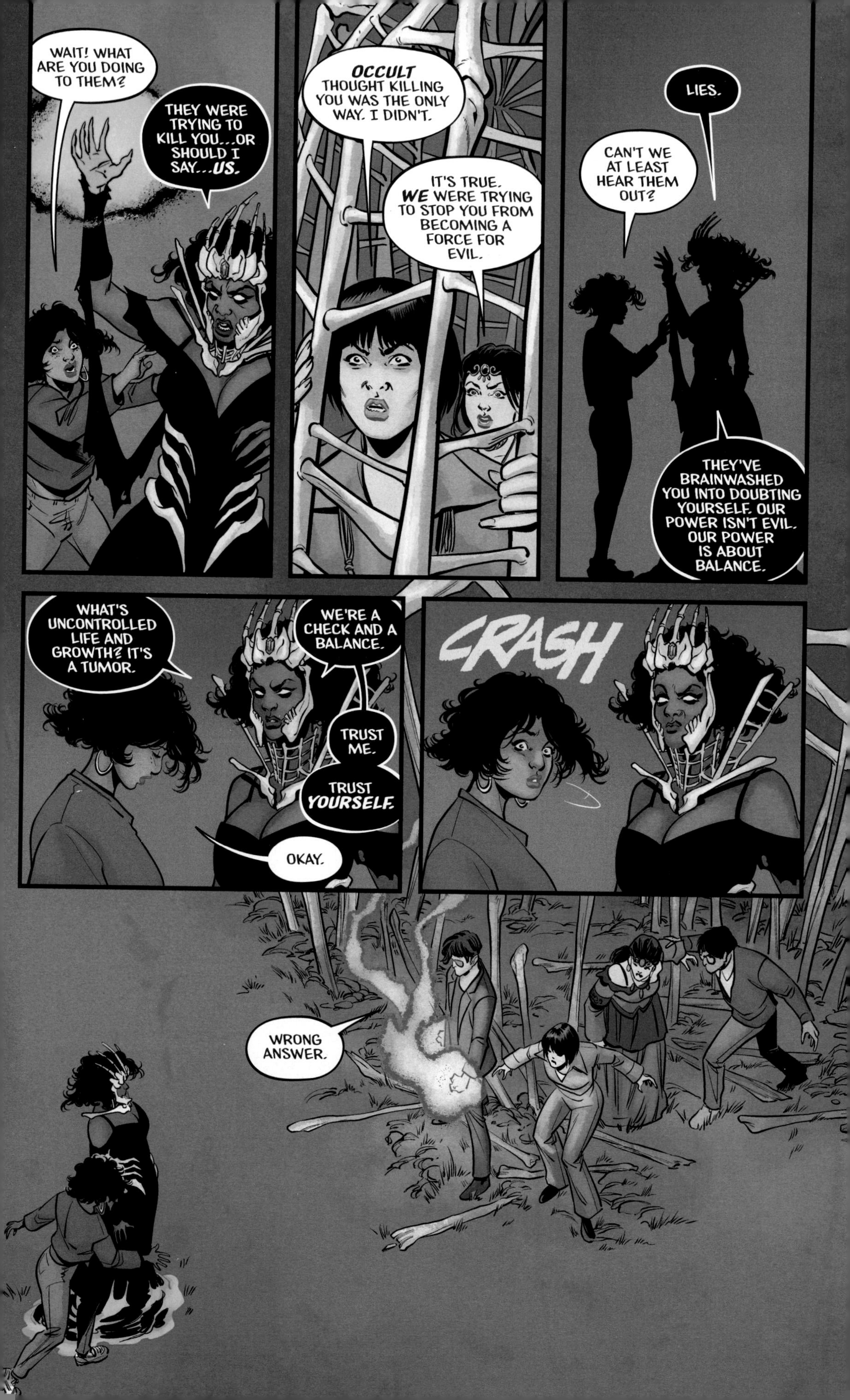
WAIT! WHAT ARE YOU DOING TO THEM?
THEY WERE TRYING TO KILL YOU...OR SHOULD I SAY...US.
OCCULT THOUGHT KILLING YOU WAS THE ONLY WAY. I DIDN'T.
IT'S TRUE. WE WERE TRYING TO STOP YOU FROM BECOMING A FORCE FOR EVIL.
LIES.
CAN'T WE AT LEAST HEAR THEM OUT?
THEY'VE BRAINWASHED YOU INTO DOUBTING YOURSELF. OUR POWER ISN'T EVIL. OUR POWER IS ABOUT BALANCE.
WHAT'S UNCONTROLLED LIFE AND GROWTH? IT'S A TUMOR.
WE'RE A CHECK AND A BALANCE.
TRUST ME.
TRUST YOURSELF.
OKAY.
CRASH
WRONG ANSWER.

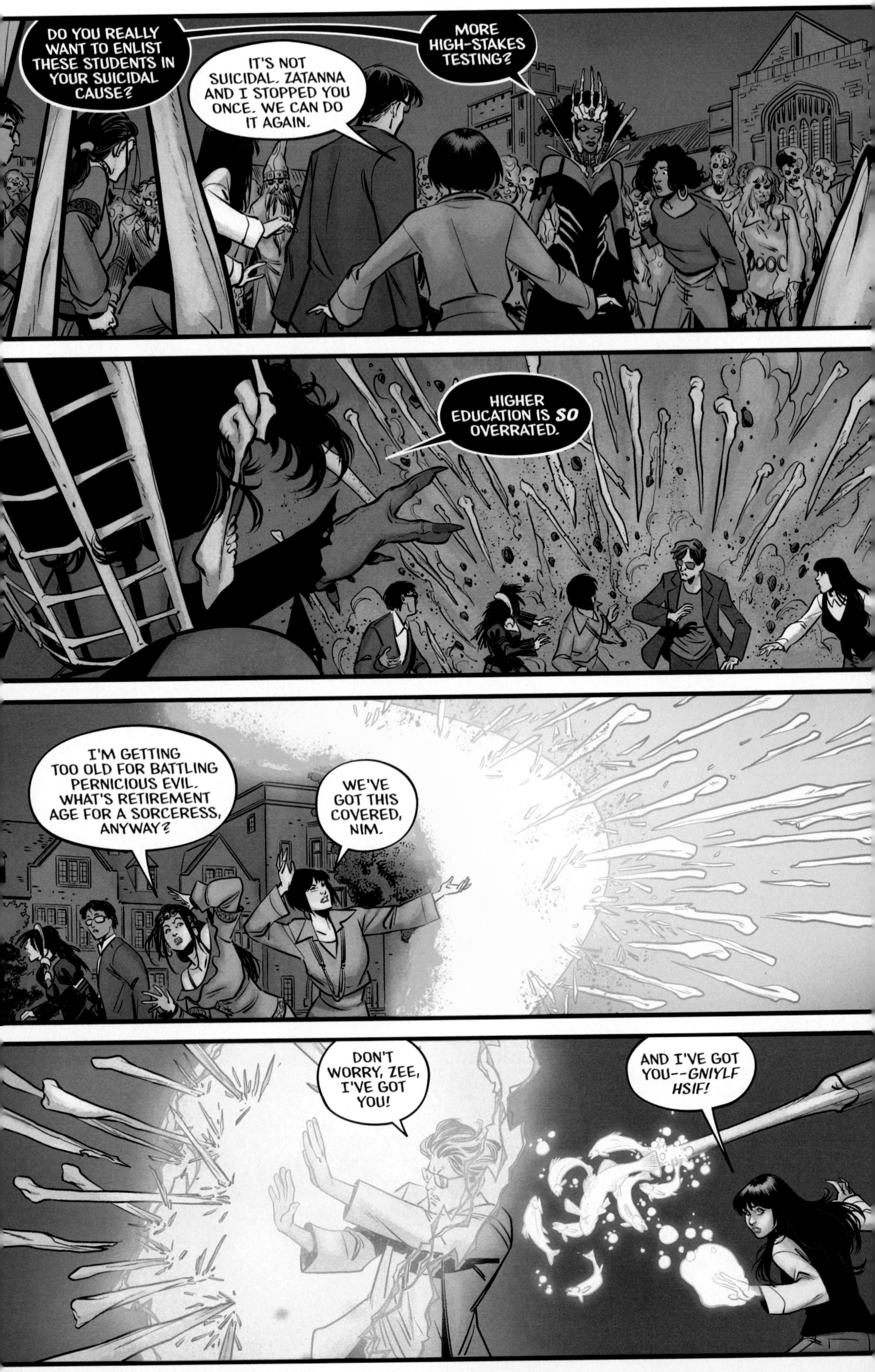
DO YOU REALLY WANT TO ENLIST THESE STUDENTS IN YOUR SUICIDAL CAUSE?
IT'S NOT SUICIDAL. ZATANNA AND I STOPPED YOU ONCE. WE CAN DO IT AGAIN.
MORE HIGH-STAKES TESTING?
HIGHER EDUCATION IS *SO* OVERRATED.
I'M GETTING TOO OLD FOR BATTLING PERNICIOUS EVIL. WHAT'S RETIREMENT AGE FOR A SORCERESS, ANYWAY?
WE'VE GOT THIS COVERED, NIM.
DON'T WORRY, ZEE, I'VE GOT YOU!
AND I'VE GOT YOU--*GNIYLF HSIF!*

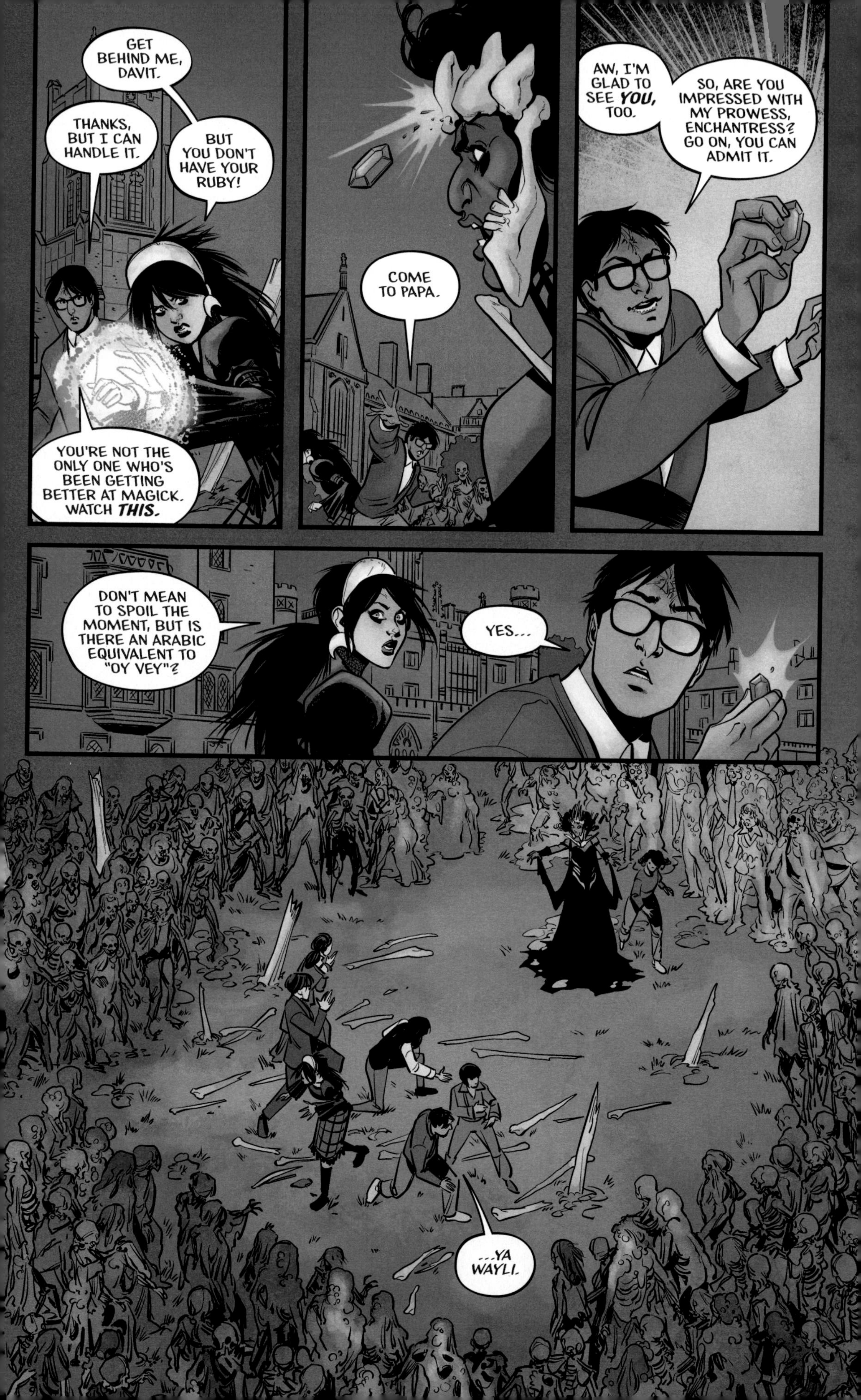
GET BEHIND ME, DAVIT.
THANKS, BUT I CAN HANDLE IT.
BUT YOU DON'T HAVE YOUR RUBY!
YOU'RE NOT THE ONLY ONE WHO'S BEEN GETTING BETTER AT MAGICK. WATCH THIS.
COME TO PAPA.
AW, I'M GLAD TO SEE YOU, TOO.
SO, ARE YOU IMPRESSED WITH MY PROWESS, ENCHANTRESS? GO ON, YOU CAN ADMIT IT.
DON'T MEAN TO SPOIL THE MOMENT, BUT IS THERE AN ARABIC EQUIVALENT TO "OY VEY"?
YES...
...YA WAYLI.

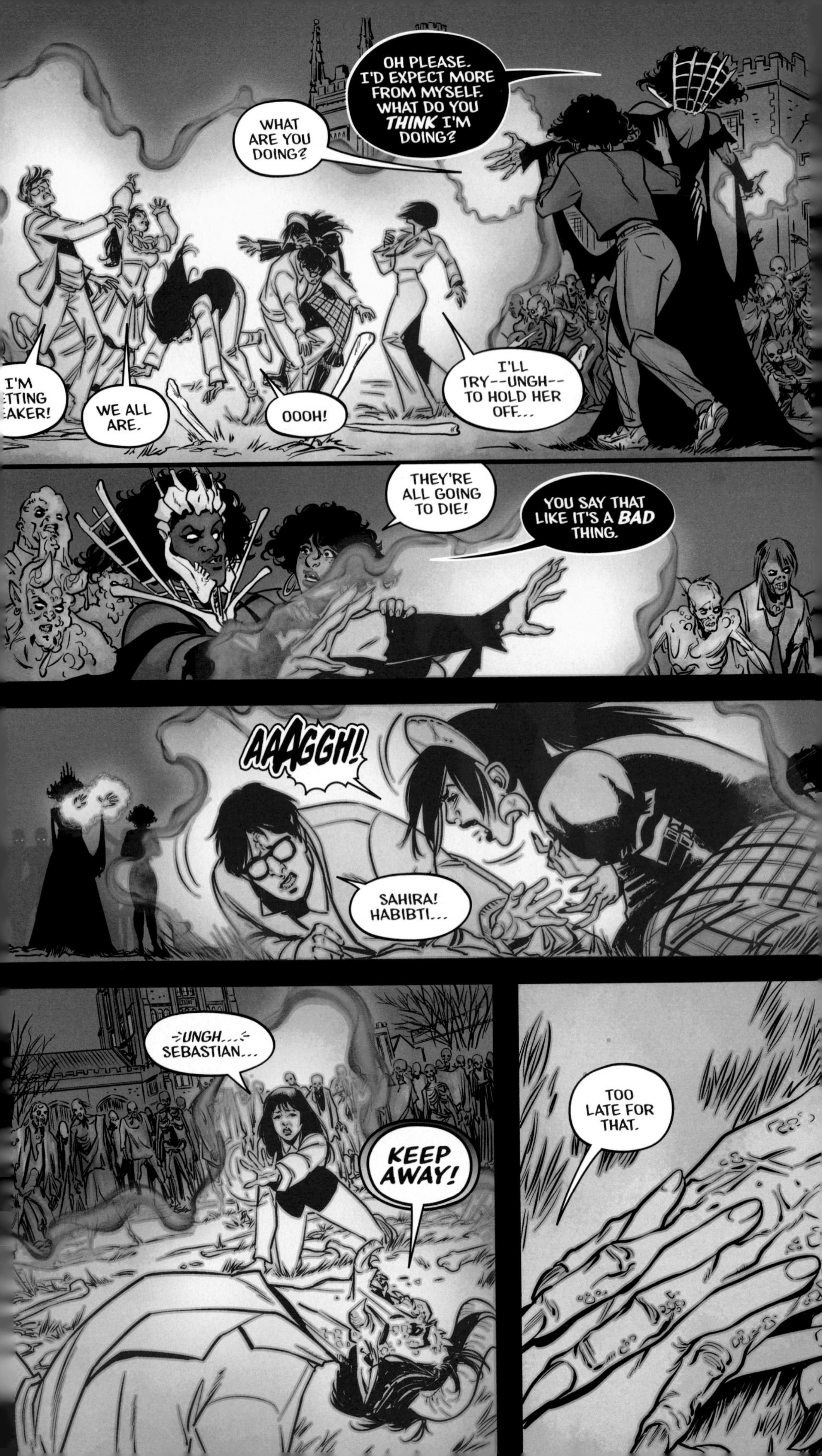
WHAT ARE YOU DOING?
OH PLEASE. I'D EXPECT MORE FROM MYSELF. WHAT DO YOU THINK I'M DOING?
I'M ETTING EAKER!
WE ALL ARE.
OOOH!
I'LL TRY--UNGH-- TO HOLD HER OFF...
THEY'RE ALL GOING TO DIE!
YOU SAY THAT LIKE IT'S A BAD THING.
AAAGGH!
SAHIRA! HABIBTI...
UNGH... SEBASTIAN...
KEEP AWAY!
TOO LATE FOR THAT.

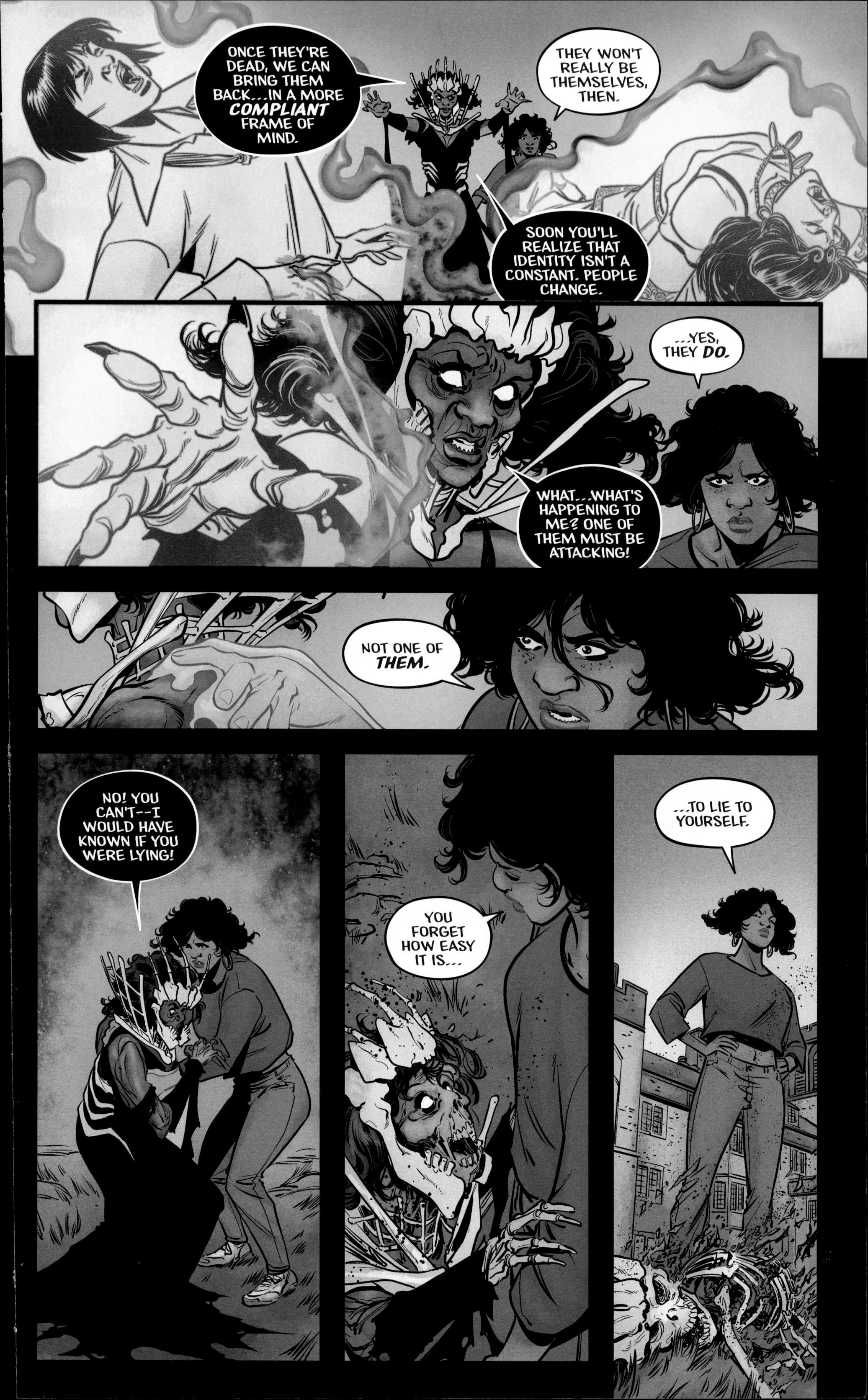
ONCE THEY'RE DEAD, WE CAN BRING THEM BACK...IN A MORE COMPLIANT FRAME OF MIND.
THEY WON'T REALLY BE THEMSELVES, THEN.
SOON YOU'LL REALIZE THAT IDENTITY ISN'T A CONSTANT. PEOPLE CHANGE.
...YES, THEY DO.
WHAT...WHAT'S HAPPENING TO ME? ONE OF THEM MUST BE ATTACKING!
NOT ONE OF THEM.
NO! YOU CAN'T--I WOULD HAVE KNOWN IF YOU WERE LYING!
YOU FORGET HOW EASY IT IS...
...TO LIE TO YOURSELF.

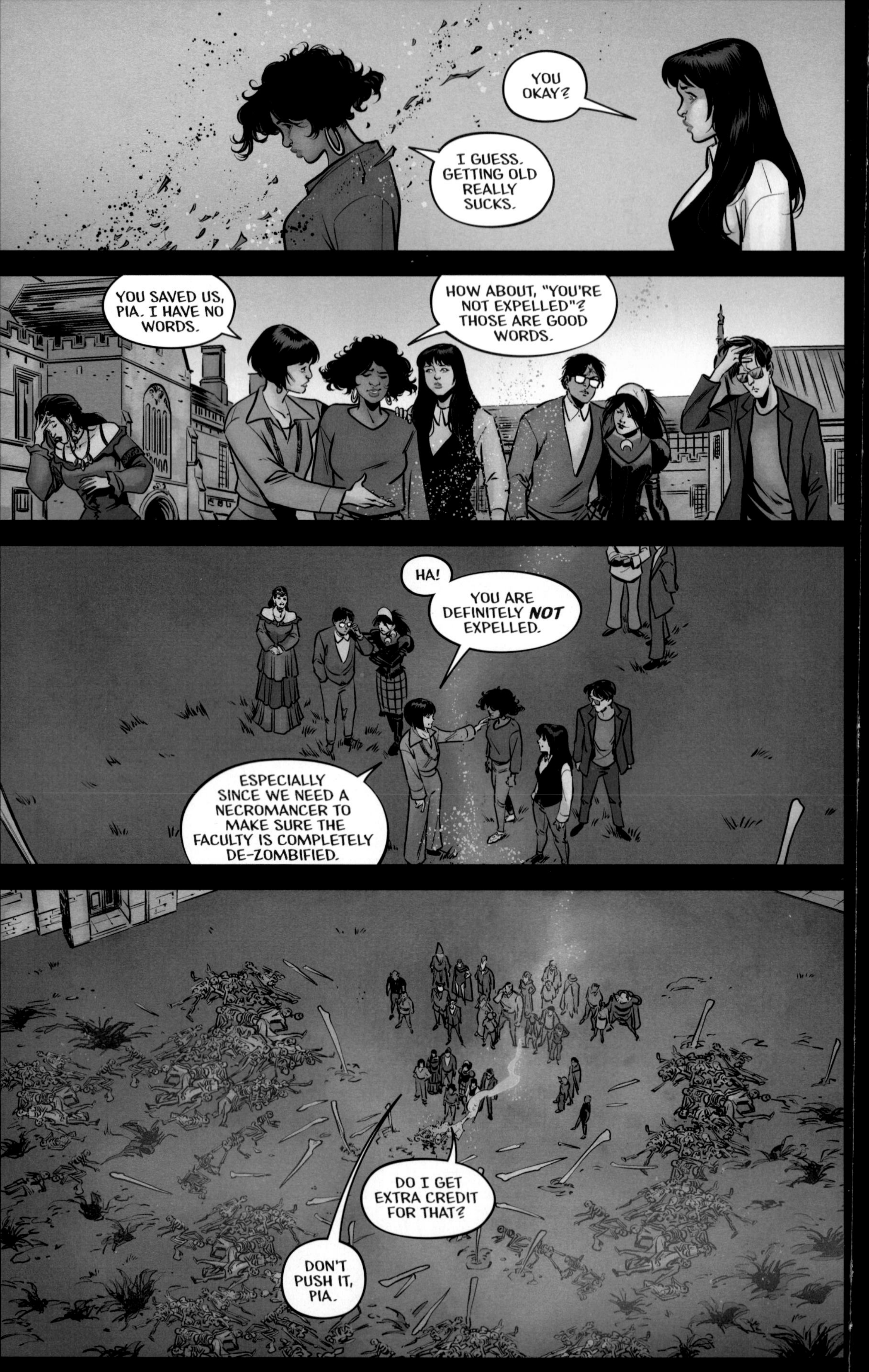
YOU OKAY?
I GUESS. GETTING OLD REALLY SUCKS.
YOU SAVED US, PIA. I HAVE NO WORDS.
HOW ABOUT, "YOU'RE NOT EXPELLED"? THOSE ARE GOOD WORDS.
HA!
YOU ARE DEFINITELY **NOT** EXPELLED.
ESPECIALLY SINCE WE NEED A NECROMANCER TO MAKE SURE THE FACULTY IS COMPLETELY DE-ZOMBIFIED.
DO I GET EXTRA CREDIT FOR THAT?
DON'T PUSH IT, PIA.

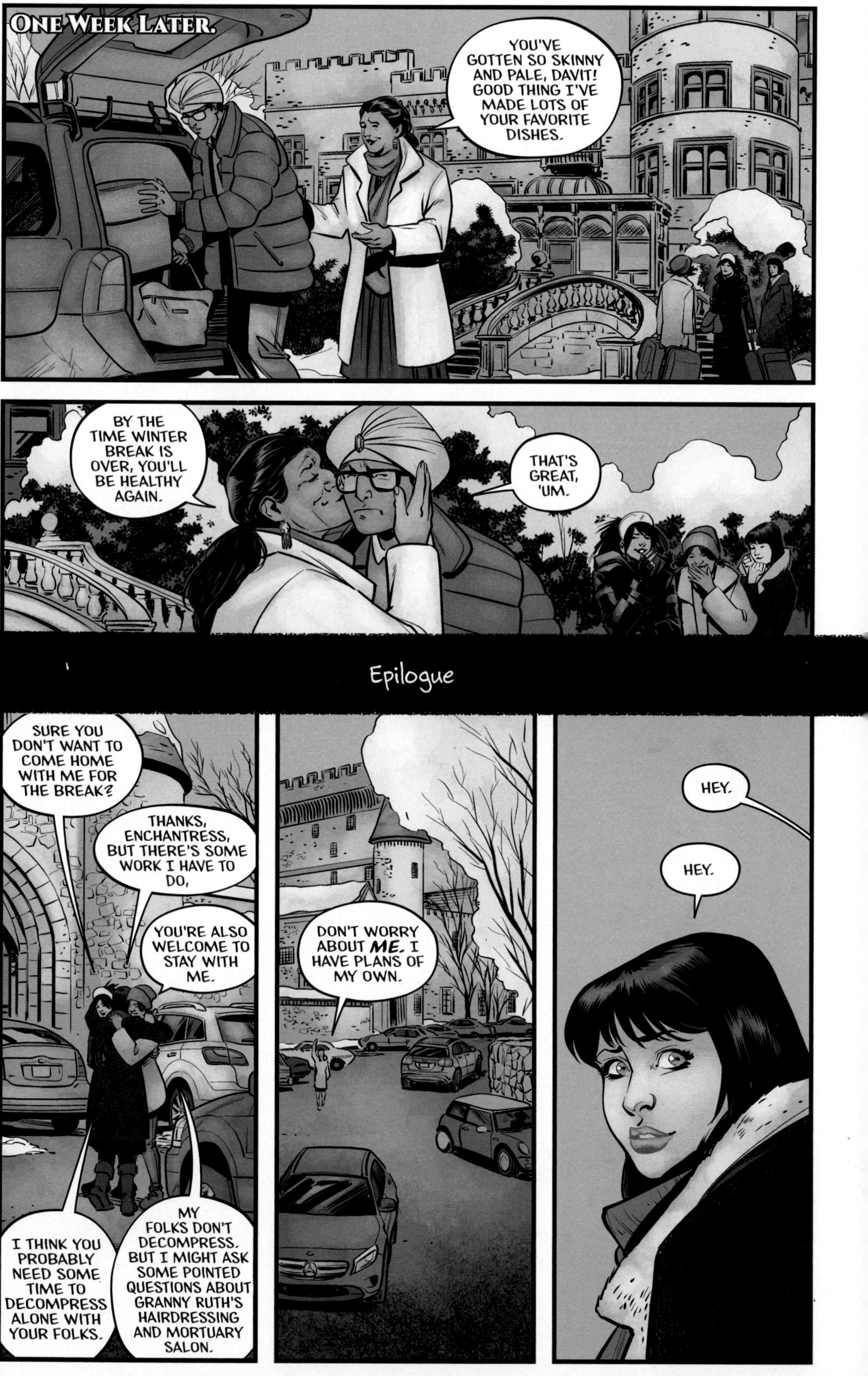
ONE WEEK LATER.
YOU'VE GOTTEN SO SKINNY AND PALE, DAVIT! GOOD THING I'VE MADE LOTS OF YOUR FAVORITE DISHES.
BY THE TIME WINTER BREAK IS OVER, YOU'LL BE HEALTHY AGAIN.
THAT'S GREAT, 'UM.
Epilogue
SURE YOU DON'T WANT TO COME HOME WITH ME FOR THE BREAK?
THANKS, ENCHANTRESS, BUT THERE'S SOME WORK I HAVE TO DO,
YOU'RE ALSO WELCOME TO STAY WITH ME.
I THINK YOU PROBABLY NEED SOME TIME TO DECOMPRESS ALONE WITH YOUR FOLKS.
MY FOLKS DON'T DECOMPRESS. BUT I MIGHT ASK SOME POINTED QUESTIONS ABOUT GRANNY RUTH'S HAIRDRESSING AND MORTUARY SALON.
DON'T WORRY ABOUT ME. I HAVE PLANS OF MY OWN.
HEY.
HEY.

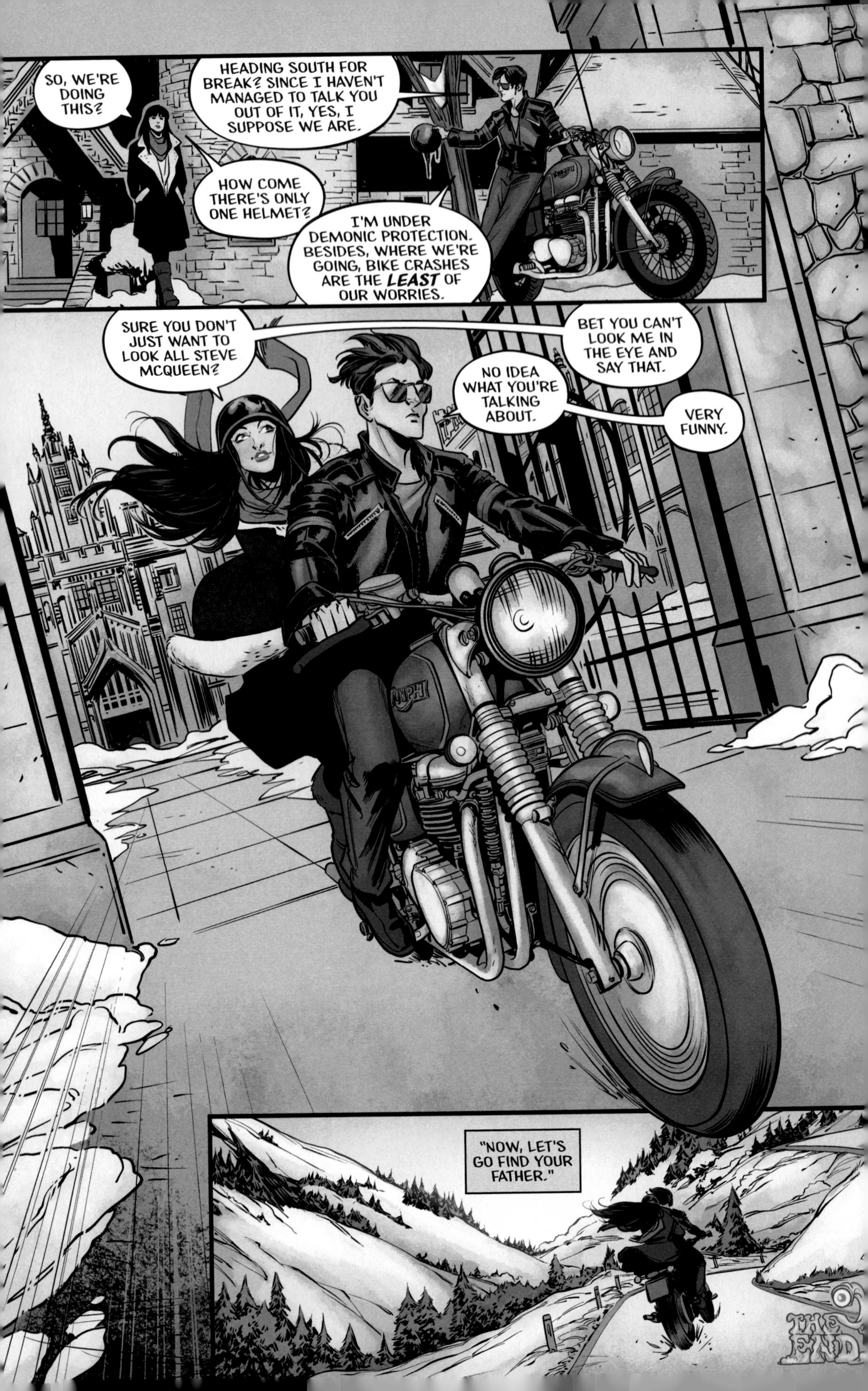
SO, WE'RE DOING THIS?
HEADING SOUTH FOR BREAK? SINCE I HAVEN'T MANAGED TO TALK YOU OUT OF IT, YES, I SUPPOSE WE ARE.
HOW COME THERE'S ONLY ONE HELMET?
I'M UNDER DEMONIC PROTECTION. BESIDES, WHERE WE'RE GOING, BIKE CRASHES ARE THE *LEAST* OF OUR WORRIES.
SURE YOU DON'T JUST WANT TO LOOK ALL STEVE MCQUEEN?
BET YOU CAN'T LOOK ME IN THE EYE AND SAY THAT.
NO IDEA WHAT YOU'RE TALKING ABOUT.
VERY FUNNY.
"NOW, LET'S GO FIND YOUR FATHER."
THE END

MYSTIK U SKETCHBOOK

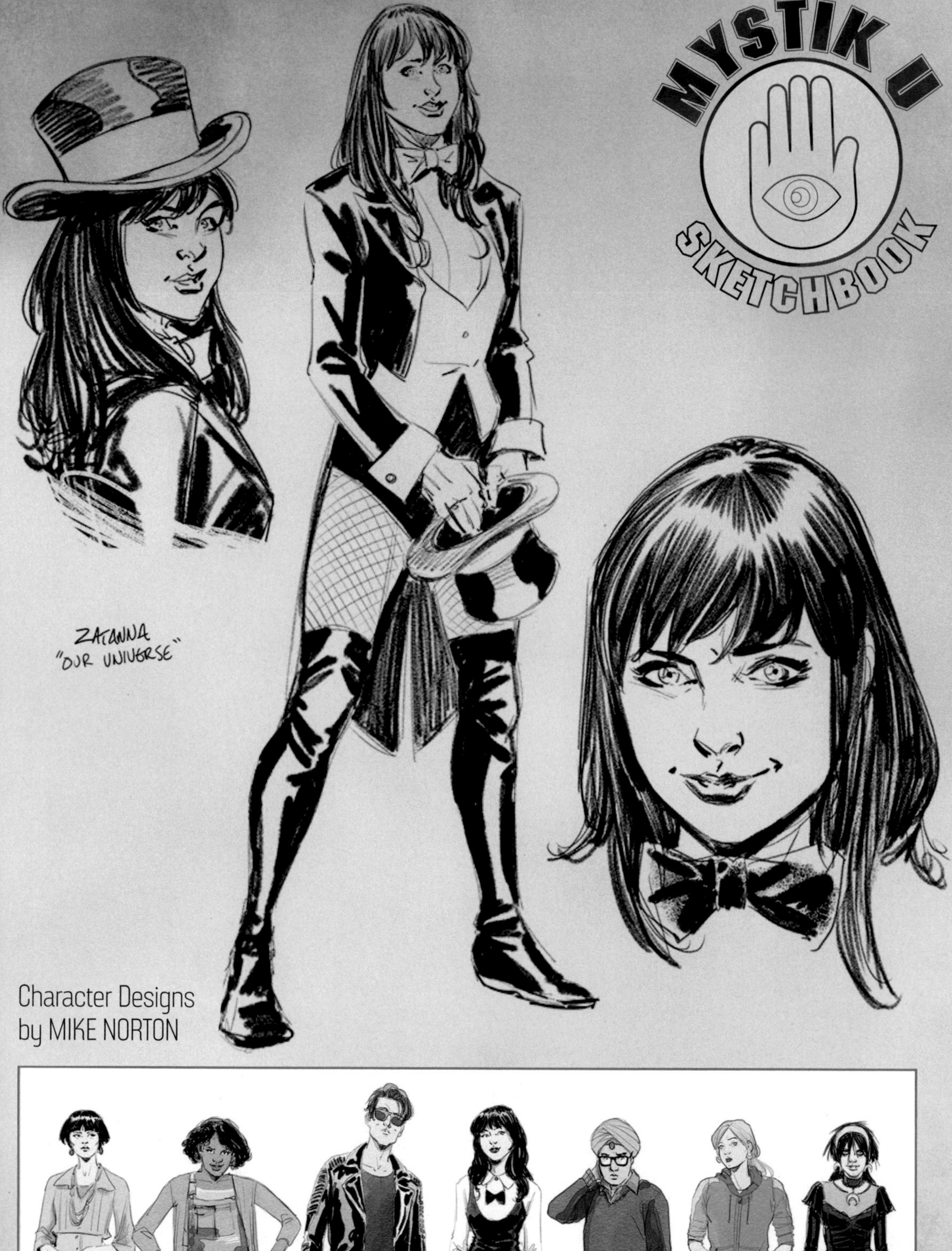
ZATANNA
"OUR UNIVERSE"

Character Designs
by MIKE NORTON

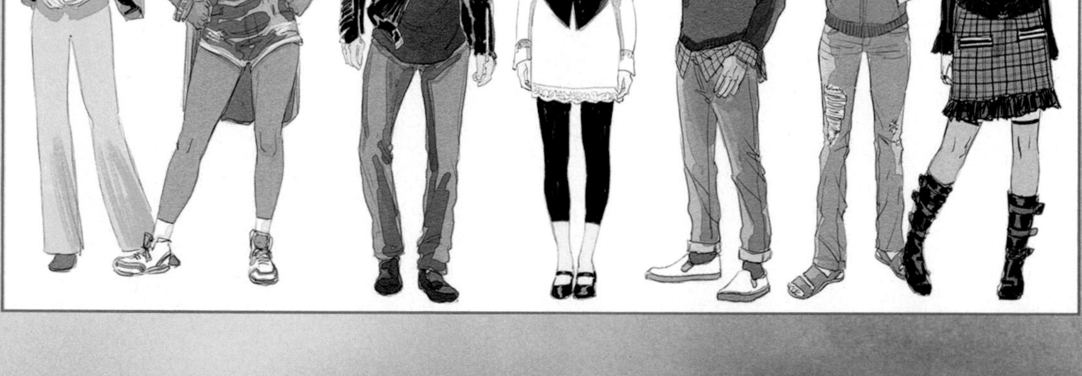

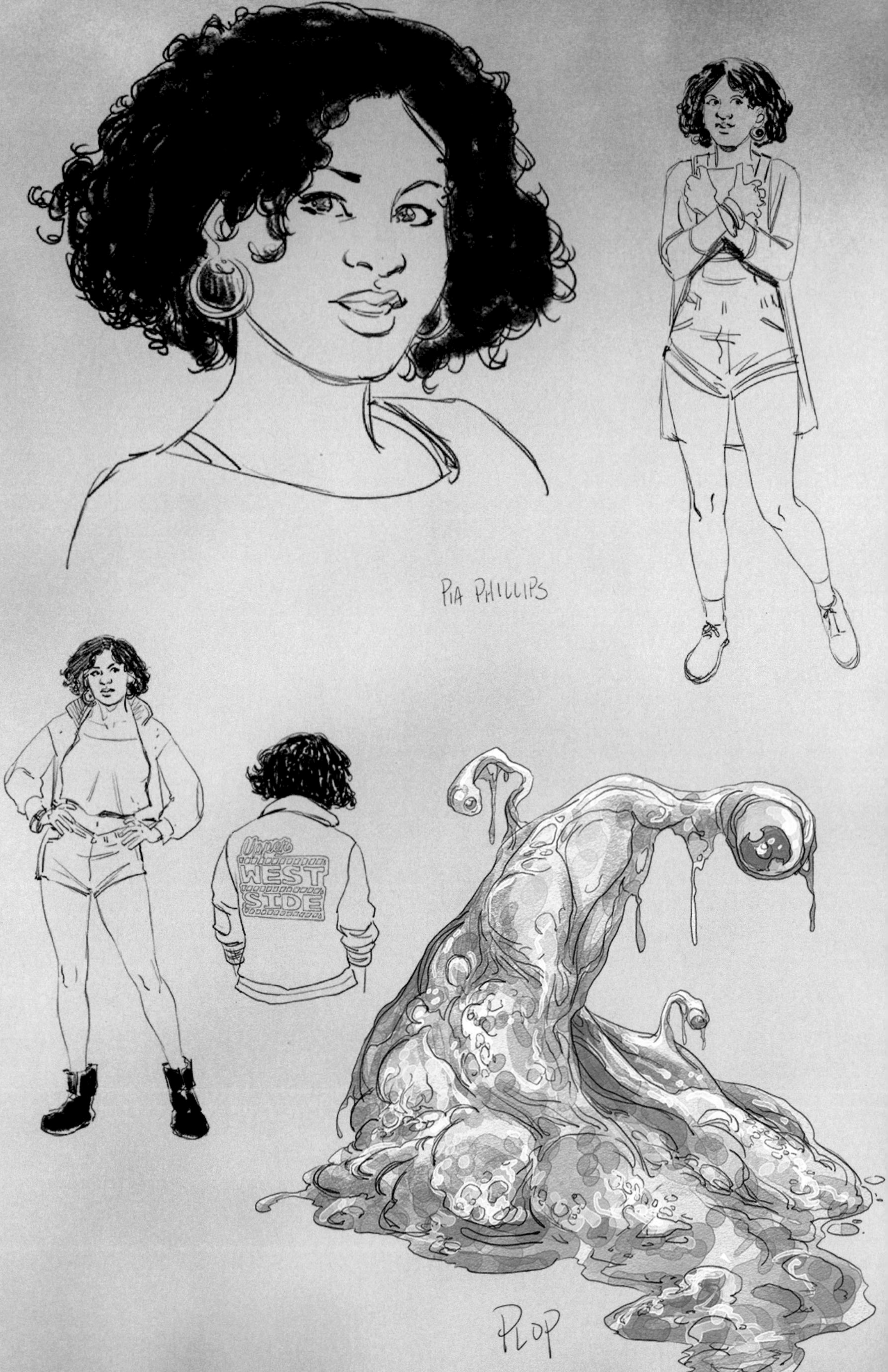
PIA PHILLIPS
Upper
WEST
SIDE
PLOP

MYSTIK U SKETCHBOOK

Cover Sketches by
JULIAN TOTINO TEDESCO

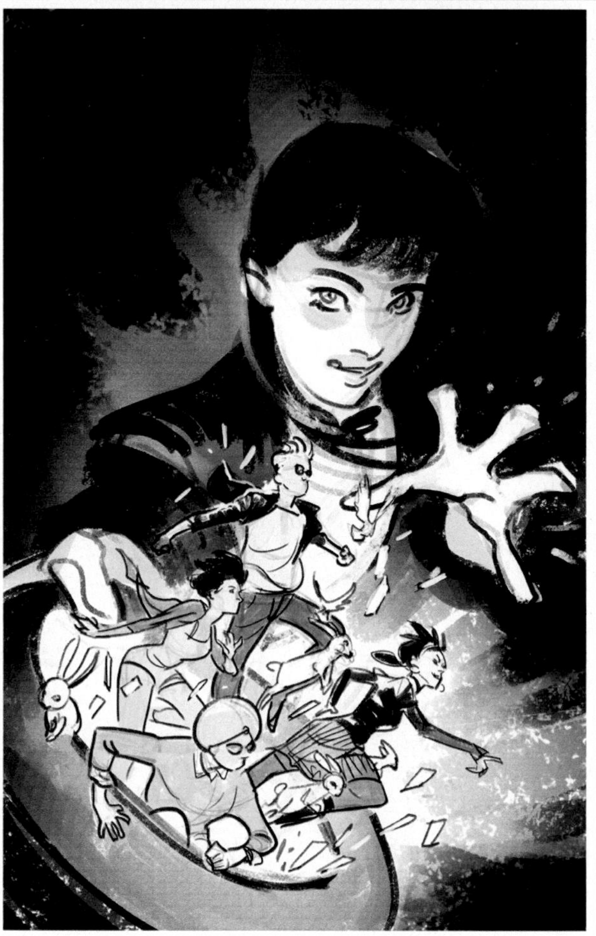

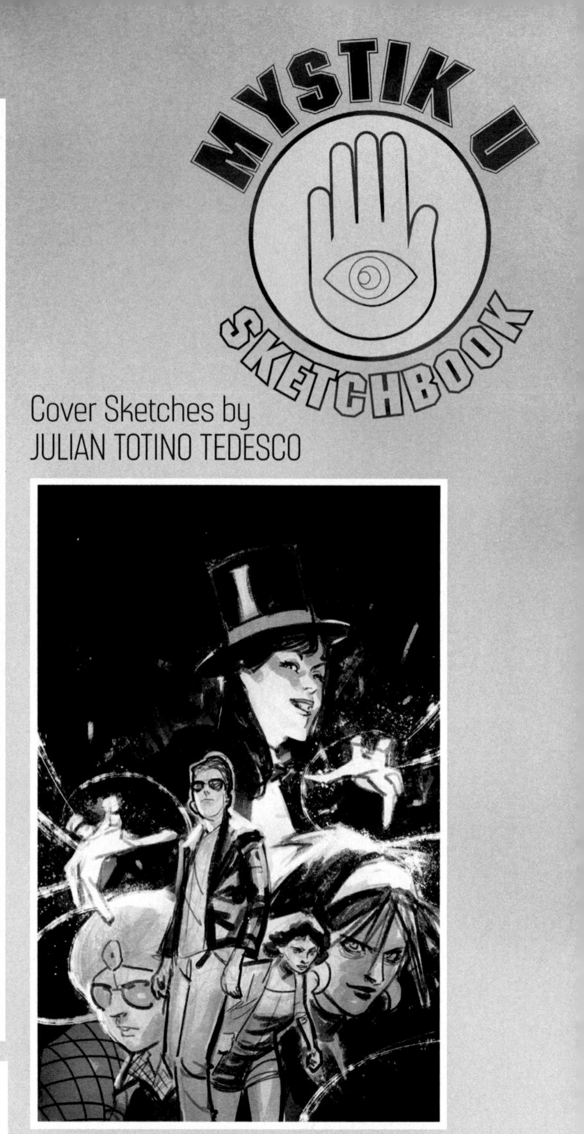

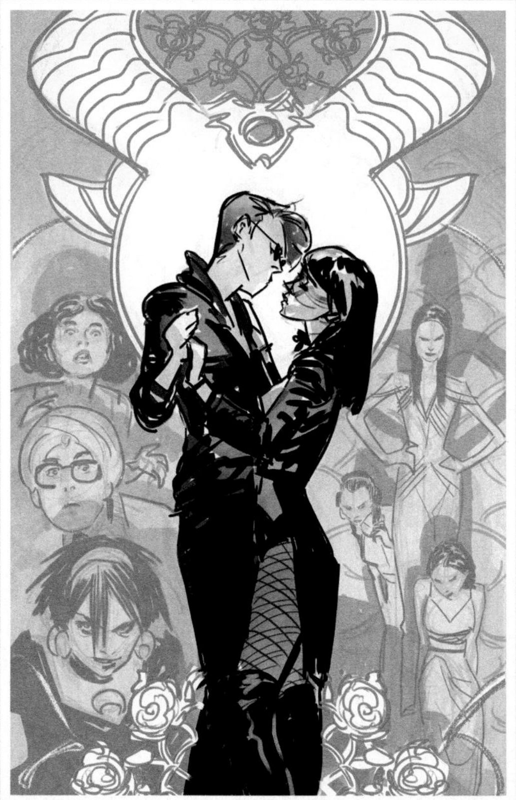

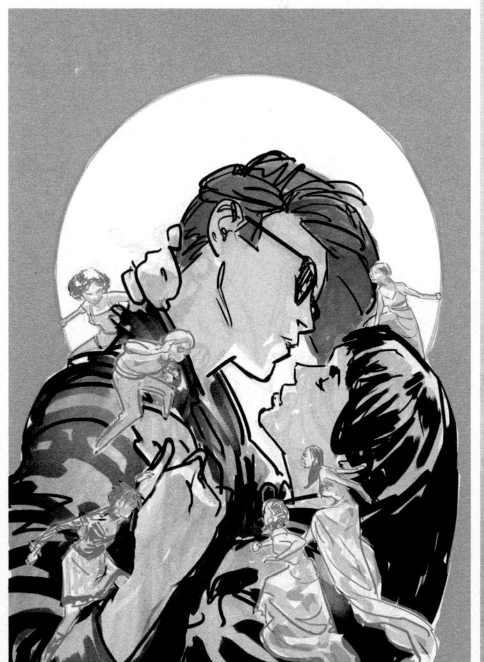

MYSTIK U SKETCHBOOK

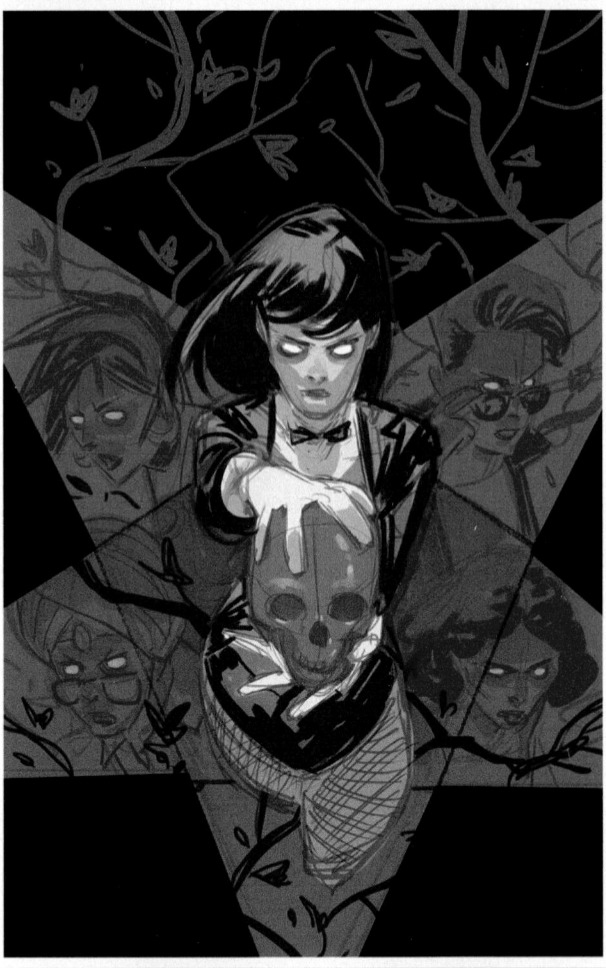

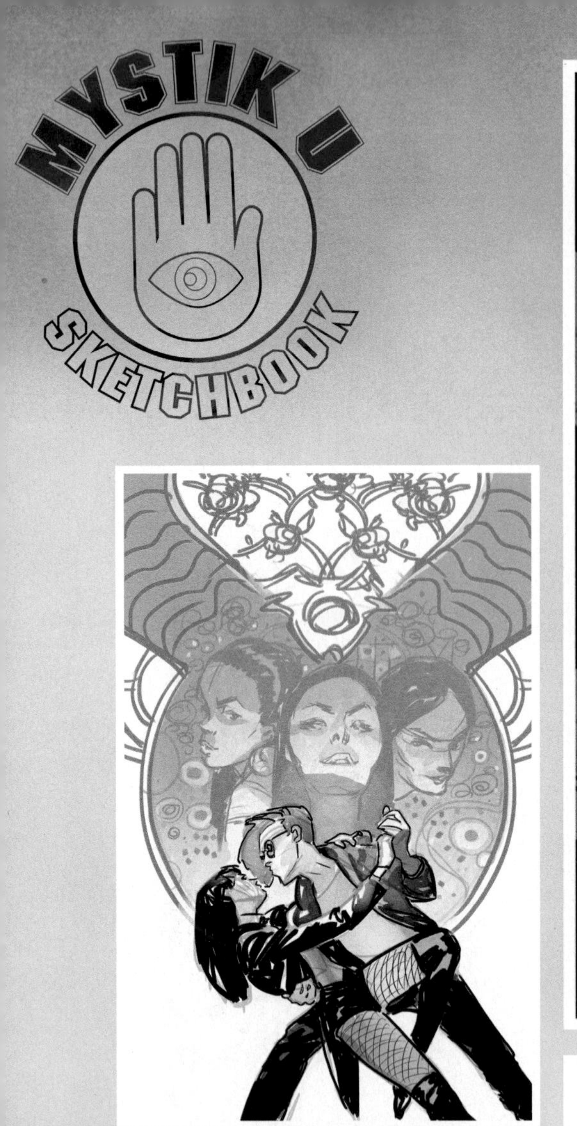

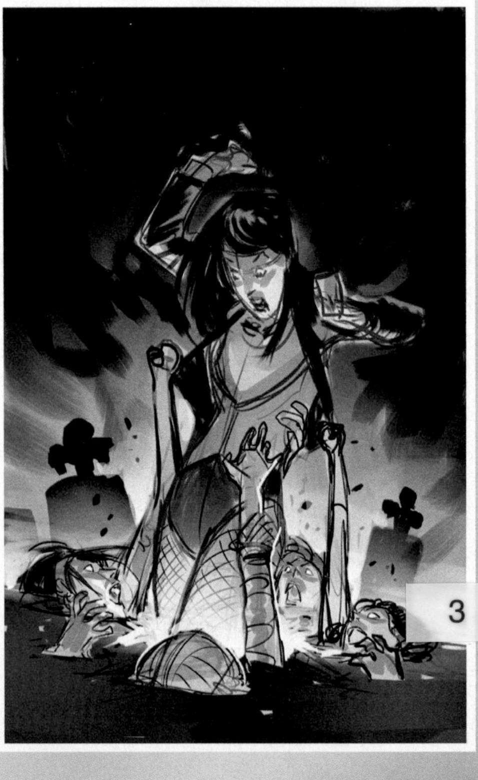

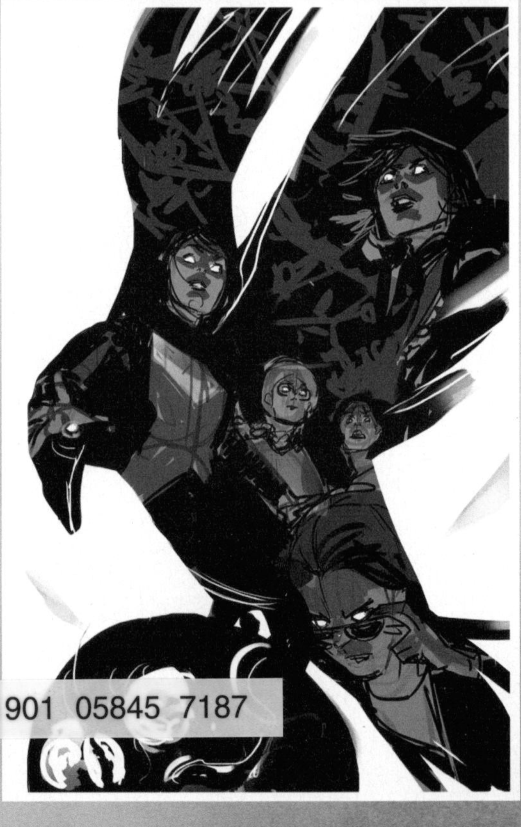